Language Myths and the History
of English

OXFORD STUDIES IN SOCIOLINGUISTICS

General Editors:

Nikolas Coupland
Adam Jaworski
Cardiff University

Recently Published in the Series:

Talking about Treatment: Recommendations for Breast Cancer Adjuvant Treatment
Felicia D. Roberts

Language in Time: The Rhythm and Tempo of Spoken Interaction
Peter Auer, Elizabeth Couper-Kuhlen, and Frank Müller

Whales, Candlelight, and Stuff Like That: General Extenders in English Discourse
Maryann Overstreet

A Place to Stand: Politics and Persuasion in a Working-Class Bar
Julie Lindquist

Sociolinguistics Variation: Critical Reflections
Edited by Carmen Fought

Prescribing under Pressure: Parent-Physician Conversations and Antibiotics
Tanya Stivers

Discourse and Practice: New Tools for Critical Discourse Analysis
Theo van Leeuwen

Beyond Yellow English: Toward a Linguistic Anthropology of Asian Pacific America
Edited by Angela Reyes and Adrienne Lo

Stance: Sociolinguistic Perspectives
Edited by Alexandra Jaffe

Investigating Variation: The Effects of Social Organization and Social Setting
Nancy C. Dorian

Television Dramatic Dialogue: A Sociolinguistic Study
Kay Richardson

Language without Rights
Lionel Wee

Paths to Post-Nationalism
Monica Heller

Language Myths and the History of English
Richard J. Watts

Language Myths and the History of English

Richard J. Watts

OXFORD
UNIVERSITY PRESS

OXFORD
UNIVERSITY PRESS

Oxford University Press, Inc., publishes works that further
Oxford University's objective of excellence
in research, scholarship, and education.

Oxford   New York
Auckland   Cape Town   Dar es Salaam   Hong Kong   Karachi
Kuala Lumpur   Madrid   Melbourne   Mexico City   Nairobi
New Delhi   Shanghai   Taipei   Toronto

With offices in
Argentina   Austria   Brazil   Chile   Czech Republic   France   Greece
Guatemala   Hungary   Italy   Japan   Poland   Portugal   Singapore
South Korea   Switzerland   Thailand   Turkey   Ukraine   Vietnam

Copyright © 2011 by Oxford University Press, Inc.

Published by Oxford University Press, Inc.
198 Madison Avenue, New York, New York 10016

www.oup.com

Oxford is a registered trademark of Oxford University Press.

Library of Congress Cataloging-in-Publication Data
Watts, Richard J.
Language myths and the history of English / Richard J. Watts.
    p.   cm. — (Oxford studies in sociolinguistics)
Includes bibliographical references and index.
ISBN 978-0-19-532760-1; 978-0-19-532761-8 (pbk.)
1. English language—History.   2. English language—Social aspects.   3. Sociolinguistics.   4. Discourse
analysis.   I. Title.
PE1098.W38 2011
420.9—dc22   2010016760

Printed in the United States of America
on acid-free paper

To all my former students with thanks and fond memories

Preface

Books take a long time to fix themselves in the mind of the author and to emerge as a (more or less) coherent text, and the present book is certainly no exception to this general pattern. The gestation period in this case, however, can be traced back very far into my own past, as far back as the time when I began to sense an interest in language, languages and the central place that language occupied in the social and cultural fabric of the communities into which I was socialised, in which I lived and grew up, and out of which I finally had to break. I remember being told, in my preadolescent days, not to say this or that, or to avoid this or that pronunciation because it sounded so "horrible", or to speak "grammatically"—the typical kinds of comment aimed at children of lower-middle-class origin in late 1940s and 1950s Britain, which unwittingly prompted many of them to do the very opposite! So I learned at an early stage in my life that people have some decidedly odd ideas about language in which they believe fervently, and I later learned, as a young university graduate, that it's not such a good idea to try to convince them of the "error" of their linguistic ways.

When, in the 1970s, I began to develop an interest in the history of the English language and then to teach the subject to Swiss undergraduates, I also realised, with the benefit of my training in second-language acquisition, pragmatics and sociolinguistics, that there were also some decidedly odd ideas about language circulating in the heads of first- and second-year students that I had to battle against. Even more dispiriting was the discovery that the canonical ways in which "the history of English" was taught, including the textbooks that were in use at university level, seemed to preserve many of the misconceptions about English which I recognised from the admonishments of my own family in my youth. As a consequence, I decided to ask awkward questions in my teaching and writing and to encourage generation after generation of students in English linguistics not only to question their own ingrained beliefs about language and the history of language, but also to submit the canonical "histories" of English to similar kinds of critical litmus test to those that I had used.

My first major attempt at asking awkward questions in print was made together with Tony Bex in the book that we edited in 1999 on the acrimonious debates over the teaching of Standard English in the new National Curriculum in England and Wales (*Standard English: The Widening Debate*). I was deeply gratified to realise that I was by no means alone in asking such questions and that a number of linguists had "been there and done that" before Tony and me. Among them were Tony Crowley, Deborah Cameron, Peter Trudgill, Jenny Cheshire, Ron Carter, Rosina Lippi-Green, Linda Mugglestone, Dennis Preston, David Crystal, Laura Wright and—above all, and with my warmest thanks and appreciation—Jim and Lesley Milroy.

My second attempt was to use different ways of conceptualising time (and thereby history) and an apolitical notion of "ideology" that I had developed in a book on language ideologies edited by Jan Blommaert in 1999 to put a little more historical meat onto the bones of the notion of *language myth*, a term used in a splendidly usable book edited by Laurie Bauer and Peter Trudgill in 1998 (*Language Myths*, London: Penguin), which I had already used with students in introductory linguistics classes. As a result, I began to unearth some of the myths underlying the canonical versions of the "history of English" (see Watts 2000).

From this point on, I became a natural convert to the idea that there was in fact no one single story of how English developed, since this would mean that the canonical history of English presented a teleology of the emergence of standard English which validated the set of myths that I was busy unearthing. A myth, however, remains a myth—a culturally important narrative means of explaining some present aspect of a cultural group. This does not mean that the myth is an untruth; myths always reveal a grain, maybe more than a grain, of "truth". But it does mean that a belief in those myths tends to bar the way to considering the sociohistorical facts that would lead to alternative histories. It was this which Peter Trudgill and I intended to show in our 2002 edited collection, *Alternative Histories of English*, and in a very real sense the present book develops that line of reasoning further. The idea of alternative histories has been picked up in David Crystal's book *The Stories of English* (London: Penguin, 2004), but *Language Myths and the History of English* attacks the issue from the point of view of the underlying myths that, it should be added, are still with us today.

In the making of the book, a number of people—colleagues, students, publisher and family—have kept up my hopes of fighting through to the end by being prepared to listen to my thoughts on language myths in the context of the history of English, by displaying immense forbearance toward my frequent impatience with myself and with the university department from which I have now been retired for two years, and by quietly and unreservedly encouraging me to continue.

My first heartfelt thanks go to my wife, Anne-Marie, who wonders, despairingly sometimes, why I still find the time to write but who, I know, understands and forgives me because she has come to realise that I cannot do otherwise. Having endured me through almost 40 years of marriage, my heart goes out to her in love and thanks for enduring it all one more time. Our son Chris and his family have been well out of the firing line for a number of years, but I would nevertheless like to express my gratitude to them for the support they have shown.

Books are not written without discussing and sometimes arguing rather forcefully about ideas with colleagues, and I should like to acknowledge the help and support of the following old friends and colleagues: Peter Trudgill, who agreed to edit the book on alternative histories with me that was published in 2002 and has given me such warm and friendly support through the years; Jim Milroy, with fond memories of discussions over convivial pints of beer in earlier years; Daniel Schreier, whose infective sense of humour and unfailing friendship always boost me to continue asking my awkward questions; Miriam Locher, whose solid common sense and enthusiasm kept my feet firmly planted on terra firma; Jürg Strässler and Franz Andres Morrissey, two old friends and erstwhile students from Zürich, who, I have no doubt, have always sensed a waywardness in me that needs humouring; and a host of others whom I will mention in fond acknowledgment of their support— Margaret Bridges, Anita Auer, Wim Vandenbussche, Stephan Elspass, Joachim Scharloth, Nils Langer, Peter Maitz and many others. I owe a special vote of thanks to Brian Hurley at Oxford University Press for being so amazingly patient and, above all, so helpful and supportive. And my list would not be complete without my thanks to Nik Coupland and Adam Jaworski for being interested in an idea that was based on those awkward questions in the first place. I simply need to add that none of those mentioned bears any responsibility for the errors in judgment, fact, or interpretation that might be found in the book.

Contents

Language Myths and the History
of English

Chapter 1

Metaphors, myths, ideologies
and archives

We are such stuff
As dreams are made on
—Shakespeare,
The Tempest, act 4, scene 1

1. DEFINING MYTHS

This book is about myths that have been told throughout the history of what is commonly referred to as "the English language", most of which are as alive and kicking today as they were centuries ago, and also about myths that are currently in the process of construction. I shall start at the obvious place—by defining what I understand by the term "myth". I argue that underlying all myths are commonly shared "conceptual metaphors" (see section 2 for a definition), and that the myths help to drive forms of ideological discourse about English and to construct "discourse archives" (see section 5 for a definition) of various kinds. This first chapter thus focuses on defining how I understand all of these terms and outlining the content of the following chapters.

To start with, consider the central term of this book, "myth". It is derived from the Greek word μύθος, which literally means "story", and the following chapters will trace out and describe that deepest urge of human beings: the urge to narrate objects, events, beliefs and explanations into being. In our modern world, myths lead an odd kind of dual existence. We talk about myths as though they are equivalent to untruths, but we should bear in mind that this is not the same as saying that they are lies. If we are told that a story we

3

have listened to or an account we are given is "just a myth", we tend to dismiss it as being fictional. Indeed, by appending the gradable adverb "just" to the assessment of that story or account, we automatically place it below what we take to be truthful, faithful to fact, in a hierarchy of believability.

But although myths are essentially fabrications, they are not lies; they are not told to deceive us. Most of the accounts and stories we believe in are venerated as part of a long cultural tradition. They are the narratives that we need to believe in to make sense of the complex world in which we exist, but as with popular folk traditions it is not possible to identify an original narrator. A myth is not a personal story or an individual act of narration; it is transferred to each of us socially in the course of our interaction with others, and culturally through a history of transference that has made it the property of a group. As we go through life, we learn to accept beliefs about aspects of the sociocultural groups to which we belong (or feel we belong), and we do this by listening to and learning to produce the legitimate narration of myths in social institutions such as the family, the education system, the church and the political system. Myths thus form an all-important part of dominant forms of "discourse" (see section 4 for a definition). In our cognition, they provide a narrative cultural embedding of beliefs, and they help us to construct a foundation for performing acts of identity in emergent social practice. For example, who would be likely to dismiss the significance of classical myths or the modern myths of nationhood or the myths at the foundation of religion, even if, deep down, we might have a sneaking suspicion that they, too, are fabrications?

Despite all the factual evidence, the major reason for the survival of myths is that they "fulfil a vital function in explaining, justifying and ratifying present behaviour by the narrated events of the past" (Watts 2000: 33). Doubting a myth to be factual can even be interpreted as an act of heresy if the story, or even only part of it, is firmly and widely believed by the group.

The French sociologist and social anthropologist Bourdieu (1977: 164–169) used Husserl's term *doxa* to refer to a set of beliefs that are taken for granted within a society: *doxa* is that which "goes without saying because it comes without saying" (1977: 169). Myths are thus part of a *doxa*. In Greek, δόξα meant a common belief or a popular opinion, and if that belief or opinion was considered incontestable, it constituted an "*ortho*dox" belief. Bourdieu's term "orthodoxa", which is derived from the Greek adjective ορθός (right, true, straight) + δόξα, thus refers to a body of beliefs and ways of thinking which are taken to be right or true. "Heterodoxa", derived from the Greek adjective ετερος (different, other) + δόξα, refers to explicit challenges to accepted ways of thinking and believing.

Introducing Bourdieu into the argument at this early point in the proceedings is not an arbitrary move. If myths articulate orthodox beliefs, they represent ways of thinking and believing that have been legitimised by a social group. They represent part of what Bourdieu calls "symbolic power", by which he means the power to make people see and believe certain visions of the world rather than others. In Bourdieu's terms, exercising symbolic power over others—using the ability to make them think and act in certain ways—is equivalent to symbolic violence, and those who attempt to exercise symbolic power are in a constant struggle with those who challenge those myths with heterodox beliefs.

My approach to the analysis of language myths can be called "sociocognitive" and constructionist, which implies a perspective on human language which is founded on three governing principles:

1. The faculty of acquiring and using human language, possessed by every individual human being, is an integral part of human cognition—that is, of what we know and use to understand ourselves and the world in which we exist. It is not a separate module of the mind, but is constructed through our interaction with others and the physical world around us and is integrated within cognition as a set of complex *cognitive frames*,[1] *scripts*[2] and *image schemata*.[3] This is the cognitive part of the term "sociocognitive".

2. The frames, scripts and image schemata in our cognition are constructed, and they can be constructed only in social interaction (what Bourdieu 1977 calls "practice") with others. The development of cognition is thus an ongoing process of learning, as Lave and Wenger (1991) understand this term. Without exposure to social practice, we cannot learn, and we can construct neither human language nor any other aspects of cognition. This is the "socio" part of the term "sociocognitive".

3. Each individual human being, although she is born into an already existent physical world, is nevertheless the centre point of that world, and her gradual experience of interaction within that world allows her to reconstruct it anew, both individually and socially. We thus construct who we are, just as others also construct us, or piece together, through the course of time, who we are. This is what is meant by the term "constructionist".

We use human language to help us in constructing our own individual worlds and in reconstructing the world into which we are born. Scannell (2002: 262) expresses this perfectly by stating that we "language the world". Language *is* in fact our world, and it is fundamental both to the development of human consciousness and also to our notion of time and our conceptualisation of the

---

1. The term "frame" is widely used in the cognitive sciences and beyond. By restricting it specifically to cognitive frames I refer to systems of structured knowledge (semantic, experiential, social, etc.) that each of us develops through interaction with the world (which obviously includes human language). Clearly, frames may differ from one person to the next, but they can be expected to be based on prototypical types of knowledge gained by interaction between an individual and the surrounding world.
2. A cognitive script can be thought of as a subtype of frame which depends on the sequential ordering of a specific type of experience, say, going to the theatre or eating or phoning someone. The term was made well known by Schank and Abelson's 1977 book *Scripts, Plans, Goals, and Understanding*.
3. An "image schema" refers to recurring structures in cognition that are constructed from our bodily interaction with the world beyond ourselves. They establish the basis on which we develop understanding and reasoning, and they may also be transferred from more abstract kinds of experience—linguistic, historical, social, and so on.

fact that each of us has a beginning and an end. In this sense, a sociocognitive approach to human language must be able to deal with variability, change, flexibility and creativity precisely because it hinges on a historical understanding of both the phylogenetic and the ontogenetic development of language. Using a sociocognitive constructionist approach to human language means that I will need to introduce terms as they prove to be necessary, but without burdening the reader with a full-scale theoretical model.

Croft (2001: 93) has coined the term "conceptual space" to refer to cognition, and he defines it as a "structured representation of functional structures and their relationships to each other". If each of us acquires language socially and if language is integrated within cognition, we will certainly need to develop a sociocognitive theory of language, one in which the social practices in which we are involved move to centre stage.[4] But the present book is not the place to take up this task. In this opening chapter, I introduce aspects of Conceptual Metaphor Theory and of Cognitive Blending Theory, and readers who are interested in learning more about these theories are encouraged to consult the references given.

One point, however, is fundamental to my analysis of English language myths in the following chapters, and I will make it quite explicit at this early point before moving on. When we talk about language, we have an automatic tendency to think in terms of "languages" and not in terms of the capacity of human language. Imagine a one-and-a-half-year-old child beginning to produce his first approximations to words. If the learning environment is bilingual, the child will learn, in the acquisition process, to distinguish which words and which constructions can be used with which communicative partners, but there will hardly be any consciousness that those words and constructions belong to different systems of human language. The child is simply using whatever form of language he[5] has at his disposal to integrate into the group and to achieve his own ends. The fact that some of the words and constructions are from, say, English and others from, say, French is not really significant for the child's acquisition. In fact, as we shall see in later chapters, the important fact is that participants use whatever language or languages they can in real-time emergent instances of social practice. The construction of individual languages (countable) from human language (uncountable) occurs at a later time, and it is a conscious decision to distinguish system A from system B. My decision to restrict myself to "English" is, in a way, artificial, but it is crucial to bear in mind that the myths presented in this book have all started from the assumption that there *are* languages, rather than from the basic assumption

---

4. Croft's book is concerned with setting up a theory of what he calls Radical Construction Grammar, but such a grammar will ultimately need to take on board elements that, strictly speaking, lie outside the purview of grammar. Hence part of his conceptual space "also represents conventional pragmatic or discourse-functional or information-structural or even stylistic or social dimensions of the use of a grammatical form or construction" (2001: 93).

5. Throughout the book I shall alternate between "he" and "she" to designate the generic third person singular pronoun.

of human language. This is an assumption which I attempt to deconstruct in several of the chapters, since the myths themselves are essential to the socio-cultural construction of individual languages.

One further word of warning is in order at this juncture. Whenever I use the term "deconstruction", I understand the systematic uncovering of a set of beliefs and the serious questioning of their validity. I do not intend to indulge in poststructuralist interpretations of the kind made famous in literary deconstructionism.

2. CONCEPTUAL METAPHORS AND MYTHS

Human beings desperately need explanations for inexplicable situations in life. After all, the only two ineluctable facts that we are aware of about life are (1) that we are born and (2) that we die. It is impossible for us to have any memory of the former event, and we have no idea of when the latter event will overtake us. Life is thus an enigma, something that we know we have or are in, but do not know why. To conceptualise "life", we have no option but to revert to what we know about ourselves, such as fundamental bodily experiences at a very early stage in life, experiences from which we construct and store image and action schemata, action frames and event scripts in cognition. However, we cannot reasonably conceptualise "life" until we have the capacity of human language. Once the conceptualisation of abstract concepts becomes possible through the acquisition of human language, we can begin to construct our own life stories. To do this we need to revert to conceptual metaphors.

Conceptual Metaphor Theory (CMT), developed in the late 1970s and early 1980s by George Lakoff, Mark Johnson, Mark Turner, Zoltán Kövecses, Rafael Núñez and others, constitutes an early version of the cognitive approach to language. This approach provides a viable alternative to ratio-nalist/essentialist accounts of cognition. It has given rise to a new philosophical perspective on knowledge and understanding which argues that the ways in which we conceptualise abstract concepts can be traced in the metaphors we continually and unconsciously use in our language.

We can understand what a conceptual metaphor is by referring to a some-what later approach to cognitive linguistics known as Cognitive Blending Theory (CBT) (Fauconnier 1994; Fauconnier & Turner 2002), so I will digress just a little to outline what CBT is. The crucial concept in CBT is that of "mental space", which Fauconnier and Turner (2002: 40) define as follows:

> Mental spaces are small conceptual packets constructed as we think and talk, for purposes of local understanding and action.... [They] are connected to long-term schematic knowledge called "frames".... Mental spaces are very partial. They contain elements and are typically structured by frames. They are interconnected, and can be modified as thought and discourse unfold. Mental spaces can be used generally to model dynamic mappings in thought and language.

Most mental spaces are constructed and used on the fly "as we think and talk" and then erased when they are no longer needed—that is, once they have served their purpose in emergent social practice. But a certain number of mental spaces are transferred to long-term memory and may be blended with other information stored in cognition, and this may lead to the reorganisation of frames and scripts. While we may be marginally conscious of online mental spaces (i.e. mental spaces that are constructed and used in ongoing interaction), the vast majority of our cognitive concepts, our frames and scripts of experience and our action schemata remain below the level of consciousness. During online interaction, mental spaces are combined with other mental spaces to form "cognitive blends" that generally create new emergent structures which can then be run in instances of emergent social practice by the participants. Sometimes these blends may seep down and become embedded in cognition.

We understand abstract concepts that have no direct connection to those bodily experiences that we have with our environment by accessing the frames, scripts and action schemata that have already been constructed. A blend is created between aspects of previously stored concepts, or previously stored blends to provide a cognitive concept for the lexeme to prompt for when it is used in the mental space of an utterance. Aspects of the previously stored cognitive concept (or cognitively embedded blend) are projected into a mental space to become the referent of the lexeme. The empty mental space is the target concept that needs to be understood, and the result is yet another cognitive blend. For example, the abstract cognitive concept of TIME in an utterance (as with all cognitive concepts, represented in the text in small caps) can be conceptualised by projecting aspects from fundamental schemata of physical movement (i.e. experiences of movement that have been stored as image schemata in cognition from our most fundamental bodily experiences). So when the lexeme *time* is used[6] in an utterance to create an emergent mental space, we are prompted, in that fleeting mental space, to access a conceptual metaphor stored in a cognitively embedded blend. We can represent this schematically as shown in figure 1.1. The conceptual metaphor is thus the blend of an empty mental space and a projection from a set of bodily experiences stored in image schematic form in an already existent cognitive frame related to bodily movement. The cognitive frame containing the image schemata is referred to as the "source domain" of the metaphor, and the empty mental space, the blend between zero information and the projection from the source domain(s), is referred to as the "target domain".

We need to bear in mind that the metaphor itself is a part of cognition, not an utterance. For this reason cognitive metaphors are represented by printing them in small caps in this text (see above). In any conceptual meta-

---

6. Or any other lexeme or construction that is perceived to be within the semantic frame of the concept TIME—for example, *week*, *three hours*, *the lesson*.

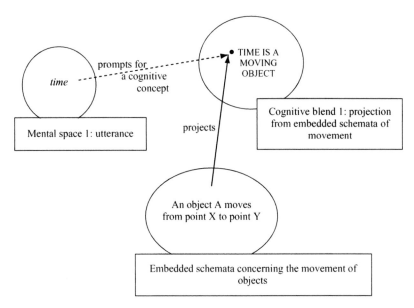

FIGURE 1.1. Representation of a conceptual metaphor in terms of Cognitive Blending Theory

phor the IS does not represent an ontological equivalence between the lexeme *time* and the image schemata, but rather those mental processes that are necessary to construct the metaphor. The assumption in CMT and CBT is that such metaphorical cognitive spaces are ubiquitous in cognition, are learned through social interaction with others and are necessarily universal to the human race, although specific to those cultures in which the metaphors are cognitively significant.

Often there is more than one conceptual metaphor that can be used as a reference point from a lexeme or grammatical construction. For example, another way of conceptualising time is to project from an already blended space containing the cognitive concept of MONEY into the empty mental space to form the conceptual metaphor TIME IS MONEY. This then accounts for utterances such as the following:

(1) I'm afraid I can't *spend* much time on that problem.

(2) There's not much time *left*.

(3) We're *running out of time*.

(4) Could you *spare* me a moment of your time, sir?

To return to our initial problem, then, how do we conceptualise the cognitive concept LIFE? I suggest that the following might be acceptable conceptual metaphors:

LIFE IS A JOURNEY   LIFE IS A PRELUDE TO PARADISE/HELL
LIFE IS A GAMBLE   LIFE IS A STRUGGLE
LIFE IS A BURDEN   LIFE IS AN ADVENTURE

From a sociocognitive perspective, if myths are communally shared stories that function in attempts at "explaining, justifying and ratifying present behaviour by the narrated events of the past" (Watts 2000: 33), they must ultimately be grounded in conceptual metaphors. Life, after all, is not a journey, it is not a gamble and it is not an adventure. However, we may perceive it to be so close to these other (often abstract) concepts that we choose to metaphorise it in this way in order to be able to understand it. But constructing stories which do not fit the matter-of-fact details can lead to the mythologisation of a discursive *orthodoxa* which may need to be deconstructed. I conclude this section by hypothesising that commonly used conceptual metaphors that lie deeply embedded within our cognition feed into and form the basis of the myths we discover. Neither the myths nor the metaphors are in any sense "rationally true", but because they are so deeply embedded in cognition, they need to be taken seriously.

3. LANGUAGE MYTHS AND CONCEPTUAL METAPHORS

We have seen in the previous section that myths are based on conceptual metaphors, but we have digressed somewhat beyond the field of language. We now need to return to the major theme of this book and to focus on the notion of "language myths" and the kinds of conceptual metaphors on which they are based.

Language myths are communally shared narratives told in the construction of an ideological set of beliefs

> about the structure of language and/or the functional uses to which language is put.... The beliefs have formed part of [a] community's overall set of beliefs and the life-styles that have evolved on the basis of those beliefs for so long that their origins seem to have been obscured or forgotten. They are thus socioculturally reproduced as constituting a set of "true" precepts in what appears to the community to be a logically coherent system. (Watts 1999a: 68)

Some of the language myths that we will look at in this book are also told about other languages, in the past as well as in the present. Others seem to be restricted to English. Many of the language myths that I attempt to deconstruct go back over a period of centuries, whereas others can be traced back only as far as the nineteenth century, specifically to the beginnings of linguistics as an academic discipline and its intimate connections with the emergence of history as an academic discipline at around the same time and to the rise of the concept of the nation-state.

3.1 The connection with history and the nation-state

The beginnings of linguistics as an academic discipline go back roughly to the end of the eighteenth and the beginning of the nineteenth century, and it is important to note that it was first conceived as a historical discipline. This corresponds neatly with the emergence of history itself as an academic discipline at around the same time. Both disciplines also coincided with the development of the concept of the nation-state, particularly in the wake of the French Revolution. Hobsbawm (1990) made the pertinent point that the concept of the French state, constructed in the early stages of the revolution, preceded that of the nation-state, in the sense that a nation-state relied (and often still does rely) on the concept of "homogeneity". A state must show homogeneity in its political system, but it does not need to show homogeneity in terms of religion, race and language. The nation-state, however, demanded a homogeneous national language, a homogeneous religion and, wherever possible, a homogeneous history.

The conceptual basis of homogeneity is grounded in abstract cognitive blends such as PURITY, PERFECTION, SYMMETRY and positive moral values. If, for the moment, we focus on the ideal of "purity", a little thought will lead to the conclusion that this quality in human beings is a metaphorical construction. In the previous section, we looked briefly at the ways in which the abstract concept LIFE is constructed cognitively. The representation of the source of the journey metaphor to conceptualise the lexeme *time* in figure 1.1 makes use of a frame of embedded schemata concerning the movement of objects. Obviously, experiences with objects in the environment, from a very early age on, include other aspects of objects than what is involved in moving them (e.g. their size, their shape, the material from which they are made).

One of the most obvious bodily experiences made with objects is that human bodies themselves are also objects, and that, like all other objects, they, too, can be *clean* or *unclean*. In addition, objects have physical substance and are composed of different kinds of material. At a later stage in our lives, we also learn that substances themselves can be unblemished, untarnished, clear and so on. Those substances can thus be either *pure* or *impure*. At a much later stage than this, long after the acquisition of language, we learn that human bodies have an internal mental/moral substance as well as an external physical substance, allowing the metaphorical projection of the cognitive concept of PURITY to human beings. So when we say that a human body is *clean* or *unclean*, this is not a metaphorical conceptualisation. But when we say that a human being is *pure* or *impure*, it most certainly is.

Let's turn to history. If history traces out a path through time along which humanity moves towards the goal of achieving homogeneity in human actions,[7] then the ultimate goal of all human communities must be to achieve such abstract metaphorical states as PURITY, PERFECTION, SYMMETRY, or even much more complex metaphorical constructs like DECORUM, GRACE and MORAL GOODNESS. History in the early nineteenth century thus attempted to construct a teleology of human progress (see Jules Michelet's early work, particularly Michelet 1833). Unfortunately, however, the metaphor A HUMAN BEING IS PURE/IMPURE was also carried across to the nation-state through the conceptual metaphor THE NATION-STATE IS A HUMAN BEING, leaving the way open for the conceptualisation of the nation-state as being either PURE or IMPURE, and by implication PERFECT or IMPERFECT, HOMOGENEOUS or NON-HOMOGENEOUS. Since the nation-state ideology promoted competition between states, the vast majority of nineteenth-century historians applied this teleology not to human progress in general but to the progress of the nation-state of which they were citizens.

If the metaphor THE NATION-STATE IS A HUMAN BEING is accepted, a whole range of "true"[8] statements can be set up, which are derived from the metaphor, such as the following:
The problematic comparison here is with the concept of death. Even though it is patently clear that previous civilisations have, in a sense, "died", it would

<A human being is born>	→	<A nation-state is born>
<A human being reaches maturity>	→	<A nation-state reaches maturity>
<A human being dies>	→	<A nation-state dies>
<A human being has a character>	→	<A nation-state has a character>

not have suited nineteenth-century historians to have stretched their teleology to the extent that their own nation-states might someday die.

3.2 Conceptual metaphors of language

Constructing the ideology of the nation-state entailed a very close association with the national language, so it is hardly surprising that the fundamental conceptual metaphor THE NATION-STATE IS A HUMAN BEING also provides the most frequently used conceptual metaphor for language: A LANGUAGE IS A HUMAN BEING. This anthropomorphic conceptualisation of language is so ubiquitous in the Western world, regardless of whether a distinction is made

7. This is of course a modern way of looking at history, one that does not correspond to medieval notions of history (as I will discuss in chapter 3) and is probably not acceptable in late modern or even postmodern ways of conceptualising history, as we shall see at the end of this book.

8. Propositions, or statements, that are considered "true" by virtue of the metaphors will be placed between < >, for example, <A nation is born>, and the myths will be formatted in bold italics, as in the *myth of the ancient language*. To say that a statement is "true" here and elsewhere in this book is to say that the statement would be accepted and believed on the basis of the conceptual metaphor. I do not to wish to suggest that such statements correspond with states in the world which are objectively true. For this reason the expression "'true' statement" will always be used with double quotation marks around the lexeme *true*.

between human language as a general cognitive faculty of human beings or different linguistic systems (i.e. languages), and it goes back so far into the past that the metaphorical conceptualisation of the nation-state can be said to be derived from it. Two related aspects of human beings from the source domain are projected into the empty blend for language:

1. A LANGUAGE IS A HUMAN BEING

which yields "true" metaphorical "statements" (or propositions) such as the following:

- <A language is born>   – <A language dies>
  <A language grows old>   – <A language is mature>
- <A language at time point x is the same language as at time point y>
- <A language has a character>
- <A language is a potential actor> (i.e. has the ability to initiate and carry out actions)
- <A language is corrupt>   – <A language is noble>

2. A LANGUAGE IS A MEMBER OF A LANGUAGE FAMILY
which yields "true" metaphorical "statements" (or propositions) such as the following:

- <Languages are related/unrelated>
- <A language is part of a genealogical family tree>
- <A language inherits features from related languages>

The only restriction on this second domain of projections is that although a language may have sisters, brothers and cousins and may also conceivably have parents, it can hardly be said to be the grandfather/grandmother/grandson/ granddaughter of another language. The element of procreation is problematic in this domain.

Within the framework of the basic metaphor of A LANGUAGE IS A HUMAN BEING, all the moral characteristics that can be attributed to a person can also be projected onto the conceptualisation of a language, with the notable exception of physical or material qualities, such as:

- <A language is noble>   – <A language is perfect>
- <A language is homogeneous> – <A language is polite>
- <A language is hesitant>   – <A language is bold>
- <A language is great>

but hardly:

- <?A language is big>   – <?A language is short>
- <?A language is bald>   – <?A language is fat>

From this list we can see that a language may be conceptualised as PERFECT or PURE, but not as CLEAN or DIRTY.

There is an exception to this restriction on the possibilities of projecting physical characteristics onto language, however. From the metaphorical conceptualisation that a language can die, we can project the concept of health or illness onto a language, such as the following:

- <A language is healthy>   - <A language is sick/ill>
- <A language is fit>   - <A language is ailing>
- <A language is dying>   - <A language is weak>
- <A language is recovering/reviving>

Several texts on language, particularly in the nineteenth century, are full of this kind of metaphorisation of language. By way of illustration, consider the following very brief selection of quotations from Richard Chevenix Trench's book *English, Past and Present*:

One who now says, "If he *call*, tell him I am out"...is seeking to detain a mood, or rather the sign of a mood, which the language is determined to get rid of. (1855: 11; from "true" metaphorical "statements" [propositions] such as <A language is a potential actor>, <A language has a will>, RJW)

It is indeed marvellous how quickly a language will create, adopt, adapt words in any particular line of things to which those who speak that language are specially addicted. (1855: 58; from "true" metaphorical "statements" [propositions] such as <A language is a potential actor>, <A language is creative>, RJW)

When we call to mind the near affinity between English and German, which, if not sisters, are at any rate first cousins, it is remarkable that almost since the day when they parted company, each to fulfil its own destiny, there has been little further commerce in the way of giving and taking between them. (1855: 136; from "true" metaphorical "statements" [propositions] and conceptual metaphors such as <A language is a member of a language family>, A LANGUAGE IS A HUMAN BEING, <A language is a potential actor>, RJW)

Its [the genitive form of the pronoun "it", i.e. "its", RJW] is, in fact, a *parvenu*, which has forced itself into good society at last, but not with the good will of those who in the end had no choice but to admit it. (1855: 149; from "true" metaphorical "statements" [propositions] such as <A language has a character>, RJW)

Before moving on, I should note that there are two further source domains for the metaphorical conceptualisation of human language, the domain of plants and planting, and the domain of geology. The first metaphorical blend is A LANGUAGE IS A PLANT, and it can occur in a number of variations—for example, that the essence of a language is like the sap of a tree, or that the language must be planted outside its normal natural environment to the good of those living there.

Texts making use of the A LANGUAGE IS A PLANT metaphor begin to occur regularly in the latter half of the sixteenth century, particularly with reference to the language contact situation in Ireland, in which the dominant but minority culture using English attempted to force English customs and the English language on the Irish, a policy that was ultimately successful at least with respect to the language. As an example, consider the following quotation from Richard Stanihurst's "A Treatise Containing a Plain and Perfect Description of Ireland" (1577, in Crowley 2000: 32):

> And truly, so long as these impaled dwellers did sunder themselves as well in land as in language from the Irish: rudeness was day by day in the country supplanted, civility engrafted, good laws established, loyalty observed, rebellion suppressed, and in fine the cornerstone of a young England was like to shoot in Ireland. But when their posterity became not altogether so wary in keeping, as their ancestors were valiant in conquering. The Irish language was free denizened in the English pale: this canker took such deep root, as the body that before was whole and sound, was by little and little festered, and in manner wholy [sic] putrified.

What we read here are the beginnings of a discourse of colonialism, in Ireland and elsewhere, in which plantation literally and metaphorically became the conventionalised way of justifying colonial domination and exploitation.

In the nineteenth century several writers on language use the A LANGUAGE IS A PLANT metaphor. As an example, consider the following quotations from Trench (1855):

> Our own is, of course, a living language still. It is therefore gaining and losing. It is a tree in which the vital sap is circulating yet. (85)

> It is true that there happened here what will happen in every attempt to transplant on a large scale the words of one language into another. (98)

> One branch of the speakers of a language engrafts on the old stock numerous words which the other does not in the same way make its own. (50)

The geological metaphor A LANGUAGE IS A GEOLOGICAL FORMATION is, strictly speaking, not directly derived from action and image schemata, but if we assume that the basis of any metaphor is some form of cognitive blend, then the way in which geologists conceptualise their discipline ultimately derives from underlying human experiences. Throughout the nineteenth century, writers on language in Britain and America frequently made use of the metaphor, providing comparisons of language as consisting of strata, or layers and deposits of sediment, or as containing fossils or skeletons. Henry Welsford's book *On the Origin and Ramifications of the English Language*, published in 1845, contains the following complex description of the history of the Indo-European languages in terms of a landscape changed over the course of time, with the "dregs" of older languages being deposited to provide the basis from which modern European languages have appeared:

> The Sanskrit may be regarded as the pure fountainhead: the streams which flowed from it remained long in a troubled state from the turbulence of the middle ages, till, having found a more spacious and secure channel, they have gradually deposited the dregs of the Frankish, the Anglo-Saxon, the Cimbric, and the Celtic and reappeared in the beautiful languages of Montesquieu and Racine, of Goete [*sic*] and Schiller, of Byron and Scott. (259)

In Champneys' book *History of English*, published in 1893, the final mute letter <e> in words such as *ride, home, take* and so on is described as a *fossil*:

> First of all, the differences in spelling may be briefly dismissed. Enough has been said before on the use of I where we now use J, on the difference of principle in the use of U and V, and about the final E, which was now a kind of fossil in the language. (327)

Oliver Farrar Emerson, in *The History of the English Language* (1894), talks of language *strata*:

> Moreover, in addition to these linguistic areas representing the words actually used by individuals or by classes of society, there are in the same linguistic area what may be called language strata, overlying one another and differing from one another. (115)

If the basis of myths is the shared conceptual metaphors that we use to refer to abstract notions such as the nation-state and language, we still need to consider how those myths form the substance of ideological discourses about language (and nation). To do this, we need an adequate concept of discourse, which I will present in the following sections.

4. FOUCAULT'S UNDERSTANDING OF DISCOURSE

If conceptual metaphors are the "stuff" of myths, myths are the "stuff" of ideological discourses. Language myths, like all other myths, are communally shared stories that, regardless of their factual basis, are believed and propagated as the cultural property of a group. Cameron (1995) argues that people cannot leave their language alone and that it is better for sociolinguists to face up to this fact than to try to convince people of the "error" of their ways. Hence, deconstructing language myths is unlikely to have much effect on how people, on an everyday basis, view language. Language myths that form the basis of discursive ideologies are always present, and no amount of effort will persuade people to relinquish them. With that in mind, I now turn to the notion of "discourse" and the related notions of "ideology" and "archive".

Foucault's understanding of a discourse is that it is a body of statements (i.e. a subset of statements) belonging to a single system in the overall formation of statements; that is, it is a system of statements markedly distinct from other systems of statements. Foucault takes statements to be historically situated "events". No human interaction can take place outside discursive formations, such that the individual comes to accept the statements, the events, as representing a "true" state of affairs, true not in the sense of logically true (i.e. true in a coherent logical system), but rather in the sense of a system of beliefs shared (or believed to be shared) by others. The process of coming to accept a system of statements can be thought of, sociocognitively, as part of the larger cognitive process of socialising individuals into sociocultural groups, and this process takes place principally, but by no means uniquely, below the level of consciousness. In this sense, we are all the prisoners of discourse, or, to put it less dramatically, none of us can avoid the cognitive process of socialisation into discursive formations.

Foucault stresses the fact that although we may feel that the system of statements constituting a discourse is coherent and is characterised by its continuity over time, the fundamental characteristic of discursive statements is their discontinuity. In other words, what we interpret to be a commonsense discursive unity is in fact a dispersion of elements displaying discontinuity, in that groups of statements may occur in any order, with any function, and correlated in any way with other groups of statements. Discontinuity is characteristic of discourse for the simple reason that discourse is constructed not simply of statements involving human language, but also of "statements" involving several other semiotic systems, such as speed of delivery and volume level, gesture and mime, pictorial and filmic representation, and so on. In addition, all of the objects, forms and themes of discursive statements are historically linked to the external conditions of discourse production.

Looked at from the point of view of emergent social interaction, or practice (Bourdieu 1977), discursive production is always conditioned by the context of that production. As we have seen, in Bourdieu's terms the symbolic power of the discourse resides in its ability to convince people of the *orthodox* nature of the statements. At the same time, however, it is important to allow for *heterodoxy*—different or perhaps even subversive or heretical opinions. Although this is never stated explicitly in Bourdieu's work, he appears to concur with Foucault in the discontinuity of discourse, for the simple reason that there will always be different opinions and beliefs.

In more recent constructionist approaches to the notion of "context" (Duranti & Goodwin 1992; Auer 1995; Silverstein & Urban 1996), context is not taken as a pregiven environment, temporal, local, or cognitive. It is actually constructed emergently by the participants, thus providing an even greater validity to the Foucauldian notion of discontinuity.

In the *Archaeology of Knowledge* (1972), Foucault represents knowledge as being constructed historically through the production of discourses which can only be pieced together from the surviving textual and non-textual evidence. The discursive evidence "unearthed" displays some of the discontinuities in discourses and may even lead to a sudden shift in the way in which a particular topic is constructed discursively. Some of these shifts are dealt with in later publications by Foucault (e.g. *Discipline and Punish: The Birth of the Prison*; *The History of Sexuality* Vol. 1). It is important to note that at any historical period and in any culture, a number of different, partially compatible or totally incompatible discourses will coexist or compete with one another, so that it is possible to talk about dominant discourses and "anti-discourses".

5. DISCOURSE ARCHIVES

It is within this mode of looking at discourse that Foucault introduces the term "archive". An archive, which I shall call a "discourse archive" to avoid misunderstandings, is not equivalent to a library or a stored collection of documents. Foucault calls it "the general system of the formation and transformation of statements" (1972: 127) or, alternatively, "the law of what can be said, the system that governs the appearance of statements as unique events" (1972: 129). In fact, the archive is of primary importance in understanding the archaeological approach to discourse:

> The never completed, never wholly achieved uncovering of the archive forms the general horizon to which the description of discursive formations, the analysis of positivities, the mapping of the enunciative field belong. The right of words—which is not that of the philologists—authorizes, therefore, the use of the term *archaeology* to describe all these searches. This term does not imply the search for a beginning; it does not relate analysis to geological excavation. It designates the general theme of a description that questions the already-said at the level of its existence: of the enunciative function that operates within it, of the discursive formation, and the general archive system to which it belongs. Archaeology describes discourses as practices specified in the element of the archive. (131)

By the "positivity" of a discourse Foucault means "that which characterizes its particular unity throughout a particular discursive time", so that the "positivity" of a discourse is to be found in the archive to which that discourse belongs: "the law of what can be said". It is the archive that determines how certain statements can be grouped together to form an apparent unity and how certain statements appear to us as historical events. Blommaert (2005: 102) suggests that the archive consists of "the macro-sociological forces and formations that define and determine what can be said, expressed, heard, and understood in particular societies, particular milieux, particular historical periods."

What, however, are the "true" statements that belong to "the general system of the formation and transformation of statements" and that constitute "the law of what can be said", and what are "the macro-sociological forces and formations that define and determine what can be said, expressed, heard, and understood"? Recall from section 3.2 on the metaphors used to conceptualise language that a metaphorisation such as A LANGUAGE IS A HUMAN BEING, or A LANGUAGE IS A MEMBER OF A LANGUAGE FAMILY, or A LANGUAGE IS A PLANT, or A LANGUAGE IS A GEOLOGICAL FORMATION gives rise to a large number of propositions, or statements that can be generated from the metaphors. If the metaphor is conceptually embedded, members of the cultural group using it as the basis of their discourse on language will automatically accept the "truth" of the statements that go to make up that discourse, and if the discourse is in the form of a narrative, the story, or the myth, will not seem incredible. Blommaert's point that the archive also consists of the macro-sociological forces defining the validity of the statements goes some way towards explaining why the conceptual metaphor A LANGUAGE IS A GEOLOGICAL FORMATION in the nineteenth century gave rise to statements which were part of an archive that has now been transformed. Geological metaphors are far less likely to be a legitimate way of talking about language in the first decade of the twenty-first century than they were in the nineteenth, when geology was not only a very popular academic discipline but was also practised by amateurs beyond the boundaries of academia. To illustrate this, I shall briefly analyse the quotation given in section 3.2 from Welsford's *On the Origin and Ramifications of the English Language*, presented this time as a set of propositions in what is clearly a narrative text:

(5)   i   <the Sanskrit may be regarded as the pure fountainhead>
      ii <the streams which flowed from it remained long in a troubled state from the turbulence of the middle ages>
      iii <till, having found a more spacious and secure channel>
      iv <they have gradually deposited the dregs of the Frankish, the Anglo-Saxon, wthe Cimbric, and the Celtic>
      v   <and reappeared in the beautiful languages of Montesquieu and Racine, of Goete [*sic*] and Schiller, of Byron and Scott>

The course of language history, the passing of time, is metaphorised as the course of a river, the source of which (the *fountainhead*) is Sanskrit. The problem here is that several streams are fed by the fountainhead, which tends to go against our conceptualisation of the geological source of a river. We could argue, however, that, within statements derived from the metaphor A LANGUAGE IS A GEOLOGICAL FORMATION, conceptualising Sanskrit as the source of a number of historical linguistic streams is a valid, "true" statement. Once this statement is accepted, statements ii. and iii. follow from it, and conceptualising the socio-geographical, sociohistorical framework within which those languages developed as a "spacious and secure channel" is also coherent with the topographic/geological metaphor of language. The next step in the story is the depositing of "the dregs of the Frankish, the Anglo-Saxon, the Cimbric, and the Celtic" within this channel (these channels?), which is again a statement deriving from the basic metaphor. Once enough material has been "deposited", statement v. is feasible within the conceptual framework constructed by Welsford; the modern languages English, French and German emerge (presumably as solid land). This is an example of what Fauconnier and Turner (2002) mean by "running the blend", the blend being the conceptual metaphor A LANGUAGE IS A GEOLOGICAL FORMATION. The story, the myth, thus gains validity within the part of the archive determining how language was conceptualised discursively in the nineteenth century.

The intimate connection between the underlying conceptual metaphors for language and the statements derived from those metaphors constitutes part of the discourse archive within which the statements emerge and which they help to construct. This understanding of the discourse archive is the motive force behind the unearthing of the language myths to be discussed in this book. Chapter 3, in particular, is based on the notion of a discourse archive and its breakdown in deconstructing the *myth of the unbroken tradition of English*.[9] However, before moving on to discuss the relationship between myths, discourse and ideologies, I will take this opportunity to disagree with some of the assumptions made by Foucault.

My first criticism concerns Foucault's statement (1972: 146–147) that "it is not possible for us to describe our own archive, since it is from within these rules that we speak .... The archive cannot be described in its totality; and in its presence it is unavoidable." In any period of time, different discourses will coexist or compete with one another, and this point is echoed by Blommaert when he talks about "macro-sociological forces and formations that define and determine what can be said, expressed, heard, and understood in particular societies, particular milieux, particular historical periods". So it is more than likely that an individual in any "particular society", any "particular milieu", or any "particular historical period" must function in more than one archive and that these archives may overlap or may be inconsistent with one another. This contradicts Foucault's idea that

---

9. Throughout this book I shall represent the myths in bold, italic type as a way of highlighting them. In doing this I am not claiming that the myths themselves have an ontological reality, but I am relating them to the sociocognitive and historical process of deriving "true" statements from metaphorical concepts, and shaping narrative discourses from these "true" statements within which ideologies of language are discursively crystallised and used in larger discourse archives. I thus wish to highlight the myths but to do so in a way different from my handling of conceptual metaphors and "true" statements.

a historical archive is a collection of statements that we cannot interpret, since that would assume that we can never be within more than one archive at the same time. If we can distance ourselves from an archive, then it should be possible to describe it even though it will never be possible do so in its entirety. And if that is the case, an archive is not always "unavoidable", in Foucault's terms.

Foucault's position leads him to the conclusion that, although we are able to piece together the archaeological remains of an archive, it will never be possible to understand it. Now, while living in a historical archive is indeed impossible, denying an understanding of it is tantamount to denying any interpretation of archaeological data. I take this to be an unacceptable conclusion, and I maintain that the heterogeneity of current discourses does indeed help us to apply interpretative methods in identifying, however tentatively, earlier historical archives, even if we will never "understand" them in the sense of having experienced or lived them.

6. MYTHS ARE THE "STUFF THAT IDEOLOGIES ARE MADE ON"

In the first section of this chapter I suggested that "the myths help to drive forms of ideological discourse about English and to construct discourse archives of various kinds". If we wish to trace out the development of a language ideology, we should be able to identify the complex of myths that form the basis of the set of beliefs constituting that ideology. We need to assess the relative strength of those myths in relation to the social factors that have exerted a formative influence in the social construction of the community for whom the ideology is significant.

Myths are essentially fictive, but they contain elements of reality in them, derived as they are from the mutually shared past experiences of the members of a community. If myths are judged solely on the basis of a present-time, commonsense point of view, they will have to be rejected as fantasy. As shared stories, they tell part of the overall "story" of the socio-cultural group. They help to reproduce and validate the group, and in this sense they fulfil a vital function in explaining, justifying and ratifying present behaviour by the narrated events of the past. Myths can also be changed, altered, lost, abandoned, or inverted. They are, in other words, continually reproduced and reconstructed socially.

What, however, do we take an ideology to be? Ideologies are constructed and reproduced through forms of discourse, which Foucault sees as an institutionalised mode of thinking, instantiated in social interaction between individuals. Such interaction may be through the medium of written or oral language, but it may also make use of other systems of signifying (e.g. pictorial, gestural), thereby allowing us to talk in the singular of *a* discourse to refer to one institutionalised mode of thinking in contrast to others. A discourse is thus a set of communally shared beliefs representing "truth" for the community concerned, but not necessarily for another community. The shared beliefs themselves may then be referred to as an ideology. Hodge and Kress (1993: 6) define ideology as "a systematic body of ideas, organized from a particular point of view". They argue that "ideology is thus a subsuming category which includes science and metaphysics, as well as political ideologies, without implying anything about their status and reliability as guides to reality". They go on to state that "ideology involves a systematically organized presentation of reality" (1993: 15). Seliger (1976: 14) defines ideology as "sets of ideas by which men [*sic*] posit, explain, and justify ends and means of social action, and specifically political action, irrespective of whether such action aims to preserve, amend, uproot or rebuild a given social order". But whichever way we define ideologies, it is crucial to see them as sets of ideas that are shared by the members of a community. I can hardly have an ideology all of my own. The content of a discourse is thus a set of beliefs of an ideological nature.

In Watts (2001: 299), I define "language ideologies" as being "constructed by discourses that have language (language attitudes, beliefs, opinions and convictions about language, etc.) as their central theme". Both Hodge and Kress's and Seliger's approaches to the study of ideology given above should be conflated, particularly with respect to "political action". The construction of "a systematically organized presentation of reality" (Hodge & Kress 1993: 6) leads to a shared belief in that "reality", within which explanation and justification of social and political action may be grounded.

Summarising the previous sections in this opening chapter, therefore, the focus of this book is to locate and deconstruct the myths underlying language ideologies which have guided our way of thinking about the history of the English language for the past century and a half. It is my aim to suggest that there are other ways to consider the materials that lie before us, but it is not my aim to suggest that these approaches are necessarily an improvement on earlier interpretations of them. It is also my aim to present ways in which a funnel view of the language can be avoided. In the funnel view of English, we have a wide range of early varieties of English situated at the wide top edge of the funnel, which are then finally distilled into modern standard English in the narrow neck of the funnel.[10] The funnel view of the history of English ignores the histories of the varieties, just as it also ignores the continued emergence of new forms of English.

The overall social process from metaphors to archives which informs the structure of this book and the discussion of the myths dealt with can be represented diagrammatically as in figure 1.2.

Myths draw on common conceptual metaphors to create stories that are then produced and reproduced socially through discourse. The stronger the

---

10. Watts and Trudgill (2002: 1) refer to the "tunnel vision" of language history, by which they mean more or less the same thing. I now believe, however, that using the lexeme *funnel* rather than *tunnel* more appropriately expresses what is meant.

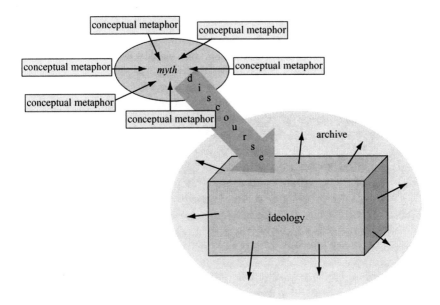

FIGURE 1.2. From conceptual metaphors to archive

myths become or the more support one myth draws from others, the greater the likelihood is that a language ideology will emerge. If this ideology becomes part of the dominant hegemonic discourse of a social group, it will give rise to statements that are equivalent to "laws", thus constructing an archive of what can and what cannot be said or believed in.

Discursively, the language myths surrounding English lie between, on the one hand, conceptual metaphors offering us an understanding of human language in general and of individual languages and language varieties in particular and, on the other hand, dominant language ideologies. For this reason it is important to locate and deconstruct the myths, but this will not be done in an effort to discredit them. No amount of logical argument or practical demonstration will prevent people from constructing and believing in myths, and any attempt to do this is doomed to failure. As linguists, however, we need to make ourselves aware of the basis of our own beliefs about language, and if we feel that there is something not quite right about those beliefs, perhaps an analysis of the myths may help us to transform them. In the final section of this opening chapter I will briefly outline the contents of each successive chapter.

7. THE STRUCTURE OF THE BOOK

Each chapter in this book will deal with language myths that have helped to construct the history of the English language ideologically. Some of them have a long history and either return from time to time to help drive an ideological discourse, or have remained fairly steady over the course of centuries. Older and more lasting myths will be introduced in chapter 5. Other myths, however, are the product of the late-nineteenth-century ideology of standard English as the only legitimate form of language.

In chapter 2, I introduce the *myth of the longevity of English*, which can be conveniently split into two kinds of story. On the one hand, we have the *myth of the ancient language*, in which English is constructed as having a very long history, in some cases well before the migration of the Angles, Saxons and Jutes to England in the fifth century. On the other hand, a second story strand connected to the notion of longevity is the *myth of the unbroken tradition*, which will be the subject of the third chapter.

The *myth of the ancient language* is illustrated here with two quotations, one from Trench (1855) and the other from Kington-Oliphant (1878). In discussing the disappearance of reduplication in the formation of the preterite of strong verbs, Trench (1881: 267) implies that the beginnings of Old English go well back into the past beyond the written evidence that we possess: "From our Old English [reduplication] had died out, leaving the very faintest traces behind it, long before the times which come within the scope of our vision." Trench only implies longevity, but Kington-Oliphant goes so far as to suggest that the *Beowulf* text reaches as far back as the fifth century or even beyond:

> In the Fifth Century our brethren overran Spain, Gaul, and Italy; becoming lords of the soil, and overlaying with their own words the old Latin dialects spoken in those provinces. To this time belongs the Beowulf, which is to us English (may I not say, to all Teutons?) what the Iliad was to the Greeks. The old Epic, written on the mainland, sets before us the doughty deeds of an Englishman, before his tribe had come to Britain. There is an unmistakable Pagan ring about the poem; and a Christian transcriber, hundreds of years afterwards, has sought to soften down this spirit, which runs through the recital of the feats of Ecgtheow's bairn. (Kington-Oliphant 1878: 18)

As we will see in chapter 2, there is no evidence at all to suggest a later date for *Beowulf* than the first decade of the eleventh century.

Chapter 3 tackles the second part of the *myth of the longevity of English*, the *myth of the unbroken tradition*. Most histories of English from the nineteenth almost up to the end of the twentieth century assume that there is an unbroken tradition of English stretching from *Beowulf* and beyond as far as the present. An unbroken tradition assumes not only that there is an uninterrupted record of texts for this period of time, but also that it is legitimate to refer to Old English as "English". To make my position absolutely clear, I shall follow James Milroy (2002) in considering the language before the Norman Conquest to be so different from what followed as to challenge this legitimacy. I shall henceforth talk of Anglo-Saxon rather than Old English. The thrust of chapter 3, however, is to deconstruct this myth by showing how the last set of Anglo-Saxon texts, the *Anglo-Saxon Chronicle(s)*, represents a break in the sociopolitical archive following the Norman Conquest, whereas the "new" archive made use of Latin and Anglo-Norman French.

This is then juxtaposed in chapter 4 to a linguistically driven demonstration that change from Anglo-Saxon to Middle English was well under way in the early eleventh century and that what emerged in the late twelfth century was not a creole, but rather the normal development of several instances of analogical levelling with the constraint of a written language removed. The myth that needs to be deconstructed in this chapter is the modern *myth of the creolisation of English*.

The focus in chapter 5 shifts to the localisation and critical discussion of a whole cluster of related myths that reach back at least as far as the twelfth century, if not further. Most of these myths are by no means restricted to English, although one of them, the *myth of the pure language of the South and the corrupted language of the North* most certainly is. The underlying myth in this cluster is the *myth of homogeneity*.

Chapter 6 looks at the *myth of "greatness"*, in which the lexeme *great* evokes such abstract notions as "remarkability", "power", "influence", "enthusiasm", and so on. At the centre of this chapter is the Great Vowel Shift, which functions conveniently to construct a dividing line between Middle English and Modern English. The division makes sense only from the point of view of the periodisation of English, which, in its turn, serves the purpose of separating modern from medieval literature and helps to construct a standard form of the language in opposition to dialectal forms. One might say that it is after the Great Vowel Shift—which, I argue, did not in reality exist—that the narrow neck of the funnel is reached and all thought of following up on the histories of other forms of English and the emergence of new varieties is closed off. In linguistic terms, vowel shifts are an inherent feature of English. They are still occurring today, and they occurred prior to the Great Vowel Shift.

I return to modern myths in chapter 7, in which I am concerned not so much to outline any specific myth but to raise an awareness of the strong possibility of Swift's *A Proposal for Correcting, Improving and Ascertaining the English Tongue* being taken as the watershed of a further potential myth. Swift's *Proposal* is the quintessential example of the Milroys' complaint tradition and is generally accepted by most scholars as representing a genuine complaint, addressed to the Earl of Oxford, about declining standards of English and the need to introduce a language academy. However, I argue that this analysis of the *Proposal* does not take full account of Swift's ubiquitous satire. It also ignores the wider sociocultural and sociopolitical framework in which the text was published. I shall give a detailed analysis of the *Proposal*, taking account of that framework, to establish an alternative reading of it that, at least potentially, places it alongside other satirical texts. If this interpretation holds its own against the canonical interpretation, it releases the *Proposal* from the simple function of a genuine complaint about English and opens it up for more interesting interpretative possibilities, which do not radically effect the Milroys' argument but tend to add greater force to it. The overall message of this chapter is that commentators should take more trouble to read carefully the central texts from which they derive their arguments, since, by doing so, myths concerning the degeneration of the standard language after a mythical Golden Age can be highlighted and deconstructed more forcefully.

In chapter 8 I restate arguments that I have made elsewhere that the development of the ideology of the standard language in the eighteenth century can be seen as a wider and socially more significant ideology of "politeness". The argument links social standards of "politeness", as this concept is interpreted in eighteenth-century terms, to the commercial interests of a relatively small group of writers and entrepreneurs in the middling orders of society in the second half of the eighteenth century. It draws on work done on the lucrative publishing market in English grammars in this period, and it argues that the ideology of prescriptivism was, at base, driven by commercial interests. At the same time, it helped to establish linguistic distinctions between the middle and upper classes of society and the working classes and the destitute in the first phase of the Industrial Revolution. The myth presented in this chapter is the *myth of the polite language*, and deconstructing it is essential if we wish to take full account of commercial, social and political factors in our attempts to unravel the ideologies of language.

Chapter 9 discusses the nineteenth-century transformation of the *myth of polite language* into the *myth of the legitimate language*, which effectively discriminates against speakers of other forms of English on an "official" basis—on the basis of the sole acceptance of standard English as the unitary, homogeneous language of the nation-state of Britain. The myth was used to promote an ideology of internal national unity in the nineteenth century in the face of the divisive class struggle exacerbated, although not created, by the Industrial Revolution.

The politicisation of language myths in the post–Second World War era in Britain is dealt with in chapter 10, in which the *myth of the legitimate language* is transformed, in not so subtle ways, into the *myth of the educated language*. In both chapters the myths have been and still are used to construct and reproduce the ideology of the standard language.

Chapter 11 tackles the modern *myth of English as a global language*, and it explicitly takes issue with attempts by linguists and non-linguists alike to construct an ideology in which English is promoted as the "world language". This myth is particularly in need of deconstruction because it has begun to infiltrate educational language policies in a large number of countries, in which the learning of other languages as a second language is being, or already has been, demoted to second place behind learning English.

The final chapter, chapter 12, takes stock of what has been presented in the book as a whole and returns to the notion of "language myth" as derived from conceptual metaphors of language and as constituting a major factor in shaping discourse ideologies and discourse archives that were constructed in the past and are presently being constructed. The principal argument in this final chapter is that, while it is certainly important to raise an awareness of the mythological underpinnings of language in a reassessment of the history of English language varieties, it is unwise to believe that we can afford to do away with myths entirely. It is even less wise to think that people can be persuaded of the potential dangers of believing in myths.

I began this first chapter by suggesting that human beings have a deep urge to narrate objects, events, beliefs and explanations into being. Myths are not lies, and they are not completely untruths. They are not consciously told to deceive us, but they are part of a long, communally shared cultural tradition by which we try to make sense of the world in which we live by means of the narrated events of the past. My aim is not to create a history of English that is devoid of myths, but one in which those myths that prevent us from having a clearer view of the relationship between the past and the present can be deconstructed. Modern myths underlying ideologies which, deliberately or not, are driven by political agendas ought to be contested rather than blindly accepted, and they need to be looked at with a critical awareness. The myth presented in chapter 2 is a nineteenth-century myth, and deconstructing it offers a route to many stories that are more fascinating than the myth itself. At the centre of the myth is the fascinating text *Beowulf* and its possible "author".

Chapter 2

Establishing a linguistic pedigree

To this time belongs the Beowulf, which is to us English (may I not say, to all Teutons?) what the Iliad was to the Greeks. The old Epic, written on the mainland, sets before us the doughty deeds of an Englishman, before his tribe had come to Britain.

—Thomas Kington-Oliphant, *The Old and Middle English*, 1878

1. THE FIRE AT ASHBURNHAM HOUSE

In the October 1731 edition of *The Gentleman's Magazine: Or, Trader's Monthly Intelligencer* (Vol. 1), under "Casualties", appeared the following brief report of a fire that had occurred on October 23:

> A Fire broke out in the House of Mr *Bently* [*sic*], adjoining to the King's School near *Westminster Abbey*, which burnt down that part of the House that contained the King's and *Cottonian* Libraries: almost all the printed Books were consumed and part of the Manuscripts. Amongst the latter, those which Dr *Bentley* had been collecting for his *Greek Testament*, for these last ten Years, valued at 2000£.

While the loss of Dr. Bentley's manuscripts, "valued at £2000", must have been a severe blow to his efforts to compile a Greek Testament, the *Gentleman's Magazine* says nothing about the loss to the British people of 114 valuable manuscript codices and the severe damage to 98 more out of a total of 958 in the Cottonian Library (Prescott 1997).

The library was originally compiled by Sir Robert Bruce Cotton (1571–1631) and bequeathed to the British people by his grandson Sir John Cotton in 1700.[1] It was kept in Cotton House in Westminster till 1722, when the dilapidated state of the building necessitated the removal of the library to Essex House in the Strand. At the end of a seven-year lease in 1729, Essex House was considered to be a firetrap, and the Cottonian Library was removed to another firetrap in Little Dean's Yard, Westminster, namely Ashburnham House.[2]

The fire at Ashburnham House, which, contrary to the brief notice in the *Gentleman's Magazine*, gutted the building, plays a central role in the present chapter. Had Dr. Bentley, the former keeper of the Royal Library, and his son, the keeper at the time of the fire, not acted as swiftly as they did, one of the most curious but also most precious manuscript codices[3] of the whole collection would have become a victim of the fire. As it was, Cotton Vitellius A xv was thrown out onto the lawn, badly singed around the edges but essentially intact. Cotton Vitellius A xv contains the only extant manuscript—quite probably the unique manuscript—of the *Beowulf* epic.

The loss of *Beowulf* would have meant the loss of the greatest literary work and one of the most puzzling and enigmatic texts produced during the Anglo-Saxon period.[4] But it would also have made one of the most powerful linguistic myths focusing on the English language, the ***myth of the longevity of English***, immeasurably more difficult to construct. This is not because other Anglo-Saxon texts have not come down to us; it is, rather, because of the perceived literary and linguistic value of *Beowulf*. To construct the longevity myth one needs to locate such texts, and the further back in time they can be located, the "older" the language becomes and the greater is the "cultural" significance that can be associated with that language.[5] The first task in this chapter will thus be to define the ***myth of the longevity of English*** within the framework set out in chapter 1. What are the archives that frame the discourse in such a way as to give evidence of the construction of the myth, and what was the sociohistorical background against which this occurred? Once we have answered those questions, we will be in a better position to discuss how the *Beowulf* manuscript—particularly in its present badly singed state—is at the heart of an alternative discourse from within which another archive may eventually emerge. The challenge from that discourse has not only engendered

---

1. Sir John Cotton died in 1702.
2. A very good account of the fire and the ensuing restoration of the Cottonian Library is given in Prescott 1997.
3. A *codex* (pl. *codices*) is a collection of manuscripts bound together to form one "book".
4. In this chapter I deliberately choose to use the term "Anglo-Saxon" rather than "Old English" to document the fact that what is usually referred to as Old English was a radically different language from that which later emerged.
5. I have placed the lexeme "cultural" in quotation marks here to indicate that the conceptualisation of *culture* as the elite goods, activities and artefacts of a civilisation are meant here rather than "the way of life for an entire society" (Jary & Jary 1991). That is, the reference is to "high" culture rather than to the social anthropological understanding of the term.

a fierce debate over the dating of the poem, but it has also put the myth itself into serious question.

2. THE *MYTH OF THE LONGEVITY OF ENGLISH*

Throughout the first half of the nineteenth century, study of the English language in the tertiary sector of the education system meant the study of what was then called "Anglo-Saxon". Although Anglo-Saxon was clearly a precursor of English, its structure was so different from that of even post-Conquest late-medieval English that it could be seen as a different language. In his prologue to *Alternative Histories of English*, James Milroy makes this point very forcefully:

> The standard view of the transition from Old to Middle English is that, although it appears in the texts to be abrupt, it was actually gradual, and this of course backs up the idea of *the ancient language and unbroken transmission*. Old English, however, is structurally very unlike Modern English or most of Middle English in a number of ways. To show that it is the "same" language on purely internal grounds requires some ingenuity. It is much easier to show that it is different. (2002: 19, emphasis mine)

When Milroy talks of the "idea of the ancient language and unbroken transmission", he is obliquely referring to the ***myth of the longevity of English***, which, in accordance with Milroy's own words, can be divided into two ideological components, the ***myth of the ancient language*** and the ***myth of the unbroken tradition***. He argues that the longevity myth depends on the linguistic ingenuity of scholars of Old English (or Anglo-Saxon) to trace an unbroken transmission from Old to Middle English. Milroy's argument can be expanded by showing, as I do in the present chapter, that although all existing manuscripts theoretically contribute to the construction of the longevity myth certain texts of an assumed literary value, like *Beowulf*, are given priority in the demonstration of the transmission of Anglo-Saxon from the fifth century AD onward.[6] In this chapter I deal more specifically with the ***myth of the ancient language***, and in chapter 3 I focus on the second ideological strand in the longevity myth, the ***myth of the unbroken tradition***, which more specifically concerns the "transition period" between Anglo-Saxon and Middle English.

Myths are constructed as part of naturalised forms of discourse, and naturalised forms of discourse generate Foucault's notion of the archive. As we saw in chapter 1, they have a narrative structure, are essentially fictive and

---

6. Cf. the quotation from Kington-Oliphant (1878) in chapter 1.

are centred on characters and events whose historical existence is assumed to be highly probable or beyond doubt. They thus contain elements of reality since they are derived from the shared experiences of a community, and they are produced, reproduced and transformed socially. The essence of a myth is that it presents a discursive point, or set of discursive points, at which an individual can identify with a common history and shared heritage.

Myths are constructed discursively to justify present actions and beliefs as being "historically" based—despite their essentially fictive nature. In this sense they are in the possession of a community as a whole and not of individuals in that community. In Watts (1999a), I suggest that myths emerge at times that are favourable to their acceptance in and reproduction by the community. The concept of time I am using here is taken from Fernand Braudel's work (1949, 1980), in which he distinguishes between at least three time scales layered one over the other: *la longue durée* (the slow, relentless, endless progress of time over which we, as human beings, have no control); *le temps conjoncturel* (the inevitable cyclic rise and fall of human institutions); and *l'évènement,* or event time (time that covers events in an individual's life but may extend beyond the events themselves and is measured against the time span, hopes, experiences, or dreams of individuals). "Conjunctural" time (*le temps conjoncturel*) refers to specific periods along the *longue durée* at which certain significant historical factors come together. The medieval concept of time/history was cyclic rather than linear, and this will form part of my argument for a change in the discourse archive represented by the *Anglo-Saxon Chronicles* in chapter 3. The Greeks used the term *kairos* to refer such periods in time, and it is at those "kairotic" moments that certain discursive strands may come together to help construct a myth.

My argument in this chapter is that the ***myth of the ancient language*** was discursively constructed from around 1830 to well into the twentieth century. We can interpret this period as the kairotic, or conjunctural, period of time at which the myth was able to emerge. It occurred at an important cyclic convergence of a number of significant elements in British history. Crowley (2003) deals extensively with this period of linguistic thought in Britain, though without mentioning either conjunctural/kairotic time or the term "myth". So I will not go into great detail here. The central part of his argument concerns the genesis of the *New English Dictionary* (which later became the *Oxford English Dictionary*). The compilers of the dictionary considered only the "best" texts as sources for the words they wished to include in the dictionary, and, as we might expect, the "best texts" were literary (Crowley 2003).

Now, while one can sympathise with this tendency in the middle of the nineteenth century, there are sound reasons to reject reliance on the "best texts" at the end of the twentieth and the beginning of the twenty-first century. In addition, the compilers of the *New English Dictionary* were acutely aware of the need to set a chronological cutoff date for what could be considered "English".[7]

---

7. In the "General Explanations" to the proposed dictionary, the date was set much earlier, at 1150, and the original suggestion was to exclude all words "that had become obsolete" prior to that date.

In their *Proposal for the Publication of a New English Dictionary* (1857), they defined the "rise" of English as occurring around the year 1250, although words in the language that could be traced back etymologically to the Anglo-Saxon period were recorded as having a longer history. The period during which "Anglo-Saxon" was discursively transformed into "Old English" was the latter half of the nineteenth century, although the term "Old English" was also used sporadically by the compilers of the *New English Dictionary* before then.

What were the driving forces that gave rise to the *myth of the ancient language*? The major nonlinguistic impetus towards its construction was the blatant contrast between, on the one hand, social inequality in Britain separating the country into Disraeli's "two nations", the wealthy to immensely wealthy upper-middle and aristocratic classes and the at times poverty-stricken working classes and, on the other hand, the rapid social and economic transformations created by the second stage of the Industrial Revolution and the growth of a colonial empire (cf. chap. 9). Squeezed between these two social classes was the rising and rapidly expanding middle class (or what Langford 1989 aptly calls "the middling orders of society") bent on assimilation into the upper end of the social scale rather than on sociopolitical solidarity with the working classes.

The late 1830s witnessed the emergence of Chartism, a proto-working-class movement campaigning for better working conditions, access to education and the right to vote. At the end of the first phase of the Industrial Revolution, the sense of class solidarity among unskilled and manual wage earners and their frequently violent protests in an effort to achieve those (and other) basic human rights created unparalleled social unrest throughout Britain. The government answered these protests with repressive and sometimes violent measures that did nothing to alleviate working-class dissatisfaction (cf. chap. 9).

We can thus interpret the development of the *myth of the ancient language* as part of a general linguistic reflex to the extreme anxiety in the upper and middling levels of the social hierarchy created by Chartism. The myth congealed around the need to provide some sort of answer to the wide and explosive social gulf between the new working classes and other social levels. If anything could bridge this gulf, it was an extension of the voting franchise, education for all and the development of a feeling of national patriotism. Of these three "solutions," the third was obviously more easily achievable than the other two, given the class tensions that divided the country socially, and, from an economic point of view, was far cheaper. Crowley (2003) points out that the two driving forces behind the implementation of the third solution were religion and language.

Part of the answer lay in diverting the focus of unrest in the underprivileged classes of society away from the demand for parliamentary reform, universal suffrage and better working conditions by promoting a sense of national patriotism. As the nineteenth century wore on, the idea that Britain had emerged preeminent among the nations as a global imperial power was used as a counter to social unrest. The notion of a "national language", which was soon to be transformed into the concept of an "imperial language", provided symbolic support for the historic consciousness of a strong nation-state whose roots could be traced back through time. If the "British state" could be traced back to pre-Norman Conquest Anglo-Saxon times, then the "national language" must have existed at that time too. An imperial power needed a unifying, unchanging, standardised imperial language that could be exported to the colonies and dominions as a material commodity and promoted as a carrier of the values of Western civilisation. It needed a language with an unbroken history alongside a history of coherent national development. It also needed a language that could boast a literary tradition, since in that way language could be seen as a cultural product on a par with cultural achievements such as law, art, education, religion and science.

At this point I invoke the modern German term *Kultursprache*, for which there is no adequate translation in English.[8] It implies a connection between language and cultural "achievements" closely related to or even created through the language concerned, and it often occurs in close collocation with the term "literature" (e.g. "Literatur- und Kultursprache"). An equivalent term used during the "long" nineteenth century in the Austrian part of the Austro-Hungarian Empire was *historische Sprache* (historical language), which neatly links the nineteenth-century preoccupation with history to the later-twentieth-century preoccupation with "culture".

German as a "historical language" was frequently invoked by Austrian politicians as a justification for its imposition as the language of the administration and education in non-German-speaking parts of the empire (see Rosita Rindler-Schjerve 2003). A "historical language", or its modern equivalent, *Kultursprache*, is a written language with a significant body of written texts, both fictional and nonfictional, literary and nonliterary. Vetter (2003) suggests that German was frequently promoted as the language of science, as the language that was meant to unify the empire and as its dominant literary language. Her arguments can be transferred almost one-to-one to refer to the development of the "English as the imperial language" discourse in the second half of the nineteenth century in Britain.

The *Kultursprache*/"historical language" ideology promotes the dominance of one language variety over others. It is imposed through specific media, first and foremost the education system, but also by the press from the eighteenth century on and in the twentieth century the broadcast media, radio and television. At least since the eighteenth century, standard English has also been imbued with the same aura of cultural dominance over nonstandard

---

8. The Wildhagen German–English dictionary (1972) does not even give a translation. The *online dictionary german–english* glosses the term into English as "language of a civilized people" (http://odge.de/index.php?ebene=Suche&kw=Kultursprache), which then forces us to define how we understand the term "civilized people". Vetter (2003: 282) uses the English expression "language of significant cultural heritage". Cf. the use of the term *Kultursprache* in chapter 5.

varieties of English (and also over Irish, Welsh, and Scots Gaelic). In this sense, English is also a *Kultursprachel*"historical language", as we shall see in chapters 8 to 10. For the moment, however, we need to discuss how the *Beowulf* text came to be separated from its manuscript representation and reified as an object of the "historical language" discourse to play a prominent role in the ancient language myth.

3. TRACING THE GROWTH OF INTEREST IN THE *BEOWULF* MANUSCRIPT

From the outset we need to make a distinction between the text of *Beowulf* and the unique (fire-damaged) manuscript of the poem contained in Cotton Vitellius A xv now kept in the British Library. The text of *Beowulf* has been hypothesised to have existed from an earlier century, sometime between the seventh and tenth centuries, by virtue of being copied over a period of time from the postulated genesis of the poem till the eleventh century. The extant manuscript contained in Cotton Vitellius A xv was dated by Ker (1957) to lie somewhere between 975 to 1025. Just how many copies there may have been and what the linguistic provenance of the "original" manuscript was remains a mystery for the simple reason that there *is* only one extant manuscript. This, in itself, is a strong argument for rejecting the postulated textual history of *Beowulf*. The arguments that I put forward are based on Kiernan's well-researched and trenchant critique of the textual history of *Beowulf* in *Beowulf and the Beowulf Manuscript* ([1981] 1996), but I wish to add a set of arguments to modify his conclusions. The major aim of the chapter is, of course, to deconstruct the use of *Beowulf* as a major argument in support of the **ancient language myth** by showing that the myth itself is an integral part of a larger hegemonic discourse archive that came under strong pressure from alternative academic archives in the last twenty years of the twentieth century.

Cotton Vitellius A xv is a composite codex that was assembled for the Cottonian library in the first half of the seventeenth century, probably under the orders of Sir Robert Cotton's librarian, Richard James, from two Anglo-Saxon codices, the Southwick Codex (some items of which were in the possession of the Augustinian priory of St. Mary in Southwick, Hampshire) and the Nowell Codex, which, in or around 1563, came into the possession of the antiquarian and Anglo-Saxonist Laurence Nowell (ca. 1515–1571). Unfortunately, there is no evidence of where Nowell had acquired the codex in the first place,[9]

---

9. Some commentators suggest that Nowell acquired the manuscript after the dissolution of a Catholic monastery during Henry VIII's dissolution of the monasteries, which began on a small scale in 1538 following the Act of Suppression (1536) and increased in intensity until 1541.

which makes it difficult, if not impossible, to reconstruct the provenance of the manuscript.[10]

Kiernan (1996) argues convincingly that both codices were also composite, but we have no information on when they may have been assembled. The *Beowulf* manuscript is the fourth item in the Nowell codex, and all five items (the first three being prose texts, whereas *Beowulf* and the *Judith* fragment [item 5] are poetic texts) were copied by the same two scribes.

Apart from the *Judith* fragment, the items deal with different kinds of monster (cf. Orchard 2003), which may have been the reason to have the two scribes copy the manuscripts in the first place. There are two arguments against this thesis, however. First, if that were the case, what is the *Judith* fragment doing in the same codex? Second, there is convincing evidence (presented in Kiernan 1996: 133–140) that the *Beowulf* manuscript was a codex in its own right and that the *Judith* fragment was added to the Nowell codex during the sixteenth century. It is much more likely that all five texts were gathered together to form a composite codex at that time.

As we shall see in a later section of this chapter, the presence of the *Judith* fragment in the codex offers interesting interpretative perspectives supporting the hypothesis of overlapping and disjunctive discourse archives. *Judith* was certainly copied by scribe B and was thus part of the output of the scriptorium in which the first four texts (including *Beowulf*) were copied. As we shall also see later, there is strong evidence that *Beowulf* was practically scribe B's own "private possession". If he had added the *Judith* fragment to the end of *Beowulf*, then anyone deciding to put the texts together later as a collection of stories about monsters could not easily have omitted *Judith*. In point of fact the way in which the Nowell codex was put together is more complex and infinitely more revealing from a sociohistorical and discursive point of view.

Sir Robert Bruce Cotton's librarian, Richard James, had difficulty in categorising *Beowulf* when he catalogued the contents of Cotton Vitellius A xv. He listed the first three items of the original Nowell codex as *4. Dialogi de Chroto et christianitate vbi interloquuntur Pilatus et alij. sicut melius visum est Legendario. Sax. 5. Dialogus inter Saturnum et Salomonem. Saxon. cum Legendis Sancti Cristoferi. 6. Defloratio siue translatio Epistolarum Alexandri ad Aristotelem cum picturis prodigiosorum. Saxonicè*

---

10. There were, unfortunately, two Laurence Nowells known to us during the second half of the sixteenth century. One of these was the owner of the codex, which we know for the simple reason that he wrote his name on the first folio of the Nowell codex, and the other was the Dean of Lichfield Cathedral, at which there was a scriptorium at the time when the extant manuscript of *Beowulf* was prepared. For the sake of Kiernan's argument it would of course be ideal to be able trace the manuscript back to that scriptorium and to hypothesise that it finally ended up in Dean Nowell's possession. The convenience of such an argument would be that it would provide a simple solution to the relatively large number of Anglian features in the poem. But the facts of history are sometimes a little unkind, and the provenance of the manuscript may remain forever a mystery to us. At one point in his book, however, Kiernan does allow himself the bold step of suggesting that either the scriptorium at Lichfield or that at Tamworth, both on the edge of Danelaw territory, could have been where the manuscript was copied.

8. *Fragmentum Saxon: de Iuditha et Holoferne.*[11] But he left a gap between numbers 6 and 8, indicating that *Beowulf* was an anomaly to him.[12] One reason may have been that the other four items had a clear Christian or pre-Christian but classical connection, whereas the first five lines of *Beowulf* almost declare it to be a story from a heathen background:

Hwæt we gardena	in geardagum
Lo! We of the spear Danes	*in the days of yore*
þeodcyninga	þrym gefrumon
of the people of the kings	*the glory heard tell*
hu þa æþelingas	eller fremedon.
of how the princes	*brave deeds accomplished.*
Oft Scyld Scefing	sceaþena þreatum
Often Scyld Scefing	*with bands of warriors*
monegum mægþum	meodosetla ofteah…
from many peoples	*mead benches seized…*

("Lo! we have heard tell of the glory of the warlike Danes, the people of the kings, in bygone days, of how the princes accomplished brave deeds. Often Scyld, son of Scef, seized mead-benches with bands of warriors from many peoples…")

Whatever the reason for the unusual gap in the catalogue, we could argue that it is hardly surprising that enthusiasm for this apparently heathen poetic text was lukewarm in the early part of the seventeenth century, to say the least.

When Thomas Smith, the unofficial guardian of the library in Sir John Cotton's days, published a catalogue of the contents of the library in 1696, he listed the contents of Cotton Vitellius A xv as having only six items, thus missing one of the items in the Southwick codex and, significantly, also missing *Beowulf*. After Sir John's death in 1702, one of the commissioners appointed by Parliament to catalogue the Cottonian library was the palaeographer Humfrey Wanley, who had previously been employed as assistant in the Bodleian Library in Oxford and had made several unsuccessful attempts to gain access to the manuscripts in Sir John Cotton's library. Wanley undertook to compile a composite catalogue of all the significant libraries in

---

11. "4. Dialogue on Christ and Christianity in which Pilate and others speak. As is better seen in a collection of legends. Saxon 5. A dialogue between Saturn and Salomon, Saxon with legends of St. Christopher 6. The interpretation or translation of the letters of Alexander to Aristotle with pictures of monsters. Saxon 8. A fragment. Saxon. On Judith and Holofernes."

12. Kiernan (1996) speculates that there are two possible reasons for this omission. Either James did not know how to categorise this part of the codex and left it blank with the intention of attempting some form of categorisation at a later date (note that he was aware that there *was* a seventh text as he makes a jump in his numbering from 6 to 8) or the manuscript was out on loan (a not unusual occurrence in Sir Robert Cotton's days, considering his generosity in allowing privileged individuals to take manuscripts out of the library on a temporary basis). Kiernan uses this conjecture to support his conviction that the *Beowulf* manuscript was in fact originally a separate (and thus separable) ms. I shall have more to say on this matter later in this chapter.

England, which was finally published in 1705 with the title *Librorum Vett. Septentrionalium, qui in Angliæ Biblioth. extant, Catalogus Historico-Criticus (Antiquæ Literaturæ Septentrionalis Libri Duo)*. In his *Catalogus Historico-Criticus*, Wanley corrected the oversights made by the previous cataloguers of Cotton Vitellius A xv by writing "In hoc libro, qui Poeseos Anglo-Saxonicæ egregium est exemplum, descripta videntur bella quæ Beowulfus, quidam Danus, ex Regio Scyldingorum stirpe Ortus, gessit contra Sueciæ Regulos." ["In this book, which is an excellent example of poetry in Anglo-Saxon, can be seen fine descriptions in which Beowulf, a certain Dane, originally from the royal line of the Scyldings, performs against the princes of Sweden" (p. 219)], which is a grossly misleading summary of what *Beowulf* is all about.

Notwithstanding and perhaps precisely because of his erroneous summary of the contents, Wanley's description came to the notice of two antiquarians from Denmark, the Dane Jakob Langebek and the Icelander Grímur Jónsson Thorkelin, Regius Professor at the University of Copenhagen from 1766 to 1808. On a trip to England in the 1780s with the express purpose of hunting down texts with any reference to Danish history, Thorkelin hired James Matthews, an employee of the British Museum, to transcribe *Beowulf* for him, this first transcription being referred to as Thorkelin A. However, Matthews's transcription was so unsatisfactory that Thorkelin, who apparently knew no Anglo-Saxon, took it upon himself to carry out a second transcription (Thorkelin B) in 1787. Thorkelin then published the first edition and translation of the poem in 1815. Oddly, however, the translation was into Latin.

The poet Sharon Turner translated some of the lines of *Beowulf* in 1805, but the first full English translation of and commentary on the poem was published by John Kemble from 1835 to 1837, a time frame that corresponds to the first beginnings of the Chartist movement in England. Although Kemble does not openly suggest a date for the original composition of the poem, his derogatory comments on the work of the two scribes who copied the extant manuscript leaves no doubt about the fact that he considered the poem to have had a long history of transmission:

> All persons who have had much experience of Anglo-Saxon MSS. know how hopelessly incorrect they are in every way...which can perhaps be accounted for by the supposition that professional copyists brought to their task (in itself confusing enough) both lack of knowledge and lack of care. (1837: xxiii–xxiv)

In addition, Kemble had nothing but scorn for Thorkelin's translation into Latin, considering it "only a copy, and a careless copy too" (xxi).

Interest in *Beowulf* developed rapidly throughout the nineteenth century, and figure 2.1 shows the number of translations and editions of the poem decade by decade after Kemble's translation. During the course of the nineteenth century the belief that *Beowulf* had a long manuscript history going back into at least the eighth century became accepted as fact, a "fact" that was first seriously challenged by Kiernan's publication in 1981 of *Beowulf and the Beowulf Manuscript*. However, before reviewing some of Kiernan's arguments, the following questions need to be put:

1. How does the Nowell codex come to be made up of three prose texts, *Beowulf* and the *Judith* fragment? (see section 7)
2. Why is the *Judith* text only a fragment, and how and when did it come to be bound together with the other texts? (see section 7)
3. Why was *Beowulf* of no apparent interest to antiquarians in the sixteenth and early seventeenth centuries? (see section 7)
4. What caused the initial interest in the manuscript?
5. Why was there a sudden surge of interest in the "text" of *Beowulf* in the latter half of the nineteenth century rather than in the manuscript itself?
6. Why, in the face of increasingly incontrovertible palaeographical and codicological evidence to the contrary—evidence that can be at least partially backed up by sociohistorical arguments—does the academic community still find it so difficult to let go of the belief in a long textual history of *Beowulf*?

Plausible answers to these questions bring us straight back to the issue of discourse archives and the myths that are used to construct them. Neither the supporters of the long textual history of *Beowulf* nor the supporters of the theory that it is an eleventh-century text can ever be proved right or wrong. We may forever be locked in the prison of conjecture, but it is precisely that prison, the prison of our own human limitations, that we need to investigate in more detail.

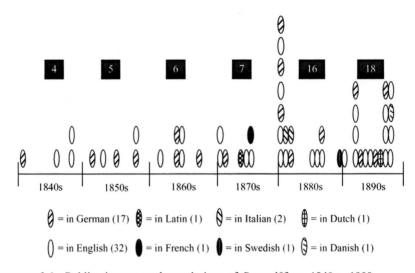

FIGURE 2.1. Publications on and translations of *Beowulf* from 1840 to 1900

4. THE DATING OF *BEOWULF*

The central text on which the **ancient language myth** was developed has always been *Beowulf*, not Anglo-Saxon recipes, chronicles, wills, charters, religious tracts and legal documents, nor even other Anglo-Saxon poems. The reason is obvious: *Beowulf* is considered to be an epic poem, which places English into the same illustrious league as the classical languages Latin and Greek. If the dating of *Beowulf* can push the genesis of the poem as far back into the Anglo-Saxon period as possible, the "classical", literary prestige of English is greatly enhanced. English might then conceivably be presented as the oldest *Kultursprache* in Europe.

In the 1980s a dispute broke out over the dating of *Beowulf* following the publication of *Beowulf and the Beowulf Manuscript* by Kevin Kiernan in 1981. As we know from Ker's meticulous dating of Anglo-Saxon manuscripts (Ker 1957), the *Beowulf* manuscript as we have it today was written within a fifty-year period from 975 to 1025. Ker was not able to be more precise than this, which has led Kiernan and his followers to propose that the manuscript dates from some time after the accession of Cnut to the throne of England in 1016 and some of Kiernan's opponents to place it within the earlier part of the fifty-year period. A crucial factor in the argument has been the consideration of the sociohistorical, sociopolitical situation of England during that time.

In 978 Æthelræd acceded to the throne as Æthelræd II upon the sudden death of his half-brother King Edward (referred to after his death as "the Martyr"). Æthelræd was not beyond suspicion of having had Edward murdered, since Edward reigned only three years after the death of his father, King Edgar. Æthelræd earned himself the pseudonym "the Unready", in Anglo-Saxon "Unræd", which means "ill advised" or "without advice". Opinions are divided as to the success of Æthelræd as a ruler (see Howard 2003), but one thing is certain; his reign was comparatively long, 38 years (to the year 1016) including a break of little more than a year after 1013, a period that Æthelræd spent in exile in Normandy.

The bane of Æthelræd's reign was the resumption of Viking raids on England in 991, after a period of peace and consolidation following Alfred's treaty with Guthrum around 890 and the establishment of the Danelaw in the northern and eastern parts of the country. There are a number of hypotheses as to why these raids resumed. The logical explanation is demographic: Scandinavia was again experiencing a population boom incommensurate with its ability to feed the population. Overpopulation often leads to migration, particularly the migration of surplus males. The victims of the Viking raids were generally more prosperous countries relatively nearby, which the raiders could plunder and, in the first stages of the migration, return home from readily. During the course of time, however, many of the raiders stayed in the territory they had plundered as mercenary troops, settlers and traders.

England, in other words, was wealthy enough to attract those in search of spoils, particularly silver bullion, plate and coin, and spacious enough to attract those looking for an opportunity to settle and make a better life for themselves. English military weakness, bad leadership and a complex system of payment (*gafol* "tribute", *metsunge* "provisioning" and *heregeld* "payment of a foreign army as a mercenary force"), which was either designed as a ploy to entice the raiders to leave English shores or to induce them to stay as mercenaries in the service of Æthelræd during the last decade of the tenth century, is assumed to have weakened the English economy considerably by creating a need for higher taxation. In 991, £10,000 was granted as *gafol* and *metsunge* to the Viking raiders and, in 994, £16,000 as *gafol* and *metsunge* and £22,000 as *heregeld*. This rather ineffective method of keeping the Viking raiders at bay continued after the turn of the century. In the year 1002, £24,000 as *gafol* and *metsunge* were paid out; in 1007, £36,000; in 1009, £3,000; in 1012, the astronomical figure of £48,000; and in 1014, £21,000 as *heregeld* (for details, see Howard 2003: 20). However, Howard argues that the overall effect of the Viking raids was to stimulate the economy:

> Billeting Scandinavian forces upon the land would have increased the value of land, as would the demand for provisions for native and foreign forces. Paying them geld, whether by way of tribute for their mercenary activities, forced the government, nobility and the Church to bring back huge amounts of stored silver into circulation as coin and it also drew silver into England from abroad.... The recipients of the payments were keen to acquire land, goods and services, and, even when the coins were taken back to Scandinavia, they served to benefit trade because they could be returned to England in exchange for manufactured goods and other produce, such as wheat, woollens, tin and honey. There was an encouragement to trade with England because the coinage had a fiduciary element and was worth more than its intrinsic silver content in England. (2003: 19–21)

During the first decade of the eleventh century, and in particular after the St. Brice's day massacre of Danes in England in 1002, sanctioned by King Æthelræd, the Danish raids on England began to take on a systematic character and, from 1003 on, were organised and led by Swein Forkbeard, king of Denmark, whose sister Gunnhild, a hostage in England at the time, had perished in the massacre. It gradually became clear that Swein's ultimate ambition was the conquest of England, which was finally achieved at the end of 1013. However, Swein died in February 1014, a few weeks after the conquest, which immediately left the question of the succession wide open. Swein's son Cnut had a claim to the throne, but the elders decided to call back Æthelræd from his exile in Normandy. After a defeat at Gainsborough, Cnut returned to Denmark. In 1015, he was back with an army which attacked Wessex from the Dorset coast. Æthelræd died in April 1016, leaving the kingdom to his son Edmund Ironside. Cnut and Edmund decided to divide the kingdom between themselves, but Edmund died in November 1016, and Cnut was proclaimed king of England, thus uniting England, Denmark, southern Sweden and southern Norway in a short-lived, embryonic

Anglo-Scandinavian "empire" until Cnut's death in 1035. Cnut's reign was peaceful, and he spent most of it in England promoting English traditions, the economy and the English Church and earning himself the pseudonym "the Great".

Kiernan argues that "it is, at least, highly unlikely that a poem so obviously sympathetic to the Danes, and indeed extolling them for their peaceful foreign policy, could have been copied in Late West Saxon during the calamitous reign of Æthelræd Unræd from 978 to 1016" (1996: 15). But if Howard is correct and the Viking raids had an overall positive effect on the English economy, it is not beyond belief that folk poetry extolling the Danes and Scandinavian legends might have flourished in precisely that part of the country that profited most during the reign of Æthelræd and whose population expanded during that time, namely the Danelaw. The *Beowulf* epic, or rather its component parts, had probably been circulating orally in the Danelaw area for many years prior to the accession of Cnut in 1016. We know that Swein's army enjoyed support from the population in the North and East of the country and that on his march south in 1013 Swein ordered that no looting or pillaging should take place in the Danelaw area. The freedom to do so was expressly given after Watling Street had been crossed. We also know that Cnut and Thorkell the Tall invaded Wessex from the south coast in 1015 because they could be absolutely sure of political support in the North and East.

Kiernan's assessment of the reign of Æthelræd as being "not years for Englishmen, least of all Anglo-Danes, to be openly betraying Danish sympathies in splendid epic poems" (1996: 16) is, on the face of things, sensible, but his systematic forensic analysis of the manuscript actually opens the way to retaining Ker's 50-year period during which it was copied and, more intriguing still, allows us to surmise that committing *Beowulf* to written form was the life work of the second scribe.

This should not surprise us if we look more closely at the nature of folk literature. The concept of the "author" or the "poet" is simply not applicable to the genesis of the songs and stories of ordinary people. There is still a very rich folk tradition throughout the British Isles today in the first decade of the twenty-first century. The songs are frequently given new melodies appropriate to the musical tastes of the age. The texts are often fused and almost certainly adapted and changed through time and from performer to performer. Some do have identifiable authors but in the performance and in the communal enjoyment of the stories they tell, they are simply "traditional". The identities of the original "authors" are not important, and the greatest accolade for anyone who has written a song is anonymity—to hear someone announce it and sing it as a song that they "picked up" from the singing of someone else in some other place. The song has then become the possession of the people. Committing such texts to written form raises the issue of authorship, and this is the issue that will be central to my deconstruction of the *ancient language myth*. Before we tackle that problem, however, we need to examine Kiernan's arguments and some of the counterarguments that have been raised against him in more detail.

5. KIERNAN'S ARGUMENTS

Kiernan's arguments are based on a painstaking forensic study of the extant manuscript and on piecing together the conclusions he has come to with respect to the original writing of the manuscript and its possible authorship, on the one hand, and the sociopolitical events in England at the time of its preparation, on the other. He begins with a meticulous examination of the constituent parts of Vitellius A xv. For the moment, we can leave the discussion of the Southwick codex on one side, since it is only associated with *Beowulf* by virtue of its inclusion in Cotton Vitellius A xv.

In copying the Nowell codex, scribe A used an Anglo-Insular script with clear influences from Carolingian script, and scribe B used an early form of Anglo-Insular script (Boyle 1997: 25). Part of the reasons for Ker's dating of the manuscript between 975 and 1025 is the use of these two scripts. Dumville (1987) argues that the script used by scribe B is not to be found beyond 1011/1012, which vitiates Kiernan's argument that the *Beowulf* codex was copied in the reign of King Cnut. However, since the Anglo-Carolingian script is not to be found in any of the manuscripts dated before 1000, the palaeographical argument for dating the *Beowulf* codex to the beginning of Cnut's reign rests entirely on similarities between scribe B's hand and examples of the later form of Anglo-Insular script. The latter, however, shows Carolingian influences, is more compact than the older form of Anglo-Insular and is not present till well into Cnut's reign. In the second edition of *Beowulf and the Beowulf Manuscript*, Kiernan presents, as comparative evidence, a Worcester vernacular, chirographic lease datable to between 1033 and 1038. Unfortunately, he restricts himself to the discussion of the letter <a>. The evidence is dismantled by Rose (1997), who shows that the later form of Anglo-Insular script, which has Carolingian influences, is closer to scribe A's hand than to scribe B's. Rose concludes that Dumville's statement about the nonoccurrence of the older form of Anglo-Insular beyond 1011/1012 is a palaeographical fact that precludes Kiernan's theory of a manuscript date for *Beowulf* after this time. Hence, the statement that *Beowulf* was commissioned by the court of Cnut the Great sometime after 1016 is pure conjecture on Kiernan's part.[13]

On the other hand, Kiernan presents four strong arguments to support his theory that the *Beowulf* manuscript, although it was copied by the same scribes who copied the first three texts in the Nowell codex (scribe A) and the final text, the *Judith* fragment (scribe B), was prepared at a different time and as a codex in its own right. The first argument concerns the different styles of the capital letters in the first three prose items in the Nowell codex and in *Beowulf*. He states (1996: 141) that "significantly, the style of the capitals does

---

13. Rose (1997: 140) argues that those texts that definitely were produced for Cnut's court were "lavish, sumptuous, skilfully-illuminated deluxe productions", and he suggests that "the *Beowulf* manuscript is pallid and pedestrian, utterly unlike the known examples of book-production in Cnut's reign".

remain constant through the prose texts, but it changes notably at the beginning of *Beowulf*", and he adds that "the letters in the *Beowulf* line are drawn with more care, more evenness, more technical draftsmanship, than those in the line from *Alexander's Letter*".

Kiernan's second argument concerns the quantity and quality of the corrections made by both scribes, but particularly by scribe B, in each other's manuscript sections. Roughly 180 corrections were made, and Kiernan describes them as "intelligent". From this we can conclude that both scribes understood exactly what they were copying. As a comparison, the prose texts display what he calls a "marked lack of interest, amounting at times to outright negligence" on the part of scribe A in copying them. Kiernan then extends this argument by giving a number of concrete examples to demonstrate this carelessness in the prose texts.

The third argument concerns the meticulous proofreading carried out by scribe B at different times of both his own work and that of scribe A. As Kiernan points out, "Surely the second scribe would have proofread the prose texts as well if *Beowulf* at the time were merely the fourth item in an English *Liber Monstrorum*" (1996: 145). The evidence shows that both scribes had a very high opinion of the *Beowulf* text and made every effort to ensure that it was faithfully and accurately copied. Carrying this argument further, Kiernan concludes that folio 145 must have been a replacement since it breaks the pattern of hair and flesh sides of the vellum[14] in that, whereas its conjugate folio 142 shows the flesh side up and the hair side down, fol. 145 has the hair side up and the flesh side down. In addition, in line 6 of the recto of folio 145 there are more words than in any other line on the page. Line 6 even spills over onto line 7, in which a new fitt[15] begins. A major blunder, probably an omission, must have been noticed on this folio leading to the replacement of the whole leaf.

The final argument is that the gatherings[16] in the *Beowulf* codex are fundamentally different from those in the prose texts. Kiernan's argument is complex, so I shall restrict myself to a statement of what he says about the arrangement of the quires[17] and to the evidence that scribe B went to a lot of trouble to squeeze the *Beowulf* text into the space available to him:

> The last two gatherings of the *Beowulf* codex are uncharacteristic in several respects: they are five-sheet gatherings from the start, their sheets are all arranged so that hair side faces outward, and they are ruled for twenty-two lines to the page instead of the normal twenty. (1996: 148)

---

14. Vellum was made from calfskin and parchment from the split skin of a sheep. The hair side of a sheet of vellum is the outer side of the skin, that side on which the animal's hair grew.

15. A fitt is a canto or portion of a ballad or an epic poem.

16. See footnote 17.

17. A quire is composed of four folded sheets of parchment or vellum to form 8 leaves, or 16 pages in all. A "gathering" is also used in the same sense.

Evidence that scribe B needed to squeeze the text onto the last quire of vellum available to him is provided by the unprecedented number of abbreviations towards the end of the text and the fact that the last word of *Beowulf*— *geornost*—spills onto the twenty-second line.

The information we have gathered so far from Kiernan's controversial book and articles critically reviewing some of his assumptions consists of the following points:

1. The manuscript itself was unlikely to have been copied any later than 1011/1012.
2. It is thus highly unlikely to have been copied during the reign of Cnut the Great.
3. Scribe A used a script that was typical of the earlier third of the eleventh century, whereas scribe B used a script that was typical of the latter part of the tenth century (and from this we may be able to conclude that scribe B was older than scribe A).
4. While they were both working on *Beowulf*, both scribes were meticulous in their correction of each other's work, and must therefore have understood the text.
5. Scribe B must have continued correcting the *Beowulf* manuscript after scribe A's mysterious disappearance in folio 175v, lines 3 to 4 (I shall return to this point below).
6. The *Beowulf* manuscript was originally a codex in its own right.
7. The three prose texts in the Nowell codex, *Beowulf* and the *Judith* fragment all came from the same scriptorium (since they were copied by scribes A and B). They were not originally part of the same codex but must have been gathered together in the Nowell codex at a much later date.

On the verso of folio 175 in the eleventh quire, scribe A suddenly stopped copying. The first four letters of *moste* are in scribe A's hand, but the <e> and the rest of the text of *Beowulf* are by scribe B. This has given rise to the speculation that scribe A suddenly fell ill and, since he did not return to complete his part of the overall manuscript, that he may have died. When scribe B took over in the eleventh quire, he must have already finished copying his part of *Beowulf*, which starts at quire 12. Hence he realised that he only had the remainder of quire 11 to use. To get the rest of the text into quire 11, however, he had to subtly squeeze in an extra line on folio 177 verso, folio 178 recto, folio 178 verso and folio 179 recto. But how did he know this was going to be necessary? In discussing the degree of compression in scribe A's and scribe B's hands when compared to the scribe of the Worcester chirographic lease, Rose (1997: 138) unwittingly provides the answer. The degree of compression in scribe A's hand was almost 1mm. per letter greater than scribe B's, which allowed scribe B to calculate how many words he would *not* get in on the remaining folios[18] of quire 11 if he stuck to the 20-line ruling. We can thus add the following point to the seven listed above:

8. The *Beowulf* poem is composed of two stories, Beowulf's adventures at the court of Hrothgar in Denmark (which scribe A must have undertaken to copy) and his final fight with the dragon as king of the Geats (which scribe B must have already copied).

From this we can conclude point 9:

9. Scribe B was already familiar with the story of Beowulf's fight with the dragon before they decided to copy the text, and possibly also knew of the story of his youthful exploits.

The weakest part of Kiernan's argument is his insistence on placing *Beowulf* within the reign of Cnut the Great. But the strongest part is the evidence, first suggested by Tilman Westphalen (1967), that folio 179 is a palimpsest.[19] When Zupitza made his facsimile of the manuscript in 1882, he assumed, according to Westphalen, that folio 179 was a damaged text that had been freshened up by a later hand. However, Zupitza made no statements on whether the "freshened up" text was in scribe B's hand or in a different hand. Kiernan argues, from a palaeographical point of view, that the "freshened up" text *was* in scribe B's hand and that the slight differences between the two hands are the result of aging: that scribe B made the palimpsest 10 to 20 years after first copying the text. The palimpsest theory has been roundly rejected by scholars who insist on a genesis of the *Beowulf* text prior to the tenth century (cf. many of the contributions in Chase 1997) and who offer somewhat unlikely explanations of how the folio became damaged. However, Westphalen's and Kiernan's arguments that it is a palimpsest cannot simply be ignored. In fact, they offer by far the most convincing explanation for the physical condition of folio 179. Why, then, should this theory meet with a storm of protest?

The reason is obvious. The idea that scribe B, long after having taken over in scribe A's absence and having completed the copying of scribe A's part of the manuscript in quire 11, should have returned to the text, erased what he had already copied and substituted it with what is effectively a shorter text is anathema to the belief that scribes simply copied texts and did not change them. If folio 179 is a palimpsest—and all the evidence points to that being the case—then scribe B partially revised the text and was therefore, on that

---

18. A folio is a sheet of vellum/parchment folded so as to give four leaves or pages, 1 verso (i.e. the outer part of the sheet folded inwards to give the first page), 2 recto (the inner or upper-facing part of the sheet), 3 recto and 4 verso.

19. A *palimpsest* is a leaf in a manuscript whose text has been scraped or washed off so that the leaf can be used for a new text.

folio at least, the author. The essence of the *ancient language myth* is the mystery surrounding the authorship of *Beowulf* and the vagueness of the evidence that supports the theory that the manuscript is the end product of a line of texts copied since the eighth (or even the seventh) century. Arguments based on the form of language used in the poem, on the metrics of Anglo-Saxon poetry, on textual references to burials such as that at Sutton Hoo and to King Offa of Mercia are ineffectual when compared with the palimpsest argument.

There are three further pieces of evidence to support the hypothesis that scribe B erased his own text. First, folio 179 could have been taken from some other codex and the text on it erased to provide an empty folio on which to copy the new text. But if this was the case and scribe B was the person who wrote the new text on the palimpsest, it was still his text on the original folio that was now replaced. Surely the easiest thing to do was to erase the text on the original folio and simply write the new text over it. In effect, scribe B either misjudged the adhesive quality of the ink or did not leave the folio enough time to dry, since many of the letters have not adhered well to the folio and have run.

Second, if the whole folio was replaced, scribe B needed to erase the first four lines at the top of folio 180 recto. Damage to folio 179 and its consequent replacement does not explain the need to continue erasing text at the top of the next folio. The third piece of evidence to support the argument that scribe B made a palimpsest of one of the folios that he himself had copied is one of textual coherence. The point at which scribe B took over from scribe A is immediately prior to the homecoming episode linking the story of the younger Beowulf at Hrothgar's court and the older Beowulf in the dragon episode. As such, it was conceptualised as a thematic link between the two parts of the epic and was originally part of scribe A's responsibility to copy.

As Kiernan points out, "The homecoming episode was written after the dragon episode, as a transitional link between two formerly unrelated *Beowulf* narratives" (1996: 259), and it contains a number of inconsistencies with respect to the story of the younger Beowulf. It is at least conceivable that the original homecoming episode did not link the two narratives as well as scribe B wished and that, long after finishing the manuscript, he decided to try and improve on it. At least in this respect scribe B was part author of *Beowulf*, and the manuscript was probably in his personal possession. In addition, it appears to have been a draft on which scribe B was still working years after copying it. Kiernan makes clear that "these arguments are systematically rejected by other scholars almost as soon as they are made, and it is safe to say that the theory is generally repudiated by Beowulfians as a group" (1996: 250). He puts this down to the belief held by most readers of the poem that this represents "an impotent assault on the artistic integrity of the poem" (250). I put it down to the inability of believers in the *ancient language myth* to give up using *Beowulf* as the central element in projecting that myth.

6. SOCIOLINGUISTIC ARGUMENTS IN FAVOUR OF A DANELAW PROVENANCE FOR *BEOWULF*

Linguists arguing for an early date of the *Beowulf* text and a long history of transmission through copying which results in the extant manuscript, despite the loss of all the hypothesised earlier manuscripts, were on relatively safe ground as long as they were looking at the manuscript from a purely linguistic point of view. But since the advent of sociolinguistic research in the 1960s, the arguments can be shown to be worthless against the background of what we now know about language change, linguistic variation, processes of standardisation, dialectal variation and stylistic differences between text genres.

Kiernan suggests that "by far the most persuasive case for an early date rests in the bewildering variety of linguistic forms, of uncertain date and dialect, embedded in the essentially Late West Saxon dialect of the preserved text" (1996: 23). However, this becomes a problem only if one firmly believes in a homogeneous linguistic system spoken by members of a socially homogeneous speech community. Since the appearance of the groundbreaking article "Empirical foundations for a theory of language change", by Weinreich, Labov, and Herzog (1968), sociolinguists have assumed the opposite. No linguistic system is ever homogeneous, no speaker (or even writer) is ever in perfect control of such a system and no linguistic system can ever be divorced from the social and cultural conditions of its use by a potentially endless number of speakers (writers). Language always varies from speaker to speaker and from one occasion of its use to the next. That variability is the essence of change in language. There may be variability without the language necessarily having to change, but there could never be change if there were no linguistic variation.

The misguided belief in linguistic homogeneity leads scholars to desperate measures in explaining the profusion of varied forms in the *Beowulf* manuscript. Many have maintained that those forms which are not West Saxon must be relics copied into the successive manuscripts of *Beowulf* by somewhat mindless scribes.[20] We have already seen that scribe A of the Nowell codex could certainly show a lackadaisical attitude towards copying if we examine his performance in the three prose texts of the codex, but his work on *Beowulf* was meticulous, and both he and scribe B provide adequate evidence that they understood perfectly what they were writing out. The only two Anglo-Saxon texts that can be shown to have a long textual history (Cædmon's hymn and Bede's death song) do not have traces of other "dialects" or earlier forms in their transition from early Northumbrian to Late West Saxon.

Klaeber (1950: cviii) suggests a syntactic test whereby progressively later texts should show an increase in the use of the old demonstratives used as the

---

20. Witness the birth of the ***mindless scribe myth***, which has severely hampered sensible discussion of sociolinguistic aspects of medieval manuscripts throughout the Anglo-Saxon and Middle English periods.

new definite determiners, a decrease in the use of weak adjective and noun inflections and an increase in the use of the determiner with a weak adjective and noun. So if the *Beowulf* manuscript has high proportions of such structures, these must be traces of the earlier manuscripts. The argument crumbles into dust, however, if we accept a predilection on the part of poets to use archaic forms of language in their work. *The Battle of Brunanburh* and *The Battle of Maldon* are both tenth-century productions, but they, too, have similar kinds of archaic, formulaic syntactic structure. Even today, songwriters in the folk idiom use archaic structures to evoke an atmosphere of the past.[21] A spurious syntactic argument such as Klaeber's is based on a disregard for variation and simply takes no account of different styles in different written genres.

A further "linguistic test" for the conjectured long manuscript history of *Beowulf* is phonetic/metrical. The argument runs as follows: certain half lines do not appear to scan well because they contain contractions. Hence in the "original" text they must have appeared with uncontracted forms; for example, *gepēon* is said to appear in place of a reconstructed original **gepihan*. The argument is spurious, however, since, in accordance with syllable theory in phonology (Roca & Johnson 1999, chap. 9; Zec 2007), both words are trisyllabic (*ge- pē- on* and *ge- pi- han*), and we can surely expect both performers and listeners (readers) to have had a good sense of the rhythmic and metrical conventions of their own poetry. In addition, if scribes were sensible enough to change **gepihan* to *gepeon* from one older manuscript to another, why did they fail to insert definite determiners into a large percentage of determinerless noun phrases in *Beowulf*?

I will not run through the story of the hypothetical "early" form *wundini*, which resulted from a blind reliance on Zupitza's facsimile, except to say that it remains the only argument left to those who wish to use linguistic evidence to prove their hypothesis of the long manuscript history of *Beowulf*. Kiernan makes the eminently commonsense point that if one were to carry out a detailed study of the manuscript rather than the text, the hypothesised word *wundini* disappears, and the word that can be suggested (and only suggested because of the damage to the vellum at this point in the manuscript) is *wunden*, which would be perfectly normal for the poetry of the early eleventh century.

How can we account for the variation of forms that occur in the *Beowulf* manuscript? First, we should remember that sociolinguists know very little indeed about dialectal variation in pre-Conquest times. The estimated population of England at the turn of the eleventh century was between 1.5 million and 1.8 million. With relatively poor means of transportation overland, goods

---

21. Irish songwriter Sean Mone recently wrote a song called "New Holland Grove" about Irish immigration to North America in the nineteenth century. The refrain is as follows: "Here's **a health unto you**, sweet Keady town, a village **of renown** / And **likewise** to New Holland Grove where pleasure could be found. / Where **lads and lasses sport and play** on the bright long summer's day, / But **I am resolved** to leave all behind, all for Americay" (archaic, formulaic structures noted in bold type). The distance in time between the fictive experience and the song itself is roughly 150 years.

were more easily carried by boat around the coasts and up the navigable rivers, which led to population clusters in coastal areas and along the courses of such rivers as the Thames, the Severn, the Humber, the Trent, the Yorkshire Ouse and the Avon. So although population in those areas was not necessarily scattered, communication between them was not always easy. We would therefore expect a reasonably broad range of spoken dialects to have evolved from the fifth to the eleventh century, but we have little to go on apart from the written documents that have survived.

There are notorious difficulties in extrapolating from written documents to hypothesised oral usage, which I will not go into here. Suffice it to say that we can very broadly accept a range of dialects reaching from the northern limits of "English"-speaking territory (present-day Northumberland and the southeastern counties of lowland Scotland) down to the River Humber. These have traditionally been called "Northumbrian", although even within this large area there must have been degrees of variation. A second area stretched from the east coast south of the Humber across to the Welsh borders and as far south as the Thames valley, constituting the varieties that have traditionally been called "Anglian". Here, however, a language contact situation existed roughly to the east of the Roman road called Watling Street and created by widespread Danish settlement in those areas. We can assume that speakers of Danish in what was called the Danelaw area would have lost their mother tongue within roughly three generations if they were in frequent contact with speakers of Anglo-Saxon, but not before Danish had exerted a considerable lexical and morphological influence on eastern Anglian forms of Anglo-Saxon. The Danish (or it might be more appropriate to talk of "Norse") influence also extended into the Northumbrian area, and there is evidence that Danish (or Norse) was still spoken in York in the tenth century.

The two remaining dialect areas were Kentish south of the River Thames in the southeastern part of the country as far as the coast, and West Saxon roughly south of the Thames to the coast and stretching west as far as the Bristol Channel coast, Cornwall and the River Severn. The struggle for the control of England after the Danish incursions of the late eighth and ninth centuries led to the hegemony of the West Saxon royal house and, from the time of King Alfred on, the imposition of a proto-standard written variety of West Saxon.

At this point, we need to be very careful about using the term "standard", which is too often and too glibly used to refer to this written variety in the literature. In chapters 8, 9 and 10, I will focus in more detail on the discourse of the "standard language", which the Milroys have rightly called "the ideology of the standard". Linguists in the twentieth century have often failed to see that their concept of a homogeneous standard variety is inapplicable to earlier varieties of English. One of the principles of the "ideology of the standard" is that there should be, as far as possible, no variation, particularly in written genres. Judging by their use of Late West Saxon, many of the scribes involved in producing the manuscripts of this era felt under no compunction to avoid orthographic and lexical variation, much of which reflected the area from which they came and in which they wrote. This is indeed the case in the *Beowulf* manuscript, and the vast majority of deviations from Late West Saxon are demonstrably of Anglian origin. In his discussion of pertinent examples of variation, Kiernan concludes that "the reversal in the mixture of forms is more likely to occur from conscious variation, or laxity in the spelling tradition, than from remarkably coincidental scribal slips in the course of transmission" (1996: 56). I agree with him in all but one point: there was probably no real "spelling tradition" that the scribe needed to adhere to.

None of the deviations in the *Beowulf* manuscript constitutes linguistic proof of a long manuscript history, and almost all of them support the socio-linguistic focus on variation and heterogeneity. If we combine these results with the contents of the poem, which are undeniably Danish/Scandinavian, it is a small and logical step to conclude that the manuscript, at least part of which was authored by scribe B, was at just one remove from and very possibly contemporaneous with the original. We can also conclude that the "Beowulf project", for want of a better term to refer to it, was scribe B's very own and that it was carried out at a scriptorium somewhere in Danelaw Anglian territory.

7. SWITCHING DISCOURSE ARCHIVES

I began this chapter with a brief description of the fire at Ashburnham House, which almost destroyed one of the most enigmatic and mysterious texts in Anglo-Saxon literature. I argued that the *Beowulf* manuscript, or perhaps more appropriately the *Beowulf* "text", is at the heart of the *ancient language myth*, which has been used since the middle of the nineteenth century to instil a feeling of pride in the long heritage of the English language for those who tell the story and for those who listen to it or read it. It has not been my intention in this chapter to disparage the belief itself but rather to deconstruct the need to use *Beowulf* as a means of reinforcing it.

It should have become clear that I support Kiernan's general argument, although I reject the idea that the manuscript was copied early in the reign of Cnut the Great. Despite Kiernan's reliance on sociopolitical facts, I maintain that these are not enough in themselves to warrant such a conjecture. Howard's suggestion that the reign of Æthelræd II was not quite as negative as the Viking raids on England from 991 on imply might provide a certain amount of credibility to the suggestion that scribe B's *Beowulf* project arose in Danelaw territory in the eastern part of the Anglian-speaking area sometime prior to 1011. In the last resort, however, we will never know the truth, and even if it should turn out that there *was* a long manuscript history after all, neither this fact nor the stronger assumption that the extant manuscript is the only manuscript and is, in modern terms, a draft of the *Beowulf* text can alter the fact that *Beowulf* is a work of genius.

To finish the chapter, however, I return to the following three questions posed in section 3 but not yet answered:

1. How does the Nowell codex come to be made up of three prose texts, *Beowulf*, and the *Judith* fragment?
2. Why is the *Judith* text only a fragment, and how and when did it come to be bound together with the other texts?
3. Why was *Beowulf* of no apparent interest to antiquarians in the sixteenth and early seventeenth centuries?

Answers to these questions reveal that different archives determined the history of the *Beowulf* manuscript from the sixteenth century on. The questions of how and why the Nowell codex came to consist of three prose texts focusing, however loosely, on monsters, the *Beowulf* manuscript, and the *Judith* fragment are crucial for an understanding of how texts from the Anglo-Saxon era were evaluated in sixteenth-century England and why so little attention was paid to *Beowulf*. Central to my argument is the *Judith* fragment.

I shall assume, for the sake of argument, that scribes A and B were busy in the first decade of the eleventh century copying texts at a scriptorium somewhere in the Danelaw area of Anglian territory. Scribe A was given the job of copying prose texts such as the *St. Christopher* fragment, *The Wonders of the East* and *Alexander's Letter to Aristotle*, while scribe B took on[22] the job of copying poetic texts based on the Vulgate version of the Bible, which would have included *Judith*. At some stage during this time scribes A and B were also engaged on their own private project putting together a composite version of the *Beowulf* stories circulating in the Danelaw area. After their deaths, all these manuscripts would then have become the property of the scriptorium in which they were working.

At the time of the dissolution of the monasteries during the reign of Henry VIII, many of the written records of the scriptoria of these monasteries were lost, burned, or otherwise destroyed. But fortunately, many came into the possession of assiduous collectors, including Matthew Parker, the first Archbishop of Canterbury in Elizabeth I's reign. Parker took the trouble to scour the country looking for old Anglo-Saxon manuscripts in private libraries that had escaped destruction. Interest in those manuscripts was specifically directed at matters of religious, legal, constitutional and historical import. The argument used by Parker and his associates was that the Reformation of the English Church represented a return to the Church as it had been prior to the Norman Conquest, in which the vernacular was liberally used.[23] This lent support to Henry VIII's break with Rome and to the

---

22. I use the verb *take on* at this juncture to suggest, tentatively, that scribe B, who was in all probability older than scribe A and hence of senior position, assigned the texts to be copied to scribe A. In other words, scribe A was working under scribe B's supervision.

23. In point of fact, the Anglo-Saxon Church in England was always a staunch supporter of the papacy.

"right" of the English monarchy to head the Church of England. The Protestant, reformed church, however, rejected the Latin Vulgate Bible, which contained a number of books that were not in the original Hebrew Bible, and the book of Judith was one of those.

It is certainly conceivable that a series of saints' lives in verse, containing a text on Judith, would have been anathema to a Protestant church. The *Judith* fragment may thus have been physically removed from the series. Kiernan is of the opinion that not much of the overall text is actually missing. If he is correct, the beginning of *Judith* may have occupied the verso, or part of the verso, of a folio. The removal of the *Judith* fragment may have been ordered by Archbishop Parker. Likewise the three prose texts at the beginning of the Nowell codex and the *Beowulf* codex deal with decidedly non-Biblical themes and were not important for Parker's purposes. Laurence Nowell was part of the circle of Anglo-Saxonists associated with Matthew Parker and may have come into possession of all five texts, which he then bound, or had bound, into one codex.

All this is of course speculation, but it is at least well-founded speculation. It also explains why all five texts were not of importance in the first stage of interest in Anglo-Saxon studies in the sixteenth century. The dominant discourse archive at this particular moment of conjunctural time was religious. It was the struggle to assert Protestantism after the break with the Church of Rome that determined the focus on religious, legal, constitutional and historical texts of the Anglo-Saxon era. The Counter-Reformation in the seventeenth century sustained this dominant discourse and relegated interest in the longevity of the language and the poetic value of texts like *Beowulf* till a much later period.

As a whole, the *longevity of English myth*, consisting of the *ancient language myth* and the *unbroken tradition myth*, was a nineteenth-century phenomenon that lasted almost till the end of the twentieth century. The need to establish a linguistic pedigree for English was an important discourse archive within the framework of the growth of the nation-state and the Age of Imperialism. In the face of competition from other European languages, particularly French, it was perhaps necessary to construct English as a *Kultursprache*, and one way to do this was to trace English back to its earliest texts.

Kiernan's book has not only created a revolution in *Beowulf* studies; perhaps more important, it has also introduced an alternative form of cultural discourse that seriously challenges the archive to which the *ancient language myth* belongs. *Beowulf* is a significant text in its own right, both from a literary and a sociohistorical and sociolinguistic perspective. Kiernan may not be completely correct in all his conjectures, and I and others (Dumville 1887; Rose 1997; Chase 1997) have challenged his dating of the poem to the first years of Cnut the Great's reign. But this does not and cannot alter the literary and sociohistorical fascination of *Beowulf*. In the following chapter I shall move a little further into the future and consider another myth that contributes to the archive of creating a pedigree for English, the *myth of the unbroken tradition*.

Chapter 3

———

Breaking the unbroken tradition

I ne can ne I ne mai tellen alle þe wunder ne alle þe pines ðat hi diden
wrecce men on þis land...
—*Peterborough Chronicle*, Second Continuation

1. LINKING TWO MYTHS

One of the methods used in this book to track down the myths that have
clouded our interpretations of the historical development of English is to find
evidence of dominant discourse archives and to interpret where they begin to
break down. Foucault's understanding of discourse (cf. chap. 1) is that it is a
set of statements that help to construct discontinuity. The very coherence
and apparent unity of a discourse is the dispersion of elements involving
discontinuity. Hence discursive formations are groups of statements in any
order, with any function and with any correlation to other statements determined by the disunity rather than the unity of the discourse. The objects, forms
and themes of discourse are crucially dependent on external conditions. In this
sense, a "discourse" is any group of statements that belongs to a single system
or a group of statements different from other groups of statements.

Foucault's understanding of discourse thus implies that any appearance
of coherence in a discourse is illusory and that discontinuity, heterogeneity
and change characterise discourse rather than continuity, homogeneity and
permanence. Looked at historically, discourses tend to appear or disappear

to accompany the rise and fall of human institutions in Braudel's *temps conjoncturel*. Braudel's focus on three timescales—*la longue durée, le temps conjoncturel* and *l'évènement*—is an attempt to move historians away from a linear conceptualisation of time in which history records a teleological movement towards the achievement of a perfect homogeneous world: a history that marks the march of human progress. The medieval conceptualisation of time was cyclical, not linear, and this insight will play an important role in the assessment of the change of archive to be discussed in this chapter.

We saw in chapter 1 that a *discourse archive* is anything but a library. It is defined by Foucault as "the law of what can be said, the system that governs the appearance of statements as unique events" (1972: 129). The archive determines how statements are grouped in accordance with "conjunctural" changes along Braudel's *longue durée*. An archive has the appearance of being a systematic collection of historical statements following a historical event, a system that determines how statements occur as historical events. According to Blommaert, an archive consists of "the macro-sociological forces and formations that define and determine what can be said, expressed, heard, and understood in particular societies, particular milieux, particular historical periods" (2005: 102).

In reconsidering the historical genesis of the *Beowulf* manuscript in the previous chapter, the **ancient language myth** was challenged by showing how *Beowulf* does not sit easily within the nineteenth-century discursive construction of the longevity of English. The dominant discourse archive to which that myth belongs is that of the nation-state, in which one homogeneous language in a supposedly homogeneous speech community symbolically represents the positive values of the state. It is an archive that has clouded our view of what *Beowulf* meant to those who copied it—or even wrote it.

It is hardly possible to assess whether the "Beowulf project" embarked upon by the two scribes represents a caesura in some pre-Conquest archive. But it is interesting to note that there is no text quite like *Beowulf* among the other Anglo-Saxon texts that have come down to us. Its subject matter is secular, its composition appears to be derived from that of folk poetry, but it displays, like no other Anglo-Saxon poetic text, an expert command of archaic forms of diction and control over the metrical conventions of alliterative poetry on the part of whoever constructed it.[1]

Textual manifestations from earlier periods of Anglo-Saxon that might help to bolster the **longevity of English myth** are certainly available. Consider, for example, the various runic inscriptions; the Anglo-Saxon translation from Bede's *Historia Ecclesiastica Gentis Anglorum*; Bede's death song; Caedmon's hymn, which can be found in ten different manuscript versions ranging from early Northumbrian to West Saxon; the early Latin–Anglo-Saxon Anglian glosses; Alfredian and other translations; the laws of England; charters in

---

1. My own hunch is that scribe B was principally responsible for putting the text together, but this doesn't necessarily mean that scribe B "wrote" *Beowulf*. The modern notion of the author is in any case inappropriate here.

English; the records from Canterbury and Worcester; lists of kings, saints and bishops; and many more. The myth itself, however, is not just about the great age of the English language; it also relies on the parallel belief that any literary tradition begins with epic poetry (cf. the significance of Homer's *Odyssey* or the Finnish *Kalevaala*), from which an unbroken literary tradition may be traced. Our own current discourse on the history of the English language, then, has become inextricably entangled with a discourse on the beginnings of "English literature". The discourse can be traced back to the antiquarians of the sixteenth century, but it began to flourish in the latter half of the nineteenth century and has lasted till the present day.

The approach to the texts that I wish to discuss in this chapter (the *Anglo-Saxon Chronicles [ASC]*) is that they were originally the textual production of a dominant sociopolitical discourse representing an archive that was already changing in the eleventh century, before the Norman Conquest, and had lost virtually all significance after the Conquest. At the centre of the discussion are the First and Second Continuations of the *Peterborough Chronicle*, which display evidence to counter the assumption that there is an unbroken tradition of "English" reaching back at least as far as the seventh century AD, and I shall call the myth lying at the heart of this ideological belief the ***myth of the unbroken tradition of English***. The myth rests on the unfounded ideological assumption that speakers of English, although oppressed by the Norman yoke after the time of the Conquest till around 1250 AD, were in some sense conscious of a "glorious past" and hung onto their language until it finally gained the upper hand over French in the fourteenth and fifteenth centuries.

The breakdown of the archive encapsulated in the *ASC* becomes evident in the increasing degree to which metapragmatic and metadiscursive linguistic expressions are used, marking a significant discursive change in that archive which did not survive after 1155. The evidence thus shows that, contrary to the recurrent insistence in histories of English that there was an unbroken English tradition, the changing discursive practices of the *ASC* and the final transformation of its sociopolitical function from a system of social control to a narrative record of anarchic violence and social injustice represents a very clear discursive discontinuity.

In the following section I shall state what I understand by metapragmatic and metadiscursive expressions and explain the term "inscribed orality". I intend to use Foucault's understanding of the discourse archive to trace some of the linguistic signs of a breakdown in a dominant archive from the end of the ninth to the twelfth century in later sections of this chapter. The basic pattern which I shall trace out is a movement away from a written/oral set of discursive practices to one in which written practices were dominant. In the period of breakdown itself, written texts show increasing features of orality in which metapragmatic and metadiscursive expressions become increasingly frequent until there is a striking discontinuation of the discourse itself. However, before I do this, I need to stress once again my criticism of the following statement by Foucault:

> It is not possible for us to describe our own archive, since it is from within these rules that we speak.... The archive cannot be described in its totality; and in its presence it is unavoidable. (1972: 146–147)

The point made in chapter 1 was that different discourses will coexist or compete with one another and that it is more than likely that an individual functions in a number of different archives, which may overlap or be inconsistent with one another, thus contradicting Foucault's idea that a historical archive is a collection of statements that we cannot interpret.

2. METAPRAGMATIC AND METADISCURSIVE LINGUISTIC EXPRESSIONS AND THEIR SIGNIFICANCE IN INSCRIBED ORALITY

2.1 Metapragmatic and metadiscursive linguistic expressions

Metapragmatic expressions in emergent social practice can be understood as linguistic expressions that lie beyond the level of the propositional structure of utterances and are used in a number of ways to position the speaker and the hearer with respect to those utterances. Discourse markers in English such as *anyway, like, well, you know, I mean*, and so on or meta-pragmatic particles in German such as *doch, aber, mal, eben*, etc. are all said to be inserted non-propositionally into an utterance to give the interlocutor(s) important clues in interpreting the speaker's position or in positioning the interlocutor(s) with respect to what is said, or in linking the utterance in specific ways to previous or upcoming utterances in the interaction. As such they are often considered to have a *procedural* rather than a propositional function (cf. Blakemore 1992, 2002). In Watts (2003: chap. 7) I use the term "expressions of procedural meaning" (EPMs) to highlight this type of metapragmatic expression, examples of which are given below:

(1) ...and he didn't ring me up at all. *Anyway*, I was only half expecting him to.

(2) A: Excuse me. Can you tell me how to get to the station from here?

   B: *Well, I think* so...

(3) ...and I didn't get it finished in time. *I mean*, I did try.

Other metapragmatic expressions may have the effect of positioning the speaker or the interlocutor outside the "world" of the discourse by commenting on it in the here-and-now of the interaction. They are thus similar to Labov and Waletsky's functional category of "evaluation" in narrative discourse ([1967] 1997), as in the following examples:

(4) …so he told me to turn round and put my hands on my head. *Now, I knew the gun didn't have any bullets in it…*

(5) The difference between the bark of the ash and that of the elm, *which we don't see all that often anymore*, is….

Since this latter category of expression positions the speaker/writer and the interlocutor/reader with respect to the overall discourse structure and orders of discourse outside the here-and-now of the ongoing discourse, I propose to call metapragmatic inserts of this kind *metadiscursive expressions.*

As we might expect, there is no clear boundary between metapragmatic and metadiscursive expressions, but I make this distinction for three reasons. First, in studying historical data, we had no access to overt orality until the advent of audiorecording technology at the end of the nineteenth and the beginning of the twentieth century, so it is not easy to classify which expressions function metapragmatically unless the discourse structure appears to simulate oral interaction or, as I intend to show, unless we have markers of what I call "inscribed orality". Second, I wish to discuss a form of discourse that lies outside our modern-day discursive practices, in which written text was, at one and the same time, oral text to be committed to memory and transferred orally to others.

2.2 Inscribed orality

The central concept in this chapter is that of "inscribed orality", which may, but does not need to include metapragmatic, metadiscursive expressions. Till relatively recently, the only evidence historical linguists had for past forms of language and discursive practices were written documents from which oral practices had to be tentatively hypothesised. However, we can extrapolate much of what we know about how interlocutors in social practice use human language in present time to hypothetical historical situations. Modern sociolinguistic and conversation-analytic research into oral practices requires close and meticulous analysis not only of language variation but also of contextualisation. So it is not unreasonable to assume that instantiations of oral social practice, whether in the present or in the past, share certain broad similarities, since they are all instantiations of on-the-spot emergent language contact. Labov (1994: 21–25) refers to this hypothesised similarity of linguistic interaction as the "uniformitarian principle".

The principle suggests that we are able to recognise elements of orality and what Koch (1997) calls "immediacy" in written texts. Koch suggests that the distinction between oral and written instantiations of discourse concerns "two aspects of communication that have to be strictly distinguished: the medium and the mode of communication" (1997: 149–150). By "medium" he understands the binary distinction between the phonic and the graphic medium, and by "mode" the degree of formality or distance between the speaker/writer and the hearer/reader. The degree of mediacy between participants in the ongoing social practice is a function of the degree of distance

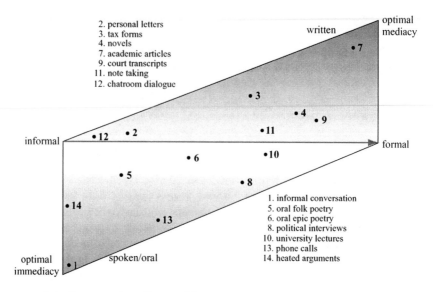

FIGURE 3.1. Degrees of mediacy and formality in written and oral text genres

between them (physical, social, referential and what Koch calls "elocutional") and the degree of formality or informality aimed at in the social interaction.

I have put these aspects together in figure 3.1 to show how we can effectively construct a communicative space within which different types of interaction using the two different media can be located prototypically. Above the horizontal informal-to-formal axis are textual instantiations of discourse in the written medium, in which optimal mediacy is attained in the top right-hand corner of the diagram. Below the horizontal informal-to-formal axis are textual instantiations of discourse in the oral medium, in which the optimal degree of immediacy is attained in the bottom left-hand corner of the diagram. As oral instantiations of discourse move from informal to formal, the degree of immediacy is reduced. The effect of this movement will be that elements typical of the written medium are more likely to occur. Similarly, as written instantiations of discourse move from formal to informal, the degree of mediacy is decreased so that linguistic expressions typical of the oral medium are more likely to occur. I have illustrated this by offering a set of instantiation types and have suggested where they might be positioned, roughly, within the communicative space given. The degree of informality in chatroom discourse (interaction type 12), for example, is almost as far to the left as are heated arguments in the oral medium or informal conversation. It is thus highly likely to contain expressions of inscribed orality, whereas a university lecture (interaction type 10), even though it is held in front of a student audience, does not have the same degree of communicative symmetry between the participants and is highly likely to contain features of formal written language.

Historical evidence is overwhelmingly more likely to come from written sources, texts from the space above the informal/formal axis. Hence, if instances of written discourse increase their degree of immediacy and become less formal—if they move from the top right-hand corner of the diagram towards the informal/formal axis and further to the left—linguistic features associated with oral forms of discourse, including an increasing number of metapragmatic/metadiscursive expressions, will occur. Since these features are still in the written medium, I wish to call them instances of "inscribed orality". For instance, there may be an increased frequency of the first-person-singular pronoun *I*, referring to the writer or the narrator of a text. The addressee may be mentioned explicitly, either by name or by the use of second-person pronouns. In narrative texts the present tense of verbs may replace the past. There will be an increase in the number of proxemic deictic expressions, such as "here," "now," "this". There will be an increase in metadiscursive comments on the text by the narrator/scribe/author. I shall use examples of inscribed orality such as these to illustrate the move of textual instantiations of the *ASC* from the mid-right of the diagram towards the left and lower towards the informal-to-formal axis. I shall argue that this movement provides evidence for the breakdown of the discourse archive, which in turn provides firm evidence to counter the **unbroken tradition myth**.

3. THE *ANGLO-SAXON CHRONICLES* AND THE ARCHIVE THEY INSTANTIATED

3.1 What were the *Anglo-Saxon Chronicles*?

What were the *Anglo-Saxon Chronicles*? What was their political and sociocultural significance in the period during which the chronicles were kept? How do these texts fit into the overall pattern of hegemonic discourse in the time between King Alfred and the Norman Conquest (e.g. legal and administrative texts such as laws, edicts, capitularies, diplomas, land grants, charters; religious texts such as sermons, homilies, hagiographic texts; poetic texts; types of narrative text other than saints' lives; and riddles, recipes, quasi-medical texts and charms)? What is the sociolinguistic and discursive significance of the *ASC*?

The *Anglo-Saxon Chronicles* are a unique set of manuscripts from scriptoria in different parts of the country, written in Anglo-Saxon, documenting events from the birth of Christ (or from Julius Caesar's abortive attempt to conquer Britain) to the time at which the scribe is entering his annal, which is generally not the immediate present of making the entry. Palaeographical evidence indicates that scribes may not always have made the entries immediately after the year that they were recording, but may have chosen to write up entries for a set of years. This appears to be the case in the central text that we shall be looking at in section 4: the Second Continuation of the so-called *Peterborough Chronicle*.

There is some dispute over whether it is more appropriate to refer to the *ASC* in the singular or to use the plural form. Those in favour of just one chronicle base their argument on the fact that successive copies were made from one master copy, and, as we shall see, there is undoubtedly more than a grain of truth in this argument. However, some scholars have found it safer and, in view of the complexity of the existing manuscript situation, more expedient to consider the manuscripts that have survived as being, at least in part, independent versions. Many of the chronicles make use of sources other than the original Alfredian Chronicle, as we shall see, and there are clear cases of changes having been made to chronicle entries at later dates in history, often for propaganda purposes.

We can piece together a history of the *ASC*, beginning at the end of the ninth century during the reign of King Alfred and stretching as far as 1154, when the last entry was made in the *Peterborough Chronicle* in a form of English that is markedly different from Anglo-Saxon and clearly an early forerunner of Middle English.[2] The origins of the *ASC* lie at the end of the ninth century, in the reign of King Alfred, and represent, as Swanton puts it, "a reflection of both the 'revival of learning' and revival of English national awareness" at that time (1996: xviii).[3] He also points out that the twelfth-century Anglo-Norman chronicler Gaimar explicitly mentions the chronicles.

The sources for the *ASC* range from local information on events in the West Country through records of world history from the beginning of the Christian era to annals taken from Bede's chronological summary of his *Ecclesiastical History*. In later copies of the *ASC* northern annals extending into the ninth century, lists of Northumbrian and Mercian kings with their genealogies, material drawn from a continental source for the years 880–890 were also added (Swanton 1996).

The texts are unique in that they are written in the vernacular at a period in European history in which chronicles were otherwise written in Latin. Later in this section I will argue that this provides evidence for suggesting that the texts themselves formed an important set of statements in a hegemonic discourse archive.

The *ASC* has survived in the following nine manuscripts:

1. The A ms., or Parker Chronicle (Corpus Christi College, Cambridge, MS. 173), since it was in the possession of Archbishop Matthew Parker, Archbishop of Canterbury from 1559 till his death in 1575.

   This was begun in the Winchester scriptorium by a scribe who copied out a genealogy of King Alfred and then began copying out the first version of the chronicle. After 891 we have a comprehensive contemporary account of the Danish invasions until 924. At this point a page is missing in the manuscript, and we come across a copy of the laws of Alfred and Ine. A new scribe then

---

2. A good source for the information provided here can be found in Swanton 1996.
3. The reader can be forgiven for detecting rather more than a faint echo of the nation-state ideology here.

took up work on the chronicle, giving surprisingly sparse entries covering the reigns from Athelstan to Æthelræd II (the Unready). On the other hand, the entries contain four occasional poems in alliterative verse on Athelstan's victory at Brunanburh, Edmund's liberation of the Five Boroughs in 942, the coronation of Edgar at Bath in 973 and on his death in 975. The manuscript was transferred to St. Augustine's Canterbury around 1011, possibly to mitigate the manuscript losses after the Danish occupation and sacking of Canterbury in 1011 and also to assure safer keeping than at Winchester, which was now also prey to invasion after the devastating Danish raids on Hampshire, Sussex and Berkshire in 1010 (Howard 2003). Very few new entries were made at Canterbury, but a privilege granted by King Cnut around 1031, an *Acta Lanfranci* in Latin, church events from 1070 to 1095, and a list of popes and archbishops of Canterbury who received the pallium were also included. The last entry in Anglo-Saxon was made in 1070.

2. The A^2, more commonly G, ms., also from the Winchester scriptorium, and sometimes called the Cottonian Otho Fragment (British Museum, Cotton MS. Otho B xi, 2), since it was in the possession of Sir Robert Cotton in the sixteenth century and was almost completely destroyed in the 1731 fire at Ashburnham House (cf. chap. 2).

A copy was made of the A manuscript before it left Winchester sometime between 1001, when the last annal was copied, and 1012–13, if we judge by the names in the episcopal lists appended to the manuscript.

3. The B ms. or the Abingdon Chronicle I (British Museum, Cotton MS. Tiberius A vi.) from the Abingdon scriptorium.

The B manuscript appears to be a copy of A made by one scribe, in that it also starts in 60 BC and contains a preface with a modified genealogy of Alfred extending the line to Edward the Martyr. It thus ends in 977 and was therefore probably copied shortly after Edward's accession to the throne. The manuscript served as the basis for the C manuscript, also copied at Abingdon, but it was transferred to Christ Church, Canterbury, in the middle of the eleventh century, where several interpolations and corrections were made and a list of popes and archbishops of Canterbury who had received the pallium was added. These lists end with Anselm in 1095.

4. The C ms. or the Abingdon Chronicle II (British Museum, Cotton MS. Tiberius B i.), again from the Abingdon scriptorium.

Swanton assumes that C was copied from B in the middle of the eleventh century at Abingdon. The manuscript begins with an Anglo-Saxon translation of Orosius's world history, a metrical calendar and a series of verse maxims on the laws of the natural world. At the bottom of the leaf on which these verses are copied, the scribe begins a version of the chronicle. As in B, he begins in 60 BC, and he copies up to 490, at which point a second scribe takes over and continues the entries as far as 1048. After the entry for 652 the second scribe apparently had access to a version other than the original, and between the entries for 915 and 934 he inserts a series of short entries known as the Mercian Register documenting the activities of Æthelflæd, Lady of the

Mercians. Thereafter he appears to go back to the original and continues as far as 1066, where the manuscript ends in the middle of the Battle of Stamford Bridge, subsequent entries being lost.

5. The D ms. or the Worcester Chronicle (British Museum, Cotton MS. Tiberius B iv.) from the Worcester scriptorium.

The D manuscript is the most puzzling of all, being copied in the middle of the eleventh century in all probability from a version of the chronicle that Archbishop Wulfstan is assumed to have had prepared in Worcester in 1016 from what may have been a York/Ripon copy. Howard (2003: 3) gives his version of how he considers the D manuscript to have come about:

As part of a propaganda campaign supporting King Edmund, Archbishop Wulfstan instructed his scribes to prepare an updated version of the *ASC*. This version of the *ASC*, which will be referred to as the *Æthelredian Exemplar* (*ÆE*), drew upon earlier versions of the *ASC* and other sources for early annals. Then annals covering the reigns of King Æthelred and King Edmund were added by one man. The scribes were probably based at Worcester, a see that Wulfstan held in plurality with York. Version D is possibly a fair copy of this updated version up to and including 1016. The annals covering the reigns of Æthelred and King Edmund in versions C and E of the *ASC* are derived from the same source.

Howard assumes, then, that the copy at York or Ripon was transferred to Worcester and was altered on Wulfstan's instructions. The D manuscript is different from the others in that, instead of a genealogy of Alfred, it contains a description of Britain taken from Bede, material from a set of eighth-century Northumbrian annals, and an amalgam of the Mercian Register. The first evidence of Wulstanian influence is a set of rhetorically coloured prose texts covering the short reign of Edgar from 973 to 975 in place of the poems in the A manuscript. The entry for 1016 does indeed read as propaganda in favour of Edmund. The last entry in the D manuscript was made for the year 1080.

6. The E ms. or the Laud (or "Peterborough") manuscript (Bodleian, MS. Laud 636) from the Peterborough scriptorium, named after its seventeenth-century owner Archbishop William Laud, Archbishop of Canterbury from 1633 to 1645.

The E manuscript, with which we are primarily concerned in this chapter, is thought to have been copied from one of the Canterbury manuscripts. The source texts from which the E manuscript may have been copied will be dealt with later. It contains several interpolations referring to local events in the Fenlands and on the affairs of the abbey, in particular an elaborate story of the building and consecration of the abbey. Since the E manuscript will interest us further in this chapter, I will not give a detailed description of it here.

7. The F ms. or the Bilingual Canterbury Epitome (British Museum, Cotton MS. Domitian A viii.).

This manuscript was copied from the original A manuscript deposited at St. Augustine's. It contains entries in both English and Latin and was begun around 1100, some 30 years after the last entry in A. The scribe was one of those who had written notes in the A manuscript at Christ Church. Its preface is also from Bede's description of Britain, and the same scribe made several interlinear annotations and insertions.

8. The H ms. or Cottonian Domitian Fragment (British Museum, Cotton MS. Domitian A ix.).

This is a single leaf covering the years 1113 and 1114, probably copied in Winchester as part of the G (or A²) manuscript from the original A manuscript.

9. The I ms. or an Easter Table Chronicle (British Museum, Cotton MS. Caligula A xv.).

This was a late addition to the chronicle containing bilingual notes from 952 to 1130 and dealing largely with the affairs of Christ Church, Canterbury.

As we have seen, there has been some discussion as to whether the manuscripts were compiled independently of one another, but because of similarities in the wording of the texts, it seems much more likely that one of them was a master copy from which the others were made and adapted. Further evidence to support this interpretation is provided by Keynes (1980), who argues that diplomas (land grants) were prepared and witnessed "on the occasion of the gathering of the king and his council" in which the "witness lists appear to be 'official' records of attendance at a *witenagemot*" and that they therefore need to be dissociated "from ecclesiastical scriptoria, since it requires that the agency was mobile and could operate...where the gatherings were commonly held" (1980: 79).

Howard (2003), who uses the *ASC* as a source text to give a historical account of the second wave of Danish invasions during the reign of Æthelræd II (the Unready), which eventually led to the conquest of England by Swein Forkbeard in 1013 and the accession to the throne of Swein's son Cnut in 1017, suggests that three texts were made from the original chronicle compiled during the latter part of Alfred's reign, two of these being copies and the third Asser's *Life of Alfred*. According to Howard one copy of the *ASC* was kept at Winchester while the second was taken to York or Ripon (presumably to be copied from the Winchester original). While the Winchester copy (the A manuscript) is certainly extant, there is no evidence of there ever having been a York/Ripon copy. However, for the sake of historical consistency Howard develops a line of "ghost" copies emanating from this supposed copy, one of which is said to have been enlarged by a set of northern annals, and another to have been enlarged by Mercian annals. Howard then suggests that the second of these gave rise to the B manuscript before the end of the tenth century and the later C manuscript, both kept at Abingdon. According to Howard, the York/Ripon manuscript, whose existence must remain pure speculation, was removed by Archbishop Wulfstan to Worcester towards the end of Æthelræd's reign and was changed to support the royal lineage in the person of Æthelræd's son Edmund

Ironside in 1016. This then became the Worcester manuscript D. The E manuscript made after Peterborough Abbey burned down in 1116 is also given a direct lineage from the York/Ripon copy, although the A manuscript, which was moved from Winchester to Canterbury around 1011, is assumed to have served as a model to be copied. Howard's schematic history of the different copies of the *ASC* is presented in figure 3.2.

Any such scheme must remain at worst pure speculation and at best a careful reconstruction of all the evidence available, and it is important to note that this evidence will be extralinguistic and social-historical as well as textual. It is clear from a close study of figure 3.2 that Howard has tried to create as coherent a history of the *ASC* as the facts will allow. In so doing, however, he helps to create a present-day discursive account of what can only be, by nature

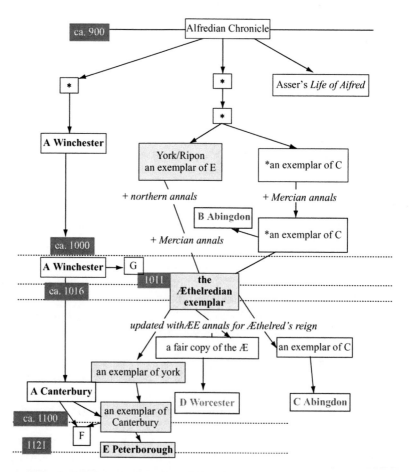

FIGURE 3.2. A slightly revised version of the schematic history of the *ASC* suggested by Howard (2003: 4)

of the "archaeological" evidence on hand, a historical discourse, which, in Foucault's terms, displays gaping discontinuities. The starred textual exemplars, none of which has ever been discovered, are fitted into the assumed historical discourse to present a continuity that probably never existed. There are thus far too many points at which continuities have been presupposed where we in fact have discontinuities.

The most problematic aspect of Howard's schematic history is the assumption that there ever was an *Æthelredian exemplar*, since this plays a central role in his overall interpretation. Howard's argument for its existence presupposes a York/Ripon copy of the *ASC* which has likewise never come to light. Part of his argument rests on the fact that Wulfstan, certainly the politically most powerful ecclesiastical figure during Æthelræd's reign, was both archbishop of York and bishop of Worcester. He was thus in the advantageous position of being able to have a York/Ripon copy of the *ASC* removed to Worcester during a period in which Danish influence in the Danelaw must have been strongly in favour of Swein Forkbeard and his son Cnut. It would have been relatively easy for the assumed "northern annals" not only to have been removed and copied, but also to have been altered in favour of the royal inheritance. Wulfstan was, after all, a loyal supporter of the royal house and of Æthelræd's son Edmund Ironside's claim to the throne.[4] There is also textual evidence that the Worcester D manuscript was subject to changes in the annals dealing with Æthelræd's reign that smack of political propaganda, although it is more than a little curious that the putative Æthelredian exemplar exerted no apparent influence on the A manuscript which had been transferred from Winchester to Canterbury. What is important from the point of view of this chapter is that the *Peterborough Chronicle*, copied shortly after a fire at the abbey in 1116, has more affinities with the D manuscript than with the A manuscript.

There is an alternative schematic history of the *ASC* that preserves the discontinuities which Howard has tried to erase, one which allows us to posit the rough outline of a discourse archive at the centre of which was the *ASC* itself. We first need to develop Keynes's analysis of diplomas written during the course of Æthelræd's reign, in which he suggests that documents were produced on the occasion of the meetings of the *witenagemote* (meetings of the wise men) in different parts of the country, thus indicating that, even if it is difficult to talk of a royal chancery, it is certainly the case that the king took his official scribes with him on his travels throughout the country. If we consider where these meetings were held from the time of King Alfred on, it immediately becomes obvious that very few indeed were held in Danelaw territory and that the overwhelming majority took place in territory under the jurisdiction of English law.

---

4. Curiously enough, however, Wulfstan continued in office after Cnut's accession to the throne and served Cnut as loyally as he had Æthelræd.

In addition, there is ample evidence that both the *ASC*, sets of laws and other "official" texts were collected in the same manuscript codices. The crucial manuscript collection is the Parker Manuscript, Corpus Christi College Cambridge MS 173, in which we have not only the A manuscript of the *ASC* but also two quires of laws, a set of papal and episcopal lists and a text of Sedulius's *Carmen Paschale*. Wormald (1999) argues that laws (both secular and ecclesiastical), other official documents such as charters and diplomas (land grants) and papal and episcopal lists were closely associated with the *ASC* and were originally deposited at the Winchester scriptorium. Despite an intensive debate about whether one can talk of a royal chancery in Winchester or whether many or most of the texts, particularly charters (cf. Keynes 1980 on the Æthelredian diplomas), were prepared by scribes accompanying the king on his travels through the country, the place in which the manuscripts were stored was still Winchester. In addition, both written laws and a written historical account of important political events were intimately bound together in an archive emanating ultimately from royal authority. The chronicle as such acquired its authoritative legitimacy from its close association with the law codes.

If we consider where the other copies of the *ASC* were stored—Worcester, Abingdon in the Thames Valley and Canterbury (to which the A manuscript

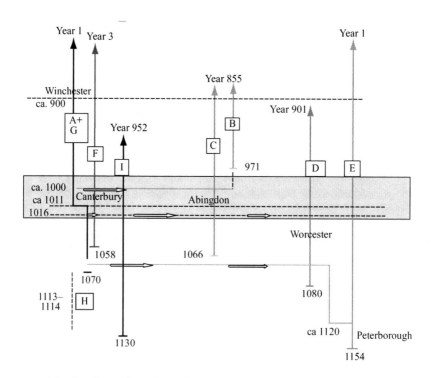

FIGURE 3.3. An alternative schematic history of the *ASC*

was transferred for safekeeping around 1011)—we can conclude that those copies were made from the A manuscript and distributed to politically strategic points throughout the English part of the country (rather than to locations in the Danelaw area).

We can thus leave the discontinuities as an unsolvable enigma if we simply assume that all other manuscripts were copied from A. In figure 3.3, I represent this way of viewing the *ASC*, which outlines the connections between A and the other copies and gives the dates at which the entries begin and the dates at which they cease.

3.2 What was the archive of which the *ASC* was an instantiation?

The first part of the *ASC* up to the time of King Alfred gives a chronological record of events in the Christian world as these affected England and tells the story of setting up the Anglo-Saxon kingdoms, the important political figures controlling the destiny of Anglo-Saxon England, and the quarrels, disputes and wars between the kingdoms. The sociopolitical purpose of these annals was not simply to give a chronological account of the events leading up to the time of Alfred, but rather to highlight his (largely successful) attempt to unite the kingdoms under West Saxon suzerainty. Important Church matters were recorded, as were other important political issues since they were also part of this overall policy.

The annals of the *ASC* were quasi-official records used for the diffusion of selected information in the service of the political aims of the West Saxon royal house. If we look at them from within our own archives, they are not what we might expect from other forms of chronicle. They certainly detail annual events in chronological order, but the way in which the events are reported and the possible use to which the reports were put are very different from the Latin chronicles of the twelfth century on, or, for example, from Holinshed's *Chronicles* in the sixteenth century.[5] They contained neither social comment on the plight of the lower orders of the social hierarchy nor information on socioeconomic conditions in the country at large, nor any overt or covert criticism of government. When this kind of information begins

---

5. Patterson (1994) argues that in the first 1577 edition of the chronicles that bear his name Holinshed makes great play on the need to report on past events "indifferently", by which he means "objectively" or not in a partisan spirit but in such a way that a variety of opinions concerning an event can be expressed. The multivocality of the chronicles is upheld by the variety of writers who wrote contributions to that mammoth project. The provenance of the contributors is evidence of the fact that "the Chronicles, especially when they deal with the sixteenth century, are an expression of citizen consciousness" (1994: xiii). The discourse instantiated by Holinshed's *Chronicles* thus forms part of an unofficial, nondominant discourse that aims at questioning the events of the past, especially the immediate past, and the official interpretations of those events. It signals the imminent breakdown of an archive, whereas the *ASC* constituted an important part of the construction of the archive at the end of the Anglo-Saxon period of English history.

to appear in the *ASC*, as indeed it does shortly before and most definitely after the time of the Norman Conquest, it can be taken as the indication of a significant change in the archive.

Official information was read out to the *witenagemote*, assemblies of so-called *witan* (wise or learned men), in the presence of the king or his representatives with the intention that the information should be diffused orally to as large a section of the population as possible. For this reason, the *ASC* needed to be in the vernacular Anglo-Saxon and not in Latin. The meaningful statements imposed by this archive were those of a dominant discourse promoting, in secular terms, the legitimacy of the monarch and his claim to rule over the whole of England and not just the area to the west and south of Watling Street (i.e. non-Danelaw England) and, in religious terms, the Christian religion and the dominance of the Church of Rome.

I argue that the *ASC* was originally the instantiation of an archive whose meaningful statements exuded royal authority and whose rules of production emanated from royal assemblies in which the written word was used as the authoritative basis on which quasi-official, historical, genealogical, documentary and religious information was meant to be spread orally among the population. But in the course of time and even before the putative *Æthelredian Exemplar* was prepared, some of the annals became less formulaic and longer, indicating that their use as a written record on which the oral diffusion of authority was based was being transformed into that of an official *written* record of events. This does not change the meaningfulness of the statements, but it does suggest a change in the rules of discourse production.

The Parker Manuscript is an interesting mixture of historical, legal and ecclesiastical texts, and it opens with the *ASC*, followed by the laws, the papal and episcopal lists and the Sedulius text. When the codex was copied and transferred to Canterbury at the beginning of the eleventh century, the lists preceded the laws and the Sedulius was ignored. By the end of the sixteenth century, when the codex came into the possession of Archbishop Parker, the order of its contents had been changed yet again, so that the Sedulius preceded the laws (Wormald 1999: 165–166). The confusion as to the order of the contents has led certain scholars to assume that there was no connection between the laws and the other texts. Wormald, however, argues on the basis of palaeographical and codicological evidence that nothing could be further from the truth:

> It is reasonably deduced, then, that the laws were written at about the time when they were added to the *Chronicle*; and it can be argued that they were copied in order to be added to the *Chronicle*. Even the most hard-headed scholar can hardly deny that the laws were consciously associated with the *Chronicle* half a century after their composition. (1999: 166–167)

What immediately becomes apparent from this analysis of the manuscript evidence is that the latter part of King Æthelræd II's reign is characterised by a decentralisation of the *ASC* (see fig. 3.3). For this to have happened, we need to assume that the sociopolitical functions of the *ASC*—the archive to which it, the charters and the law codes belonged—had changed significantly between the time of Æthelræd's accession to his death in 1016. Chronicle writing had become dissociated from the writing of laws. This corresponds to the increasing length and linguistic complexity of the annals themselves. If it is correct to say that they had changed from being, like the laws, a written record on which the oral diffusion of authority was based to an official written documentation of historical events, then it is also feasible to suggest that they may have become open to political propaganda (cf. Wulfstan's *Æthelredian Exemplar*).

4. THE BREAKDOWN OF THE ARCHIVE AND INSCRIBED ORALITY

The alternative interpretation of the significance of the *ASC* and the archive that it instantiates, given in the previous section, does not attempt to create continuity or coherence. In contrast to Howard's interpretation, it allows us to posit that all the manuscript copies of the *ASC* were copied from the same original source, whether or not items were added from other sources (e.g. from Bede's *Ecclesiastical History*, from northern or Mercian annals) or altered after the original copy had been made (e.g. the changes made to the genealogy of the Wessex royal dynasty or the possibility that Wulfstan did have the Worcester D manuscript rewritten in favour of Edmund Ironside). It also allows us to suggest that the copies were made later than Howard assumes, and it relieves us of having to speculate on the existence of exemplars such as the York/Ripon copy. More important than Howard's schematic history is a clear indication of when each version of the chronicle begins and ends its reporting, even though this destroys the attempt to impose chronological continuity and coherence. The alternative interpretation presented in figure 3.3 also documents the decentralisation of the records from the beginning of the renewed Danish invasions in 991 and Æthelræd's death in 1016, a decentralisation which indicates changes in the archive.

In this section I shall argue that the First and Second Continuations of the *Peterborough Chronicle* show a movement away from a degree of mediacy[6] in the written medium (see the top half of fig. 3.1) towards a degree of immediacy and informality typical of the oral medium (i.e. there is a movement closer to the line separating texts in the written and those in the oral medium and farther towards the left of the figure). This can be shown by the increase in the number of forms of inscribed orality represented by metapragmatic and metadiscursive

---

6. The mediacy is nowhere near optimal mediacy in the top right-hand corner of figure 3.1, for the simple reason that the texts of the *ASC* had to be formulaic and short enough to be consigned to memory for oral transmission later.

expressions, the general effect of which is to create a narrative persona that is not appropriate to the dominant sociopolitical archive originally instantiated in the *ASC*. Before I give examples of inscribed orality, however, the following subsection will give more information about the source text to be used for the analysis, the *Peterborough Chronicle*.

4.1 What was or is the *Peterborough Chronicle?*

The central text in assessing how the archive lost its significance as "the law of what can be said, the system that governs the appearance of statements as unique events" (Foucault 1972: 129) is the *Peterborough Chronicle*, the E manuscript of the *ASC* copied around 1120 at Peterborough after the reconstruction of those parts of the abbey destroyed by a fire in 1116. In that year Peterborough Abbey burned to the ground, and with it one of the most important scriptoria in the country was destroyed. All but the chapter house and the dormitory burned, and we have no information as to whether any manuscripts were rescued from the flames.

There is no way of knowing whether a version of the *ASC* was kept at Peterborough, and perhaps the conviction that a copy of the *ASC* was destroyed rests on the same kinds of belief as those that spawned the fictive predecessors of the *Beowulf* manuscript (see chap. 2). Stories are, after all, the discursive framework of myths, and those myths are the backbone of ideological discourses. If there had been a copy of the *ASC* at Peterborough prior to the fire, this would make the *Peterborough Chronicle* unique in being the only copy made and stored in the Danelaw area of the country (on the assumption, of course, that there was no York/Ripon copy).

Four puzzling questions present themselves:

1. Why was a copy (or new copy) needed more than 50 years after the Norman Conquest of England?
2. If the A and D manuscripts were used to make the Peterborough copy, why were both those exemplars discontinued shortly after the Conquest, A in 1070 and D in 1080?
3. If D and A were not the models, what was?
4. What sources did the first scribe use to create the entries after 1080?

A facsimile of the E manuscript with a detailed account of its palaeographical and codicological characteristics was published in 1954 by Dorothy Whitelock, and Cecily Clark used Whitelock's work as the basis for her 1958 edition of the years from 1070 to 1154. Clark describes the manuscript as follows:

It is a parchment manuscript of ninety-one folios (interleaved with paper), in quires of ten, except that f. 81 is an odd leaf added after the eighth quire. The original size of the book is probably shown by ff. 86–90, which are 9½ x 6½ in. (24 x 17 cm.) and bear on their wide margins (the original written space is 6¾ x 4 in.) a thirteenth-century Anglo-Norman Chronicle. Ff. 1–85 and 91 have been cut down to 8¼ x 5½ in. (21 x 14 cm.), with the result that parts of many old marginal notes have been cut through. Since the uncut folios are creased all round as if they had been folded down to the smaller format, the cutting may have taken place some time before the interleaving with paper 12¼ x 8 in. (31 x 20.5 cm.). The binding (in spite of modern rebacking) is still substantially the seventeenth-century Laudian one. (Clark 1958: xi)

The information about the cutting could well indicate that the interleaving of the so-called "Peterborough Interpolations" was carried out after the text had first been copied from the exemplars and then continued till 1121 and some time before the First Continuation ends in 1131, since the hand is that of a scribe writing up the events between 1122 and 1131. From a linguistic point of view, the interpolations are most definitely not the work of the final scribe from 1132 to 1154.

Palaeographically, the overall manuscript falls into three distinct sections. The first section contains all the entries from the topographical preface (which is based on Bede) and the year 1 to 1121. From around 1000 the entries are very similar to annals such as those in the Latin *Waverley Annals* (*Annales Monastici*) from 1000 to 1121, and entries after 1070 are particularly similar to the Latin chronicle compiled by Henry of Huntingdon, the *Historia Anglorum* (ca. 1125). The scribe may have drawn liberally on Henry of Huntingdon, although it is equally likely that Henry drew much of his material from the *Chronicle*. Beyond roughly 1090, assuming our scribe to have joined the abbey as a young man, we can posit that his firsthand experience plus that of other monks forms the basis of the entries up to 1121. However, since the ink and the hand are uniform up to that year, the entries must have been put together in one go, say at the end of 1121 after the abbey had been reconstructed. Whether the scribe added comments on the events with knowledgeable hindsight (see the examples in the next subsection) or whether these comments were in the original exemplar that the scribe was copying is unknown.

The second section of the *Peterborough Chronicle*, often called the First Continuation, takes us from 1122 to 1131. Clark (1958) maintains that because of the frequent changes in ink and hand these entries must have been written up in six blocks (1122, 1123, 1124, 1125–1126, 1126–1127, 1128–1131), and were thus on-the-spot reports of the events of those years. Rather than six different scribes being entrusted with the writing up of the annals, however, Ker (1957) believes that the same scribe who copied out the first section was also responsible for the First Continuation. The variations in writing are minimal and can easily be explained by the simple fact that a person's handwriting is indeed variable throughout the course of his life. The last section of the manuscript, often called the Second Continuation, takes us from

1132 to 1154, where the *Chronicle* ends. The hand is completely different from the first part of the *Peterborough Chronicle* up to 1121 and the First Continuation, and the language has changed considerably. From a linguistic point of view, the first scribe, who, following Ker (1957), I shall take to be responsible for the first part of the chronicle up to 1121 and the First Continuation, is at pains to reproduce the language of the other copies of the *ASC*—that is, quasi-standard West Saxon[7]—but very frequently introduces Anglian forms, mixes up gender and case inflections and sometimes seems a little unsure of his use of demonstratives and relative pronouns (see chap. 4). Linguistically, the second scribe is a veritable revelation and has turned out to be the historical linguist's dream: a missing link between "Old English" and "Middle English". If the first scribe at least tried to reproduce older forms, the second appears to write as he spoke.

To return to the four puzzling questions, at first sight, the only extant copies that continued reporting after 1080 and that could have served as the source were the I manuscript (an Easter Table Chronicle, British Museum, Cotton MS Caligula A xv) and the H manuscript or Cottonian Fragment (British Museum, Cotton MS. Domitian A ix.). However, from the point of view of text type, the I manuscript is definitely not the model from which the *Peterborough Chronicle* was (re-)created. This leaves us with one of the two Cottonian Fragments (A[2] [or G] and H). It is thought that H was prepared from A in Canterbury, but it exists as only one leaf covering the years 1113 and 1114. Both fragments are the remains of manuscripts that were almost entirely destroyed by the fire at Ashburnham House in 1731, which, as discussed in chapter 2, destroyed a large part of the Cottonian library. However, since there is no record of how far into the eleventh century the A[2] manuscript reaches, there is no way of knowing whether one of these two fragments served as the basis on which the events of the years from 1080 till the turn of the twelfth century were reconstructed.

From the point of view of my argument, however, we can conclude that the chronicle part of the discourse forming the dominant archive became decentralised toward the end of Æthelræd's reign. In addition the entries became longer and more detailed throughout the eleventh century, making them decidedly unsuitable as the written basis of oral transference, and indicating that the *ASC* had taken on the function of an official or semiofficial written record of events. But question 1, concerning the need for a copy of the *ASC* as late as roughly 1120, remains. If, as seems quite likely, it no longer served its purpose in the new dominant sociopolitical discourse archive after the Conquest, did it serve the purpose of an alternative antidiscourse, a form of linguistic subversion in a world of increasingly Latin texts in the ecclesias-

---

7. I hesitate to suggest, as many have done, that West Saxon was a standard literary language. The scribe may have been aiming at conformity with forms of language that he could still read but that had changed quite considerably in the 50 years since the Conquest, and the refreshing thing is that he never quite makes it. Talking of a "standard" is not really appropriate here, so I have chosen the halfway stage—"quasi-standard".

tical and legal worlds and Anglo-Norman French in the world of administration and bureaucracy? This is what I intend to investigate in the following subsection.

4.2 Inscribed orality in the first section and First Continuation of the *Peterborough Chronicle*

The first section of the *Peterborough Chronicle* written by the first scribe consists of the copy (or, if the text had had to be replaced, the recopying) of the chronicle from other chronicle sources or the scribe's own knowledge of events up to and beyond 1080 as far as 1120. As we might expect, there are virtually no examples of inscribed orality until after the Conquest (with the exception of the interpolations describing the founding of the abbey in the seventh century). Those that we see in the entries after the Conquest are of a metadiscursive nature offering, with the benefit of hindsight, an evaluative scribal/ narratorial commentary on events of the past, which may also have been in the text(s) from which the copy was made. The entry for 1077 begins as follows:

> (6) Her on þisum geare wurdon sæhte Franca cyng and Willelm Englalandes cyng: *ac hit heold litle hwile.*
>
> "Here in this year the king of the French and William, the king of England, made peace: *but it did not last long.*"

The use of the proxemic spatiotemporal deictic adverb *her* ("here") is typical of the *ASC* in general and is an indication that the texts were meant to be reproduced orally to larger audiences. By this time, of course, the *her* had become completely ritualised. The only signs of Anglian influence here are the unrounding of [y] to [i] in *litle* and the lowering of [ɛ] to [æ] in *sæhte*. The metadiscursive comment on the event is negative.

We have similarly negative comments in the entries for 1091 and 1093, although in these two entries, the scribe's written language displays more Anglian features (bold type) and clear signs of insecurity with respect to the language model used (single underlining),[8] both indicating that the scribe may have been aiming at West Saxon without having had a written source to copy from:

> (7) Ðas forewarde **geswor**an <u>xii þa betste</u> of þes cynges healfe and xii of þes eorles, *þeah hit syððan litle hwile stode.*

---

8. The elements underlined in (7) involve a wrongly imagined spelling of the third-person plural past inflection of the strong verb *geswerian* (*gesworan* for *gesworon*), which could indicate that the scribe in any case pronounced the final syllable as [ən], the nominative instead of the genitive case in the NP *þa betste* plus the use of the strong adjective instead of the weak adjective after the determiner, and in (8) confusion as to how to represent the dative plural in the NP *manegan mynstren* for *manegum mynstrum*, again indicating that the scribe pronounced the inflections with a schwa [ə].

"Twelve of the best of the king's half and 12 of the earl's swore on those agreements, *though it stood* [i.e. held or lasted] *afterwards only a little while*".

(8) ...to <u>manegan mynstren</u> land geuðe—*ac þet he syððan ætbræd, þa him gebotad wæs.*

"...granted land to several minsters—*but he afterwards took away what was offered.*"

As in (6), the negative comments in (7) and (8) are also aimed at secular authority, and in (8), which is the least formulaic of the criticisms, it is significant that the comment concerns land grants to ecclesiastical institutions.

The First Continuation is characterised by a marked change in the narrative style of the annals indicating the presence of a narratorial persona and by a further shift away from the linguistic model of the West Saxon of the other versions of the *ASC* towards the scribe's own language.[9] The style is lively and flowing, and the text reveals a narrator who was involved in what he was reporting and was not averse to making critical remarks on events and characters. As might be expected from the definition of inscribed orality given in section 3, there is a marked increase of metapragmatic and metadiscursive linguistic expressions that indicate a shift towards informality and orality, three examples of which I will analyse below.

In the annal for 1123 the scribe relates the pilgrimage of the archbishop of Canterbury to Rome:

(9) Ða com se ærcebiscop of Cantwarabyrig and wæs ðære fulle seouenniht ær he mihte cumen to þes Papes spræce: þet wæs forþan þet hit wæs don þone Pape to understanden þet he hæfde underfangen ðone ærcebiscoprice togeanes þe muneces of þe mynstre and togeanes rihte. *Ac þet ofercom Rome þet <u>ofercumeð eall weoruld—þet is gold and seolure</u>.*

"Then the archbishop of Canterbury arrived and was there for a full week before he was able to have an audience with the pope. That was because the pope was given to understand that he had received the archbishopric against [the wishes of] the monks of the minster and unjustly. *But that which overcame Rome <u>overcomes the whole world—that is gold and silver</u>.*"

The italicised passage indicates the narratorial metadiscursive comment on the fact that the pope finally agreed to grant an audience to the archbishop of Canterbury, and it is framed as tongue-in-cheek irony (single underlining). The archbishop must have bribed the pope to grant the audience, which indicates that the Church of Rome, like the rest of the world, is open to worldly corruption.

---

9. Since I am not concerned primarily with the structural shifts in the language in this chapter, but rather the effects of inscribed orality, I shall not go into any further detail concerning those shifts. However, I argue that an increase in inscribed orality automatically involves such structural changes, particularly in the absence of a standard language.

The annal for 1127 describes the actions of a French abbot who had whatever he found of value in his monastery shipped to France. The first comment (in bold type) is similar to those in the first part of the chronicle insofar as it is a metadiscursive evaluation, with the benefit of hindsight, on the uselessness of the abbot's actions. But this is then justified by a lengthy metadiscursive commentary (which I have not presented in full) that warns readers not to doubt the veracity of the narrator's information (marked by use of the first-person plural pronoun *we*). The narrator states that it was well known throughout the country that the action itself (which I have left out here) took place on the Sunday on which "Exurge, quare obdormis, Domine?" is sung (i.e. Sexagesima Sunday). The biting irony here is that the Latin text means "Wake up! Why are you sleeping, Lord?" The reader is not quite addressed by the second-person singular *þu*, but the impersonal pronoun *man* is certainly a form of pronominal address, and we can perceive a move towards direct reference to the addressee:

(10) Eall þet he mihte tacen wiðinnen and wiðuten, of læred and of læwed, swa he sende ouer sæ; **and ne god þær dide ne na god ðær læuede.** *Ne þince man na sellice þet we soð seggen; for hit wæs ful cuð ofer eall land swa radlice swa he þær com—þet wæs þes Sunnendæies þet man singað "Exurge, quare obdormis, Domine?"*

"Everything that he could take, inside and outside, of learned and unlearned things he sent over the sea; **and it didn't do any good there nor did it leave anything good there.** *Nor may one think wondrously that we are not telling the truth; for it was well known across the whole land that as prudently as he came there—that was on the Sunday when you sing 'Exurge, quare obdormis, Domine?'"*

Excerpt (11) is the annal for the year 1130, and it tells the story of the abbot of Cluny, who spent a great deal of energy, against the will of the monks of Peterborough and ultimately to no avail, trying to persuade King Henry I to place the abbey of Peterborough under the jurisdiction of Cluny:[10]

(11) To Burch he com, and þær behet se abbot Heanri him þet he scolde beieton him þone mynstre of Burch þet hit scolde beon underðed into Clunni: *oc man seið to biworde, "Hæge sitteð þa aceres dæleth!" God ælmihtig adylege iuele ræde! Sone þæræfter ferde se abbot of Clunni ham to his ærde.*

"He came to Peterborough, and there Abbot Henry asked him [the king] to take the minster of Peterborough for him [and] to subjoin [it] to Cluny: *but they say in the proverb, 'Hedges sit there that separate acres!' May God Almighty blot out evil speech! Soon thereafter the abbot of Cluny went home to his own earth.*"

10. The abbot's name was also Henry, which does not help to resolve the coreferencing of the actors in this passage.

The commentary is again ironic (single underlining) in that the narrator uses an imprecation to God to forgive evil speech; if God should interpret his quotation of the proverb as "evil" in relation to the abbot of Cluny, he pleads forgiveness. The fact is that his criticism is meant seriously, which is subtly signalled by a move to the prosaic statement that the abbot of Cluny left England soon afterwards, and it includes the sting in the tail (*to his own earth*) referring to the earth on his own side of the hedge. The introduction of a proverb commonly used at that period (*"Hedges sit there that separate acres"*) is introduced by the discourse marker *but*, and the proverb itself can be understood as a metapragmatic marker. The density of metadiscursive commentary and metapragmatic expressions in this brief excerpt creates undeniable humour.

4.3 Inscribed orality in the Second Continuation of the *Peterborough Chronicle*

My final excerpts are taken from the Second Continuation, in which the scribe's English is noticeably different from the first scribe's, and in which we see a distinct movement towards inscribed orality. In section 5, I shall argue that it is precisely the marked shift towards inscribed orality that indicates the end of the archive of which the *ASC* was part, thus constituting a strong argument against the **unbroken tradition myth**.

The second scribe picks up the narration from 1132 and includes the information that the king solved the dissension concerning the succession to the abbey of Peterborough, after Abbot Henry's return to Cluny, by choosing Martin (*an prior of Sanct Neod*, "a prior of St. Neot's") as the new abbot. There is then a gap of three years till 1135 in which Henry I's death and Stephen's accession to the throne are reported. The next entry is for 1137, and it effectively covers the whole of Stephen's disastrous reign. It is followed by an entry for 1138 giving a very brief report of King David of Scotland's abortive attempt to conquer England and then describes in great detail, under the year 1140, the civil war between Stephen and Matilda and the agreement finally reached that Henry of Anjou—Stephen's nephew and Matilda's son—would succeed to the throne after Stephen's death. Stephen's death and the accession of Henry II are then described in the annal for 1154, and the chronicle closes with the death of Abbot Martin and the election of a new abbot, William de Vatteville. Thus, while it could have been the case that the entries for 1132 and 1135 were written up during the reign of Stephen, it is much more likely that the whole reign was written up in 1155.

From a narrative point of view, the Second Continuation is framed by the election of Martin as the abbot of Peterborough in 1132 and Martin's death in 1154. In addition, after the gruesome description of anarchic violence under the entry for 1137, which the second scribe finishes with the sentence

Suilc and mare þanne we cunnen sæin we þol[ed]en xix winter for ure sinnes ("Such and more than we can tell we suffered for 19 years for our sins"), we then read the following: *On al þis yuele time heold Martin abbot his abbotrice xx winter and half gær and viii dæis mid micel suinc* ("During all this evil time Abbot Martin held his abbacy for 20 and a half years and eight days with much effort"). Abbot Martin thus appears to be the unsung hero of the narrative. The final sentence of the *Peterborough Chronicle*—and indeed the final sentence of the *ASC*—after reporting the election of William de Vatteville as the new abbot, is as follows:

(12) And nu is abbot and fair haued begunnon: Xpist[11] him unne þ[us] enden!

"And now [he] is abbot and has begun well: may Christ grant him that it should end that way!"

This is a very decisive ending, rounding off a period of civil war, anarchy and violence, and I return to it in section 5 of this chapter when I assess the disappearance of the discourse archive.

The long entry for 1137 is full of narrative commentary, subjective evaluation and metapragmatic expressions—all the tell-tale signs of inscribed orality. I discuss some of these in the present subsection. The first type of metadiscursive insert consists of forms of evaluative narrative commentary, such as the following:

(13) Þa namen hi þa men þe hi wenden ðat ani gold hefden, bathe be nihtes and be dæies, carlmen and wimmen, and diden heom in prisun and pined heom efter gold and syluer untellendlice pining; *for ne uuaren næure nan martyrs swa pined alse hi wæron.*

"Then they took the men that they thought had any gold, both by night and by day, rustics and women, and threw them into prison and subjected them to indescribable torture for gold and silver; *for there were never any martyrs as tortured as they were.*"

The second type is that of a metapragmatic explanatory insertion for the benefit of the reader, as in (14):

(14) Sume hi diden in crucethus—*ðat is, in an cęste þat was scort and nareu and undep*—and dide scærpe stanes þerinne and þrengde þe man þærinne ðat him bræcon alle þe limes.

"Some they put into a 'crucethus'—*that is, in a chest that was short and narrow and shallow*—and put sharp stones into it and forced the man into it so that all his limbs were broken."

---

11. The spelling of the lexeme *Christ* here is most unusual. The first two letters would appear to be from the Greek, representing the phoneme /X/ and the phoneme /r/.

Perhaps the most obvious features of inscribed orality, and those which have (or simulate) a direct connection to the ongoing interaction, are first- and second-person pronoun reference; explicit examples of modality, particularly deontic modality; and instances of verbs that are not past tense. Such insertions are metapragmatic in that they position the speaker/writer or the interlocutor/reader outside the world of the discourse by commenting on it in the here-and-now of the interaction, and they are also metadiscursive in that they position the speaker/writer and the interlocutor/reader with respect to the overall discourse structure and orders of discourse. Within the Labovian high-point model of narrative structure they represent strongly evaluative commentary. Excerpt (15) contains the first-person pronoun *I* and two modal verbs that are not past tense, one representing epistemic modality (*can*) and the other deontic modality (*mai*).[12] It is rounded off with a subjective evaluation of the overall situation. Excerpt (16) goes so far as to imagine a fictive addressee who is addressed with the second-person singular pronoun *þu*:

> (15) *I ne **can** ne I ne **mai** tellen* alle þe wunder ne alle þe pines ðat hi diden wrecce men on þis land; and ðat lastede þa xix wintre wile Stephne was king, and *æuvre it was uuerse and uuerse.*
>
> "*I **can** not nor **may** I tell* all the terrible things nor all the torture that they did to wretched men in this land; and that lasted 19 winters while Stephen was king, and *all the time it got worse and worse.*"
>
> (16) Þa þe uurecce men ne hadden nammore to gyuen, þa ræueden hi and brendon alle þe tunes, ðat wel *þu mihtes faren al a dæies fare, sculdest þu neure finden* man in tune sittende ne land tiled.
>
> "When the wretched men had no more to give, they plundered and burned down all the towns so *that you might well travel for a whole day, but you would never find* a man living in the town nor the land tilled."

The whole of the entry under 1137 is highly unusual for entries in the *ASC* in its personal tone, but, as we have seen, it was certainly anticipated by the increase of inscribed orality in the first scribe's narrative in the First Continuation. The second scribe/narrator expresses a sense of social outrage at the arbitrary violence caused by the anarchic state of England during Stephen's reign and sympathy for the sufferings of the common people. It contains horrifying descriptions of the tortures that the narrator maintains the common people were subjected to and outrage at the fact that God looked on and did nothing. In a word, it is a damning assessment of the reign of King Stephen. The major question at this point is the following: Who were meant to be the recipients of the narrative? Who was the intended *þu*?

---

12. The expression of deontic modality will be significant in assessing the breakdown of the discourse archive in section 5.

5. THE DISAPPEARANCE OF THE *ASC*:
THE END OF A DISCOURSE ARCHIVE

The identity of the second scribe's/narrator's listener/reader obviously cannot be reconstructed. The pronoun *þu* could just as easily have been a variant for the impersonal *man*, or even for the scribe himself. But *þu* is still a much more personal form of address than *man*, and is to be found nowhere else throughout the rest of the *ASC*. Whoever the imagined addressee was, it most certainly was not the same to whom the texts were read out at the old *witenagemote*. By the twelfth century, writing a chronicle annal in English (rather than in Latin) had become writing a narrative, with a beginning and an end and, as in the case of the 1137 annal, with a frame of reference. The story told in the *Peterborough Chronicle* is no longer about politically significant events and personages in the kingdom, but about the fate of the abbey of Peterborough, which narrows the circle of possible co-referents for *þu* quite considerably. But it is also about the horrors of the anarchy during King Stephen's reign, and it thus becomes a narrative offering rich opportunities for evaluation, narrative embellishment, narrative perspective and—ultimately—condemnation of King Stephen himself and of the whole Norman royal house on the accession of the first Angevin/Plantagenet king, Henry II. It is therefore feasible that the propaganda effect was welcome to Henry, but certainly not the continuation of a potentially subversive voice in the vernacular. This may explain why the scribe/narrator phrases the last sentence of the *ASC* in so final a way and also why he uses the deontic modality in *ne mai* ("may not") in the 1137 annal.

There is, however, a deeper reason that the disappearance of the *ASC* can be interpreted as the end of an archive, and it has to do with the late medieval conceptualisation of history as a cyclic progression of states ranging on a cline from good to evil and from order to disorder. After the Conquest, feudal society established itself through the church and the monarch, and with it an archive developed that differed considerably from that which was discursively supported by the *ASC*.

What was that new archive? In the late medieval world a person's life on earth was considered to be transitory, a state of existence in which she earned either an eternal life in heaven or eternal damnation in hell. Social life on earth was ordered hierarchically in terms of estates, the first of these being the clergy, the second the nobility and the third the common people.[13] The first estate and the second and third estates together were organised in pyramidal form, each with a representative of God at the top apex of the pyramid, the pope representing the first estate and the sovereign (king, prince, etc.) representing the second estate. History thus concerned itself with a chronological

---

13. The duty of the first estate (the clergy) was to take care of the spiritual well-being of others—to see to it that as many as possible did achieve eternal life in heaven and not eternal damnation in hell. The duty of the second estate was to physically protect others from outside aggression and to ensure order (i.e. to fight). The duty of the third estate was to work to provide the means to survive while alive on earth.

succession of popes and kings, some of whom carried out their duties in exemplary fashion, whereas others did not. A "bad" king, who was unable to preserve order and protect his subjects, might be followed by a "good" king. History was thus not concerned with the linearity of time, since time meant nothing when compared to the eternity of the hereafter, and the pyramidal structure of society was meant to stay in place and remain static rather than to develop and change.

The cyclic succession of secular and religious leaders between the two poles of "good" and "bad" was to be written in the sacred language Latin rather than in the vernacular English. As a result, chronicles began to be written in the scriptoria across England in Latin, their subject matter being the whole history of Britain from earliest mythical times to the present including stories devoted to legendary kings such as Brutus (hence the term "Brut chronicle"), Lear and Arthur.[14] As such, the Brut chronicles were a guarantee that the structure of society could be preserved as it was, with the king at its apex, good or bad, and with the values of chivalry upheld in the second estate. Brut chroniclers were clerics, and they were uniquely concerned with the deeds—in Latin, *gesta*—of kings, princes, nobility, bishops and popes, but most definitely not with the sufferings of the common people. Narrative was called for, but not the personal, author-centred local narrative that we see in the Second Continuation.

Developments in the *ASC* from the late tenth century on show the following tendencies:

- longer and less easily memorised annals
- a move towards more narrative structure with the increasing use of metapragmatic linguistic expressions to effect narrative evaluation; that is, an increase in inscribed orality ending, as we have seen, in the narrator-centred history of the Second Continuation
- an increase, particularly in the *Peterborough Chronicle*, in the focus on local rather than national topics
- an empathetic, critical narrative persona, particularly in the First and Second Continuations of the *Peterborough Chronicle*
- an overt sympathy for common people, specifically in the Second Continuation

When we reach the Second Continuation, we find that the *ASC* presents an *un*official historical record of a period of anarchy and civil war in a highly personalised account, a form of "antidiscourse". It points an accusing finger at a king who allowed his kingdom to get out of control. The scribe has now

14. There is one notable exception to the condition that they should be written in Latin, and that is *Layamon's Brut*, also known as the *Chronicle of Britain*, written around 1190 in verse by the English priest Layamon and based on the Anglo-Norman poem *Roman de Brut* by Wace. Translations into English of Brut chronicles do not appear until the late fourteenth century, the first of these being John de Trevisa's translation of Ranulph Higden's popular *Polychronicon*.

taken over the role of a narrator, rather than an "official" scribe, so that the *ASC* can no longer be seen as part of a hegemonic discourse archive. We might speculate that this last chronicle text written in vernacular prose was sanctioned by royal authority to put a final, nonauthoritative seal on the Anglo-Saxon and Norman periods of English history. This would, of course, be pure speculation, but it would certainly fit the facts, given that the beginning of Henry II's reign heralded the official institutionalisation of common law, introducing trial by jury and a centralised system of judges sent out regularly to different parts of the country to resolve legal disputes (the so-called assizes). Law texts had long become divorced from chronicle writing. Thus the *ASC* no longer represented an official archive that "[imposed] restrictions on what can be said meaningfully".

Foucault's conceptualistion of discourse, in which "all of the objects, forms and themes of discursive statements are historically linked to the external conditions of discourse production" implies not only that no discourse is sociohistorically decontextualised but also that the extralinguistic historical context plays a not insignificant role with respect to the form that the discourse takes. I have shown how the movement towards increased instances of inscribed orality can be interpreted as signs that the original archive to which the discourse belonged had become moribund by the early twelfth century. I have also shown how the Second Continuation might be viewed as politically subversive in its criticism of King Stephen. We now need to reconsider this interpretation in a possible contextualisation of the text.

In section 4.1, I questioned whether the last surviving copy of the *ASC*, the *Peterborough Chronicle*, might not have become an alternative antidiscourse at least in the Second Continuation. When the historical facts are reviewed, this argument becomes even more plausible. First, the Second Continuation was, in all probability, written up after the death of King Stephen in the first year of Henry II's reign. Second, the whole period from 1132 to 1154 is framed within Martin's service as abbot of Peterborough. Third, as we know, Martin was a "prior at St. Neot's" and probably of English extraction, whereas the new abbot had a distinctly French name, William de Vatteville, indicating provenance from the Continent. Fourth, the final sentence wishes William well in his position as abbot and has an odd finality to it. Fifth, Henry II was Matilda's son from her second marriage, to the Count of Anjou, and Matilda was Henry I's daughter and the rightful heir to the throne of England. And sixth, the hegemonic discourse archive at the beginning of Henry II's reign supported statements to the effect that history should be presented cyclically and should have no effect on the static nature of social structure, and it rejected statements that history should concern itself with the common people rather than those in the first and second estates.

One further intriguing piece of speculation might be suggested here. Might it have been the case that Henry commissioned this last part of the *ASC* to discredit not only Stephen but also the Norman royal dynasty? We will never know, but the *ASC* had been used before for propaganda purposes, and at this time it had run its race as a significant part of a dominant discourse archive.

Other forms of chronicle writing in Latin, the Brut chronicles, had developed from the late eleventh century on, and they were continued into the fourteenth century. Works documenting history, topography, culture, legend, and so on were of a nonpolitical nature and did not therefore endanger the new dominant discourse archive, particularly as they were produced in an ecclesiastical context in which the majority of high-ranking clerics were of Anglo-Norman or French extraction and the language of the church was Latin.

On the other hand, the officially permitted (or at least overlooked) subversive context of the Second Continuation, in which the narrative voice is so close to the reader and so full of a feeling of outrage and righteousness, is characterised by metapragmatic and metadiscursive expressions that are typical of inscribed orality, and, I would suggest, the inscribed orality of an antidiscourse. The urge to tell the stories of a people from perspectives other than the officially permitted is again—and in the vernacular language, English—evident in the London chronicles of the fifteenth century (see McLaren 2002), and it emerges in full force in the sixteenth century. This new tradition of chronicle writing in English insisted, if not on objectivity, then at least on multivocality, and it is no exaggeration to suggest that the Second Continuation of the *Peterborough Chronicle*, 400 years earlier, provides a foretaste, perhaps even a model, for writing outside the dominant discourse archive.

One final postscript is in order to conclude this chapter. Cecily Clark (1958: xii) makes the following interesting observation concerning the *Peterborough Chronicle*:

> That this is, as tradition claims, a Peterborough book is beyond question, in spite of its apparent omission from the medieval Peterborough catalogues (unless indeed it is disguised as *Elfredi regis liber anglicus* in the twelfth-century booklist in MS. Bodley 163).

Why should it have been omitted? Or if it was included, why under disguise? Perhaps this is a further piece of evidence that it was, or had become, subversive!

Chapter 4

The construction of a modern
myth: Middle English
as a creole

Not long after the study of pidgins and creoles had begun to establish itself
in its own right, a rumor started that English, too, was a candidate for this
discipline. The rumor soon turned into a full-fledged linguistic discussion
which had two main directions.
                                    —Christiane Dalton-Puffer, "Middle English
                                                is a creole and its opposite"

1. THE CREOLISATION HYPOTHESIS

Three chapters in this book deal with intentional or unintentional myth-
building on the part of linguists themselves. In chapter 7, I take a look at the
so-called complaint tradition suggested by James and Lesley Milroy in their
influential book *Authority in Language*. Chapter 11 discusses the "talking-
into-being" of a global form of English that underlies such labels as "English
as a Lingua Franca" or "English as a World Language".

The present chapter is closely linked to chapter 3 in that it deals with the
far-reaching and rapid changes that took place in English from the twelfth to
the fifteenth century. My main purpose, however, is to discuss the curious but
often heated debate that has raged in the historical linguistics literature over
the past 30 years on the results of the changes themselves. As with all debates,
two opposing sides are concerned to present two apparently irreconcilable
points of view (cf. Dalton-Puffer 1995). In the one camp, we find a group of
linguists who argue that the form of language resulting from contact situations between speakers of English and speakers of Anglo-Norman French (or

at an earlier stage with speakers of Old Norse) can best be classified as a creole. In the opposite camp, we find linguists who vehemently reject this hypothesis, arguing instead that the changes can be adequately explained as natural processes of levelling and simplification without having to resort to the term "creole" at all.

The bone of contention in this dispute is the use of the relatively harmless linguistic term "creole", and, somewhat surprisingly, it has generated unusual amounts of emotional involvement on the side of the opponents. Evidence that the debate, as a debate, might have got a little out of hand is provided by the generation of a number of stories and counter-stories on whether English—and in particular Middle English—actually *is* a creole. Heated discussion threads can be found on the Internet among both language "experts" and language "novices", and the arguments in both camps display a problematic lack of self-reflexivity and distance. We are dealing here with an embryonic modern myth, and the purpose of this chapter is to reveal its discursive origins.

The incipient myth may be called the ***myth of the creolisation of English***,[1] and in this chapter I aim to show how the construction of meanings prompted by the linguistic term "creole" has tended to cloud our ability to assess linguistic change, variability, heterogeneity and hybridity as universal features of all language varieties. Ultimately, then, the dispute derives from the ***linguistic homogeneity myth*** presented in chapter 1, which lies at the heart of all the other myths in this book.

In chapter 3, I sketched out the sociohistorical framework within which the *ASC* emerged as a text type central to the dominant sociopolitical discourse in post-Alfredian Anglo-Saxon England. The archive that it helped to construct consisted of "meaningful statements" that determined the social structure of pre-Conquest England. The entries in the *ASC* from the last quarter of the eleventh century provide evidence that the archive was under the pressure of an alternative dominant archive, so it is hardly surprising that entries are only sporadic after the Norman Conquest of England and appeared to die out around 1080—with the exception of the *Peterborough Chronicle*; the "Bilingual Canterbury Epitome" (the F ms.); the single remaining leaf of the "Cottonian Domitian Fragment" (the H ms.), the rest of which was destroyed in the fire at Ashburton House in 1731; and the "Easter Table Chronicle" (the I ms.). The Second Continuation of the *Peterborough Chronicle* shows the greatest transformation from the "older" archive, and we can state with certainty that by 1154–55 a break had occurred in sociocultural transmission.

The following two questions can be asked about the language of the *Peterborough Chronicle*:

---

1. In the body of the text I shall consistently shorten the terminology such that the ***myth of x*** becomes the ***x myth***.

1. Do the differences between, on the one hand, the language of the first scribe copying out the entries of the *Peterborough Chronicle* prior to 1116, together with the entries from 1121 to 1132 and, on the other hand, the language of the second scribe probably writing in 1154–55 and recording the events of Stephen's reign in the Second Continuation constitute evidence of a process of creolisation in early Middle English?
2. Are there continuities or similarities in linguistic constructions arising from two major language contact situations between Anglo-Saxon and Old Norse from the early ninth century on and Middle English and Norman French after 1066 that would invalidate this thesis?

The second question hinges on the assumption that there is an unbroken development of the English language from Anglo-Saxon through Middle English to Modern English, whereas the first question concerns the belief that this supposed continuity was disrupted twice in the history of English, once during the period of Scandinavian encroachments into England resulting in a de facto division of the country into the Danelaw and the rest and again after the Norman Conquest of England, in which French language varieties were brought to England. Those who support the theory of linguistic disruption tend to evoke the notion of creolisation to explain what may have happened, and in doing so they may have helped to construct an embryonic modern myth, the ***creolisation of English myth***. Those who support linguistic continuity are often, but not necessarily always, those who believe in the ***longevity of English myth*** as it is represented in the submyth of the ***ancient language*** discussed in chapter 2. Looked at from a discursive rather than from a purely linguistic point of view, however, it is perfectly possible to reject a theory of the unbroken tradition of English (as demonstrated in chapter 3) while retaining a linguistic theory of the unbroken tradition.

Myths are discursively constructed from sets of beliefs that may or may not derive from or contain a few grains of "truth". But they are still fictive constructions, and they form the basis of ideological discourses of English that may become dominant and hegemonic. My aim is to show that even a modern theory that is no older that 30 to 35 years and is located in a well-researched and well-established area of sociolinguistic research, creolistics, is open to being mythologised when it is made to challenge more solidly entrenched myths such as that of the ***longevity of English***. At the same time, however, I wish to argue that continuity in language development need not always be equated with the longevity myth. The unfortunate fact is that, despite a number of written texts in Anglo-Saxon, we have relatively little in the way of reliable firsthand data with which we can reconstruct linguistic changes during the period between 800 and the advent of the Black Death (the plague) in England in 1348. We have a reasonably solid sociohistorical profile of living conditions and social structures during that period, but we have no information on how people used language in going about their daily lives, which is just what intensive language contact involves.

The dispute over the creole origins of Middle English can also be extended to refer to Modern English, and it currently reaches beyond the confines of the academic linguistic community. The major problems concern the nature of language contact situations and conflicting definitions of the term "creole" itself. But before we take a closer look at the scholarly dispute on whether or not Middle English *was* a creole, it might help to consider some of the points made in the Internet discussion I referred to earlier in this section.

2. THE DISCUSSION THREAD "IS ENGLISH A CREOLE?"

The question that gave rise to the discussion "Is English a creole?" was originally posted on 20 September 2006 by V** on the Web site WordReference. com/Language Forums.[2] In all, there were 25 postings in the thread within the space of almost 29 hours. V** asks others in the forum whether they would consider English to be "a creole language, a formalized French-like language with a Germanic substrate". He immediately modifies this question by restricting the term "creole" to Middle English and then goes on to mention the large number of French-based borrowings in English. But he does not explain what he understands by the term "creole".

The first six responses react positively in two postings and negatively in four to V**'s original question, but there is not much attempt to define what a creole is until the third poster uses a definition taken from an Oxford Dictionaries Web site as "a pidgin language which has become a mother tongue". This same poster, B**, refers to the original posting by suggesting that what V** is really talking about is the phenomenon of lexical borrowing into English. Poster number 5 (who does not give a name but only a set of punctuation marks) then offers a definition of a creole as being "a language that forms from extended contact between two languages", and suggests that this is what has happened in the case of English. The sixth poster, M**, denies that English is a creole but seems to feel that creole languages are in any case only based on French: "Creole, on the other hand is highly modelled on French".

So far, then, we have a selection of lay interpretations of whether or not English (or Middle English) is a creole, and two somewhat different definitions of a creole emerge:

1. A creole is "a pidgin language which has become a mother tongue".
2. A creole is "a language that forms from extended contact between two languages".

2. I first accessed this Web site in December 2007, and it is still currently available at http://forum. wordreference.com/showthread.php?t=240473. Should the discussion thread be erased from the Web site or the Web site address be changed, I am in possession of a copy of it that I can make available to readers who would like to read it for themselves (contact email: watts@ens.unibe.ch). All names of the participants in the discussion thread have been anonymised.

As the thread progresses, posters become more and more confused about how to define a creole. In posting number 7, B** offers a Wikipedia definition that clearly contradicts the earlier definition she or he offered concerning the relationship between pidgins and creoles. This new definition seems to fit the second definition offered above:

3. A creole is "the result of a nontrivial mixture of two or more languages, usually with radical morphological changes and a syntax which is not obviously borrowed from either of the parent tongues".

However, this poster then goes on to suggest that perhaps a more appropriate term to use to characterise such a phenomenon would be "koiné" and backs up this argument by referring to the earlier period of contact between Anglo-Saxon and varieties of Old Norse.

The following definitions are also offered:

4. A creole is a language that shows "simplification of the grammar", which does not necessarily depend on whether it has been in contact "with one or more other languages".
5. A creole is not "simply a mishmash of languages". A creole "usually arises when speakers of one language become economically or politically dominant over speakers of another".
6. A creole is "a mother tongue formed from the contact of a European language with another language, especially an African language". (The poster of this definition, L**, who does not agree that Middle English is a creole, then goes on to seriously compromise his or her point of view by writing that "there are very good arguments for considering Old English a pidgin". This poster also calls for a poll on the opinions given in the thread, which in itself indicates a considerable degree of confusion. Defining a creole does not, after all, depend on a popular vote. The poll is never taken.)

The question of whether English is or is not a creole finally peters out in a three-way discussion between J**, B** and O**, but not before some interesting statements have been made. One participant suggests that English is a "BAstard [sic] rather than a creole". "Creole" for this poster indicates "a non-standard form of a known standard",[3] but she or he maintains that "English is not a 'colorfully messed up' version of some other more 'legitimate' standard". The confusion between "standard", "non-standard", "creole" and "legitimate' standard" displays a lack of expertise in matters of sociolinguistics, even though all the contributors to the discussion are obviously interested in the subject of language and the history of language. It is interesting to note that O**'s opinion that English is a "bastard" reveals the degree to which the participants revert to the

---

3. This is a distinctly odd point of view which would lead every dialect or sociostylistic variety of a language to be classified as a "creole".

anthropomorphic conceptual metaphor for language (A LANGUAGE IS A HUMAN BEING). It is, of course, not possible to tell whether the term "bastard", when ascribed to English, is meant to be taken seriously. In any event, the question of whether English is a creole appears to have prompted a more than average number of negatively affective comments. Another participant considers English to be "a pastiche", which implies that it is a linguistic system that has been hurriedly put together from bits and pieces. Towards the end of the thread, B** says, "I don't think there [*sic*] anything bad or disrespectful about it [being called a 'creole']", and, once again using the anthropomorphic metaphor, O** asks, "So what does a language have to do to suddenly upgrade from a creole to a 'proper' language?" One inference to be drawn from this question is that there are "proper" and "nonproper" languages.

It is obvious that not all the participants in the discussion have English as their first language, but all have a more than average interest in linguistic issues. The majority appear not to be professional linguists, although one or two could be, and they all seem to be aware that people outside the discussion could also read the discussion thread (cf. the comment "While I believe that words mean what people mean them to be, if people out there think that a creole is any language that has alot [*sic*] of foreign words then linguists need a new word for what they are under the impression 'creole' means").

Four interesting points emerge from the Internet discussion:

1. The suggestion that English is a creole provokes strong feelings not only among professional linguists, but also among lay persons who are interested in human language.
2. Six different definitions of the term "creole" emerge.
3. Most of the definitions veer either towards the opinion that a creole is a simplified form of language arising from language contact situations or towards the opinion that a creole is a nativised pidgin; they come surprisingly close to the two definitions I shall deal with in the following section.
4. All the discussants consider language contact to be significant in some way or another.

3. THE "MIDDLE ENGLISH IS A CREOLE" DEBATE IN THE ACADEMIC LITERATURE

3.1 Beginnings of the debate: Bailey and Maroldt (1977)

The debate began in 1977 with Charles-James Bailey and Kurt Maroldt's contribution to a collection of articles on pidgins and creoles edited by Jürgen Meisel. It was given the deceptive title "The French lineage of English", which, rather than declare itself openly as an argument for the creole status of

Middle English, uses the well-worn heredity and family-tree metaphor for the conceptualisation of the history of languages. This, in its turn, is also part of the anthropomorphic metaphor (A LANGUAGE IS A HUMAN BEING), which was used in the Internet discussion in the previous section.

Bailey and Maroldt waste no time in making clear which of the two conflicting definitions of the term "creole" they support. On the first page of their article they make the following unequivocal statement: "By creolization the authors wish to indicate gradient mixture of two or more languages; in a narrow sense, a *creole* is the result of mixing which is substantial enough to result in a new system, a system that is separate from its antecedent parent systems" (1977: 21).

They go on to make absolutely clear that their understanding of a creole has nothing to do with the nativisation of a pidgin: "We make no claim that Middle English developed out of a pidgin" (22). The confusion that has arisen in the "Middle-English-is-a-creole" debate, a confusion that has gone well beyond the field of professional sociolinguistics, is directly attributable to two apparently irreconcilable definitions of the term.

Bailey and Maroldt's major argument concerns the claim that, while "internal language-change will result only in new subsystems", creolisation "is required for the creation of a new system, i.e. a new node on a family tree". The onus of proof now lies on their shoulders to show that prolonged language contact with Anglo-Norman and other varieties of French actually did result in a new language system, and this can only be shown if we accept the categorisation of human language into uniquely distinct systems. It is also worth noting that they again resort to the family tree metaphor and the metaphorical anthropomorphisation of human language.[4]

Calling Middle English (or any other stage in the development of English or indeed any other language system) a creole is certainly one way of accounting for the remarkable changes—most of these morphological simplifications and an extensive amount of lexical borrowing from French—which occurred in English in the roughly 300 years after the Norman Conquest. However, it becomes problematic when placed against the nativisation hypothesis proposed by what Bailey and Maroldt call "traditionalists" (1977: 23) and when compared with other explanations of "a mixed language" that do not need to use the term "creole". They make their point somewhat forcefully as follows:

> It cannot be doubted that [Middle English] is a mixed language, or creole. The only question is whether Old French was creolized with Anglo-Saxon...whether Anglo-Saxon was creolized with Old French, or whether the mixture was of so thorough-going a nature that it makes little sense even to pose the question at all. (22–23)

---

4. This becomes even clearer in the following sentence, in which they state that "each node on a family tree therefore has to have, like humans, at least two parents".

Evidence that they are fully conscious of the provocative nature of their hypothesis is given when they state that they "naturally expect to meet with much opposition from traditionalists, who will find it hard to see the matter in such a new, if convincing, light" (23). No one can reasonably doubt that "the basic fact of mixture...does not seem to be rationally disputable", but they may wish to doubt that the use of the term "creole" to explain this mixing is presented in a "convincing light", despite the wealth of detail they give in the article.

Their purpose is to argue for two stages in the "French creolisation" of English, one prior to 1200 from Anglo-Norman French and the other involving massive lexical borrowing in the thirteenth and fourteenth centuries from what they call "Central French", but they also maintain that these two stages of creolisation under the influence of French had already been preceded from the ninth century on by a period of Old Norse/Anglo-Saxon creolisation. This assumption goes a little too far, as I aim to demonstrate in a later section of this chapter. For the moment, however, we need to focus on the reactions to Bailey and Maroldt's article.

3.2 First opponents

In the same year in which Bailey and Maroldt's contribution appeared in Meisel's collection, an article by Nicole Z. Domingue titled "Middle English: Another creole?" was published in the first volume of the *Journal of Creole Studies*. In that article, Domingue correctly points out that prior to the obvious influence of French on English after the Conquest there is no substantial evidence on which to base the assumption that a mixed language involving English ever existed in Britain. It is a strong argument against the hypothesis that creolisation, or even pidginisation, was a significant factor in the history of the language. Even using the term "mixed language" is assuming what we simply do not know. She makes a careful analysis of the sociocultural conditions under which the creolisation scenario might have taken place, if we were to accept Bailey and Maroldt's definition of the term in preference to the nativisation-of-a-pidgin hypothesis. After also looking closely at those linguistic features that characterise creoles, she concludes that there are few features that would even warrant the classification of Middle English as a creole, and she ends by simply classifying it as a *hybrid* language.

Now, what elements in these two obviously conflicting analyses indicate that we may have the beginnings of a linguistic myth that has found favour beyond the academic linguistic community? In the first place, Domingue's reaction, like that of Edgar Polomé in 1980, to which I shall turn shortly, is evidence of a long-standing dispute over the two definitions of creole. Creolists have been somewhat strict in positing that creoles develop from sociolinguistic situations in which a pidgin, very often an elaborated pidgin, becomes the native language of a generation of speakers. There is a strong feeling that sociolinguistic articles such as Whinnom's "Linguistic hybridization and the 'special case' of pidgins and creoles" (1971), in which simplification processes in certain kinds of language contact situations are equated with pidginisation and creolisation without fulfilling the typical sociocultural conditions necessary for the development of pidgins, constitute a misleading use of both terms. In 1974 Todd, in her survey *Pidgins and Creoles*, had even suggested that modern English displays "features consistent with pidginisation" when compared to Anglo-Saxon. But to be fair to Bailey and Maroldt, Whinnom and Todd, the suggestion that the theoretical apparatus of creolistics may be of some help in opening up new research pathways that historical linguistics might take up was perfectly reasonable. We have here a classical case of *noli me tangere* on the part of creolists and historical linguists with respect to perceived encroachments of sociolinguists into the academic territory of historical linguistics.

In addition, and possibly more important in explaining how the myth has spread beyond academia, people do not take too kindly to having their languages associated with pidgins or creoles. The study of pidgin languages began at the beginning of the twentieth century with the pioneering work by Schuchardt, but pidgins were always thought of as simplified, incomplete versions of their lexifier languages that were not worth paying any attention to. It was not until the late 1950s and early 1960s that Robert Hall Jr. resurrected pidgins and creoles as a respectable and important area of research in linguistics. Since that time the study of pidgin and creole languages has burgeoned into an important and insightful area of research. Lay attitudes towards pidgins and creoles, however, have lagged far behind the development of pidgin and creole studies. For many scholars specialising in the English language, to read Bailey and Maroldt seriously arguing for a process of creolisation in Middle English is almost equivalent to being told that the language is somehow inferior or has at least sprung from lowly origins.

One of the most convincing arguments against the Middle-English-is-a-creole hypothesis, but at the same time one of the most difficult to read because of his extraordinarily wide-ranging use of evidence from languages belonging to different language families, was made in 1980 by Polomé in an edited collection of contributions to creole studies titled *Theoretical Contributions to Creole Studies* (Valdman & Highfield 1980). The crux of the problem for Polomé is the tendency "to assume pidginization or language simplification for a large number of cases where languages come into contact" (1980: 185), and, if this is the case, he suggests that studying "the linguistic features that are common to pidgins and creoles may prove as valuable a parameter in the study of the history of languages as the study of sound changes was in the past" (185). He proceeds to demonstrate that in those instances in which pidginisation and creolisation processes have been claimed as part of the history of various languages, insufficient evidence is at hand to support those claims, and if, as Bailey and Maroldt claim, creolisation results in the substitution of one linguistic system for another, the first points that the researcher needs to consider are whether "a new language is acquired, with the impact of the other language(s) limited essentially to phonology and the lexicon" and whether "pidginization and creolization [have taken place] with thorough restructurization by the native population of the language introduced by the invaders" (192–193). Referring to Domingue's 1977 paper, he argues that she demonstrates convincingly that the hypothesis of the creolisation of Middle English fails to show the features of a creole syntax.

Polomé also urges readers to consider three conditions in the language contact situation that need to be met to argue in favour of creolisation. To begin with, "there must be clear evidence of a break in continuity in language development", which, as I shall demonstrate for the Anglo-Saxon period, holds neither for the Anglo-Saxon–Old Norse contact situation nor for the Anglo-Norman French/French–Middle English situation. Second, "there must be linguistic features characteristic of *creolization* (successive phases of *simplification*...and *restructuration*", which is only partially the case in the Middle English period. And third, "there must be adequate evidence of the socio-economic or politico-cultural conditions by which *deculturation/acculturation* processes of outsiders acquiring the language can be documented" (197). In the case of both Anglo-Saxon–Old Norse and Middle English, this kind of evidence is also lacking.

3.3 Confusion reigns

The kinds of difficulty that may arise through the confusion of two distinctly different definitions of pidgin and creole can be illustrated with an article by Patricia Poussa, "The evolution of early standard English" (1982). On the one hand, Poussa defines a pidgin as "a language which has been drastically simplified in structure and vocabulary, in order to serve restricted communication needs. A pidgin is no-one's native language" (69), and she suggests that pidgins tend to emerge through "sudden direct contact" such as "military invasion or trade contact". This is the standard explanation of a pidgin, although one should go a little further and also mention that the language which is "pidginised" is the non-native language of the nondominant language group. There are, in other words, social-cultural constraints on the development of a pidgin. She also presents the standard explanation of a creole as being derived from a pidgin when she says that a pidgin is adopted "as the first language of a community" (70). She then goes on to say that such an adoption leads to elaboration, which she equates with creolisation. In point of fact, in most nativisation scenarios, the original pidgin has already undergone considerable elaboration before being adopted as a native language (cf. the case of Tok Pisin). However, in the very next paragraph, she states that "I shall use the term *creolization* to cover the pidginization–creolization processes which take place in the *spoken* form <u>when two languages hybridize to form a creole as a result of direct contact between two speech communities</u>" (70, my emphasis).

This is a notion of creole decidedly different from the one she has presented, and it is one that leads her into difficulties.

Poussa rightly criticises Bailey and Maroldt for using written sources to support their creole hypothesis. Any language contact situation is primarily oral, and we simply have no linguistic evidence as to how people spoke to one another on an everyday basis during either the period of French–Middle English contact or the period of Anglo-Saxon–Old Norse contact. At least for the Middle English period we can find useful clues, often from the writings of Chaucer, but certainly not enough to be able to define the contact situation in any detail. For the Old Norse situation, we have no clues at all.

This indisputable fact is important in assessing the path that Poussa takes in her article. First she focuses on precisely that period in which linguistic evidence is virtually nonexistent, and she fictionalises a situation of contact that, even if it might represent some element of reality, certainly fails to cover the "normal" situation of Danish settlers farming land close to Anglian or Northumbrian farmers. It is worth quoting this passage in full with my comments added:

> The civilian population of the East Midlands [What about the North Midlands and Northumbria up as far as the River Tees?], caught between two Danish armies [At what time would this have been the case and how long would this population have been caught in comparison with the long period of peaceful cohabitation?], consisting largely of women and children and men too old to have served in the levy, must have been in complete disarray [Yes, but for how long? Surely only during the hostilities, but quite apart from anything else there is no evidence to back up this story]. The settlement of the area by the Danish army and later arrivals must have involved intermarriage with the local women on a large scale [This could have been the case, I admit, but settlers might also have arrived with their families. Again we simply do not know, nor do we know the size of the Danish army, although it could hardly have been more than 10,000 at an absolute maximum]. The children of such unions [which could hardly have been that numerous] would be compound bilinguals, hearing both languages in the home [The crux of my later argument is that we are probably dealing not with two different languages, but rather with two "dialectal" varieties that were to a large extent mutually intelligible. In that kind of situation, is it feasible to talk of "compound bilingualism"?]. In this kind of bilingual [bidialectal] society, language mixing and switching is normal behaviour. Some families or villages would have maintained their "pure" Danish or English [Even if Poussa puts the lexeme *pure* between quotation marks, this is still an ideological statement prompted by the **myth of the pure language** (cf. chap. 5)] longer than others, but separation from both parent speech-communities would favour the development of a hybrid language, a creole. (1982: 74)

My final comment on Poussa's "story" is that she has now given up the principle that a creole derives from the nativisation of a pidgin and has shifted to the principle that a hybrid language constitutes a pidgin regardless of the social situation which, in all probability, governed the language-mixing situation in the first place.

3.4 Clarity returns

In 1986 Görlach published an article in the first volume of a Festschrift for Jacek Fisiak titled "Middle English—A creole?" in which he stresses the point already made by Polomé (1980: 185) that studying "the linguistic features that are common to pidgins and creoles may prove as valuable a parameter in the study of the history of languages as the study of sound changes was in the past". However, since Polomé is not referred to explicitly, we may safely assume that Görlach simply comes to the same conclusion: he asks whether "the methods of creolists—drawing, as they do, their data from a sociolinguistics laboratory under the eyes of the participant observer—[can] help us to understand the motivation for linguistic changes observed in the early histories of modern languages", or whether "such methods [can] be more helpful than the traditional methods of historical linguistics have been" (1986: 328). Görlach makes the valid point that a creole provenance has also been suggested for several other languages (e.g. the Romance languages, Yiddish and Bulgarian). He insists that linguists should provide answers to the following questions before a creolisation hypothesis can be advanced for any language, including, of course, Middle English:

1. How are, or can the central terms used in classification be defined?;
2. What features are thought to be constitutive for creole languages?;
3. What contact situations are recorded in the history of English and its speakers (to see whether the sociolinguistic conditions can be equated with those that gave rise to pidgins, creoles, creoloids, etc.)? (1986: 330)

He also makes the point that "the term 'creole' is used quite vaguely by some scholars" and that "others have redefined it to make it satisfy the specific needs of their arguments", and he evaluates Bailey and Maroldt's use of the term "creole" as "an idiosyncratic redefinition" (330). It is hardly surprising that Görlach criticises Poussa along lines similar to those I have presented above, but when he comes to dismantling Bailey and Maroldt's claim, he needs to refer very specifically to those points at which the syntax and morphology of Middle English fail to show the features of a creole syntax. After summarily dealing with most of the major creole features and showing that Middle English cannot be interpreted as showing any of them fully, he comes to the following tentative conclusion:

> Unless simplification and language mixture are thought to be sufficient criteria for the definition of a creole or creoloid (and I do not think they are, since this would make most languages of the world creoles, and the term

would consequently lose its distinctiveness), then Middle English does not appear to be a creole. (1986: 335)

Of course, it still remains open for creolists to dispute this point and to argue that simplification and language mixture do constitute sufficient criteria for defining a creole or a creoloid. He insists that the sociopolitical and sociocultural relationship between Anglo-Saxon and Old Norse from the ninth century on and between varieties of French and Middle English in the first three centuries following the Conquest must be adequately taken into account. If we do this with reference to French, we note that Anglo-Norman French was a written language in England after the Conquest and was used as a native language by a small but immensely powerful elite of royalty, nobles, clergy and merchants, which enabled it to linger on as a native language till well into the fifteenth century. With respect to the language contact between Anglo-Saxon and Scandinavian, however, Görlach makes the following eminently sensible point:

> The great concentration of northern settlers in some Midland areas...and the fact that Scandinavian and Anglian dialects were of similarly low prestige and largely unused in written form is likely to have led to forms of communication quite unlike those between speakers of English and French: with no lingua franca available, Scandinavians and Anglians had to use both languages in order to communicate—an objective greatly facilitated by the similarity between the two varieties. There was no norm that a speaker could have aimed at: West Saxon was, for a speaker of Anglian, a dialect almost as remote as that spoken by his Scandinavian neighbour, and its limited use in writing made it much less present than Danish. (1986: 338)

Görlach's argument is simply that the term "creole" should not be bent to such an extent that it can be pressed into service to define all the results of all language contact situations. If it is, it becomes meaningless. In addition, the language changes affecting Anglo-Saxon can be shown to have been under way well before the Conquest. Those that are on record in written texts from the Danelaw part of the country reach back as far as the tenth century, as I shall show later, and the logical outcome of the kind of simplification processes that were already under way may or may not have been caused by the contact situation itself, but was certainly encouraged by it. In this sense we can still argue for a continual process and a linguistic continuity in the ultimate development of varieties of English without having to revert to the *longevity of English myth* and its submyth, the *ancient language myth*.

Other articles support the creolisation hypothesis (e.g. Wallmannsberger 1988) or refute it (e.g. the sections of Thomason & Kaufmann 1988 that specifically deal with the history of English; Danchev 1997; Dalton-Puffer 1995; Dawson 2003). Still others deal with the borrowings from Anglo-Norman French and French into English from the perspective of researchers into

Anglo-Norman French (e.g. Short 1980; Rothwell 1998), who advise researchers into English to look at the Middle-English-as-a-creole hypothesis from both sides of the coin—from the point of view of French as well as from the point of view of English. Berndt ([1965] 1969) approaches the language contact situation between Anglo-Norman French and Middle English from a demographic point of view and shows convincingly that the number of French speakers in England was never at any time in the period after the Conquest large enough to "oust" English, as Legge (1941) maintained. Bailey and Maroldt make light of Berndt's arguments, but his arguments are strong enough to throw a considerable amount of doubt on the creolisation hypothesis.

What evidence is there, then, that the change from Anglo-Saxon to Middle English was by no means so great as to warrant the hypothesis of a decisive break in linguistic continuity? And why is this controversy on the point of becoming yet another myth? In the following three sections I will deal with these problems. The first point we need to consider in section 4 is what the nature of a language contact situation is and whether there are other alternative scenarios that would correspond to the sparse data that we have so that we can avoid falling into the trap of the *longevity of English myth* and can factually dismantle the myth that modern English has creole origins.

4. ALL LANGUAGE IS LANGUAGE
IN CONTACT

In section 3 we saw that, of the two definitions of a creole at the heart of the confusion over the possible creole origins of Middle (and thereby also Modern) English, the definition that allows a creole to result from a contact situation between two or more languages is the bone of contention. For obvious reasons, the definition that a creole is a nativised pidgin has not been seriously entertained to explain the origins of Middle English, and no scholar has yet been bold enough to suggest that Anglo-Saxon was a pidgin from which Middle English was nativised.[5]

The problem with the first definition resides in the very wide range of possible language contact situations, each depending on the sociocultural conditions under which contact is made between individuals speaking different language varieties in instantiations of emergent social practice. In addition, each instantiation of social practice, precisely because it is emergent, is both guided by prior experience of similar social practices and forms a locus of negotiation between the participants as to how that particular social practice should be carried out. If the participants have no prior experience of the

---

5. This suggestion was made during the Internet discussion dealt with in section 2 of this chapter, however, which is just one indication that embryonic narratives are in the process of discursively constructing a new myth about English: the *creolisation of English myth*. I discuss this in the final section of this chapter.

sociocommunicative situation in which they are involved, they will have two alternatives: they can either break off communication, or they can negotiate and construct a set of practices according to which they can attempt to communicate with one another.

Let us now assume that the participants in an instantiation of emergent social practice use a very high proportion of the same linguistic constructions that evoke meanings that they share in common—or rather that they assume they share in common. They might then be said to "speak the same language variety". Does this then mean that the communicative situation is not characterised by language contact? Quite the opposite is the case. Two interlocutors may use the same linguistic constructions, and yet those constructions may evoke slightly different meanings. This, in turn, implies that all instantiations of emergent social practice involving language are characterised by a shared negotiation of meanings, that all human language is reconstructed and reproduced in emergent interaction and therefore, strictly speaking, that no two interlocutors ever speak the same language, although they may of course share it. Two conclusions emerge from this line of thinking: (1) that "languages" or "linguistic varieties" are a second-order cognitive construct from the emergent use of human language—they are, cognitively speaking, deeply entrenched mental blends; and (2) that every instantiation of emergent social practice in which human language is used is a language contact situation.

However, the fact that we are accustomed to assuming the truth of statements such as "x and y speak the same language / x and y speak different languages" makes it difficult to accept this line of argumentation. The premise of "speaking the same language" lies at the heart of all sociolinguistic definitions of language contact, and to question that premise, as I have done above, is to admit that whenever we enter into communication with an interlocutor, we re-create a language contact situation. Language contact situations are generally thought of as situations in which two or more interlocutors communicate using different language varieties.

But what do we mean when we speak of "different language varieties"? The linguistic differences between speaker A and speaker B, even if we assume that they speak the same language, will always be on a cline from total intelligibility of the linguistic constructions used in the contact situation to total unintelligibility. For example, the interlocutors may be of a very different social status so that power differentials, authority and types of social control are likely to influence different kinds of linguistic construction used by A and B. If social status between the participants is equal, differences in linguistic constructions between A and B may be virtually nonexistent. Speakers A and B may come from different ethnic groups in the overall population that are demographically strong or demographically weak, and the status of members of these groups may also differ considerably. The type of social interaction in which the interlocutors are engaged may be of a formal or an informal nature and may or may not be institutionally significant. The frequency of the interaction type in which A and B are engaged may also be low or high.

If we consider all these parameters, and many more,[6] we arrive at an immensely complex set of potential language contact situations, each defined within the overall communicative space within which individuals may interact. During the course of one single instantiation of emergent social practice, the value of any of those parameters may also change. Given the potential complexity of individual language contact situations in the endless multiplicity of instances of emergent social practice, statements by language contact researchers to the effect that language A was in a state of extended contact with language B over a certain period of time sound rather hollow. What they really mean is that speakers of language variety A and language variety B frequently had recourse to social interaction using one or both of those varieties during that time.[7] To illustrate this complexity, the reader is invited to imagine the following three fictional language contact situations, one in the tenth-century Danelaw, the other two anywhere in rural England in the thirteenth century.

Two farmers in the tenth century Danelaw area of England: Imagine a Danish farmer in the tenth century enjoying a jug of some form of alcoholic beverage with his Anglo-Saxon-speaking neighbour after both have been busy at the local cattle market. The likelihood of this fictional representation being a reflection of real interactions is high. The social status of both participants must have been one of relative equality wherever it is placed on the social status cline. The function or type of interaction is decidedly nonformal. The demographic strength of the ethnic groups to which each farmer belongs was probably tipped in favour of the Anglo-Saxon neighbour, although this would ultimately depend on where in the Danelaw area the interaction took place. It can be shown that constructions in Old Norse were linguistically not very far from those in Anglo-Saxon (cf. Dance 2004; Davis 2006), so intelligibility would have been relatively high, particularly with respect to the topics that they might have chosen to talk about. In addition, although they must have been aware that each of them spoke somewhat differently from the other, there would probably have been little consciousness of the one speaking "Old Norse" and the other speaking "Anglo-Saxon". The main point of interest for both of them was to enjoy one another's company and to talk.

If this kind of situation is multiplied over the whole area of the Danelaw through a period of 150 to 200 years, the resulting forms of language that must have emerged from such extended language contact would be similar to those resulting from processes of koïneisation in which two mutually intelli-

---

6. One of these would be whether there is some standard written language in a community acting as a kind of authoritative reference for people who interact with each other.

7. Readers are asked to bear in mind the point made above that the existence of language varieties A and B is in any case a second-order cognitive construct from the emergent use of human language. It is an abstraction away from the reality of using forms of human language in real-time instantiations of social practice.

gible language varieties contribute towards a new variety over a period of roughly three generations of speakers. Kerswill (2002) refers to two kinds of koïné, "regional" and "immigrant". A "regional koïné" develops when a strong regional dialect comes into contact with dialects of speakers who move into the region. An "immigrant koïné" emerges in the situation in which speakers of a related language variety settle as immigrants in the territory occupied by speakers of another variety, and this is, in all probability, what happened between Old Norse and Anglo-Saxon from the ninth century on.[8] There is no question of the creolisation of either the Danish variety of Old Norse or of Anglo-Saxon. In each case we are likely to have had mutual simplification and lexical borrowing on both sides, but with the dice loaded in favour of the demographically stronger ethnic group, speakers of Anglo-Saxon.

A Middle English–speaking peasant summoned to testify in a case of theft at the local assizes: In this language contact situation, the magistrate at the court, who is likely to have been a native speaker of Anglo-Norman French, belonged to a demographically weak ethnic group (cf. Berndt [1965] 1969), but this was largely offset by the magistrate's social status in comparison with the peasant's and by the institutional power he must have wielded. The situation would probably have led to the need for an interpreter, or, at the very least, the magistrate may have used whatever Middle English he could.

The likelihood of this language contact situation occurring would have been low for the peasant but high for the magistrate, and the degree of formality would have been high. This is decidedly not the kind of social interaction that would have favoured much intelligibility unless an interpreter was used. How can it be said to have encouraged the creolisation of Middle English? And even if this had been the case, whose Middle English would we be talking about, the peasant's or the magistrate's?

A Middle English–speaking clerk discussing the accounts of the demesne with his employer, the lord of the manor: In this second fictional case of thirteenth-century language contact, the clerk would have been far more likely to use whatever French he could. He may have been bilingual, or—and this was a strong possibility—both may have reverted to Latin. The clerk, however, would have had the opportunity to import French terms into his written English, and within his own circle of acquaintances, he may even have used these terms in face-to-face oral interaction. However,

---

8. Note that Kerswill refers to "dialects" that are mutually intelligible, whereas I am still referring, perhaps rather loosely, to "Old Norse" and "Anglo-Saxon". To take my argument in this section seriously, however, we are in reality confronted with two closely related Germanic forms of language regardless of whether we refer to them as "dialects", "varieties", or "languages".

this phenomenon represents a case of extensive borrowing, and the clerk's English was probably very different from the peasant's, even if they interacted socially.

The first fictional situation involving contact between speakers of Old Norse and Anglo-Saxon is so radically different from either of the two Middle English situations that to refer to both forms of contact as resulting in a creole is patently absurd. Equally, and for different reasons, when one searches within the sociocultural space in which language contact situations can occur, any suggestion that language contact always results in creoles tends to disregard the very sociocultural conditions under which language contact takes place.

The next part of my argument consists in producing evidence to show that Anglo-Saxon, particularly from the Danelaw part of the country, shows clear signs of simplification well before the Norman Conquest, presumably under the influence of the koïneisation process created by language contact situations involving both Anglo-Saxon and Old Norse. In addition, texts from the transition period from Anglo-Saxon to Middle English after the Conquest show how quickly these simplification processes progressed without the presence of a standard form of the language. The central texts in this demonstration will again be the First and Second Continuations of the *Peterborough Chronicle*.

5. SIMPLIFICATION PROCESSES NOT RESULTING IN A CREOLE

At the outset we need to consider the huge differences between oral instantiations of language produced in emergent situations of language contact, examples of which are no longer possible to unearth, and the paucity of written texts that evidence simplification. Given the restrictions on any such investigation, however, certain texts may still be considered crucial.

My first example is taken from an Anglo-Saxon will written approximately ten years before the Conquest. Judging by the place names referred to in the will, it was probably taken down in Essex or Suffolk, since land in Stisted, a village lying quite close to Braintree in Essex, is referred to as well as Bury St. Edmunds in Suffolk. The will was made on behalf of a man called Ketel, and was, in all probability, taken down by a scribe from dictation.

5.1 The will of Ketel

Her is **on þis write** Keteles quide þat ic an Stistede
after mine tyme for mine fader soule and for Selfledan.

And ic wille þat mine men ben ben alle fre
and Mann myne refe þat he sitte **on þe fre lond** þat ic him to honde habbe leten his time euer fre
and **after his time** folege þat lond þen oþere.
And ic an into þere kirke þat lond þat Withrich hauede under hande and Lewine and Siric and Goding so so geard goð to Leueriches hyge.
And þat no man him ne forwerne þan vtgang.
And ic wille þat alle þo men þe ic an fre

þat hi habben alle þinge þe he vnder hande habben **buten þat lond**.
And ic an þat lond at Herlinge Stigand Arche- bisscop **mine louerd** so it stant buten þo men ben alle fre
and ten acres ic an **into þe kirke**
and gif ic ongein ne cume þan an ic him to **min heregete**
an helm and **a** bronie and hors and gereade and sverd and spere
and ic wille **after þe forwarde** þat Eadwine and Wulfric **after my time** fon **to alkere þinge** þe min ower is þer on tune buten
so mikel so ic an **into þe kirke**,

þat is þat erninglond þat Alfwold *mine* **man** haueð vnder hande
and he sitte **on þat** other his time.

And sithen al þat lond þat him to honde begeð folege **mid þe oþere into þe kirke**.

Here in this document is Ketel's will:that I bequeath Stisted after my days to Christ's church for the sake of my father's soul and Selfledan's soul.

It is my will that my men should all be free and that my reeve Mann should occupy the free land that I have left him to hold during his life and after his death may the land follow in his line.

And I bequeath the land that Withrich, Lewin, Siric and Goding worked on as far as Leverich's hedge, to the Church.

And it is my will that no man shall deny them exit.

It is also my will that all the men to whom I grant freedom should keep all the things in their possession except for the land.

And I bequeath the land at Herling as it stands to my Lord Archbishop Stigand except that the men should all be free, and I bequeath ten acres to the. church.

If I should not return again I bequeath him [them?] in my household a helmet, a bridle, a horse and harness and a sword and spear, and it is my will that, by agreement, Edwin and Wulfrich after my death should acquire other things that are mine in the town except as much as I bequeath to the church,

i.e., the freehold land that my man Alfwold works,

and it is my wll that he occupy that land for the rest of his days,

and from then on that all the land that he works should follow the other into the church.

Gif Eadwine min Em wille helden se	*If my Uncle Edwin keep faith with me and*
felageschipe mid me and Wulfric min em	*my Uncle Wulfric concerning the land at*
ymbe þat lond at Meþeltune	*Methelton*
gif wit him ouerbiden, fon we **to þat**	*if the two of us outlive him we succeed to*
londe at Thorpe	*the land at Thorpe*
into þat forwarde þat vre boþere time go	*on condition that after both of our lives the*
þat lond at Metheltone	*land at Methelton*
for vre heldren soule and vre awene	*should go to St. Benedict's at Holme for*
soule into seint Benedicte at Holme.	*our parents' souls and the sake of our own*
	souls.
And þat lond at Thorpe into saynt	*And the land at Thorpe should go to Bury*
Eadmundes biri.	*St. Edmund's.*
And þat is min and mine *sustres* boten þat	*And it is my and my sister's bidding that if*
forwarde gif ic mine day do her his þat ic	*I do obey his (will) that I should succeed to*
fon **to þat lond** at Keteringham	*the land at Keteringham*
and an marc goldes oþer be wyrth,	*and inherit one mark of gold or the value*
	thereof,
and gif ic hire ouerbide þanne schal ic	*and if I outlive her then I shall have the*
habben þat lond at Somerledetone	*land at Somerledeton,*
and þat ilke forwarde Ic and Gode mine	*and by virtue of the same agreement made*
suster habbed speken	*between me and my sister God,*
gif he me ouerbide gripe he **to þat lond**	*if she outlive she will succeed to the land*
at Walsingham	*at Walsingham*
buten ten acres þo schulen into þere	*except for ten acres which will go to the*
kirke.	*Church.*
And gif ic libbe leng þanne hio þanne	*And if I live longer than her, then I shall*
schal ic habben þat lond at Prestone.[9]	*have the land at Preston.*

Apart from a number of phonological features that give immediate testimony to its Anglian origins, three major morphosyntactic changes are in evidence:

1. Dative cases after prepositions are virtually nonexistent (bold typeface) either in the singular or in the plural (e.g. sg. *on þis write* or *buten þat lond* and pl. *to alkere þinge* or *buten ten acres*).
2. The indeclinable defining relative pronoun *þe* functions in a number of instances as a definite article (single underlining), and not merely in the nominative case (e.g. *on þe fre lond* for which we would have expected (a) the

---

9. Single underlining indicates occurrences of the uninflected definite article *þe* in place of an inflected form, or the digraph *th* used in place of *þ/ð*. Bold typeface indicates retention or loss of the dative case, and italic typeface indicates confusion with respect to the gender of the noun. Double underlining indicates confusion between the pronouns *he* (he) and *heo* (she).

dative singular *þam*, (b) a weak dative inflection on the adjective and (c) a dative singular inflection -*e* on the neuter noun *lond*; *after þe forwarde* for which we would have expected the Anglian singular feminine dative form of the definite article *þere*; three instances of *into þe kirke* for which we would have expected *þere*; and *mid þe opere* for which we would have expected the dative plural form of the definite article *þam* [or in Anglian, at least, *þan*] and a weak dative plural adjective inflection on *oper-*, and *þe wyrth* for which we would have expected *þa wyrth*).

3. Some confusion is apparent with respect to the marking of grammatical gender on nouns (italic typeface) for which we would have expected clarity from the point of view of natural gender, for example, *mine mann* for *min mann* and *mine sustres boten*, which has a strong masculine declension marking for the genitive (*sustres*) rather than a weak feminine declension marking (*sustren*).

4. There is also a phonologically weakened form of the indefinite article *a* for *an* governing the noun *bronie* (bold italic) which has been borrowed from Old French—even at this stage in the language prior to the Norman Conquest!

5. And, interestingly, <*eo*> is monophthongised to <*e*> which leads to ambiguity between "he" (*he*) and "she" (*he* in place of *heo*) (double underlining).

Normally these phenomena would be accounted for by resorting to simplification processes, but they may sometimes cause difficulty here by generating possible ambiguity, particularly in the case of the third-person singular pronoun (i.e. they lead to greater complexity in that the reader has to rely solely on the context to resolve the intended meaning). Resorting to the koïneisation argument might help to explain the disappearance of an explicit morphological marking of the dative case, since a drastic reduction in the number of cases had also taken place in the Scandinavian languages. But there is no way we can resort even to koïneisation to explain the gradual spread of *þe* in place of *se*/*seo*/*þæt*, since the Old Norse definite article appeared (and still does appear in the Scandinavian languages) as a suffix added to the noun. Clearly, this does not exclude the introduction of *þe* as a simplification that would have helped speakers of the Danish variety of Old Norse to communicate with speakers of Anglo-Saxon. In fact this is very likely to have been the case. But neither does it exclude the possibility that this substitution was under way in any case and was simply speeded up by the language contact situation involving both language varieties.

Let us now make a jump of roughly 70 years to the language of the two scribes in the First and Second Continuations of the Peterborough Chronicle, where we see an advanced state of all three major areas of simplification that were already under way in the first half of the eleventh century.

5.2 The First and Second Continuations of the *Peterborough Chronicle*

Before we look at part of the entry for 1137, here is a list of the some of the changes already present in the first scribe's work (cf. chap. 3):

1. There is a regular weakening of vowels in non-tonic syllables to the central vowel [ə]:

   Examples: *griðode* > *griðede*; *þæt* > *þet*; *comon* > *comen*; *denisca* > *densce*; *secgan* > *sægen (sæcgen)*; *cuman* > *cumen*; *huscarlas* > *huscarles*

2. There is strong evidence of a confusion of gender:

   Examples: *þa densce biscop* (West Saxon *se denisca biscop*), in which the feminine accusative singular definite article *þa* has been used for the masculine *se*; *feonlandes* (WS *feonland*) where the plural inflection reclassifies the noun as masculine rather than neuter; *þone mynstre* (WS *þæt mynster*), where the masculine singular accusative form of the definite article *þone* is used instead of the neuter singular accusative form *þæt*; *reafes* (WS *reaf*), where like *feonlandes* the neuter noun *reaf* has been reclassified as masculine.

3. The reanalysis of cases resulting in the loss of the dative:

   Examples: *of eall þa feonlandes* (WS *of eallum þam feonlandum*), where the preposition *of*, which normally governs the dative case, now governs the nominative/accusative; *an frencisce abbot* (WS *anum frenciscum abbote*) as the indirect object of the verb; *to þone abbot* (WS *to þam abbote*), where the accusative case substitutes for the dative.

This is just a brief selection from one or two entries, but even here we can see the continuing disappearance of the dative case and the tendency for the category of masculine nouns to attract neuter and even feminine nouns. The developments noted in the *Will of Ketel* appear to have progressed further here. If we now look at the language of the second scribe, the same tendencies become even more noticeable, and the language seems to have already gone over the breach between Anglo-Saxon and Middle English.[10]

A.D. 1137 Ðis gære for þe king Stephne ofer sæ to Normandi; and ther was underfangen, forþi ðat hi wenden ðat he schulden ben alswic alse the eom wes, and for he hadde get his tresor; ac he todeld it and scatered sotlice. Micel hadde Henri king gadered gold and syluer, and na god ne dide him *for his saule* þarof. Þa þe king Stephne	def. article in place of *se* <th> digraph for <þ/ð> def. article in place of *se* +<th> digraph for <þ/ð> borrowing from French remnant of the dative + def. article in place of *se*

10. Single underlining indicates occurrences of the uninflected definite article *þe* in place of an inflected form. Double underlining th indicates the digraph *th* used in place of *þ/ð*. Thick underlining (e.g. tresor) indicates borrowings from French or Latin. Bold typeface with single underlining indicates use of the *s*-plural (e.g. sinnes). Noun phrases (mostly in prepositional phrases) in italics show loss of the dative case.

to Englaland com, þa macod he his gadering
æt Oxenford. Þar nam he be biscop Roger of
Serebyri and Alexander biscop of Lincol
and te canceler, his neues, and dide ælle in

prisun til hi iafen up here castles. Þa þe

suikes undergæton ðat he milde man was
and softe and god, and na iustice ne dide, þa
diden hi alle wunder. Hi hadden him manred
maked and athes suoren, ac hi nan treuthe
ne heolden. Alle hi wæron forsworen and
here treothes forloren, for æueric rice man
his castles makede and agænes him heolden;
and fylden þe land ful *of* castles. Hi

suencten swyðe þe wrecce men *of þe land
mid castelweorces*; þa þe castles waren

maked, þa fylden hi *mid deovles and yuele
men.* Þa namen hi þa men þe hi wenden ðat
ani god hefden, bathe *be nihtes* and *be
dæies,* carlmen and wimmen, and diden
heom in prisun and pined heom *efter gold
and syluer* untellendliche pining; for ne
waren nævre nan martyrs swa pined alse hi
wæron. Me henged up *bi the fet* and smoked

heom mid ful smoke. Me henged *bi the
þumbes* other *bi the hefed* and hengen

bryniges on her fet. Me dide cnotted
strenges abuton here hæved and wrythen it
ðat it gæde *to þe hærnes.* Hi diden heom in

quarterne þar nadres and snakes and pades
wæron inne, and drapen heom swa. Sume hi
diden in crucethus—ðat is, in an ceste þat
was scort and nareu and undep—and dide
scærpe stanes þerinne ðat him bræcon alle
þe limes. *In mani of þe castles* wæron lof

---

no dative
no dative | def. art. in place of *þone*
def. art. in place of *þone* + <th>
digraph for <þ/ð> borrowing from
French | s-plural
borrowing from French x2 | s-plural |
def. article in place of *þa*
s-plural
borrowing from French

s-plural | <th> digraph for <þ/ð>

<th> digraph for <þ/ð>
borrowing from French+s-plural
def. article in place of *þæt* | borrowing
from French+ s-plural | no dative
def. article in place of *þa* | def. article in
place of *þam*
no dative | borrowing from French |
s-plural | def. article in place of *þa* |
borrowing from French + s-plural
s-plural | no dative

<th> digraph for <þ/ð> | no dative | no
dative
borrowing from French | no dative

borrowing from French + s-plural
def. article in place of *þa* + <th>
digraph for <þ/ð> | no dative
def. article in place of *þa* | no dative
s-plural | def. article in place of *þam* |
no dative
s-plural
s-plural
def. article in place of *þa* | s-plural | no
dative
borrowing from French | s-plural x3

s-plural

def. article in place of *þa* x2 | no dative
| borrowing from French+ s-plural

and grin; ðat wæron rachenteges ðat twa
oþer thre men hadden onoh to bæron onne,
þat was swa maked, þat is, fæstned *to an*
beom—and diden an scærp iren abuton þa
mannes throte and his hals. Mani þusen hi
drapen *mid hungær*. I ne can ne I ne mai
tellen all þe wunder ne alle þe pines ðat hi
diden *wrecce men on þis land*; and ðat
lastede þa xix wintre wile Stephne was king,
and ævre it was werse and werse. Hi læiden
gældes on the tunes ævre um wile, and

> s-plural
> <th> digraph for <þ/ð>
> no dative
>
> <th> digraph for <þ/ð>
> no dative
> def. article in place of *þa* x2 | s-plural
> no dative | no dative
>
> s-plural | def. article in place of
> *þa*+<th> | digraph for <þ/ð> | s-plural

clepeden it "tenserie". Þa þe wrecce men
ne hadden nammore to gyven, þa ræveden
hi and brendon all the tunes, ðat wel þu
myhtes

> def. article in place of *þa*
> def. article in place of *þa*+<th>
> digraph for <þ/ð> | s-plural
> <th> digraph for <þ/ð>

faren al a dæies fare, schuldest thu nevre
finden man *in tune* sittende ne land tiled. Þa
was corn dære, and flesc and cæse and
butere, for nan wæs o þe land. Wrecce men
sturven *of hungær*. Sume ieden on ælmes þa
waren sum wile rice men; sum flugen *ut of*
lande. Wes nævre gæt mare wreccehed *on*
land, ne nævre heþen men werse ne diden
þan hi diden, for ouer siþon ne forbaren
nouþer circe ne circe-iærd oc namen al þe
god þat þarinne was, and brenden syþen
þe circe and al tegædere. Ne hi ne forbaren
biscopes land ne abbotes ne preostes ac
ræveden munekes and clerekes, and ævric
man oþer þe overmyhte. Gif twa men oþþe
þrie coman ridend *to an tun*, al þe tunscipe
flugæn for heom, wenden þat he wæron
ræveres. Þe biscopes and leredmen heom
cursede ævre, oc was heom naht þarof, for
hi weron al forcursæd and forsworen and
forloren. War-sæ me tilede, þe erþe ne bar
nan corn, for þe land was al fordon *mid*
swilce dædes, and hi sæden openlice þat
Crist slep and his halechen. Swilc, and
mare þanne we cunnen sæin, we þoleden
nientiene wintre *for ure sinnes*.

> remnant of a dative
>
> def. article in place of *þam*
> no dative | s-plural
> remnant of a dative
> no dative
>
> def. article in place of *þæt*
> def. article in place of *þa*
>
> s-plural | borrowing from Latin+
> s-plural
> no dative | def. article in place of *þa*
>
> s-plural | def. article in place of *þa* |
> s-plural
>
> def. article in place of *þa*
> def. article in place of *þæt* | no dative
> s-plural
>
> s-plural | no dative

In the analysis of this text extract I have focused on those features of simplification evident in the first text (plus also the brief comments on scribe 1 of the *Peterborough Chronicle*), but I have also added a change that appears to be under way in this scribe's orthography: the substitution of <þ/ð> with the digraph <th>,[11] and borrowings from French and Latin, of which there are eight in all: *prisun, canceler, justice, castle, quarterne, clerek, tresor,* and *martyr.* The first significant point to comment on is the almost complete disappearance of the inflections in the definite article system, which leads to a wholesale breakdown of the system of grammatical gender. In this text extract there are, in all, 30 tokens of a definite article, but only three of these retain the former inflections. So we see 90 percent occurrences of *þe, the,* or *te* and only 10 percent occurrences of inflected definite articles in this short text extract alone. If we were to take a longer extract, the 10 percent might even dwindle to around 5 percent or less. The breakdown of the gender system is also reflected in the large number of plurals ending in *-s,* 31 out 50, making 52.5 percent in this extract alone. The other 47.5 percent consist of occurrences of umlaut in the frequently used nouns *man>men* and *fot>fet,* which make up 13 of the 19 non-*s*-plurals. Apart from these we have *wunder* twice, *wintre* twice, *quarterne* once and *halechen* once.

Nouns and noun phrases in the dative case have almost disappeared with the exception of the personal pronouns, the only remnants being the *-e* inflection on the nouns *saule (for his saule), lande (ut of lande)* and *tune (in tune).* I do not wish to comment on whether the almost wholesale introduction of *the* into the article system hastened the demise of the case system or whether the breakdown of the case system encouraged the introduction of *the.* However, the virtual disappearance of the dative is a very marked feature of the second scribe's language. It would seem, therefore, that this is only the continuation of a process that had begun well before any language contact situations involving Anglo-Norman French and Anglo-Saxon were likely on English soil and, judging by Ketel's will, long after the assimilation of that section of the population of the Danelaw speaking the Danish variety of Old Norse. So even though a koïneisation of the varieties of Anglo-Saxon spoken in the Danelaw and the Danish variety of Old Norse probably resulted in new dialects of Anglo-Saxon with a relatively high percentage of lexemes from Old Norse used in everyday contacts between the two sections of the population, the koïneisation process seems only to have speeded up the morpho-phonological simplification of Anglo-Saxon. My conclusion is that it is more than a little bold to suggest creolisation here.

One problem remains, however. Why is it that the first scribe's language in the *Peterborough Chronicle* was much closer to Anglo-Saxon than the second scribe's when a period of only 20 years separates the end of the First Continuation from the end of the Second? If we consider the breakdown of the discourse archive discussed in chapter 3, this problem is not insoluble.

11. This substitution even occurs once in Ketel's will, which has *Thorpe* instead of *þorpe.*

Scribe 1 was given the job of copying out a version (or possible two versions) of the *ASC* that was written in a form of Anglo-Saxon that attempted to reproduce the quasi-standard West Saxon. He also continued after 1080, which led us to posit in chapter 3 that he may have had access to a version that was continued into the twelfth century but was almost completely destroyed in the fire at Ashburnham House (possibly the H ms.). The entries after 1121 were obviously his own (he was then the author), but he attempted to reproduce the no longer existent "standard" model till the end. If that was the case, his use of language in face-to-face instantiations of emergent language contact might have been relatively similar to that of the second scribe.

Scribe 2, on the other hand, was most definitely more than just a scribe. He was the author of a colourful and moving narrative of Stephen's reign, which lay completely outside the dominant discourse archive. The amount of inscribed orality that we identified in his reporting of events is considerably higher than anywhere else in the *ASC*, and we are justified in positing that the difference between his oral and his written language production could not have been that great.

5.3 The *Ormulum* and *Havelok the Dane*

My final two texts were written in the thirteenth century and also come from the Lincolnshire–East Midland area, the *Ormulum* around the year 1200 (roughly 50 years after the *Peterborough Chronicle*), and *Havelok the Dane* around 1280. I shall again focus on case structure, the definite article, plural forms, adjective inflections and borrowings from the Scandinavian and the French:[12]

Prologue of The *Ormulum*[13]	Beginning of *Havelok the Dane*
Nu, broþerr Wallterr, broþerr min	Herkneth to me, gode men,
Affterr þe flæshess kinde;	Wiues, maydnes, and alle men.
Annd broþerr min i Cristenndomm	Of a tale ich you wil telle,
Þurrh fulluhht annd þurrh trowwþe;	Hwo-so it wile here, and þer-to dwelle.
Annd broþerr min i Godes hus,	þe tale of Hauelok is i-maked;
ȝet o. *þe þride wise*, Yet in the third way	Hwil he was **litel**, he yede ful naked.

12. Single underlining indicates occurrences of the uninflected definite article *þe* in place of an inflected form. Double underlining indicates <t> used in place of <þ/ð>. Thick underlining (e.g. þeȝȝm) indicates borrowings from Scandinavian (i.e. the Danish variety of Old Norse). Small caps indicate borrowings from Anglo-Norman French. Bold, italic typeface indicates use of the *s*-plural. A noun phase (mostly in prepositional phrases) in italics indicates possible remnants of the dative case. Bold typeface with single underlining indicates predicative and attributive adjectives with no inflection. Bold typeface with double underlining indicates adjective inflection in -*e* (in most cases dictated by the prosody).

13. The monk who is credited with writing the *Ormulum*, Orm by name, has a peculiar but phonologically helpful habit of doubling all his consonants following short vowels, as he did in the first line, with *broþerr Wallterr*.

Þurrh þatt witt hafenn takenn ba
An reȝhellboc to follȝhenn,
Unnderr KANUNNKESS had annd lif,
Swa summ Sannt Awwstin sette;
Icc hafe don swa summ þu badd,
Annd forþedd *te þin wille,*
Icc hafe wennd inntill Ennglissh
Goddspell*ess* hallȝhe lare,
Affterr þatt little witt ţatt me
Min Drihhtin hafeþþ lenedd.
Þu þohhtesst ţatt itt mihhte wel Thou
thought ţhat it might well
Till mikell frame turrnenn,
ȝiff Ennglisshe follk, forr lufe off Crist,
Itt wollde ȝerne lernenn,
And follȝhenn itt, annd fillenn itt
Wiþþ þohht, wiþþ word, wiþþ dede.
Annd forrþi ȝerrndesst ţu þatt icc
Þiss werrc þe shollde wirrkenn;
Annd icc itt hafe forþedd ţe,
Acc all þurrh
Annd uncc birrþ baþe þannkenn Crist
Þatt itt iss brohht *till ende.*
Icc hafe sammnedd o þiss boc
Þa Goddspell*ess* neh alle,
Þatt sinndenn o þe messeboc
Inn all þe ȝer *att messe.*
Annd aȝ after þe Goddspell stannt
Þatt ţatt ţe Goddspell meneþþ,
Þatt mann birrþ spellenn to þe follc
Off þeȝȝre sawle nede; of
Annd ȝet ţær tekenn mare inoh
Þu shallt ţæronne findenn,
Off þatt ţatt Cristess hallȝhe þed
Birrþ trowwen wel annd follȝhenn.
Icc hafe sett her o þiss boc
Amang Goddspelles word*ess,*
All þurrh me sellfenn, maniȝ word
Þe rime swa to fillenn;
Acc þu shallt finndenn þatt min word,
Maȝȝ hellpenn þa þatt redenn itt
All þess ţe bettre hu þeȝȝm birrþ
Þe Goddspell unnderstanndenn;
Annd forrþi trowwe icc þatt ţe birrþ
Wel þolenn mine word*ess,*

Hauelok was a ful <u>god</u> <u>gome</u>, < gumi: man
He was ful **god** in eueri trome,
He was <u>þe</u> wihtest man at need
Þat þurte riden on ani stede.
Þat ye mowen nou y-here,
And <u>þe</u> tale ye mowen y-lere.
At <u>þe</u> biginning of vre tale,
Fil me a cuppe of ful **god** ale;
And y wile drinken, er y spelle,
Þat Crist vs shilde alle *fro helle!*
Krist lat us euere so to do

Þat we moten comen him to;
And with-þat it mot ben so,
Benedicamus domino!
Here y schal biginnen a rym,
Krist us yeue wel **god** fyn!
<u>The</u> rym is maked of Hauelok,
A **stalworþi** man in a flok;
He was <u>þe</u> wihtest man at need
Þat may riden on ani stede.
It was a king in are daw*es,*
Þat in his time were god*e* laws
He dede maken, and ful wel holden;
Him louede <u>**yung**</u>, him loueden old*e,*
Erl and barun, dreng and thayn,
Knicht, and <u>**bondeman**</u>, and swain,
Widu*es,* maydn*es,* prest*es* and clerk*es,*
And al for his god*e* werk*es.*
He louede god with al his miht,
And **holi** <u>kirke</u>, and soth, and riht;
Riht-wis*e* men he louede alle,
And oueral made hem forto calle;
Wreier*es* and robber*es* made he falle,
<u>Vtlawes</u> and theu*es* made he bynde,
Alle that he mihte fynde,
And heye hengen on galwe-<u>tre;</u>
For hem ne yede gold ne fe.
In þat time a man þat bore
Wel fifty pund, y wot, or more,
Of rede gold up-on his back,
In a male **hwit** or **blac**,
Ne funde he non þat him missseyde,
Ne hond on him with iuele leyde.
Þanne mihte chapmen fare

E33whær þær þu shallt finndenn Hemm.   Þurhut Englond with here ware,
And baldelike beye and sellen,
Oueral þer he willen dwellen,
In gode burwes, and þer-fram
Ne funden he non þat dede hem sham,
þat he weren to sorwe brought, And
POUERe marked, and brought to nought.

In the *Ormulum*, only one definite article *þa* (in the noun phrase *þa Goddspelless*) is inflected, the original plural form of the article, here governing the plural noun *Goddspelles* (Gospels). Every other definite article is now the uninflected form *þe*. In *Havelok* inflected definite articles are nonexistent, and, as we have seen, this leads inevitably to the complete erasure of grammatical gender in the determiner system of the language. In both texts, apart from frequently used nouns with the umlaut plural (here *man/men*), the plural forms are universally with the *s*-suffix indicating that the tendency already evident in the Second Continuation of the *Peterborough Chronicle* has ousted other plural forms.

Dative nouns in prepositional phrases still show possible remnants of the old dative case in the final *e*-suffix (e.g. *affterr þe flæshess kinde, o þe þride wise, te þin wille* [although here we would have expected a remnant of the dative in *þin*, e.g. as *þine*], *till mikell frame, till ende* and *att messe*), but we could also argue that the *e*-suffix might have been used for prosodic reasons. There is even a remnant of the old genitive case in *off þe33re sawle need*, but again it might have been used for prosodic reasons. Otherwise there are no remaining dative case nouns. By the time we reach *Havelok*, all trace of the dative has disappeared (except, of course, in the personal pronoun system). Two other features are marginally significant in the *Ormulum*. As with the second scribe in the *Peterborough Chronicle*, the author (Orm) has a strong tendency to vary between <þ> and <t>, and there are a few clear influences from the Danish in the form of the third-person plural pronoun (and the preposition *till*). In *Havelok the Dane* we also find that adjectives, whether predicative or attributive have largely lost their inflections. Exceptions in the text are *gode* (three occurrences) and *pouere, rede* and *olde* (one occurrence each). But here, as in the *Ormulum*, we can just as easily argue for their retention on the basis of prosody and rhyme. There are also a relatively small number of borrowings from the Danish variety of Old Norse (*gome, kirke, vtlawes, tre* and *bondeman*), but only one from French (*pouere*, from *pauvre*). In the *Ormulum*, too, only one word is derived from Anglo-Norman French (*kanunnkess*, from *canun*).

It is of course true that the percentage of words in texts from the fourteenth century shows a marked increase of French borrowings. It could also be argued that this brief outline of simplifications in the noun phrase displays only a small and selective cross-section of constructions from Anglo-Saxon into early Middle English, but it can hardly be denied that they represent a significant section of the grammar, which is almost always referred to by those supporting the creolisation hypothesis. Neither can it be denied from the texts presented here that those changes in the East Midland area were in evidence in the first half of the eleventh century before the advent of French influence and reached completion well before the flood of French borrowings in the fourteenth century. The borrowings from Old Norse and from Anglo-Norman French (and later from other varieties of French) appear to have had little or nothing to do with simplification processes from Anglo-Saxon into Middle English, whether or not these were speeded up by the koïneisation of Anglo-Saxon and Old Norse in the area of the Danelaw.

6. CREOLISATION OR NO CREOLISATION?

The idea of a sociocultural space for language contact situations presented in section 4 makes use of the insight that language is only in evidence, at least in its primary oral function, in actual instantiations of social practice between people as they interact. Language in this constructionist approach to interaction is always a part of individual and social performances in which social relationships, forms of identity and, ultimately, social institutions themselves are constructed, reconstructed and transformed. Language is, in other words, always emergent but always cognitively embedded in individuals through their mutual engagement in social practice. It is by no means the only system of signification open to human beings to construct their worlds, but it is arguably the most powerful and the most important system. It is in this sense that I wish to argue that every instantiation of social practice in which language is used is a situation of language contact, and the sociocultural space posited for the enactment of those situations involves varying degrees of intelligibility, varying levels of social status and functions of the interaction, varying frequencies of occurrence, and varying degrees of demographic strength of the groups to which the participants belong.

The linguistic results of language contact will thus be as varied as the parameters which go to make up that space, and not enough research has yet been carried out on the linguistic systems of individuals and, through them, the groups with which they identify to see exactly what goes on when languages change or appear to change. The speakers themselves, the actors in the social performance, are responsible for the changes, not the systems. Obviously some combinations of those parameters may well result in pidginised forms of human language, and pidgin and creole studies have done magnificent work in tracing out developments in repeated instances of language contact situations to show how a pidgin may become highly elaborated and yet not be anyone's first language. Likewise, the theory that creoles emerge from very specific sociocultural and sociohistorical situations is convincing.

The second way of defining a creole, however, tends to ignore the sociocultural space of language contact and to assume that processes of simplification almost automatically lead to the formation of creoles. What proponents of this theory too often ignore is that creoles evince typical kinds of construction, which are not present in the results of creolisation as defined by Bailey and Maroldt. We have seen how grammatical gender was ultimately lost in Middle English, possibly as a result of language contact situations, but this only applies to the noun system. Personal pronouns still exhibit grammatical gender. We have seen how the various ways of forming the plural were all but lost to the *s*-suffix, but the important construction in this last sentence is "all but", since a small number of frequently used nouns still have umlaut plurals (*mouse/mice, louse/lice, man/men, foot/feet, tooth/teeth*, etc.) or *en-* plurals (*ox/oxen, child/ children*, etc.) or no inflection in the plural (*sheep/sheep, fish/fish*, etc.). If we had looked at the verb system, we would have seen that English, like creoles, has developed aspect systems, but, unlike creoles, it has retained tense. These and other examples are given in most of the articles that argue against the creolisation hypothesis.

In accounting for language change, there is no reason why we should not resort to the principles of pidgin and creole studies, but, if we consider the complexity of the sociocultural space of language contact, it can only be useful in certain well-defined contact types. To avoid the kind of problem that the creolisation hypothesis has created, some researchers have coined the term "creoloid", but this only shifts the problem away from looking at language contact as a highly complex area of concern in sociolinguistics.

The major point of this whole chapter, however, has been to argue that the creolisation hypothesis has created discursive openings for mythologisation. Linguists and sociolinguists may continue to argue for decades to come about how useful aspects of the theories of pidgin and creole studies are for historical linguistics, but it is when nonlinguists access this discourse that myths may arise. When we read in the Internet discussion described in section 2 that certain interested participants think that a creole has something to do with French, the Middle English-as-a-creole argument put forward by Bailey and Maroldt unwittingly offers a reason for saying that English is a creole language because it came under French influence. Alternatively, when another participant believes that a creole is "a language that forms from extended contact between two languages", then this would virtually mean that every language involved in situations of colonisation automatically becomes a creole. Or when we read that a creole is not "simply a mishmash of languages", we must conclude that there are people who believe that that is the case, and this automatically plays into the *myth of language purity*, which I will deal with in the next chapter. On the other hand, when we hear that English is a "bastard rather than a creole", we note a moral, evaluative tone suggesting that it is even lower than a creole. One participant suggests that a creole is "a non-standard form of a known standard," thus implying that the only "valid" languages as such are standard languages. All nonstandard varieties would automatically become creoles. The same participant, however, maintains that "English is not a 'colorfully messed up' version of some other more 'legitimate' standard", which of course implies that this is what a creole would be.

The reader may have noted that the incipient ***creolisation of English myth*** tends to partake of other forms of language ideology to do with standardisation, language purity, possibly also the need to prevent languages from changing at all. The implication is that there is something "unclean" or at least inferior about a language being a creole, and this is decidedly not the result that Bailey and Maroldt could have wished for. What we can say, however, is that looking at this incipient myth has ultimately led us to consider other, more deeply ingrained myths about English and other languages that have a long history, and this is the topic of chapter 5.

Barbarians and others

Therefore if I know not the meaning of the voice,
I shall be unto him that speaketh a barbarian,
and he that speaketh shall be a barbarian unto me.
—1 Cor. 14:11

1. THE NATION-STATE AND THE NOTION OF *KULTURSPRACHE*

Lying at the crossroads of a number of disciplines within what are tradition-ally called "the social sciences" is a mental building that has been under construction by practitioners of those disciplines for at least 250 years. The building has been erected through the conscious collaboration of those prac-titioners, but it has always received the enthusiastic help of persons and insti-tutions that do not normally travel the roads of the disciplines themselves. Historians of the social sciences are uncertain as to when construction first began, but they are generally in agreement that it has not yet been completed. The building has not been erected by the side of one of the roads leading to the disciplines themselves, but in the middle of the square formed by the con-fluence of roads. The building has been given a name, the "nation-state", and the roads leading away from the square lead to sociology, political science, religion, linguistics, history, anthropology, economics and law, to name the most obvious.

Critical interest in how the building has been (and indeed is still being) constructed seems to be a rather recent phenomenon and was begun by the philosopher, sociologist and social anthropologist Ernest Gellner in his book *Nations and Nationalism* in 1983. The critical thread was taken up in the same year by political scientist Benedict Anderson's *Imagined Communities*. In 1987 sociologist and social anthropologist Anthony Smith turned his attention from nationalism as a process (1971) to focus on the ethnic origins of the building, and has continued researching in this field ever since (see, e.g., Smith 1991, 2004). In 1990 historian and political scientist Eric Hobsbawm contributed his own critical assessment of the construction in his book *Nations and Nationalism since 1780: Programme, Myth, Reality*, and it is in this book that the term "myth" appears in this connection for the first time. Ali Khan, professor of law at Washburn University in Topeka, Kansas, prophesied the dismantling of the building in his 1992 book *The Extinction of Nation States: A World without Borders*. His argument was that the building had become dysfunctional and should be superseded by free movement between states in an increasingly globalised society. This argument is taken up by Philip White in an article that, like Hobsbawm's book, declares that the building of the nation-state is nothing more than a myth ("Globalization and the mythology of the nation state", 2006).

To take leave of our extended metaphor just for a moment, the idea of the nation-state, as we understand it today, is that of a state (i.e. a political entity or polity) deriving its legitimacy from the political representation of an ethnic group or a nation. So the territory occupied by that nation, the square on which the building stands (that is, if the building is ever completed), ideally represents the extent of sovereignty of that type of state. We have here the geographical fusion of a cultural, ethnic notion (the nation) with a political notion (the state). A classical nation-state would thus be a political entity which, in a one-to-one fashion, coincides geographically with an ethnic group, and since this is a rare situation indeed in the modern world (aside from, e.g., Iceland, Tonga, Tuvalu), perhaps the building will never be completed after all. Population movements have always tended to erode this imagined and longed-for unity, sometimes shaking the foundations of the building like an earthquake. There is some discussion in the literature of whether the concept of nation historically precedes that of the state or vice versa, indicating that more thought should have gone into planning the building before construction began. The term "nation" in reference to an ethnic unity does seem to precede that of "state", but different forms of state, such as political sovereignty over territory, certainly preceded the nation-state, even if the term "state" itself was not commonly used. Hobsbawm, for example, maintains that the French state, as this was envisaged in the early stages of the French Revolution, preceded the French "nation", a term which had to be discursively constructed after the event, as it were, and a similar point may also be made about Britain and the tendentious notion of a British nation.

Creating a state that was coterminous with a nation demanded a considerable amount of discursive ingenuity, and it is hardly surprising that myths played a major role in squaring this particular circle. Foremost among the myths that were used in creating the imagined community of the "nation-state" was the *myth of homogeneity*. If the state and the nation were bounded by the same geographical borders, the characteristics of the nation had to be uniform. Social institutions had to be created that were unique to the state, and in particular one variety of language was needed to serve as the uniform language. Following in the wake of language and closely associated with it, both religion and racial characteristics also had to conform to the demand for homogeneity.

In states in which minority languages existed, every effort needed to be made, largely through education systems, to impose the national standard language over those minority languages and other varieties closely related to the standard. Unfortunately, attempts to impose a uniform religion were apt to produce cataclysmic consequences, and it is hardly surprising that, in the name of the edifice "nation-state", religion has sometimes been reduced to a level of insignificance, only to return at a later stage of history in all its destructive power (as the fate of former Yugoslavia attests).

A nation-state that is in every respect homogeneous would have a uniform state religion, one ethnicity, one political system, uniform state institutions and one homogeneous language. But what would a homogeneous language be? It would have to be a totally standardised variety of language admitting of no variability and no change. It would be a language variety which has been elevated above the level of a local variety and is therefore usable and used by the whole population of a nation-state. It would serve all the communicative functions of the state in the written and the oral media. It would be the cultural carrier of history, education, religion, politics, law and literature. In other words, it would be an impossible, unworkable form of human language. But this is just what the *homogeneity myth*, when applied to language, entails—a language of total uniformity in both written and oral form, a language of stasis, and yet one that could be adapted (or rather manipulated) to cover the communicative needs of the future, largely in the expansion of its lexicon.

Curiously enough, though, this was the aim of nation-state builders throughout the nineteenth and twentieth centuries, and I will deal with the problems that this ideal has raised in more detail in chapters 8, 9 and 10. In the nineteenth century, the German language had a word to refer to this ideal of the homogeneous language—*Kultursprache* (loosely translatable as "language of culture"; cf. the discussion of this term in chap. 2). Vetter (2003: 282) defines a *Kultursprache* as "a language of significant cultural heritage", and she gives the example of German in the Austrian part of the late-nineteenth-century Habsburg Empire. She characterises the *Kultursprache* German as "the language of science", "the language as a political instrument", "the language which unifies the Empire" (i.e. in terms of the nation-state, the language that allows an equation to be made between state and nation within the same territory), and as "the dominant literary language of the Empire" (2003:

283). Put differently, a *Kultursprache* is always a written language with a significant body of written texts, both fictional and nonfictional, literary and nonliterary, which enshrine the cultural values of the nation-state.

The *Kultursprache* ideology promotes the dominance of one language variety over others. It is imposed through specific media, first and foremost the education system, but also the press from the eighteenth century on, in the twentieth century the broadcast media, radio and television and, most recently, the Internet. At least since the eighteenth century, standard English[1] has also been imbued with the same aura of cultural domination over nonstandard varieties of English (and also over Irish, Welsh and Scots Gaelic). In this sense, English can also be seen as a *Kultursprache*. Ironically, however, emphasising the assumed *cultural* superiority of one variety of language over others does not always lead to a strengthened sense of national unity, just as in the mid-nineteenth-century Habsburg Empire it did not lead to a "powerful Empire". The *Kultursprache* ideology is oblivious of the simple fact that the faculty of language, rather than *a* specific language variety, is acquired by all of us as a cognitive system that becomes part of the set of social identities that each of us develops.

The discursive creation of the idea of a *Kultursprache* is a way of imposing that language on the citizens of the nation-state, which will be the topic of later chapters. But the myths that constitute the **homogeneity myth** must be identifiable, and they must also have a long history allowing them to be used over the course of time to lay the foundations for the unbuildable and unfinished edifice of the nation-state from the eighteenth century on. In this chapter I will investigate into the origins of those myths, and attempt to show how they coalesce in the **linguistic homogeneity myth**. In the following section I shall present arguments that oppose the notion of homogeneity in language, after which I shall search for the myths I am looking for in what I call the "other" chronicle tradition and locate those myths in the most popular Latin chronicle of the fourteenth century, Ranulph Higden's *Polychronicon*.

2. LANGUAGE VERSUS *A* LANGUAGE VERSUS *THE* LANGUAGE

In 1968 Weinreich, Labov and Herzog published a long contribution to a book edited by Lehmann and Malkiel titled *Directions for Historical Linguistics: A Symposium*. The title of their contribution was "Empirical foundations for a theory of language change", and it was an extended rewrite of a lecture given at the symposium referred to in the title of the book. It has since become one of the most significant sets of statements on how we should

---

1. Since I am hesitant to accept that there is such an entity as "standard English", I prefer to write "standard" lowercase in the rest of this book.

go about researching the problems of language change, and it contains the recognition of an archetypal language myth that sociolinguists seriously need to acknowledge, the *linguistic homogeneity myth*.

In a nutshell, Weinreich et al.'s argument starts from the following premise: Trying to develop theories of how language change occurs is hampered if those theories are based on structuralist and generative approaches to language. They state quite explicitly at one point in the article that "structural theories of language, so fruitful in synchronic investigation, have saddled historical linguistics with [four basic paradoxes] which have not been fully overcome" (1968: 98). The first three of these paradoxes are listed below. All will be important for the argument I now wish to develop:

1. the "*language as a homogeneous system*" paradox,
2. the paradox that *language change always involves a change from one homogeneous synchronic state of the language in question to another*,
3. the paradox that looking at language as a homogeneous system and taking change to be change from one homogeneous state to another does not allow the researcher to consider what Weinreich et al. call the "orderly differentiation" displayed in all language.

2.1 Explaining the paradoxes

The first paradox is the belief that "language is a homogeneous system". Language, understood as the overall ability to acquire, store and cognitively use a set of abstract constructions of whatever kind—phonological, morphological, semantic, and so on—is certainly systematic. No one would deny this. But that ability must also enable speakers and listeners to manipulate the system as and when the need arises, which is what Weinreich et al. mean by "orderly differentiation". Homogeneity, on the other hand, implies a regularity that would contradict differentiation, and herein lies the paradox. We need a system that we share with other members of the community to which we belong or within which we are communicating, but we also need the freedom to manipulate and change the system.

Human language enables us to use the variety of language we have acquired to mediate our physical, social and mental worlds and the worlds of others. It allows us to enlarge and expand our own individual mental worlds in infinite ways. In doing this, "the actual production of syntax is locally managed" (Cumming & Ono 1997: 132), and its "'rules' are the construction of particular speakers" (Bex 2008: 222). In this sense, as Bex maintains, "grammars are 'emergent' at the moment of utterance" (224).

For the moment, imagine an isolated community of speakers with no or minimal contact with anyone outside that community, a rare occurrence in the modern world but still possible (see Schreier 2003). The linguistic constructions that they learn to produce in prompting for and negotiating meanings with others are used automatically without those speakers having to think twice about them. There are no "mistakes" that can be made, only meanings that are not, or not fully, negotiated. For the purposes of coexistence, collaboration and occasional conflict in the isolated community, it is immaterial what the speakers themselves call the variety of language they are using, as long as the linguistic constructions they share with others can be put to use in social practice. Why, then, is it so important to insist on homogeneous language systems when it is more important for speakers to be able to use the potential heterogeneity of human language in use?

Thus the first paradox resides in the hypostasisation of individual languages—looking for homogeneous linguistic systems rather than studying how "grammars are 'emergent' at the moment of utterance". Weinreich et al. take linguistic systems themselves to show heterogeneity as well as homogeneity, but they are aware of the paradox in this assumption. In addition, they characterise the approach to language that looks for linguistic "competence" without admitting to the creative variability of language in use[2] as leading to the attempt to create total homogeneity where it does not exist. For this reason, it is hardly surprising that Weinreich et al. characterise the approach as "needlessly unrealistic" and as "a backward step" (1968: 100).

The second and the third paradoxes are directly derivable from the paradox of a homogeneous linguistic system. The second presupposes two homogeneous states of language, distinguished by a change and ignores the variability inherent in language use in which speakers may use both the prechange and the postchange structure. The third paradox is that this way of looking at language prevents us from thinking in terms of the heterogeneity inherent within it when used in instances of social practice. It completely forecloses any notion of heterogeneity and variability.

2.2 The cognitive approach to language: Human language versus different languages

In chapter 1, I sketched out a cognitive approach to language that sees it as a cognitive faculty intimately connected with and ultimately derived from other cognitive faculties (cf. Feldman 2006) and not as an independent module of the mind. It is activated only in instances of social interaction—that is, emergently— and is in this sense subject to the immediate needs of the context of use, which is also in the process of being constructed during the course of the interaction.[3] Why, then, do we still talk in terms of individual languages rather than simply human language?

---

2. This is the major problem, of course, with all forms of theoretical linguistic model, not just with generative models of the Chomskyan kind.

3. This is also the case when we are talking to ourselves or when we are reading a book. We project ourselves or an imaginary partner as the person we are communicating with.

It is clear that we all need to function as "ratified" members of a social group, and to be ratified we are constrained to acquire the linguistic constructions that others use. In point of fact, we cannot do otherwise. The step from language to *a* language involves the projection of a blend from one mental space to another, in which the constructions we use and perceive others to use are mapped onto a cognitive frame that then becomes embedded in our long-term memory (see chap. 1 and Fauconnier & Turner 2002). The frame is then metaphorically projected as "the property" of the group: its "language". So the shift from human language to *a* language is essentially the construction of a metaphorical blend in the minds of the members participating in the group's activities.

If this account of how we cognitively construct the concept of *a* language in place of human language is feasible, it is hardly surprising that we accept the "truth" of the existence of languages. Nor is it surprising that the group or groups that perceive themselves to be using a language construct communal stories (myths) to explain, justify and ratify its existence. The myths themselves belong to the archetypal *linguistic homogeneity myth*, and they provide a means of distinguishing the group from other groups.

2.3 A focus on *the* language

In language standardisation processes, one variety emerges over time or is "selected" to serve as the mythical homogeneous variety or *Kultursprache*. But the selection not only denies other varieties any sociocultural validity; it also denies the validity of variability and heterogeneity with respect to human language in general. This final step constitutes the mythical construction of *the* language from *a* language—that is, the construction of the only legitimate language for the group and by extension for the nation-state. Legitimacy is then characterised in terms of homogeneity and immutability. Obviously, the mythical construction of *the* language feeds negative value judgments of other languages (or language varieties) and of those who do not speak *the* language. It is, in other words, a process of "othering". The myths that are used to validate the superiority of *the* language as a homogeneous system form part of the discursive ideology of standardisation (cf. Milroy & Milroy 1999; Bex & Watts 1999; Cameron 1995; Crowley 2003; Bonfiglio 2002; Grillo 1989), and they will be dealt with in more detail in later chapters. Essentially, however, a belief in a homogeneous legitimate language is (somewhat perversely) linked to the belief in a homogeneous polity within a homogeneous territory, what we now know as the "nation-state". The questions that occupy us in this chapter are thus the following:

1. How far back in the history of what we call "English" can the myths that form the archetypal *linguistic homogeneity myth* be traced?
2. What are those myths and can they be related to myths about other "languages"?

I shall begin by considering where we might find statements concerning language in another chronicle tradition than that of the *ASC* in the following section and then by looking closely at a frequently quoted and central passage from Higden's *Polychronicon*.

3. THE "OTHER" CHRONICLE TRADITION

In chapter 3 the *Anglo-Saxon Chronicle* was interpreted as one secular textual instantiation, among others, of a dominant discourse archive that stretched from the time of Alfred at the end of the ninth century to the end of the tenth century. As we saw in chapters 1 to 3, the statements of a dominant discourse archive represent "the law of what can be said, the system that governs the appearance of statements as unique events" (Foucault 1972: 129). In the *ASC* they exercise a form of control over social structure and, within the social structure of early medieval England, acted as an important instrument in the exercise of secular sociopolitical control. Other types of text, such as ecclesiastical laws, homilies, hagiographies and sermons exercised control over the spiritual practices of the population. Through the discourse archive, the "state", if we can call it such, exercised spiritual, ecclesiastical and secular political power over its subjects. However, the dual nature of secular and ecclesiastical political control over territory[4] tends to mask the fact that secular power was nominally subordinate to the ecclesiastical power wielded by Roman Catholic Church, at least in western and later in northern Europe. Local rulers were the guardians of the power of the church.

Anderson ([1983] 2006) makes a distinction between "sacred" and "dynastic" languages before the advent of the printing press in the fifteenth century. Throughout the Christian world Latin was the sacred language. Anderson refers to dynastic languages, some of them deriving from Latin, as those of the ruling royal houses across Europe. Till the seventeenth century they were referred to as mere "vernaculars". The codification and functional extension of dynastic languages such as Italian, French, Spanish, English, Portuguese, German and Russian developed only after the invention of printing and the subsequent spread of the availability of texts throughout the population. So it is all the more remarkable that Anglo-Saxon was widely used for the dissemination of texts from the archive before the Conquest.

After the Conquest, however, varieties of Anglo-Saxon were superseded[5] by Anglo-Norman French and Latin in the textual manifestations of laws,

---

4. It would be inaccurate to refer to the term "state" here, and for this reason I shall avoid using that lexeme. However, it is indisputable that stretches of territory were under the nominal or actual political control of potentates of various status from kings to dukes to counts, and it is also indisputable that the territories over which they ruled were frequently challenged by others and used as bargaining power in arranged marriages to extend territorial power.

5. Although not necessarily on a local level.

charters, land grants, and so on and almost entirely by Latin in ecclesiastical texts. Since, in the immediate post-Conquest period, religious houses were still the seats of learning and the repositories of written documents, it is hardly surprising that there was also a firm tradition of chronicle writing in Latin. After the Conquest, a veritable flood of Latin chronicles appeared, some reporting on the deeds of the kings of England (Britain), fictional or real, some on ecclesiastical dignitaries (archbishops, bishops, abbots, etc.), and some on the deeds of selected individuals (including but not restricted to royal persons or church figures) (cf. Walter Map's *De Nugis Curialium* [Courtiers' trifles], written sometime during the last 30 years of the twelfth century).

Chronicles whose aim was to trace the "history" of Britain back to its mythological sources are generally referred to as *Brut* chronicles (see the discussion in chap. 3). *Brut* chronicles presented the progress of time as a cyclic succession of good and bad rule and consequent states of order and disorder that exerted positive and negative influence over the static feudal structure of society. Perhaps the most well-known of these chronicles was Geoffrey of Monmouth's *Historia Regum Britanniæ* (History of the kings of Britain, completed around 1136), described by its translator for the Penguin edition, Lewis Thorpe, as a "strange, uneven and yet extraordinarily influential book...which may be said to bear the same relationship to the story of the early British inhabitants of our own island as do the seventeen historical books in the Old Testament...to the early history of the Israelites in Palestine" (1966: 9).

Some of the *Brut* chronicles, like that by Geoffrey of Monmouth, are predominantly narrative, whereas others plot out the history of England within a larger history of the known world. Others not only chronicle events but also give geographical descriptions of significant regions, particularly Britain, part of which consists of describing the climate, the inhabitants and their languages. These last two factors are significant in that they sometimes contain evaluative comments on the perceived degree of civilisation of those peoples and the languages they speak, and it is here that we discover a nexus of language myths that are still with us today.

To locate that nexus of myths and unravel the different mythical strands that go to make up the *linguistic homogeneity myth*, I shall begin by looking at Ranulph Higden's *Polychronicon*, which was completed by the middle of the fourteenth century.

4. MYTHS IN THE *POLYCHRONICON*

The *Polychronicon* is a central text in locating the myths concerning English that go to make up the *linguistic homogeneity myth*. In following chapters we shall see how these myths have lasted right down to the present, have been added to by metaphorically based myths and have been transformed in the process. In this chapter, most of the myths we can identify in Higden's text were actually taken from earlier texts, pushing the history of the myths even further back in time. In the fourteenth century, the *Polychronicon* was the most popular and most frequently copied *Brut* chronicle in a long line of chronicles stretching well into the fifteenth century. It was compiled by Ranulph Hidgen, a Benedictine monk at the monastery of St. Werburg in Chester, and its full title is *Ranulphi Castrensis, cognomine Higdon, Polychronicon (sive Historia Polycratica) ab initio mundi usque ad mortem Edwardi III. in septem libros dispositum* (The Polychronicon of Ranulph of Chester, named Higden, [or the Polychratic History] from the beginning of the world to the death of Edward III, put into seven Books).

The first of *Polychronicon*'s seven books presents a geography of the known world; books 2 to 4, a history of the world from the Creation to the time of the arrival of the Saxons in England; the fifth, the invasion of the Danes; the sixth, the history of England up to the Norman Conquest; and the final book, the history as far as the time of Edward III, Higden's own time.[6]

In all, there were three translations of the work from Latin into English. The first and most famous of these was completed by John de Trevisa in 1387. The second was an anonymous translation written before 1432, possibly by Osbern Bokenham, since it is known that he translated certain sections of the *Polychronicon*. The third was Caxton's reworking and printing of Trevisa's translation in 1482. The number of translations and the fact that more than 100 copies of the manuscript were made from the original in the fourteenth and fifteenth centuries, prior to the advent of printing, attest to the popularity of this work.

In 1865 Churchill Babington published the Latin text together with Trevisa's translation and the anonymous translation mentioned above. In chapter 59 of book 2, titled "De incolarum linguis" (Of the languages of the inhabitants), Higden deals with the languages of Britain, and it is here that we find evidence of a complex of myths. I shall quote the passage in Latin with my own (somewhat free) translation into English:

Ranulphus. Ut patet ad sensum, quot in hac insula sunt gentes, tot gentium sunt linguæ; Scoti tamen et Wallani, uptote cum aliis nationibus impermixti, ad purum pæne pritinum retinent idioma: nisi forsan Scoti ex convictu Pictorum, cum quibus olim confœderati cohabitant, quippiam contraxerint in sermone.

Ranulphus. As is obvious to the understanding, there are as many races in this island as there are languages of the races. The Scots as well as the Welsh, even though they are intermixed with other nations, retain their languages almost in their former purity. It might be the case that the Scots have taken on something in conversation from their intercourse with the Picts, with whom they lived together for some time.

6. There is some controversy as to whether Higden completed the history from 1342 to 1357 or whether it was continued by others from 1327 on, but this does not concern us here.

Flandrenses vero, qui occidua Walliæ incolunt, dimissa jam barbariæ, Saxonice satis proloquuntur. Angli quoque, quamquam ab initio tripartitam sortirentur linguam, austrinam scilicet, mediterraneam, et borealam, veluti ex tribus Germaniæ populis procedentes, ex commixtione tamen primo cum Danis, deinde Normannis, corrupta in multis patria lingua peregrinos jam captant boatus et garritus.

Hæc quidem nativæ linguæ corruptio provenit hodie multum ex duobus; quod videlicet pueri in scholis contra morem cæterum nationum a primo Normannorum adventu, derelicto proprio vulgari, cosntruere Gallice compelluntur; item quod filii nobilium ab ipsis cunabulorum crepundiis ad Gallicum idioma informantur.

Quibus profecto rurales homines assimilari volentes, ut per hoc spectabiliores videantur, francigenare satagunt omni nisu.
Ubi nempe mirandum videtur, quomodo nativa et propria Anglorum lingua, in unica insula coartata, pronunicaitione ipsa sit tam diversa; cum tamen Normannica lingua, quæ adventitia est, univocal maneat penes cunctos.

De prædicta quoque lingua Saxonica tripartita, quæ in paucis adhuc agrestibus vix remansit, orientales cum occiduis tanquam sub eodem cœli climate lineati plus consonant in sermone quam boreales cum austrinis.

Indeed the Flemings who live in the west of Wales, who set aside barbarism long ago, speak Saxon well enough. The English, too, were given three types of speech from the beginning, i.e., southern, midland, and northern, as proceeding from three peoples of Germany, but mainly from a mixture with the Danes, and then with the Normans, but their native language has been corrupted in so many ways that they now produce foreign-sounding chattering and bellowing.

Indeed this corruption of the native tongue today is largely the result of two factors. Contrary to the custom of other nations, boys in schools, from the first arrival of the Normans, leave their own common tongue to one side and are compelled to construe their lessons in French. On the other hand, the sons of the nobles are taught the language of the French from the very rocking of their cradles.

Certainly, rural men who desire to assimilate with these nobles and to be seen as remarkable, labour with every effort to speak French.
Of course, where something is seen as being admirable, like the real native language of the English enclosed within one island, it is as diverse in pronunciation as the Norman language, a language that is foreign, remains "univocal" in the possession of everyone.

In addition, with respect to the aforesaid tripartite Saxon language, which lingers on with difficulty in a few wild rustics, the speech of those in the East sounds more like that of the men of the West who live under the same climate of the heavens as that of the men of the North compared with the speech of those in the South.

Inde est quod Mercii sive Mediterranei Angli, tanquam participantes naturam extremorum, collaterales linguas arcticam melius intelligant quam adinvicem se intelligunt jam extremi.

The reason for this is that the Mercians or the Southern English, although they share nature at the extremities, understand languages close to them, northern and southern, better than those at the extremities understand one another.

Willelmus de Pontificibus, libro tertio. Tota lingua Northimbrorum, maxime inEboraco, ita stridet incondite, quod nos australes eam vix intelligere possumus; quod puto propter viciniam barbarorum contigisse, et etiam proper jugem remotionem regum Anglorum ab illis partibus, qui magis ad austrum diversati, si quando boreales partes adeunt, non nisi magno auxiliatorum manu pergunt.

Willelmus de Pontificibus, libro tertio. The whole language of the Northumbrians, especially in York, hisses so confusedly that we of the south can scarcely understand it, so that I suppose it to have bordered on the vicinity of the barbarians, and even the perpetual removal of the kings of England from those parts, who have turned to the south, whenever they return to the northern parts they do not go there without a large group of auxiliary troops.

This short passage on the languages of the British Isles from the *Polychronicon* is frequently quoted in the literature, perhaps because it displays traces of several interconnected and overlapping linguistic myths, many of which, in one form or another, are still with us today. Higden also makes explicit reference to the third book of William of Malmesbury's chronicle *Gesta Pontificum Anglorum* (Deeds of the English bishops, 1125), which he simply calls *De Pontificibus*. This allows us to surmise that some, if not all, of the myths go back at least to the twelfth century if not even further. In addition, many of these myths can also be found in reference to other languages and other cultures than English; the ***myth of the barbarians having no language***, for example, can be traced back at least to Greek antiquity.

A closer look at the text reveals the following points. Although Higden does not say explicitly what languages the Welsh and the Scots speak, we must assume that he is referring, in the case of the Welsh, to the Welsh language itself. But it is unclear whether, in referring to the Scots, he means earlier forms of Gaelic or Lowland Scots dialects of English. Both the Scots and the Welsh are said to have "intermixed with other nations"—that is, language contact situations led the languages away from a state of "purity" (they are "almost in their former purity"). In the case of Scots this is modified in the statement that "Scots" has "taken on something" as a consequence of conversational "intercourse with the Picts". We can infer that Scots is further away from a state of "purity" than Welsh. The state of purity is equivalent to the state of homogeneity, from which we can infer that speakers have a duty to retain the supposed "purity" of their languages. In situations of language contact, however, this becomes impossible.

When Higden turns to English, he first takes Bede's split into three types of English brought to England by three "peoples of Germany": the Angles, the Jutes and the Saxons.[7] English, however, has moved further from a state of purity than either Welsh or Scots because of "a mixture with the Danes, afterwards with the Normans". Higden uses a new epithet to refer to the state of English in his day: "corrupt". Those who do not speak a pure language speak a "corrupted" language, which turns out to be no better than "foreign sounding chattering and bellowing". "Chattering" and "bellowing" are hardly features of human language at all but are reminiscent of animal sounds.

Higden suggests two reasons for the corruption of English:

1. English children can only receive their schooling in French and do not have the benefit of having French as their mother tongue, and
2. English has too much variation.

The "pure" Saxon language is said to be spoken only by a "few wild rustics". Other than these rustics, speakers of English no longer speak a "pure" homogeneous language. If any "rural men" wish to assimilate, says Higden, they make "every effort to speak French", the implication being that they should not bother.

Higden then compares English with Norman French, stating that there is no variation in the latter (it is "univocal"), but there is a variation of pronunciation in English, which of course implies that Norman French is homogeneous whereas English is variable and heterogeneous. He then makes the statement that the "men of the East" and those of the West sound relatively similar, whereas those of the North and the South sound radically different, suggesting that the difference in climate between the South and the North must be responsible for these differences since those from the East and the West, who do not differ much at all, have the same climate. At the end of the extract he uses William of Malmesbury's statement that the language of Northumbria, particularly in York, "hisses so confusedly" that those from the South can scarcely understand it. William is also quoted as assuming that northern English is tainted by "the vicinity of the barbarians". The "we southerners" in Higden's text refers to William as a southerner, not to Higden himself, but what Higden gives vent to here is the long-standing prejudice against the north of England held by those living in the South.

---

7. There is a slight difference from Bede, however, as we now have a tripartite layering of English between southern, midland and northern forms, whereas Bede's account of where the three tribes settled in England does not correspond to this simple division.

In this short passage from Higden's *Polychronicon* we can tease out a nexus of myths that ultimately go back to the archetypal myth that homogeneity is superior to heterogeneity:

1. the *myth of the pure language*
   - "The Scots as well as the Welsh...retain their languages *almost in their former purity.*"
2. the *myth of contamination through contact*
   - "Even though they are *intermixed* with other nations..."
   - "The English, too, were given three types of speech from the beginning... but mainly from *a mixture* with the Danes, and then with the Normans, but their native language has been corrupted in so many ways that they now produce foreign-sounding chattering and bellowing."
   - From William of Malmesbury: "The whole language of the Northumbrians, especially in York, *hisses so confusedly* that we of the south can scarcely understand it"
3. the *myth of barbarians not having a (proper) language*
   - "The Flemings who live in the west of Wales, who set aside *barbarism* long ago, speak Saxon well enough."
   - "The aforesaid tripartite Saxon language, which lingers on with difficulty *in a few wild rustics...*"
   - From William of Malmesbury: "So that I suppose it to have bordered on the vicinity of the *barbarians...*"
4. the *myth of a good climate providing fertile ground for a "pure" language*
   - "The speech of those in the East sounds more like that of the men of the West *who live under the same climate of the heavens as that of the men of the North compared with the speech of those in the South.*"
5. the *myth of the pure language of the South and the corrupted language of the North*
   - From William of Malmesbury: "The whole language of the Northumbrians, especially in York, hisses so confusedly that *we of the south can scarcely understand it.*"

The first three of these myths are derived directly from the archetypal *linguistic homogeneity myth*, and myths 4 and 5 are indirectly connected to it.

The text extract shows that the *pure language myth* transforms seamlessly into the *contamination through contact myth*. Higden is referring specifically to the English language at this point, but throughout the passage, speakers of English shift into the language "English" and back again, creating the strong impression that the qualities of the language are attributed to its speakers and vice versa. Hence, any corruption of the language through language contact situations also entails that the speakers have been corrupted. There are strong similarities here between Higden's assessment of language contact situations and those of the contributors to the Internet discussion thread on Middle-English-as-a-creole in chapter 4. Given the negative evaluations of creoles frequently met with in nonlinguistic quarters, the Middle-English-as-a-creole hypothesis not only leads to the *pure language myth* but also feeds the *contamination through contact myth*. In fact, the nexus of myths and metaphors associated with the *pure language myth* is surprisingly complex, as we shall see in the next section.

The second nexus of myths focuses on the *barbarians myth*. The myth is used as a means of identifying the Other as being inferior to people in one's own culture, and its roots go back at least as far as classical Greece. The Other (the "foreigner", the "enemy", the "stranger") was referred to as βάρβαρος (*barbaros*) which derives from the Proto-Indo-European base **barbar-* referring to the unintelligible speech of foreigners (cf. Sanskrit *barbara*, meaning "stammering"). A barbarian was thus someone who did not speak the "legitimate" language, someone who did not conform to the speaker's conceptualisation of what was cultivated, but was, on the contrary, ignorant or rude. The step from this assessment of the Other to one in which the Other does not use language at all is small. Higden's text does not explicitly make this connection, but it certainly strongly implies it, particularly when Higden quotes William of Malmesbury as suggesting that the unintelligible language produced in York has something to do with the fact that it borders "on the vicinity of the barbarians". The fifth myth—the *pure language of the South and the corrupted language of the North myth*—is also taken from William of Malmesbury's text and is intimately tied up with the *barbarians myth*. I shall deal with this nexus of myths in the following section.

The final myth contained within this short passage is the *good climate/soil myth*, and, once again, it is linked in interesting ways to the myths associated with both the *pure language myth* and the *barbarians myth*. The assumption here is that there is some connection between language and the climate, and language and the soil. The "best" ("purest", most "perfect") languages are assumed to be spoken by those who live in a climate that favours the growth of those plants from which we derive our staple nutrition—varieties of cereal, vines, and fruits of various kinds. The favourable climate, however, has to be combined with favourable soils, so land that provides good grazing is still inferior to land that can be used for crop production.

Higden's text provides an excellent example of this connection, when he refers to Saxon as lingering on in *paucis...agrestibus*. I have translated the Latin *agrestis* as "a (or the) rustic" for the sake of convenience, but the term has a number of negative connotations in Latin, such as "wild", "unmannered", "boorish", "untamed", "pertaining to the fields", indicating that Higden may have been referring not to someone who cultivated the fields but to someone who drove sheep or cattle out into the fields. Confirmation of this interpretation is given by Trevisa, who translates in *paucis... agrestibus* as *wiþ fewe vplondisshe men*, that is, men who live in the hills. We thus have an interesting contrast between pastoralists, who can then be associated with barbarians who do not speak the legitimate language, and agriculturalists who till the land and do speak the legitimate language.

5. LINKING UP AND EXTENDING THE MYTHS

The *linguistic homogeneity myth*, which drives the ideology of the *Kultursprache* and the related ideology of the standard language, is made up of a complex web of myths that are interwoven and continually open to further extension. They are all derived from the common, possibly universal conceptual anthropomorphic metaphor used to understand the nature of human language and introduced in chapter 1: A LANGUAGE IS A HUMAN BEING. We saw in section 2 of this chapter how the concept of a language is derived from an awareness that different communities of human beings use different variations of the capacity for human language. Once the concept of a language is established, the need to understand it can only be satisfied by reverting to conceptual blends in which projections are made from the source domain of a human being onto the language itself. The reason for the projection is simple. Like TIME or LOVE, our abstract concept of language constrains us to rely on our fundamental bodily experiences with the immediate environment and to project these onto the abstract concept of human language. From the day we are born we are surrounded by human beings who use language to communicate with us. It is obvious that those same human beings also use other means of communication—facial expressions, laughter, physical contact, and so on—but language is the most fundamental human characteristic. The projection from the source domain HUMAN BEING to the target LANGUAGE is thus self-explanatory.[8]

All conceptual metaphors are mental blends, and once they are firmly entrenched in cognition, they can be run to generate as many "true" statements as are required, as we saw in chapter 1. Human beings have physical qualities such as size, strength, state of growth, and they are subject to maturity, age, infirmity, decay and death. So in terms of the conceptual metaphor, languages are also metaphorically subject to these phenomena. Human beings have personal characteristics such as honesty, civility, charm, agreeability, and so on, so once again such qualities can be projected onto language. It has often been noted in the literature (see, e.g., Milroy & Milroy 1999; J. Milroy 1999; Cameron 1995)[9] that there is a strong tendency to attribute the qualities associated with a language to the speaker. If the variety of language used is judged to be morally imperfect, degenerate or faulty, then these attributes tend to be automatically transferred to the speakers themselves.

Once a language is assigned a human feature from a metaphorical blend, the blend may also be run. For example, a language that is considered contaminated must be infected by some negative agent or other, and the infection

8. There is also an obvious sense in which the metaphor is partially metonymic in that human beings are where language is produced—they are the source of language.

9. Consider also the method of the matched guise in sociolinguistics to empirically test subjects' attribution of qualities to speakers on the strength of the language variety they use (Gardner & Lambert 1972).

must have been transferred through close physical contact. A language that is contaminated, infected, or diseased can be purified by undergoing treatment of some kind, and it is also thought to be potentially dangerous to a healthy language such that any contact with it should be avoided. Alternatively, a language that is considered noble is of course automatically considered to be superior to other languages.

Linguistic myths are discursively produced stories about language that feed on the welter of "true" statements deriving from the fundamental anthropomorphic metaphor A LANGUAGE IS A HUMAN BEING. Some of them, like the myth of the North versus the South, are specific to English in England, whereas others are of a more general nature, as evidenced in the **contamination through contact myth**. In the following subsections I will comment on the three central myths used by Higden (the **pure language myth**, the **contamination through contact myth**, and the **barbarians myth**) and the two local or peripheral myths (the **pure language of the South and the corrupted language of the North myth** and the **good climate/soil myth**) to show how they can be derived by running the conceptual metaphor of language A LANGUAGE IS A HUMAN BEING. In figure 5.1, the oval in the centre of the page towards the top represents the conceptual metaphor A LANGUAGE IS A HUMAN BEING. This yields a set of physical properties of a language on the left and at the top of the figure and a number of nonphysical, moral qualities of a language on the right and at the top of the figure, each group being potentially endless and deriving from the central conceptual metaphor. Running each of these blends yields different kinds of supplementary "true" statements, as shown on each side of the figure, which then feed into the myths used by Higden given in the centre of the figure.

5.1 The central myths

I use the term "central myth" to indicate a myth that is either directly derivable from the "true" statements generated from the conceptual metaphor or is commonly held with respect to a wide range of languages (see Grillo 1989). As we saw in section 4, the etymology of *barbarian* is closely related to language insofar as barbarians (foreigners or Others) are said not to have an intelligible language. An unintelligible language is one that is not legitimate, one that is thus not a "proper" language. The "true" statement <a language with a blemish is imperfect> is derived from running the metaphorical blend and can be used to refer to Other's language. It is also applicable to the language of the North, as we shall see in the next subsection.

If the language of the barbarians has some form of moral blemish, it can also be said to be contaminated, and should therefore be avoided; language contact is not advisable. At the same time, the language is also corrupt, and this reflects the corrupt nature of the barbarians themselves. We can easily see how the **barbarians myth** can be extended to refer to groups of individuals who are within the community supposedly encompassed by the nation state. Milroy (2007: 137) gives the following quotation from a school inspector in 1925:

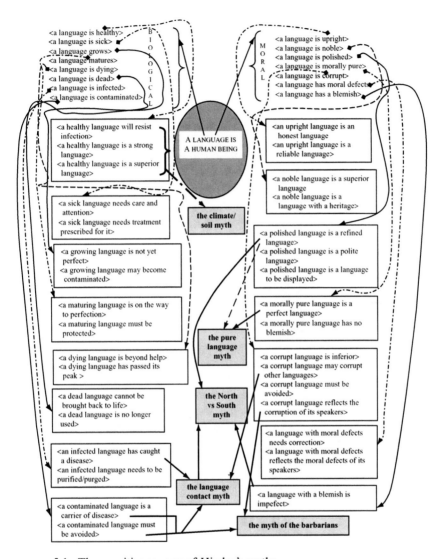

FIGURE 5.1. The cognitive sources of Higden's myths

Come into a London elementary school and...[and] you will notice that the boys and girls are almost inarticulate. They can make noises, but they cannot speak.... Listen to them as they "play at schools"; you can barely recognise your native language.

Although the expression "barbarians" is not used explicitly by the school inspector, his comments lie squarely within the discourse of the *barbarians myth*.

Related to this myth is the *contamination through contact myth*, which is more salient in Higden's text than is the myth of the barbarians. The two "true" statements derived from the conceptual metaphor—<a contaminated language is a carrier of disease> and <a contaminated language must be avoided>—can be run as the central pillars of the *contamination through contact myth*. Any language other than the "pure language" must be imperfect, a possible bearer of disease to the "pure language", and the only way to prevent this from happening is to avoid contact with it. Indirectly, of course, this includes the language of barbarians, since, as we have seen, their language is not proper. Similarly, the "true" statement <an infected language has caught a disease>, which may of course refer to the infected state of the "pure language," which then has to undergo treatment to cure it, also feeds into the *contamination through contact myth*. The "true" statements derived from the central metaphor on the right-hand side of figure 5.1 refer to the moral qualities of a language, but these also feed into the *language contact myth*, particularly the statements <a corrupt language may corrupt other languages> and <a corrupt language reflects the corruption of its speakers>, in which the attribution of moral failings assigned to the Other's language, by running the blend, endangers the speakers of the "pure" language through language contact. The interesting feature about the *contamination through contact myth* is that it also contributes a rationale for the construction of the local myth disparaging the English used in the north of England.

The third and possibly the most central myth in Higden's text is the *pure language myth*. It is central because, through it, Higden creates the impression that Anglo-Norman French is in some sense more homogeneous than English, which is looked at in an altogether more ambiguous way. There are speakers who still speak English "purely", but there are equally speakers who are equivalent to barbarians. The idea of a pure, or perfect, language is supported exclusively by running the "true" statements attributing moral character to language rather than physical attributes, and it will be a central concern in my deconstruction of Swift's *Proposal* presented in chapter 7, and also in chapters 8, 9 and 10. Although Higden does not express this idea in his text, the statement <a polished language is a refined language> will constitute a fundamental rationale for the development of "standard English" through the notion of politeness, as shown in chapter 8. For this reason I have represented the line between the blend and the *pure language myth* as a dotted line in figure 5.1. The idea of a morally pure language being a perfect language most definitely feeds into the construction of the myth.

5.2 Three later myths of the sixteenth century

The *pure language myth* becomes properly active at the very beginning of the move towards the creation of a standard at the end of the sixteenth century. At roughly the same time, two other closely related myths appear based on "true" statements derived from the conceptual metaphor A LANGUAGE IS A HUMAN BEING:

1. <a noble language is a superior language>, <a noble language is a language with a heritage>, from which we can trace the **myth of the superiority of English**, and

2. <a morally pure language is a perfect language>, <a morally pure language has no blemish>, from which we can trace the **myth of the perfect language**.

The first realisation of the **pure language myth** is to be found in book 3, chapter 4, of George Puttenham's *The Arte of English Poesie* (1588), titled "Of Language", although, as is usual in the late medieval and early modern periods, Puttenham might very well have taken over or "translated" his ideas from previous texts. Puttenham describes the language to which budding poets should aspire as follows:

Neither shall he follow the speech of a craftes man or carter, or other of the inferior sort, though he be inhabitant or bred in the best towne and Citie in this Realme, for such persons doe abuse good speaches by strange accents or ill shapen soundes, and false ortographie. But he shall follow generally the better brought vp sort, such as the Greeks call [*charientes*] men ciuill and graciously behauoured and bred. Our maker therfore at these dayes shall not follow *Piers Plowman* nor *Gower* nor *Lydgate* nor yet *Chaucer*, for their language is now out of vse with vs: neither shall he take the termes of Northern-men, such as they vse in dayly talke, whether they be noble men or gentlemen, or of their best clarkes all is a matter: nor in effect any speach vsed beyond the riuer of Trent, though no man can deny but that theirs is the purer English Saxon at this day, yet it is not so Courtly nor so currant as our Southerne English is, no more is the far Westerne mans speech: ye shall therfore take the vsuall speech of the Court, and that of London and the shires lying about London within lx. myles, and not much aboue. I say not this but that in euery shyre of England there be gentlemen and others that speake but specially write as good Southerne as we of Middlesex or Surrey do, but not the common people of euery shire, to whom the gentlemen, and also their learned clarkes do for the most part condescend, but herein we are already ruled by th'English Dictionaries and other bookes written by learned men, and therefore it needeth none other than direction in that behalfe. Albeit peraduenture some small admonition be not impertinent, for we finde in our English writers many wordes and speaches amendable, & ye shall see in some many inkhorne termes so ill affected brought in by men of learning as preachers and schoolemasters: and many straunge termes of other languages by Secretaries and Marchaunts and trauailors, and many dark wordes and not vsuall nor well sounding though they be dayly spoken in Court.

The pure language that Puttenham holds up as the model to be followed by writers is "the vsuall speech of the Court, and that of London and the shires lying about London within lx. myles, and not much aboue".

The *superiority of English myth* extols the superiority of English above all other languages. Superiority is generally located in a number of characteristics ascribing greater beauty, greater logical powers of expression, greater nobility, greater simplicity of expression and greater variety. It can be traced back to the following section of the extract from Higden's *Polychronicon* quoted above:

> *Ubi nempe mirandem videtur, quomodo nativa et propria Anglorum lingua, in unica insula coartata, pronunciatione ipsa sit tam diversa; cum tamen Normannica lingua, quæ adventitia est, univoca maneat penes cunctos.*

> [When surely it is seen as a wonder how the true and native language of the English, compressed within one island, is so diverse in its very pronunciation; the Norman language, however, which has been brought here, retains the one sound with all.]

Higden characterises this variety as a "wonder", but like Caxton's story of the eggs in the preface to the *Eneidos*, it is unclear whether this attribute is meant to be understood as a positive, negative, or simply a neutral evaluation of the "facts".

A positive evaluation is given by Richard Carew in his essay "An Epistle concerning the Excellencies of the English Tongue", which appeared in 1605 in the first edition of William Camden's *Remains Concerning Britain*. I quote from a publication of Carew's *The Svrvey of Cornwall. And An Epistle concerning the Excellencies of the English Tongue* in 1769:

> Moreover the copiousness of our Language appeareth in the diversity of our Dialects, for we have Court and we have Countrey English, we have Northern and Southern English, gross and ordinary, which differ from each other, not only in the terminations, but also in many words, terms, and phrases, and express the same thing in divers sorts, yet all write English alike. (1769: 11)

Carew's passage was taken over almost word for word, or, using today's terminology, plagiarised, by Guy Miège (a Huguenot refugee from Lausanne in Switzerland) in his *English Grammar; or the Grounds and Genius of the English Tongue* in 1688 and then again by Victor Peyton in his *Elements of the English Language* in 1779.

The *perfection myth* is represented in a text by William Harrison titled "On the languages spoken in this land" in Holinshed's *Chronicles* (1577):

> Afterward also, by diligent travel of Geffray Chaucer, and John Gower, in the time of Richard the second, and after then Iohn Scogan, and John Lydgate, monke of Berrie, our said toong was brought to an excellent passe, notwithstanding that it neuer came vnto perfection, vntill the time of Queen Elizabeth. ([1577] 1965: 25)

In the centuries to follow, the reign of Queen Elizabeth was taken by several commentators on language to be the Golden Age of English, and this notion is expressed by Swift in his *A Proposal for Correcting, Improving, and Ascertaining the English Tongue*, as we shall see in chapter 7.

5.3 Local and peripheral myths

Two myths in Higden's text—the *climate/soil myth* and the *pure language of the South and the corrupted language of the North myth*—can be said to be local, and hence peripheral. In considering the ideologies driven by these myths in England itself, however, they are pivotal. The *climate/soil myth* is also derived from a conceptual metaphor discussed in chapter 1: A LANGUAGE IS A PLANT. We shall see it used in Swift's *Proposal*, although there is evidence from Swift's text that he uses it satirically. Even so, the fact that Swift can be interpreted as satirising the myth is itself evidence of its popularity, and it may still be heard in nonlinguistic circles to explain a supposed difficulty in learning and lack of aesthetic attraction of languages containing complex consonant clusters or velar, uvular and pharyngeal affricates.[10]

The *pure language of the South and the corrupted language of the North myth* is as alive today as it was in William of Malmesbury's time although it is not easy to find explicit references to the myth in written sources. In my own data corpus of family discourse, I have located an interesting reference made by one of the participants in a conversation about the use of discourse markers such as *well, you know, like, anyway,* and so on to the effect that *like* and *you know* are expressions used in the North—which is blatantly false, as they are used just as frequently throughout Britain. Needless to say, the participants were all from the South, and their evaluation of the use of these elements by "northerners" was uniformly negative (see Watts 1989). Wales (2006) has written a social and cultural history of northern English in which she argues that the myth is actually part of a general North-South cultural divide structured from the perspective of southerners, in which aspects of the North are represented in negative terms in opposition to the positive evaluations of the South:

> This book will also reveal how the polarity between Northern English and Southern English is also intertwined with a deep-rooted cultural opposition between the North and the South, comprising a mish-mash of mythologies of Northernness accrued in different phases of the North's history.... Basic even to this cultural opposition is a more pervasive semiotic of a North–South divide based on temperature: consider phrases like "the frozen North" or "the warm South". (25)

---

10. I have even heard it used by speakers of standard German, nota bene linguists, to explain the existence of affricates and consonant clusters in the Swiss German dialects. I might add that there was also a hint of the *barbarians myth* associated with this evaluation.

The semiotic extends to such oppositions as wealth (South) versus poverty (North), agriculturalism (South) versus pastoralism (North), and industrialisation (North) versus commerce (South). Wales (2006: 25) also mentions that "the weather, and the mists from the Irish Sea, are popularly believed to account for the adenoidal quality of the Scouse [Liverpool] accent".

6. THE CENTRAL NEXUS OF LANGUAGE MYTHS

This chapter lies almost at the centre of the book for a good reason. By looking closely at a short and, within the context of the whole work, not particularly significant extract from Higden's *Polychronicon*, we were able to locate a rich nexus of language myths reaching further back than the fourteenth century, when Higden wrote the text. The myths dealt with in this chapter form the centre of a group of myths, some of a universal nature and others more specifically geared towards English, which drive ideological discourses on language. For this reason I have decided to represent the nexus of myths which represent the content of the present book in diagrammatic fashion at the end of this chapter (see fig. 5.2), indicating the overlaps and links between them. I have also indicated in which chapter each myth is dealt with, although some run like a red thread throughout the whole text.

The reader should not be too concerned if the myths that might be of more interest to her are only to be found in the chapters to follow. What is important at this stage is to demonstrate a discernible structure emerging out of the myths presented in this chapter, since those myths can be traced back furthest in time. It is of course no accident that the myth at the very centre of the diagram, the *linguistic homogeneity myth* drives the myths immediately contiguous to it and most of those myths are also present in this chapter. Apart from the *superiority of English myth*, which did not begin to emerge till the sixteenth century, the myths dealt with in this chapter are bunched closer to the centre of the diagram, the exceptions being the *immutability myth* and the *death and decay myth*, which appear in the analysis of Swift's text in chapter 7.

Toward the bottom right of the diagram appears the central myth in relation to English, the *superiority of English myth*, two major components of which were dealt with in chapters 2 and 3. The following chapter deals with another aspect of superiority in the *greatness myth*. To the top left of the diagram I have arranged myths that will be discussed in chapters 8, 9 and 10, and they revolve around the third central myth, the *legitimate language myth* (which is, of course, standard English), either feeding into it or derived from it—for example, the *polite language myth* and the *educated language*

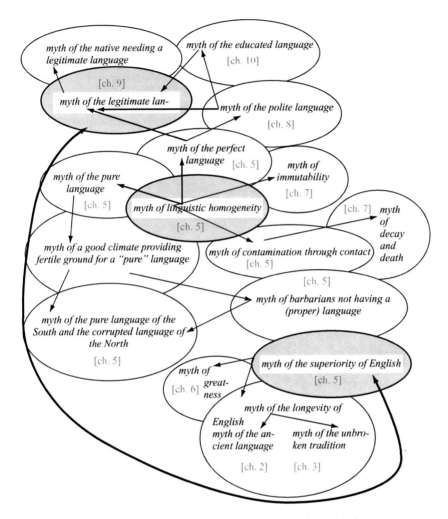

FIGURE 5.2. Contacts between the myths and the chapters in which they appear (N.B. the "modern" and potential myths presented in chapters 4 and 11 have been omitted here)

myth. All three central myths are linked together and form the scaffolding into which the other myths are fitted.

The myths help to drive specific but interrelated ideological discourses on language and to construct discourse archives. For example, the ideology of the standard language (see Milroy & Milroy 1985) is driven by the myths above the **linguistic homogeneity myth**. The discourse of the North–South cultural divide is driven by the myths below and to the left of the **linguistic homogeneity myth**, and the ideological discourse of the superiority of the

English language, which is central to the present-day perception that English is the "global language" is driven by the myths below and to the right of the *linguistic homogeneity myth*. I have not related any of the myths in the diagram to chapters 4 and 11, since it is there that modern myths are in the process of formation. The following chapter focuses on the area of the superiority of English myths and deals with what I call the *myth of greatness.*

Chapter 6

―――

The myth of "greatness"

Neither can any Tongue, as I am perswaded, deliver a Matter with more
Variety than ours, both plainly, and by Proverbes and Metaphors.
                    —Richard Carew, *An Epistle concerning the Excellencies*
                                        of the English Tongue, 1605

1. INTRODUCTION

In chapters 2 and 3, I argued that the commonly held assumption that the
history of English represents an unbroken line between Old English (Anglo-
Saxon) through Middle English and Early Modern English to Modern English
is the product of two linguistic myths that arose in the nineteenth century and
have persisted in textbooks on the history of English down to the present: the
ancient language myth and the *unbroken tradition myth*. Such a presentation
of the periodisation of English is focused on the emergence of standard
English and automatically cancels out any alternative efforts to tell the stories
of other varieties. It ultimately derives from the central myth of the homogeneity of language, society, and culture, and as such has no truck with heterogeneity and variability.

In this chapter, I turn my attention to a myth which, like the *ancient lan-*
guage myth and the *unbroken tradition myth*, also forms part of the cluster of

This chapter is a reworking and revision of my contribution to the book *English Core Linguistics: Essays*
in Honour of D. J. Allerton (2003) edited by Cornelia Tschichold.

139

myths circling around the *linguistic homogeneity myth*, the *myth of greatness*. All three myths are derived from the *superiority of English myth*, as we saw in the previous chapter. Modifying a noun with the adjective "great" in English prompts for a range of meanings that only marginally include the cognitive concept of LARGE SIZE. "Great" can also prompt for concepts such as REMARK-ABILITY, EXCELLENCE, POWER, INFLUENCE, ENTHUSIASM, and so on. There is always a sense of uniqueness, of grandiose proportions and perhaps even of historical significance associated with the term, which allows it to be used in the context of the nation-state to refer to events, institutions, objects, and so on that are infused with a mythical aura of superiority in comparison with similar events, institutions and objects in other nation-states. Within the framework of the industrial age in the nineteenth century, in which the con-cept of the nation-state was at its height, such expressions as the "Great Western Railway" or the "Great North Road" were meant to inspire stories of national achievement and admiration.

Outside the mythical sphere of the nation-state, "great" can still be used to refer to remarkable objects or events such as the "Great Wall of China", the "Great War", or the "Great Trek", which also inspire awe and admiration. And, obviously, it can be used ironically, as in expressions like the "Great Train Robbery", or—possibly familiar in linguistic circles—Geoffrey Pullum's expression the "Great Eskimo Vocabulary Hoax", used as the title of a collec-tion of brilliant satirical squibs written by him for the journal *Natural Language and Linguistics*. The cognitive sense of the lexeme *great* in these last two instances is clearly that of REMARKABILITY.

The *greatness myth* has also been projected onto national languages as the official languages of nation-states, as an integral component of what is assumed to make those nation-states more influential, powerful and admi-rable than others. English is definitely not immune to this myth. On the other hand, the only case in which historians of the language have explicitly had recourse to the epithet "great" as an integral part of their terminology is in the expression "the Great Vowel Shift" (GVS), and it is with the deconstruc-tion of this term that I shall be concerned in this chapter. The interpretation of the mythical import of the GVS is that it is used as a convenient major watershed between the hypothesised periods in the assumed history of English referred to as "Middle English" and "Early Modern English", and the decon-struction of this watershed is part of an attempt to demystify the significance of the vowel shift itself.

I shall not focus on what might have caused the vowel shift to occur nor on the merits or demerits of the drag-chain and push-chain accounts of the phenomenon of vowel shifting in general, although these problems are central to any theory of phonological variation and change. Instead, I shall focus on the disputes revolving around the GVS, which primarily concern its dating, and I shall touch on the linguistic processes involved in the development of the GVS. The major question here is whether the GVS can be properly seen as a unitary phenomenon.

Linguistic disputes on the processes involved in vowel shifting and, in particular, on whether the GVS may be seen as a unitary phenomenon are, of course, not unimportant. In this chapter, however, my focus is different: I wish to reconstruct the ideological discourse of the GVS to show that a series of smaller vowel shifts took place at different times in different parts of the country, and that there were certain geographical areas in which some (or even many) of those shifts did not take place at all. If my arguments are valid, we have a strong justification for looking at language change on a more local level—that is, for looking at language history from below rather than from above. My point is that the tradition of presenting the GVS as one "great" unitary phenomenon constitutes another ideology naturalised within the discourse of "the history of the language" (cf. Alexander Ellis 1869; Henry Sweet [1873–74] 1888), and, as we saw in chapter 1, myths are a major component driving all forms of ideological discourse.

2. DATING THE GVS

The period during which the GVS is canonically assumed to have taken place covers almost 300 years from the early fifteenth to the late eighteenth century, although most commentators restrict this period even further so that the GVS simply lies between the time of Chaucer and that of Shakespeare (Jespersen 1933; Barber 1976; Wells 1982; Claiborne 1983; Nixon & Honey 1988; Freeborn 1992; Macaulay 1994; Smith 1996; Campbell 2004; van Lier 2004; Nevalainen 2006).[1] The second of these two dates is interesting inasmuch as it is only in the last 40 years of the eighteenth century that we see attempts to construct and prescribe a standard oral language, evident in, for example, Thomas Sheridan's *A Course of Lectures on Elocution* (1762) and John Walker's *Elements of Elocution* (1781) and *A Critical Pronouncing Dictionary and Expositor of the English Language* (1791).[2] The latter part of the nineteenth century and the first 25 years of the twentieth century saw concerted efforts to locate that oral standard socially (see Wyld 1906, 1913; Jones 1909, 1917). The legacy of those efforts is the continued drive towards the homogenisation of oral English, a homogenisation that haunts the requirement written into the current National Curriculum for English that pupils be given access to standard oral English. As Bex and Watts point out

---

1. Claiborne (1983) and van Lier (2004) even restrict it to the sixteenth century, but at least Nixon and Honey suggest that the dating they give, which is similar to all the other datings in the works referred to here, has been challenged. Other linguists who discuss the GVS are prudent enough to avoid stating any time periods (cf., e.g., Labov 1994 and van Gelderen 2006).
   2. George Puttenham, in *The Arte of English Poesie* (1589; book 3, chap. 4, "Of Language"), was certainly aware of differences in pronunciation and even expressed an outright derogatory opinion of the pronunciation of "the inferior sort" (not "the better brought vp sort") associated with the royal court, as containing "strange accents or ill shapen soundes".

in *Standard English: The Widening Debate* (1999: 116), "To teach standard spoken English requires that we take on the task of showing what it is". This has never been adequately done, and I suggest that this is because it cannot be done.[3]

Let us now consider the first of the two dates marking the presumed beginning of the GVS, the early fifteenth century. Giancarlo (2001) argues that this date allows us to construct a convenient borderline between the outgoing Middle Ages as represented by the literary genius of Chaucer and the period of early modern English as represented by Shakespeare. It allows us to claim Shakespeare as "one of us" and, while not disclaiming Chaucer's greatness, to place him into the camp of those who did not speak English as we do. Such a demarcation allows us to define the language of Shakespeare as "early *modern* English" and to locate the "true" beginning of standard English at the end of the sixteenth century. Giancarlo's argument thus supports my interpretation of the discursive ideology of the "history of the language" built on a nexus of myths associated with the ***linguistic homogeneity myth*** such as those dealt with in the previous chapter. It provides evidence that the "funnel view" of the history of English focuses narrowly on the development of standard English to the detriment of the dialects, creoles and other colonial varieties. As Milroy (2002) astutely points out, the ideology works towards the exclusion of viewing the historical development of varieties of English in relation to its Germanic neighbours.

The traditional accounts of the GVS have not gone unchallenged. The work of deconstructing the ***greatness myth*** underlying the term "*Great* Vowel Shift" was begun in the 1980s by Stockwell and Minkova (1988a, 1988b, 1990, 1997), and it has been continued by a number of important articles in the 1990s (notably, Johnston 1992; J. Smith 1993; and Guzman 1994). The most detailed of these is Johnston's article, which gives well-documented evidence to suggest that, in the Plain of York, low-vowel raising preceded not only the chain shift in the long high vowels, but that it also preceded Open Syllable Lengthening itself in the thirteenth century—perhaps even earlier.

If we are interested in researching into how the traditional discourse of "the history of the language" has been constructed, the fundamental question of what the GVS was and how it should be deconstructed loses none of its compulsive power.[4]

---

3. Crowley (2003: chap. 6) presents an extended discussion of some of the current attempts in the literature to define what standard Spoken English is. He concludes with the suggestion that it should only be used "in the sense of being able to share sense and meaning through common effort and communication" (2003: 266). Standard Spoken English is thus "what each of us creates every time we use any of the various spoken forms of English and make meaning with them".

4. We might add here that sociolinguistic research into other varieties of English in the United States (Boberg 2000; Labov, Ash & Boberg 2006) and New Zealand (Bauer et al. 2007; Trudgill & Hannah 2002) gives undisputed present-day evidence of other vowel shifts taking place. It seems that speakers of English, wherever they are, whichever variety they speak, are simply inveterate vowel shifters.

3. A REAPPRAISAL OF RESEARCH WORK ON AN ELUSIVE PHENOMENON

The GVS is obviously not unimportant in explaining the historical development of the phonological construction(s) of present-day varieties of English. However, I shall argue throughout this chapter that, if we conceptualise the GVS as a unitary phenomenon and restrict ourselves to purely phonetic/phonological aspects of the vowel shift, its mythical function within the discourse of the historical development of "Standard English" will go unnoticed.

The vigorous debate over the past 15 years between Stockwell and Minkova's work and that of Lass (1988, 1999b) has engendered a more cautious approach to the phonological/phonetic phenomena encompassed by the term "Great Vowel Shift" than was the case as late as the early 1980s. Most serious researchers in English historical linguistics since the beginning of the '90s have become somewhat sceptical about most of the arguments put forward to explain those phenomena (see Labov 1994; Kiparsky 2003a, b), and they appear to question the "greatness" of the GVS. Stockwell and Minkova themselves tend to stop short of explaining why any vowel shift in the varieties of native-speaker English across the world would fail to merit the ascription of greatness, and it is precisely the point at which they stop that needs to be transcended if we wish to achieve a more realistic account of vowel shifting in English.

In part, this has already been attempted by meticulous researchers such as Paul Johnston Jr. (1992) with the overall result that the GVS does indeed appear to disintegrate into a number of smaller shifts whose importance is not thereby weakened, but certainly is more realistically contextualised. I argue here that we need to enter the world of sociolinguistics and discourse analysis, in addition to researching into the phonetic conditions that trigger off the phenomenon of vowel shifting, to give the research a more solid explanatory foundation.

3.1 How has the GVS traditionally been presented?

The GVS is a term used to refer to a series of phonological changes affecting the long vowel system of Middle English stretching from around the middle of the fourteenth century[5] to the beginning of the eighteenth. The term "Great Vowel Shift" is generally attributed to Otto Jespersen, who gave chapter 8 in the first volume of his monumental work *A Modern English Grammar on Historical Principles* (1909–1949) the title "The Great Vowel-shift". However,

---

5. Johnston (1992) actually suggests that the shift had already begun on the Plain of York in the thirteenth century. The evidence he provides supports this assumption and allows us to see the GVS in a rather different light.

Karl Luick, in his *Historische Grammatik der englischen Sprache* ([1914–21] 1964), also mentions *die grosse Lautverschiebung*, so whether Jespersen took the term from Luick or Luick from Jespersen is a minor matter of contention. In his earlier work on English phonetics, however, it is clear that Luick *was* aware of the details of the vowel shift, since these had already been amply documented by both Alexander Ellis (1869) and Henry Sweet (1874).

The period during which the GVS is assumed to have taken place thus covers almost 400 years. However, Johnston's arguments that some of the first shifts should be moved back time-wise into the thirteenth century have the effect of lengthening the period of the GVS to around 500 years. If this is the case, it is somewhat surprising to find researchers, following Jespersen and Luick, who have attempted to restrict it to the period from the beginning of the fifteenth to, at latest, the end of the seventeenth century. Those researchers have set the tone for the canonical—and essentially mythical—account of the GVS presented in standard histories of the English language to the effect that it spans the much shorter period of roughly 200 years.

Why has this interpretation of the GVS restricted it to a period of just 200 years? As I argued in section 2, it creates a convenient borderline between the Middle Ages and the period of early "modernism". Shakespeare is "rescued" as an "early modern" playwright, and Chaucer is consigned to the late Middle Ages.

The standard explanation of the GVS presents it as a systematically near-perfect construct. However, as such it assumes an odd teleology, in which speakers within those 200 years are interpreted as striving to bring about the creation of standard English. After all, 200 years represent roughly ten generations of speakers! The counter questions might very well be: "Once the GVS was completed, why did those speakers stop? Was it because they 'knew', in some mythically intuitive sense, that standard English had been achieved, or was it simply because the GVS had exhausted itself?"

It is relatively easy to show how all these points are interlinked and how this tendency in the traditional, "conventional" way of teaching the history of English leads to the fiction of *an* English language to the complete disregard of heterogeneity in the emergent process of sociocommunicative interaction and of other varieties of English.[6] The "conventional" way of presenting *the* history of English is revealed at other places in Jespersen's work, as for example in the following quotation from *Essentials of English Grammar* (1933: 16):

> In old [*sic*] times, when communication between various parts of the country was not easy and when the population was, on the whole, very stationary, a great many local dialects arose which differed very considerably from one another; the divergencies naturally became greater among the uneducated than among the educated and richer classes, as the latter moved more about and had more

---

6. The collection of contributions in Watts and Trudgill 2002 is aimed at counteracting precisely this tendency.

intercourse with people from other parts of the country. In recent times the enormously increased facilities of communication have to a great extent counteracted the tendency towards the splitting up of the language into dialects—class dialects and local dialects.... Our chief concern will be with the normal speech of the educated class, what may be called Standard English.

The message comes through clearly enough, but it turns out to be a somewhat contradictory message when one considers Jespersen's earlier interest in dialects. Here, as in Puttenham's work, dialects are out-of-date (a thing of "old times"); they are spoken by the "uneducated"; they "split up" and endanger the homogeneity of *the* language; and they are not "normal" speech, a form of speech which is in any case attributed only to the "educated class", as we shall see in chapters 9 and 10.

Conceptualising the GVS as "great", as a unifying movement, as the impulse towards the inevitable development of Standard English, and as a way of somehow "overcoming" the disruptive effect of dialects on efficient communication lent philological and, later, linguistic support to the ideology of the standard, which is equivalent to what Bourdieu would call the exercise of symbolic power to legitimise the standard language. What, after all, could be better than finding as "pure" a justification of standard speech as the coherent, unitary system of phonological changes represented by the GVS?

3.2 What was the "Great Vowel Shift"?

Before we consider the mythical nature of the GVS, we need to know in more detail what it consisted of. Conventional wisdom—which is by no means an accurate account of what actually happened—maintains that the GVS was a series of phonological changes affecting the long vowel system of Middle English, in which the high front vowel [i:] was shifted (eventually, of course) to the modern diphthong [aɪ] and the high back vowel [u:] was shifted to the modern diphthong [aʊ].[7] This is represented diagrammatically in figure 6.1 without my suggesting which shift followed which but with the two principle theories of drag-chain and push-chain movement indicated. The mid-high long vowels [e:] and [o:] were shifted to [i:] and [u:]. The low front long vowel [a:] then moved higher towards [æ:], and the mid-low long vowels [ɛ:] and [ɔ:] shifted first to [e:] and [o:] and were then diphthongised to [eɪ] and [oʊ] at a later stage of the shift. The half-low long vowel [æ:] was shifted to [e:] and

---

7. The interesting point about these movements is that they were breakings of the long vowels into diphthongs that shifted through the area of the associated short vowels [ɪ] and [ʊ], picking these up as the second half of the diphthong as they moved through this area of the vowel trapezoid (cf. fig. 6.2). The closer they moved to the central schwa vowel [ə] they temporarily picked up this vowel as the first half of the diphthong. At a later stage they moved further down the trapezoid, the [ə] becoming [a] as they moved into the area of that short low front vowel.

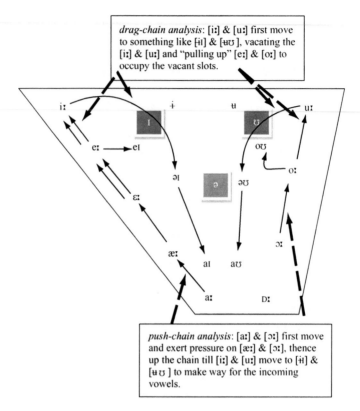

> *drag-chain analysis:* [iː] & [uː] first move to something like [ɨi] & [ʉʊ], vacating the [iː] & [uː] and "pulling up" [eː] & [oː] to occupy the vacant slots.

> *push-chain analysis:* [aː] & [ɔː] first move and exert pressure on [æː] & [ɔː], thence up the chain till [iː] & [uː] move to [ɨ] & [ʉʊ] to make way for the incoming vowels.

FIGURE 6.1. Two conventional explanations of the GVS, drag-chain and push-chain, both of which were probably involved in the shifts

then moved along with [ɛː] to [eː] and then to [eɪ]. The final shifts were from [eː] to [eɪ] and [oː] to [ou], although it is a moot point which of the shifts preceded the others.

There are, of course, several irregularities that can be observed even in "Standard British English",[8] and the stages that these shifts went through before they reached their modern positions in the vowel trapezoid are a matter of continual dispute. In addition, the conventional account represents only the result of the GVS in the standard, and it completely leaves out all other varieties of English, in which either the shift did not occur, or, if it did, the end product is varied. It is thus a product of the funnel vision of English. For example, the end point of the shift from [iː] results in a range of possibilities, for example, [aɪ], [ɔɪ], [ɒɪ]. This would then give us variable shifting as in figure 6.2 for [iː].

---

8. However, like Trudgill (1999), I am extremely unwilling to use this term at this particular juncture. I have thus chosen to place it between quotation marks.

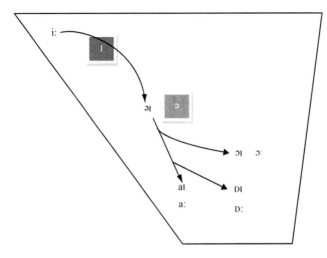

FIGURE 6.2. The variable shifting of [ɪ:]

Disregarding these irregularities and disputes, however, the GVS, when seen in this light, does indeed give all the appearances of being a unified phonetic movement producing homogenised "modern Standard English" from "late Middle English". As a heuristic principle, it has served its purpose in teaching "the history of English", but, in doing so, it has also helped to mythologise this putative historical development as "awe-inspiring", "remarkable", "influential", and so on and has contributed towards the aura of "superiority" and homogeneity constructed for "modern Standard English" (see the "true" statements derived from the conceptual metaphors for language presented in fig. 5.1, chap. 5).

In several chapters, I have challenged the very legitimacy of talking about "a language" as a unique system, since that presupposes the ability to distinguish between different homogeneous language systems and denies the validity of heterogeneity and variability in human language as a sociocognitive phenomenon. Clyne (1992) talks of "pluricentric languages"—those that are not restricted to one central geographical area—and even if we were to remain on the level of standard languages, there are by now a number of different "standard Englishes" (Standard British English, Standard American English, possibly also Standard Australian English), and there are plenty of candidates waiting in the wings to receive the accolade of "standardness" (e.g. Standard Scottish English, which is not the same thing as Scots; Standard Irish English; and even Standard Indian English).

For argument's sake, let us now assume that the unifying factor that has, along with other powerful arguments, allowed this particular kind of symbolic power to be constructed can be shown to be, if not a chimera, then at the very least a much more complicated set of vowel shifts that is always potentially part and parcel of varieties of English. Let us also assume that this more complicated set of vowel shifts is as active today as it always has been. In that case, would we not then lose the beauty, the simplicity of that heuristic principle? Would we not lose the ability to present the history of English as a series of coherent developmental steps towards a homogeneous English language? My argument will be that this is precisely what it does imply.

4. GVS DISPUTES

Giancarlo (2001) discusses the ways in which the GVS has been represented by others in diagrammatic and tabular form as a way of simplifying, visualising, and generally making palatable to the uninitiated student the phonetic complexities of the shifts that it covers. His overall point is that it is a way of telling "the story" of English. However, he admits that it is the story of the development of standard English that is at stake rather than the story of the GVS itself. The dispute that the diagrams have generated—possibly precisely *because* vowel shifts have been represented as diagrams—is whether we have a chain reaction in the whole of the vowel system and whether the set of movements was sparked off by the shift of the long high vowels [iː] and [uː]. That is, at issue is whether this movement "dragged" the mid-high vowels [eː] and [oː] into the places vacated in the vowel trapezoid by the diphthongisation of the long high vowels, or whether the initial movement was the raising of the mid-high vowels [eː] and [oː] and the mid-low vowels [ɛː] and [ɔː] into the upper slots, "pushing" the occupants of those slots out. In any event, we have a mixture of "drag-chain" and "push-chain" effects that can be represented in the form of a diagram without really knowing whether the conventional wisdom reflects the facts. This dispute can still be found in literature on the GVS today, and, since it is not my purpose to argue about the fine points of historical phonology in this chapter, I will not discuss the merits of the two explanatory camps of drag-chainers and push-chainers (cf. fig. 6.1 above).

The other major issue concerns the process of the diphthongisation of the high vowels. Did [iː] move to a more central position, say, something like [ɨ] and thence to [əɪ], or did it move to [eɪ] first? Did [uː] move to something like [ʉʊ] and thence to [əʊ], or did it move to [oʊ] first? In addition, there are varieties of English in northern England and Scotland in which certain parts of the "chain" shifts did not occur, a point that is not lost either on Stockwell and Minkova or on Lass. The classic example is the failure of [uː] to shift to [aʊ] in Lowland Scottish English, the Northumberland dialect and Tyneside Geordie.

The explanation for this failure neatly exemplifies the kind of arguments that are used to bolster the drag-chain or push-chain theories. Push-chainers such as Lass maintain that because [oː] was fronted to [øː] in these northern dialects, it did not come under pressure to diphthongise. But it is relatively easy to imagine a drag-chainer claiming that if a dialect could be found in which [oː] was fronted and [uː] nevertheless diphthongised, the push-chainer's argument disintegrates.

Further dispute revolves around the nature of the evidence used to support different interpretations of what, how and when shifts in the GVS took place. Wolfe (1972) and Lass (1989) both rely on the real-time evidence of orthoepists such as Hart, Gil and Bullokar in the sixteenth century and Cooper, Daines and Wallis in the seventeenth, whereas Stockwell and Minkova challenge the phonetic accuracy of the orthoepists' observations and instead rely on spellings and rhymes. This leads them to posit much earlier datings for the first shifts in the GVS, and it also leads them to challenge the push-chain theory. To find orthographic evidence of this kind, Stockwell and Minkova need to examine texts that are written in localised varieties of English. But even Lass's argument on the partial failure of [uː] to shift forces him to consider northern varieties of English.

As we saw above, several varieties of English, both within Great Britain and in the wider English-speaking world, also show different end points in the diphthongisation process, [əɪ], [ɒɪ] or [ɔɪ] for [aɪ] and [əʊ] and [ɒʊ] for [aʊ]. If we add to this the fact that since the GVS a number of shortening and lengthening processes have taken place together with the fact that certain dialects in the United States (Boberg 2000; Labov, Ash & Boberg 2006) and in New Zealand (Bauer et al. 2007; Trudgill & Hannah 2002) are currently undergoing shifts in the short back and front vowels, then it is time to start reconsidering the significance of the GVS and to give up the teaching heuristic as a simplistic justification of the development of the standard.

In the following section I indicate how conventional representations of the GVS have been challenged and how this leads to the need for a much more careful analysis of the phonetic processes involved in vowel shifting in general. The final link in my argumentative chain concerns the producers of the vowels themselves. After all, even if we believe with Weinreich, Labov and Herzog (1968) that languages do not change, but that people change languages, we still need to fix the dialectological and phonetic evidence to a theory of how speakers perceive innovations, of how they adopt them and of how those newly adopted innovations are diffused through space and time. This problem will be tackled in the final section.

5. CHALLENGING THE GVS

Of the various writers who in the 1990s carried on Stockwell and Minkova's work of deconstructing the traditional conceptualisation of the GVE, Paul Johnston presents the most detailed argument and, to my mind, the most plausible one. I shall focus on it almost exclusively in this section.

Before we examine Johnston's argument, however, we need to consider a few hard facts about standard languages. In effect standard languages are nothing more or less than "synecdochic dialects" (Joseph 1987). That is, they are dialects that are "chosen"—generally, but not always, by chance[9]—to "represent" all the others in the construction of the "language" itself. During the process of standardisation a synecdochic dialect is also prey to the introduction into its lexical, grammatical and phonological systems of elements from other dialects and other "languages". In this sense, a standard language is never free from innovations introduced either naturally or by force of codification processes that are often controlled institutionally by language academies, education systems and political engineering.

In addition, many standard languages begin life as written variants synecdochically representing the dialect varieties, both social and geographical, which exist within the territory in which they are destined to become a sociopolitical "standard". The final stage in the standardisation process is often, but not always, the construction of an oral standard, and this final stage can lead to divisive dispute over what is or is not part of that oral standard (see, e.g., Crowley 2003; Milroy & Milroy 1985; Honey 1997; Carter 1999). This has been the case within the last 30 years in Britain, as we shall see in chapter 10, and the dispute has by no means reached a settlement (Bex & Watts 1999). In the case of English, the beginnings of a concern with the oral standard can be traced back to the second half of the eighteenth century (Sheridan 1762; Walker 1791), although much of the groundwork had already been laid by the orthoepists in the late sixteenth and seventeenth centuries.

If we accept this very brief sketch of the standardisation of English, it follows that even if we were to restrict the GVS to the sixteenth and seventeenth centuries, we would still need to look closely at the dialects to find evidence of vowel shifts, since there was no standard *oral* English at all till, at the very earliest, the latter half of the eighteenth century—that is, of course, if we are prepared to accept the existence of an oral standard at all. There is also evidence in the present-day dialects that vowel shifts are still continuing, and if we consider some of the currently more prestigious varieties of English in the United Kingdom (the "infamous" Estuary English) and the United States (parts of the Midwest), it is noticeable that they may be exerting a significant influence on the shifting of vowels in oral standard English English (to use a term coined by Trudgill [1999]) and oral standard American English. If we carry this argument back into the past beyond the sixteenth century, which is what we need to do to identify the beginnings of the GVS, the only place we will ever be able to locate those vowel changes will be in localised forms of writing: in the dialects. This, in turn, means accepting the validity of occasional spellings as evidence for vowel shifting, which is what Wolfe (1972: chap. 4) rejects in favour of a close study of the orthoepists.

---

9. Two examples of a standard's being "artificially" constructed from the dialects making up a language are Nynorsk (created by Ivar Åsen in the nineteenth century) and Rhaeto-Rumantsch (created by Heinrich Schmid in the early 1980s).

Johnston, on the other hand, argues that, if we seriously intend to look for the beginnings of the GVS, "orthoepic evidence is, in fact, too late" (1992: 205). He supports his argument by locating the likely areas of vowel shifting in the dialects through a close study of important sources of evidence such as the *Survey of English Dialects*, Anderson's *A Structural Atlas of the English Dialects* (1987), Kristensson's *Survey of Middle English Dialects* ([1967] 1988), and McIntosh, Samuels and Benskin's *A Linguistic Atlas of Late Mediaeval English* (1986).

Johnston is well aware of the vagaries of relying on occasional spellings. The first difficulty in interpreting possible phonological realisations from graphological evidence is the limited representational power of the Roman alphabet, complicated after the Conquest by the adoption of Norman-based spelling conventions. "Middle English" length interchange processes followed by short vowel raisings make it almost impossible to differentiate between long vowels that have gone through this process and those that may have been raised without shortening during the GVS. If we add to these difficulties in using occasional spellings the simple fact that what we are looking for is spellings that are "necessarily 'occasional' and sporadic" (Johnston 1992: 206), it is not difficult to appreciate the unwillingness of such researchers as Patricia Wolfe to consider this sort of evidence.

Indeed, even Johnston suggests that occasional spellings are hard to distinguish from "simple errors". This comment by Johnston, however, is a distinctly odd one to make. Surely an "error" in spelling presupposes a well established set of conventions for spelling. Even Wolfe's refusal to take spellings into account on the grounds that "anyone who has corrected many high school essays will be reluctant to ascribe much...phonetic accuracy to occasional spellings" (1972: 115) becomes vacuous if we consider that most of those "incorrect" spellings are an attempt to represent graphologically the way the speller pronounces the word.[10] I would argue that precisely because they are "errors"—a point that in any case has little substance in the absence of a generally accepted set of spelling conventions—they are the kind of evidence we should be looking for. Attempts by local scribes to find a way of representing graphologically what they say provide invaluable insights into the earlier phonological structure of the dialects.

Johnston's careful analysis of occasional spellings from all parts of the country (see his table 2) reveals the need to reinterpret the GVS as two (possibly more) smaller chain shifts that must have taken place in different parts of the country at different periods of time. In general, he is able to differentiate a shift in the high front and back vowels in two areas that would hardly warrant the assumption of frequent sociolinguistic contact among their speakers, the Midlands and East Anglia, on the one hand, and the Southwest, on the other.

---

10. Voeste (2008), who has looked in detail at variant spellings in German texts in the sixteenth century, comes to the conclusion that writers may actually have gained prestige in spelling a word in as many different ways as possible, which is further evidence of the lack of conventionalised standards of orthography.

For these areas the focus of attention in terms of trade, migration, prestige, and so on must have been, primarily, local centres such as Norwich, Exeter, Chester, Stafford and, secondarily, London. The second chain shift affects the bottom half of the vowel trapezoid and overlaps the shift in the high vowels in the northern Midlands. The focus of attention here becomes Yorkshire and in particular the Plain of York, which lay outside the area of overlap. Evidence from occasional spellings from this area allows Johnston to surmise that "at least on the Plain of York, low-vowel raising occurred so early that it not only precedes the high-vowel raising chain but also Open Syllable Lengthening" (1992: 214). That is, the shifting can be traced to the early thirteenth century or earlier.

This is strong evidence to support Stockwell and Minkova's rejection of the GVS as a coherent, unitary phenomenon. It is also strong evidence on which to base a rejection of interpretations of the GVS that see it as an element in the process of the standardisation of English, even if, as in the case of Jespersen, Wolfe and also Chomsky and Halle in *The Sound Pattern of English* (1968), this is not their explicit averred purpose. Johnston, however, goes further than this. In support of the statement that "Vowel shifting...can be described as a continuous process rather than as something unique to a specific, long-past period, and the consequent reduction in the number of explanations needed to account for all the data a gain in simplicity rather than a loss" (1992: 219), he suggests that studying the phonetic processes involved in any vowel shifting in the present can help us to gain a fuller picture of vowel shifting in the past. Some of this work has already been done by Labov, Yaeger and Steiner (1972) in their discussion of the connections between peripherality (or tensing) of vowels and raising, on the one hand, and deperipheralisation (laxing) of long vowels resulting in double-mora nuclei and consequent diphthongisation, on the other. Johnston suggests that more attention should be paid to phonetic environments such as final or pre-pausal position, added stress (often for emphasis) and slower speech rate, all of which tend to produce an increase in vowel length rather than peripherality. Lengthening "pure" vowels is likely to produce an increase in sonority. In the case of the high vowels this opens up one mora of the vowel to produce nuclei such as [ɪi] and [ʉʊ].

All of these processes are involved in the apparent, and in all likelihood necessary, instability of vowel systems. They might lead us to suggest that, no matter how we try to explain the GVS, we are ultimately forced to admit that it really was not quite as "great" as has been assumed in the literature on the history of the language following Ellis, Sweet, Jespersen and Luick. Johnston's work provides strong evidence of at least two partially independent, but at some stage interlocking, small vowel shifts, and it is quite possible that further research of this kind will necessitate the introduction of more small vowel shifts. At this point, however, the option that this leaves us of denying that the GVS ever took place at all makes me a little uneasy, and this is the final step in my argument.

6. SOCIOLINGUISTIC ASPECTS OF THE GVS

Denying that the GVS ever took place is a dangerous step to take if it involves denying that there was ever an ideology of the GVS based on the **greatness myth** and ultimately the central **linguistic homogeneity myth** that formed part of the Milroys' ideology of the standardisation of English (1999). It is important to recognise the existence of certain powerful discourses and to investigate how they could have come into existence. If we carry out such an investigation, we are automatically involved in opening up the historicity of those discourses, and, in the case of the GVS discourse, this ultimately takes us into the realm of historical sociolinguistics.

The major aspect of the GVS that is consistently ignored, although often mentioned briefly by researchers as a desideratum, is the question of the actuation of the changes that took place in the vowel systems of the varieties of English from around the thirteenth century (if Johnston's analysis is sound) to the end of the eighteenth century. This is not to say, of course, that vowel shifts were not occurring prior to the thirteenth century, or that they have not occurred since the end of the eighteenth and are still in progress today. Weinreich, Labov and Herzog's (1968) actuation problem concerns the mechanisms involved in the introduction into a language variety of an innovative construction, its adoption by members of a community of practice[11] and its diffusion to other communities of practice, and although we know that it is almost impossible to observe these processes historically, we do know enough about what happens in present-day speech communities to be sure that they are always active (Milroy 1992; Labov 2001). From sociolinguistic research, we also know that the slenderest of differences in the quality of a vowel can operate as a salient marker of social and geographical differentiation between speakers.

Let us now apply these insights to a possible scenario of text types and everyday communicative situations on the Plain of York in the thirteenth century, on the well-founded assumption that Johnston's occasional spellings are indeed signs of a shift in the low vowels that had already taken place before Open Syllable Lengthening. We first need to know more about the kinds of texts that would have been produced locally in English in that area and for what purpose. But even without access to Johnston's sources, we can be reasonably certain that "official" texts would have been produced in Anglo-Norman French and possibly Latin. Writing a text in English would thus have been aimed primarily at an English-speaking audience. Literacy in the thirteenth century is not likely to have been common in the English-speaking community, so those texts would have been produced for oral performance of some kind. It is therefore highly likely that a scribe would introduce spellings

---

11. Weinreich, Labov and Herzog referred to the phenomenon of the "speech community", but more recent research by Eckert (2000) and Eckert and McConnell-Ginet (2003) has developed and worked more fruitfully with the concept of the "community of practice", taken from the work of Wenger (1998) and Lave and Wenger (1991).

that reflected the phonological constructions of the language in his local area. But that scribe will have been privileged enough to be one of the few who were literate. If the texts were largely for oral communication, why were there not more spellings that reflected the vowel shifts? It is here that we begin to see the tensions between oral communication and communication through writing— what I called *inscribed orality* in chapter 3. The logical assumption is that the scribe must have been writing within the framework of orthographic conventions which regulated the ways in which English was to be represented in written form and at the same time within the framework of patterns of oral communication within the English-speaking community. But judging by the haphazard nature of orthography before the advent of its standardisation from the end of the sixteenth century on and taking into account Voeste's (2008) evidence of the prestige of spelling variation, this may be a false assumption to make. Producing the "mis-spelling" of a word by reflecting the oral quality of the vowel may thus be interpreted as a way of—unconsciously—documenting membership in a community of practice and, at the same time, as documenting membership in the community of "writers in English".

Tensions such as these become more obvious the more closely the texts approach oral communication, as in the case of personal letters. This is well documented in the Paston letters, the problem here being that they date from the fifteenth century (N. Davis 1971 and 1976; R. Barber 1981). If the beginnings of one of the chain shifts of the GVS are locatable in the thirteenth century, then evidence of the social tensions between a writer and his reading public in terms of whether he documents identity in a community of practice or a discourse community[12] through written texts becomes even harder to find. On the assumption that the salience of vowel shifts may mark social distinctions of various kinds and that these distinctions frequently lead to accommodation to the language of socially more prestigious speakers (J. Smith 1993), the area in which the two shifts overlapped, the Northeast, suddenly becomes crucial in investigating the geographical diffusion of the shifts, particularly in the direction of East Anglia and London.

The major problem in dealing with written texts from the fifteenth century on is that the orthographic conventions, haphazard as they often are, generally reflect the language of areas prior to the vowel shifts that lie outside the domain of the GVS, which Chomsky and Halle (1968) make abundantly clear. There are two points that we can derive from this fact. First, we desperately need to access texts written prior to the fifteenth century in those areas in which we know the shifts associated with the GVS were either already completed or were well under way. The introduction of the printing press in the last three decades of the fifteenth century focused the orthographic conventions of printing on the phonologically more conservative varieties of London and the Southeast. Second, precisely because of this intensified focus on the language of the

---

12. See Watts 2008 for an explanation of these terms in reference to the grammarians of the eighteenth century.

capital, the work of the orthoepists takes on a radically new significance. Orthoepists such as Hart, Gil, Cooper, Daines and Wallis, however good or deficient they were as phoneticians, were primarily concerned with standardising the orthographic conventions of written English. Their comments on how various vowels were pronounced were prompted by an acute awareness of the discrepancy between phonological structures and the graphology with which they were represented, not by a desire to standardise pronunciation. In striving to promote a standardised orthography, they were simultaneously promoting the language variety of London and the area around London as their model and thereby taking the first steps towards making that variety the synecdochic dialect that ultimately became "Standard English English". Unwittingly, therefore, they may have been the first to champion the funnel vision of equating the history of English with the history of the standard variety.

Let us now turn the wheel full circle. In the first section of this chapter I suggested that the adjective "great" with reference to the vowel shifts that are generally subsumed under the GVS refers to the assumed grandiose proportions, the uniqueness, the coherence and the historical significance of those shifts. Stockwell and Minkova, Giancarlo, Johnston and others would probably not want to admit the term "great" to the vowel shift for the simple reason that it was not one vowel shift and that vowels, in any case, are always shifting. If we are interested in researching critically into how the traditional discourse of the history of English has been constructed, however, the GVS loses none of its compulsive power. It certainly does become something of a chimera, but one that we reject at our peril if we are at all interested in putting a number of records straight in the history—and here I would in fact prefer to say "histories"—of English.

One of our aims as sociolinguists should be to shift our attention to an examination of the GVS from two perspectives other than the purely linguistic. First we need to look more closely at the discursive construction of the GVS and link it explicitly to the discursive construction of the standard. In doing so, we reveal other myths that underlie and permeate the discourse, some of which were dealt with in chapter 5 and others that will appear in chapter 7. Second, we need to consider speakers of the many varieties of English within England and Scotland in the period from the thirteenth to the eighteenth century and what they were actually doing with language; in other words, we need to look at vowel shifts from a more sociolinguistic perspective. This second goal lies outside the scope of the present book. The first, however, will be considered in more detail later.

7. THE *MYTH OF GREATNESS* RECONSIDERED

Examining the GVS from the perspective of how it is discursively constructed leads to the deconstruction of a linguistic phenomenon, or, as I now wish to argue, a set of linguistic phenomena, as the crucial historical watershed between a precursor of "modern Standard English" and "modern Standard English" itself. The stories told in constructing the *greatness myth* thus have little to do with the vowel shift itself, since vowel shifting is an ever-present phenomenon throughout all varieties of English. It may even be an inherent feature of human language in general. It is not the vowel shift, or vowel shifts, or the phenomenon of vowel shifting as a linguistic universal which is held up as a unique historical phenomenon inspiring the admiration and awe of the modern student of English linguistics, but rather the presumed result of the shift(s): the emergence of "modern standard English".

Constructing the GVS was thus necessary to crystallise a historical pedigree for the English language as the homogeneous national language of a sociohistorically homogeneous nation-state in the twentieth century. The GVS also served its purpose in raising English to the same national language status in other states in the late nineteenth and twentieth centuries, notably the United States, Australia, New Zealand and Canada.

The danger of using the GVS as a useful heuristic in teaching the history of English is that, unless the instructor is perfectly clear about the true dimensions and the ubiquity of vowel shifts in varieties of English, the history presented will focus inevitably on the rise of "modern standard English". The GVS will thus become instrumental in presenting a funnel view of English, obscuring the heterogeneity of forms of language when used in social practice and the rich array of varieties of what we choose to call English across the world. Studying what leads to vowel shifting is a fascinating area of phonetics and phonology, and in its own right deserves a great deal more consideration of what people actually do with language in the cut-and-thrust of emergent social practice. Embarking on that kind of study in this chapter would have diverted us from the purpose of the book, which is to reveal the myths that lie at the basis of traditional constructions of the history of English.

In chapters 8, 9 and 10 I consider in more detail the close connection between a homogeneous national language and the fiction of a socially homogeneous nation-state, in which, as Jespersen perceived the situation, there was a danger of a "tendency towards the splitting up of the language into dialects—class dialects and local dialects". In chapters 9 and 10, I shall raise the issue of what Jespersen calls, in conjunction with what he considers to be the undesirability of the language splitting up into dialects, "the normal speech of the educated class, what may be called Standard English". The *greatness myth*, like all the other myths discussed in this book, is derived from the archetypal *linguistic homogeneity myth*. The following chapter refocuses our attention on the possible construction of modern myths about English. The central text to which I shall turn my attention is Swift's *Proposal for Correcting, Improving and Ascertaining the English Tongue*, published in 1712.

Chapter 7

Reinterpreting Swift's *A Proposal for Correcting, Improving and Ascertaining the English Tongue*

Challenging an embryonic modern myth

And as for the Dean, you know what I mean,
If a printer will print him he'll scarce come off clean.
—from "The Dean's Pamphlet",
a popular eighteenth-century Irish song

1. POTENTIAL NEW MYTHS

Not all myths have a long history. Some may have been constructed in the relatively recent past, and others may still be in the process of construction. Sociolinguists must be careful to recognise, in their own interpretations of their research findings, the potential the evidence may have for the discursive construction of myths about the past or present state of a language. One of these potential myths, the *creolisation of English myth*, was discussed in chapter 4, in which we observed how (socio)linguistic discourse may be carried beyond the discursive practices of the academic linguistic community and become part of the overall system of beliefs about language that are shared or contested.

One of the principal arguments in this book has been that the prototypical myth in English (but, by wider implication, in any "language") is that of a homogeneous, structurally perfect linguistic system, and I have classified

I would like to thank Regula Koenig, one of my former students, for allowing me to use her investigation into the historical framework without which Swift's pamphlet cannot be properly understood. Her paper on this subject was excellent and has greatly assisted me in locating the connections between what appear on the surface to be Swift's ideas and his satirical intentions in voicing them.

157

this prototypical myth as the *linguistic homogeneity myth*. I have taken pains to link it to the ways in which the idea of homogeneity can be applied just as easily to other cultural categories such as social structure and social institutions, political systems, the nation-state, religion and race. My intention has been not merely to deconstruct some of the more common linguistic myths concerning the history of English, but also to focus on three potential new myths:

1. the argument that Middle English (and by extension modern English) or even other earlier forms of language contact involving English can be classified as a creole or creole-like language (see chap. 4);
2. the focus on a complaint tradition in tracing out the ideology of standardisation in English, which will be dealt with in this chapter; and
3. the current insistence that English is the "global language" par excellence (which I'll discuss in chap. 11).

However, rather than trace out the development of a new myth, this chapter sets out to identify the myths that have been discussed so far (particularly in chap. 5) in Jonathan Swift's pamphlet *A Proposal for Correcting, Improving and Ascertaining the English Tongue*, written in 1712. My central aim is to deconstruct the interpretation of this pamphlet as "the great classic of complaint literature in English" (Milroy & Milroy 1999: 27) by interpreting how Swift makes skilful use of language myths for his own political and polemical purposes. It highlights the danger of assuming that Swift's text—and perhaps others—lies within the tradition of complaining about language, and it does this by relating significant sections of the *Proposal* in which the myths occur to the sociohistorical, sociopolitical and sociocultural context within which Swift was writing. It argues that Swift may well have been aware of the myths and was primarily using them for his own purposes in the *Proposal*. My interpretation of the pamphlet thus goes against the grain of "official" interpretations offered in historical sociolinguistics, and my major point is that ignoring the sociopolitical framework within which Swift wrote the pamphlet and his underlying purpose in writing it could easily lead to interpretations that lend themselves to mythologisation. It can be dangerous to view the discourse that forms part of the archive of an earlier historical period as constituting a coherent whole from the perspective of one's own archives. Without drawing on important sociohistorical evidence, this is always a latent danger.

2. THE "IDEOLOGY OF THE STANDARD LANGUAGE" AND THE COMPLAINT TRADITION

I provide an interpretation of Swift's proposal that goes against the grain, but I also need to make the following point clear: there is no doubt in my mind that James and Lesley Milroy's book *Authority in Language: Investigating Standard English* is a classic in the sociolinguistic and sociohistorical literature. First published in 1985, it has already gone into two further editions since then (1991 and 1999). In his own contributions to work on the "ideology of the standard language" (1996, 1999, 2000, 2001, 2002, 2005, 2007), James Milroy repeatedly emphasises the distinction between two very different approaches towards the phenomenon of human language. On the one hand, theoretical linguists hold that language is a cognitive phenomenon in that it is developed mentally by each individual; on the other hand, standard language cultures tend to believe that language is "the possession of only a few persons...who have the authority to impose the rules of language on everyone else" (Milroy 2007: 135). The first view of language is not just cognitive; it is also social, since none of us, as socially functioning human beings, can escape from acquiring language. In chapter 1, I argued that we should thus categorise that view as *sociocognitive*. The second view of language, however, is committed to the belief that language is a cultural product on a par with such cultural "achievements" as law, art, education, religion and science (see the discussion of the term *Kultursprache* in chaps. 2 and 5). In this second sense, language is outside the individual and is imposed as an overarching set of rules and constraints that pressure her to acquire forms of linguistic behaviour that are in some sense appropriate to conventionalised social norms. Milroy and Milroy (1999) call this second view of language the "ideology of the standard language", and its major overlapping characteristics are a belief in the notion of *correctness*, the importance of some form of *authority*, the significance of *social prestige* and a belief in the idea of *legitimacy*.

Their general arguments are well founded and acceptable, but I shall carry the main argument further and show that the ideology of the standard language should be seen as a subtext of the wider eighteenth-century *ideology of politeness*, which functioned as a discourse archive for the social life of the upper and middling orders of society in Britain from around the time of the Glorious Revolution in 1688 till the first half of the twentieth century. In the course of time, the two ideologies became so interwoven that the standard language grew into a rallying point of strongly nationalistic discourse that was transformed into colonialist and imperialist discursive practices, which only began to break down in the 1950s. Crowley (2003), Mugglestone (1995) and I (2002, 2003a) have made this argument a little more explicitly than Milroy, although the first edition of *Authority in Language* acted as a catalyst in studying the ideological discourse of standard English more critically than hitherto.[1]

Once a standard has emerged, or even while it is in the process of formation, its advocates tend to criticise any variety of language that does not measure

---

1. To show how the language question was taken up as part of the ideological discourse of politeness, I shall argue in chapter 8 that the "question" itself acquired an almost mythical validation, which, when fused with the ideology of politeness, helped to create the potent modern myth that language *is* a cultural product rather than an individual sociocognitive possession (cf. the discussion of the term *Kultursprache* in chap. 5).

up to their conceptualisation of what the legitimate language should be; they complain about deficiencies in language structure and language use. The Milroys ([1985] 1999) propose that there is a tradition of complaining that can be located in different kinds of discourse focusing on language. Self-elected defenders of the legitimate language rely on the conceptual metaphor A LANGUAGE IS A HUMAN BEING. They automatically transfer the failings of the language to the speakers themselves, particularly if those failings concern assumed moral qualities of both the language and the speakers. For example, one of the "true" statements derived from the conceptual metaphor is <An upright language is an honest language>. If any fault can be found with the language used by a set of speakers, the negative quality of dishonesty can automatically be attributed to those speakers. The statement <A polished language is a polite language>, which is associated with the statement <A language is polished>, leads to the ascription of lack of politeness in those speakers whose language is considered to display moral defects of any kind, that is, if the statement <A corrupt language reflects the corruption of its speakers> is operative.

The complaint tradition therefore draws on this conceptual metaphor and the statements about language obtained by running it. As Cameron (1995) argues, however, native speakers are generally not aware of such entrenched conceptualisations, since they have been subject since early childhood to a form of socialisation that has constructed them as being "normal" and "correct". Speakers are ideologically predisposed towards accepting them as naturalised (see Fairclough 1989) and as true, so that they form part of a system of symbolic power which is simply accepted as fact (see Bourdieu 1991). Attempts to correct this line of thought are ultimately futile, and Cameron suggests that researchers would be well advised to face up to this fact. However, the complaint tradition itself reaches much further back than the period of time during which the ideology of the standard language has been in evidence. In chapter 5, I suggested that the same kinds of statement were also present in Higden's *Polychronicon*. This leads to the suggestion that all that is needed for a complaint tradition to emerge is a language that is considered to be superior to other languages. In Higden's case, the superior, or legitimate, language in terms of religion was clearly Latin, and there is a slight indication from the short excerpt from the *Polychronicon* analysed in chapter 5 that (Anglo-Norman) French functioned as a quasi-official language beyond Church circles.

3. SWIFT'S *PROPOSAL* AS THE BEGINNING OF A COMPLAINT TRADITION

Although the Milroys ([1985] 1999) certainly do suggest that possible complaints about English go as far back as Higden and Caxton (see also chap. 5), J. Milroy (1999) states very specifically that Swift's *Proposal* represents the beginning of "the ideological basis of the extreme complaints" about English in the tradition of "the battle against evil and corruption". The myths presented in chapter 5 show that this is not the case. The cultural reifications of all the language myths discussed in that chapter are present in Swift's *Proposal*, but, without the catalyst fusing them together, they cannot properly become part of the ideology of the standard language. In addition, what Milroy and Milroy (1999) and J. Milroy (1999) do not mention is the opposite tendency to extol the supposed virtues of English rather than complain about its insufficiencies and corruption.

An early representative of the discourse of praise is Richard Carew's "An Epistle concerning the Excellencies of the English Tongue" (cf. chap. 5). In the Epistle, Carew maintains that "whateuer Tongue will gain the Race of Perfection must run upon these four wheeles, *SIGNIFICANCIE, EASINESS, COPIOUSNESS,* and *SWEETNESS*" (1769: 4), which he then proceeds to demonstrate by comparing English with other languages. There are signs in Swift's *Proposal* that, even if he had not been acquainted with Carew's text, Swift was certainly well acquainted with ideas extolling the superiority of English over other European languages—as we shall see. There are thus elements of the discourse of praise as well as those of the discourse of complaint to be found in the *Proposal*.

The text consists of the following 24 paragraphs. For each, I give a brief summary of the contents (see fig. 7.1).

The Milroys maintain that the *Proposal* begins in paragraph 2 (cf. line 26 in the text as presented above) with the following explicit complaint:

> My Lord; I do here in the Name of all the Learned and Polite Persons of the Nation, complain to your Lordship, as *First Minister*, that our Language is extremely imperfect...

They omit the rest of the paragraph, however, which runs as follows:

> ...that its daily Improvements are by no means in proportion to its daily Corruptions; and the Pretenders to polish and refine it, have chiefly multiplied Abuses and Absurdities; and, that in many Instances, it offends against every Part of Grammar. But lest Your Lordship should think my Censure to be too severe, I shall take leave to be more particular.

Although Swift explicitly declares his statement to be a complaint ("I do here...complain to your Lordship...that our Language is extremely imperfect..."), that does not necessarily mean that the whole text should be literally taken as a complaint. Contemporary readers of Swift must have expected that anything written by him would be either satire or satirical narrative (cf. *Gulliver's Travels*). The complaint that the language is "extremely imperfect" consciously sets up the metaphorical blend A MORALLY PURE LANGUAGE IS A PERFECT LANGUAGE, through which we can assume that (a) the

A Proposal for Correcting, Improving, and Ascertaining the English Tongue, in a Letter to the Most Honourable Robert Earl of Oxford and Mortimer, Lord High Treasurer of Great Britain, Printed from Benjamin Tooke, at the Middle Temple Gate, Fleetstreet, 1712

Para. 1: Direct address to the Earl of Oxford pointing out what has led him to write the letter

1 To the Most Honourable Robert Earl of Oxford, &c.
2 My Lord,
3 What I had the Honour of mentioning to Your Lordship some time ago in Conversation, was not
4 a new Thought, just then started by Accident or, Occasion but the Result of long Reflection; and
5 I have been confirmed in my Sentiments by the Opinion of some very judicious Persons, with
6 whom I consulted. They all agreed, That nothing would be of greater Use towards the
7 Improvement of Knowledge and Politeness, than some effectual Method for *Correcting*,
8 *Enlarging, and Ascertaining our Language*; and they think it a Work very possible to be
9 compassed, under the Protection of a Prince, the Countenance and Encouragement of a
10 Ministry, and the Care of Proper Persons chosen for such an Undertaking. I was glad to find
11 Your Lordship's Answer in so different a Style, from what hath been commonly made use of
12 on the like Occasions, for some Years past, that all such Thoughts must be deferred to a
13 Time of Peace: A Topick which some have carried so far, that they would not have us, by any
14 means, think of preserving our Civil or Religious Constitution, because we were engaged in a
15 War abroad. It will be among the distinguishing Marks of your Ministry, My Lord, that you
16 had the Genius above all such Regards, and that no reasonable Proposal for the Honour, the
17 Advantage, or the Ornament of Your Country, however foreign to Your immediate Office was
18 ever neglected by You. I confess, the Merit of this Candor and Condescension is very much
19 lessened, because Your Lordship hardly leaves us room to offer our good Wishes, removing all
20 our Difficulties, and supplying all our Wants, faster than the most visionary Projector can
21 adjust his Schemes. And therefore, My Lord, the Design of this Paper is not so much to offer
22 You *Ways and Means*, as to complain of a *Grievance*, the redressing of which is to be Your
23 own Work, as much as that of paying the *Nation's Debts*, or opening a Trade into the *South*
24 Sea; and though not of such immediate Benefit as either of these, or any other of Your glorious
25 Actions, yet perhaps, in future Ages, not less to Your Honour.

Para. 2: The statement of the complaint

26 My Lord; I do here in the Name of all the Learned and Polite Persons of the Nation, complain
27 to your Lordship, as *First Minister*, the our Language is extremely imperfect; that its daily
28 Improvements are by no means in proportion to its daily Corruptions; and the Pretenders to
29 polish and refine it, have chiefly multiplied Abuses and Absurdities; and, that in many
30 Instances, it offends against every Part of Grammar. But lest Your Lordship should think my
31 Censure to be too severe, I shall take leave to be more particular.

Paras. 3 & 4: Reasons English is less refined than Italian, Spanish or French:
**   a. (Para. 3) The period between the Roman occupation till just before the Norman Conquest**

32 I Believe Your Lordship will agree with me in the Reason, Why our Language is less Refined
33 than those of Italy, *Spain*, or *France*. 'Tis plain that the *Latin* Tongue, in its Purity, was never
34 in this Island, towards the Conquest of which few or no Attempts were made till the Time of
35 *Claudius*; neither was that Language ever so vulgar in *Britain*, as it is known to have been in
36 *Gaul* and *Spain*. Further, we find, that the *Roman* Legions here, were at length all recalled to
37 help their Country against the Goths, and other barbarous Invaders. Mean time, the *Britains*,
38 *left to shift for themselves, and daily harassed by cruel Inroads from the* Picts, were forced to
39 call in the Saxons for their Defense; who, consequently, reduced the greatest Part of the Island
40 to their own Power, drove the Britains into the most remote and mountainous Parts, and the rest
41 of the Country, in Customs, Religion, and Language, became wholly *Saxon*. This I take to be
42 the Reason why there are more *Latin* words remaining in the *British* Tongue, than in the old
43 *Saxon*; which, excepting some few Variations in the Orthography, is the same, in most original
44 Words, with our present *English*, as well as with the *German*, and other *Northern* Dialects.

FIGURE 7.1. Contents of Swift's *Proposal* paragraph by paragraph

b. (Para. 4) the period from Edward the Confessor to the time of Elizabeth

45 *Edward the Confessor* having lived long in *France*, appears to be the first who introduced any
46 mixture of the *French* Tongue with the Saxon; the Court affecting what the Prince was fond of,
47 and others taking it up for a Fashion, as it is now with us. *William the Conqueror* proceeded
48 much further; bringing over with him vast numbers of that Nation; scattering them in every
49 Monastery; giving them great Quantities of Land, directing all Pleadings to be in that
50 Language, and endeavouring to make it universal in the Kingdom. This, at least, is the Opinion
51 generally received. But Your Lordship hath fully convinced me, that the *French* Tongue made
52 yet a greater Progress here under *Harry the Second*, who had large Territories on that
53 Continent, both from his Father and his Wife, made frequent Journeys and Expeditions there,
54 and was always attended with a number of his Countrymen, Retainers at his Court. For some
55 Centuries after, there was a constant Intercourse between *France* and *England*, by the
56 Dominions we possessed there, and the Conquests we made; so that our Language, between
57 two and three hundred Years ago, seems to have had a greater mixture with French. than at
58 present; many Words having been afterwards rejected, and some since the time of *Spencer*;
59 although we have still retained not a few, which have been long antiquated in *France*. I could
60 produce several Instances of both kinds, if it were of any Use or Entertainment.

Para. 5: Reasons for the decline of Latin

61 TO examine into the several Circumstances by which the Language of a Country may be
62 altered, would force me to enter into a wide Field. I shall only observe, That the *Latin*, the
63 *French*, and the *English*, seem to have undergone the same Fortune. The first, from the Days of
64 *Romulus* to those of *Julius Caesar*, suffered perpetual Changes, and by what we meet in those
65 Authors who occasionally speak on that Subject, as well as from certain Fragments of old
66 Laws, it is manifest, that the *Latin*, Three hundred Years before *Tully*, was as unintelligible in
67 his Time, as the English and *French* of the same Period are now; and these two have changed
68 as much since William the *Conqueror* (which is but little less than Seven hundred Years) as the
69 *Latin* appears to have done in the like Term. Whether our Language or the *French* will decline
70 as fast as the *Roman* did, is a Question that would perhaps admit more Debate than it is worth.
71 There were many Reasons for the Corruptions of the last: As, the Change of their Government
72 into a Tyranny, which ruined the Study of Eloquence, there being no further Use of
73 Encouragement for popular Orators: Their giving not only the Freedom of the City, but
74 Capacity for Employments, to several Towns in *Gaul*, *Spain*, and *Germany*, and other distant
75 Parts, as far as Asia; which brought a great Number of foreign Pretenders into *Rome* : The
76 slavish Disposition of the Senate and the People, by which the Wit and Eloquence of the Age
77 were wholly turned into Panegyrick, the most barren of all Subjects: The great Corruption of
78 Manners, and Introduction of foreign Luxury, with foreign Terms to express it; with several
79 others that might be assigned: Not to mention those Invasions from the *Goths* and *Vandals*,
80 which are too obvious to insist on.

Para. 6: The concepts of language perfection and language decay

81 THE *Roman* Language arrived at great Perfection before it began to decay: And the *French* for
82 these last Fifty Years hath been polishing as much as it will bear, and appears to be declining
83 by the natural Inconstancy of that People, and the Affection of some late Authors to introduce
84 and multiply *Cant* Words, which is the most ruinous Corruption in any Language. *La Bruyere* a
85 late celebrated Writer among them, makes use of many hundred new Terms, which are not to be
86 found in any of the common Dictionaries before his Time. But the *English* Tongue is not arrived
87 to such a Degree of Perfection, as to make us apprehend any Thoughts of its Decay; and if it
88 were once refined to a certain Standard, perhaps there might be Ways found out to fix it for
89 ever; or at least till we are invaded and made a Conquest by some other State; and even then our
90 best Writings might probably be preserved with Care, and grow into Esteem, and the Authors
91 have a Chance of Immortality.

FIGURE 7.1. Continued

Para. 7: Arguments against perpetual change in language

92 BUT without such great Revolutions as these, (to which we are, I think less subject than
93 Kingdoms upon the Continent) I see no absolute Necessity why any Language would be
94 perpetually ; for we find many Example to the contrary. From *Homer* to *Plutarch* are above a
95 Thousand Years; so long at least the Purity of the *Greek* Tongue may be allowed to last, and we
96 know not how far before. The Grecians spread their Colonies round all the Coasts of *Asia*
97 *Minor*, even to the *Northern* Parts, lying towards the *Euxine*; in every Island of the *Aegean Sea*,
98 and several others in the *Mediterranean*, where the Language was preserved entire for many
99 Ages, after they themselves became Colonies to *Rome*, and till they were over-run by the
100 barbarous Nations, upon the Fall of that Empire. The *Chinese* have Books in their Language
101 above two Thousand Years old, neither have the frequent Conquests of the *Tartars* been able
102 to alter it. The *German*, *Spanish*, and *Italian*, have admitted few or no Changes for some Ages
103 past. The other Languages of *Europe* I know nothing of, neither is there any occasion to
104 consider them.

Para. 8: Return to English: Corruptions in English since the time of Elizabeth

105 HAVING taken this compass, I return to those Considerations upon our own Language, which
106 I would humbly offer Your Lordship. The Period wherein the *English* Tongue received most
107 Improvement, I take to commence with the beginning of Queen *Elizabeth's* Reign, and to
108 conclude with the Great Rebellion in Forty Two. 'Tis true, there was a very ill Taste both of
109 Style and Wit, which prevailed under King *James* the First, but that seems to have been
110 corrected in the first Years of his Successor, who among many other qualifications of an
111 excellent Prince, was a great Patron of Learning. From the Civil War to this present Time, I am
112 apt to doubt whether the Corruptions in our Language have not at least equalled the
113 Refinements of it; and these Corruptions very few of the best Authors of our Age have wholly
114 escaped During the Usurpation, such and Infusion of Enthusiastick Jargon prevailed in every
115 Writing, as was not shook off in many Years after. To this succeeded that Licentiousness
116 which entered with the *Restoration*, and from infecting our Religion and Morals, fell to corrupt
117 our Language; which last was not like to be much improved by those who at that Time made
118 up the Court of King *Charles* the Second; either such who had followed Him in His
119 Banishment, or who had been altogether conversant in the Dialect of those *Fanatick Times*; or
120 young Men, who had been educated in the same Company; so that the *Court*, which used to be
121 the Standard of Propriety and Correctness of Speech, was then, and, I think, hath ever since
122 continued the worst School in *England* for that Accomplishment; and so will remain, till better
123 Care be taken in the Education of our your Nobility, that they may set out into the World with
124 some Foundation of Literature, in order to qualify them for Patterns of Politeness. The
125 Consequence of this Defect, upon our Language, may appear from Plays, and other
126 Compositions, written for Entertainment with the Fifty Years past; filled with a Secession of
127 affected Phrases, and new, conceited Words, either borrowed from the current Style of the
128 Court, or from those who, under the Character of Men of Wit and Pleasure, pretended to give
129 the Law. Many of these Refinements have already been long antiquated, and are now hardly
130 intelligible; which is no wonder, when they were the Product only of Ignorance and Caprice.

Para. 9: Attack on unnamed writers in London

131 I HAVE never known this great Town without one or more *Dunces* of Figure, who had Credit
132 enough to give Rise to some new Word, and propagate it in most Conversations, though it had
133 neither Humor, nor Significancy. If it struck the present Taste, it was soon transferred into the
134 Plays and current Scribbles of the Week, and became an Addition to our Language; while the
135 Men of Wit and Learning, instead of early obviating such Corruptions, were too often seduced
136 to imitate and comply with them.

Para. 10: Attack on poets since the time of the Restoration

137 THERE is another Set of Men who have contributed very must to the spoiling of the *English*
138 Tongue; I mean the Poets, from the Time of the Restoration. These Gentlemen, although they
139 could not be insensible how much our Language was already overstocked with Monosyllables;

FIGURE 7.1. Continued

140 yet, to same Time and Pains, introduced that barbarous Custom of abbreviating Words, to fit
141 them to the Measure of their Verses; and this they have frequently done, so very injudiciously,
142 as to form such harsh unharmonious Sounds, that none but a *Northern* Ear could endure: They
143 have joined the most obdurate Consonants without one intervening Vowel, only to shorten a
144 Syllable: And their Taste in time became so depraved, that what was a first a Poetical License
145 not to be justified, they made their Choice, alledging, that the Words pronounced at length,
146 sounded faint and languid. This was a Pretence to take up the same Custom in Prose; so that
147 most of the Books we see now a-days, are full of those Manglings and Abbreviations.
148 Instances of this Abuse are innumerable: What does Your Lordship think of the Words,
149 *Drudg'd, Disturb'd, Rebuk't, Fledg'd*, and a thousand others, every where to be met in Prose
150 as well as Verse? Where, by leaving out a Vowel to save a Syllable, we form so jarring a
151 Sound, and so difficult to utter, that I have often wondered how it could ever obtain.

Para. 11: A further reason for the corruption of English: Spelling reforms

152 ANOTHER Cause (and perhaps borrowed from the former) which hath contributed not a little
153 to the maiming of our Language, is a foolish Opinion, advanced of late Years, that we ought to
154 spell exactly as we speak; which beside the obvious Inconvenience of utterly destroying our
155 Etymology, would be a thing we should never see an End of. Not only the several Towns and
156 Countries of *England*, have a different way of Pronouncing, but even here in *London*, they clip
157 their Words after one Manner about the Court, another in the City, and a third in the Suburbs;
158 and in a few Years, it is probable, will all differ from themselves, as Fancy or Fashion shall
159 direct: All which reduced to Writing would entirely confound Orthography. Yet many People
160 are so fond of this Conceit, that is sometimes a difficult matter to read modern Books and
161 Pamphlets, where the Words are so curtailed, and varied from their original Spelling, that
162 whoever hath been used to plain *English*, will hardly know them by sight.

Para. 12: A final reason for corruption: Young men at the universities

163 SEVERAL young Men at the Universities, terribly possessed with the fear of Pedantry, run
164 into a worse Extream, and think all Politeness to consist in reading the daily Trash sent down
165 to them from hence: This they call *knowing the World*, and *reading Men and Manners*. Thus
166 furnished they come up to Town, reckon all their Errors for Accomplishments, borrow the
167 newest Set of Phrases, and if they take a Pen into their Hands, all the odd Words they have
168 picked up in a Coffee-House, or a Gaming Ordinary, are produced as Flowers of Style; and the
169 Orthography refined to the utmost. To this we owe those monstrous Productions, which under
170 the Names of *Trips, Spies, Amusements*, and other conceited Appellations, have over- run us
171 for some Years past. To this we owe that strange Race of Wits, who tell us, they Write to the
172 *Humour of the Age*: And I wish I could say, these quaint Fopperies were wholly absent from
173 graver Subjects. In short, I would undertake to shew Your Lordship several Pieces, where the
174 Beauties of this kind are so prominent, that with all your Skill in Languages, you could never
175 be able either to read or understand them.

Para. 13: Attack on the craze for politeness and praise for the language of women

176 BUT I am very much mistaken, if many of these false Refinements among us, do not arise
177 from a Principle which would quite destroy their Credit, if it were well understood and
178 considered. For I am afraid, My Lord, that with all the real good Qualities of our Country, we
179 are naturally not very Polite. This perpetual Disposition to shorten our Words, by retrenching
180 the Vowels, is nothing else but a tendency to lapse into the Barbarity of those *Northern*
181 Nations from whom we are descended, and whose Languages labour all under the same
182 Defect. For it is worthy our Observation, that the *Spaniard*, the *French*, and the *Italians*,
183 although derived from the same *Northern* Ancestors with our selves, are, with the utmost
184 Difficulty, taught to pronounce our Words, which the *Suedes* and *Danes*, as well as the
185 *Germans* and the *Dutch*, attain to with Ease, because our Syllables resemble theirs in the
186 Roughness and Frequency of Consonants. Now, as we struggle with an ill Climate to improve
187 the nobler kinds of Fruit, are at the Expence of Walls to receive and reverberated the faint Rays

FIGURE 7.1. Continued

188 of the Sun, and fence against the *Northern* Blasts; we sometimes by the help of a good Soil
189 equal the Production of warmer Countries, who have no need to be at so much Cost or Care. It
190 is the same thing with respect to the politer Arts among us; and the same Defect of Heat which
191 gives a Fierceness to our Natures, may contribute to that Roughness of our Language, which
192 bears some Analogy to the harsh Fruit of colder Countries. For I do not reckon that we want a
193 *Genius* more than the rest of our Neighbours: But Your Lordship will be of my Opinion, that
194 we ought to struggle with these natural Disadvantages as much as we can, and be careful
195 whom we employ, whenever we design to correct them, which is a Work that has hitherto been
196 assumed by the least qualified Hands. So that if the Choice had been left to me, I would rather
197 have trusted the Refinement of our Language, as far as it relates to Sound, to the Judgment of
198 the Women, than of illiterate Court- Fops, half-witted Poets, and University-Boys. For, it is
199 plain that Women in their manner of corrupting Words, do naturally discard the Consonants, as
200 we do the Vowels. What I am going to tell Your Lordship, appears very trifling; that more than
201 once, where some of both Sexes were in Company, I have persuaded two or three of each, to
202 take a Pen, and write down a number of Letters joyned together, just as it came into their
203 Heads, and upon reading this Gibberish we have found that which the Men had writ, by the
204 frequent encountering of rough Consonants, to sound like *High Dutch*; and the other by the
205 Women, like *Italian*, abounding in Vowels and Liquids. Now, though I would by no means
206 give Ladies the Trouble of advising us in the Reformation of our Language; yet I cannot help
207 thinking, that since they have been left out of all Meetings, except Parties at Play, or where
208 worse Designs are carried on, our Conversation hath very much degenerated.

Para. 14: Suggestion that there should be a society to reform the language

209 IN order to reform our Language, I conceive, My Lord, that a free judicious Choice should be
210 made of such Persons, as are generally allowed to be best qualified for such a Work, without
211 any regard to Quality, Party, or Profession. These, to a certain Number at least, should
212 assemble at some appointed Time and Place, and fix on Rules by which they design to
213 proceed. What Methods they will take, is not for me to prescribe. Your Lordship, and other
214 Persons in great Employment, might please to be of the Number; and I am afraid, such a
215 Society would want Your Instruction and Example, as much as Your Protection: For, I have,
216 not without a little Envy, observed of late, the Style of some great Ministers very much to
217 exceed that of any other Productions.

Para. 15: What needs to be done

218 THE Persons who are to undertake this Work, will have the Example of the French before
219 them, to imitate where these have proceeded right, and to avoid their Mistakes. Besides the
220 Grammar-part, wherein we are allowed to be very defective, they will observe many gross
221 Improprieties, which however authorised by Practice, and grown familiar, ought to be
222 discarded. They will find many Words that deserve to be utterly thrown out of our Language,
223 many more to be corrected; and perhaps not a few, long since antiquated, which ought to be
224 restored, on account of their Energy and Sound.

Para. 16: What he has at heart: A method for preventing change in English

225 BUT what I have most at Heart is, that some Method should be thought on for *ascertaining*
226 and *fixing* our Language for ever, after such Alterations are made in it as shall be thought
227 requisite. For I am of Opinion, that it is better a Language should not be wholly perfect, that it
228 should be perpetually changing; and we must give over at one Time, or at length infallibly
229 change for the worse: As the *Romans* did, when they began to quit their *Simplicity* of Style for
230 affected Refinements; such as we meet in *Tacitus* and other Authors, which ended by degrees
231 in many Barbarities, even before the *Goths* had invaded *Italy*.

Para. 17: The textual models that should be followed

232 THE Fame our Writers is usually confined to these two Islands, and it is hard it should be
233 limited in *Time*, as much as *Place*, by the perpetual Variations of our Speech. It is Your
234 Lordship's Observation, that if it were not for the *Bible* and *Common Prayer Book* in the

FIGURE 7.1. Continued

235 vulgar Tongue, we should hardly be able to understand any Thing that was written among us
236 an hundred Years ago: Which is certainly true: For those Books being perpetually read in
237 Churches, have proved a kind of Standard for Language, especially to the common People.
238 And I doubt whether the Alterations since introduced, have added much to the Beauty or 239
239 Strength of the *English* Tongue, though they have taken off a great deal from that *Simplicity*
240 which is one of the greatest Perfections in any Language. You, My Lord, who are so
241 conversant in the Sacred Writings, and so great a Judge of them in their Original, will agree,
242 that no Translation our Country ever yet produced, hath come up to that of the *Old and New*
243 *Testament*: And by the many beautiful Passages, which I have often had the Honor to hear
244 Your Lordship cite from thence, I am persuaded that the Translators of the Bible were Masters
245 of an *English* Style much fitter for that Work, than any we see in our present Writings, which I
246 take to be owing to the *Simplicity* that runs through the whole. Then, as to the greatest part of
247 our *Liturgy*, compiled long before the Translation of the *Bible* now in use, and little altered
248 since; there seem to be in it as great strains of true sublime Eloquence, as are any where to be
249 found in our Language; which every Man of good Taste will observe in the *Communion*
250 *Service*, that of Burial, and other Parts.

Para. 18: Argument for "enlarging" the language

251 BUT where I say, that I would have our Language, after it is duly correct, always to last; I do
252 not mean that is should never by enlarged: Provided, that no Word which a Society shall give a
253 Sanction to, be afterwards antiquated and exploded, that they may have liberty to receive
254 whatever new ones they shall find occasion for: Because then the old Books will yet be always
255 valuable, according to their intrinsick Worth, and not thrown aside on account of unintelligible
256 Words and Phrases, which appear harsh and uncouth, only because they are out of Fashion.
257 Had the *Roman* Tongue continued vulgar in that City till this Time; it would have been
258 absolutely necessary from the mighty Changes that have been made in Law and Religion; from
259 the many Terms of Art required in Trade and in War; from the new Inventions that have
260 happened in the World: From the vast spreading of Navigation and Commerce, with many
261 other obvious Circumstances, to have made Great Additions to that Language; yet the Ancients
262 would still have been read, and understood with Pleasure and Ease. The *Greek* Tongue
263 received many Enlargements between the Time of *Homer*, and that of *Plutarch*, yet the former
264 Author was probably as well understood in *Trajan's* Time, as the latter. What *Horace* says of
265 *Words going off and perishing like Leaves, and new ones coming in their Place*, is a
266 Misfortune he laments, rather than a Thing he approves; But I cannot see why this should be
267 absolutely necessary, or if it were, what would have become of his *Monumentum aere*
268 *perennuus*.

Para. 19: Support for the scheme

269 WRITING by Memory only, as I do at present, I would gladly keep within my Depth; and
270 therefore shall not enter into further Particulars. Neither do I pretend more than to shew the
271 Usefulness of this Design, and to make some general Observations, leaving the rest to that of
272 Society, which I hope will owe its Institution and Patronage to Your Lordship. Besides, I
273 would willingly avoid Repetition, having about a Year ago, communicated to the Publick,
274 much of what I had to offer upon this Subject, by the hands of an ingenious Gentleman, who
275 for a long Time did thrice a Week divert or instruct the Kingdom by his Papers; and is
276 supposed to pursue the same Design at present under the Title of *Spectator*. This Author, who
277 hath tried the Force and Compass of our Language with so much Success, agrees entirely with
278 me in most of my Sentiments relating to it; so do the greatest part of the Men of Wit and
279 Learning, whom I have had the Happiness to converse with; and therefore I imagine that such
280 a Society would be pretty unanimous in the main Points.

Para. 20: Flattery of the Earl of Oxford to gain his patronage

281 YOUR Lordship must allow, that such a Work as this, brought to Perfection, would very much
282 contribute to the Glory of Her Majesty's Reign; which ought to be recorded in Words more
283 durable than Brass, and such as our Posterity may read a thousand Years hence, with Pleasure

FIGURE 7.1. Continued

284 as well as Admiration. I have always disapproved that false Compliment to Princes, that the
285 most lasting Monument they can have, is the Hearts of their Subjects. It is indeed their greatest
286 present Felicity to reign in their Subjects Hearts; but these are too perishable to preserve their
287 Memories, which can only be done by the Pens of able and faithful Historians. And I take it to
288 be Your Lordship's Duty, as *Prime Minister*, to give order for inspecting our Language, and
289 rendring it fit to record the History of so great and good a Princess. Besides, My Lord, as
290 disinterested as You appear to the World, I am convinced, that no Man is more in the Power of
291 a prevailing favorite Passion that Your Self; I mean that Desire of true and lasting Honor,
292 which you have born along with You through every Stage of Your Life. To this You have
293 often sacrificed Your Interest, Your Ease and Your Health: For preserving and encreasing this,
294 you have exposed Your Person to secret Treachery, and open Violence. There is not perhaps
295 an Example in History of any Minister, who in so short a time hath performed so many great
296 Things, and overcome so many great Difficulties. Now, tho' I am fully convinced, that You
297 fear God, honor Your QUEEN, and love Your Country, as much as any of Your Fellow-
298 Subjects; yet I must believe that the Desire of Fame hath been no inconsiderable Motive to
299 quicken You in the Pursuit of those Actions which will best deserve it. But at the same time, I
300 must be so plain as to tell Your Lordship, that if You will not take some Care to settle our
301 Language, and put it into a state of Continuance, I cannot promise that Your Memory shall be
302 preserved above an hundred Years, further than by imperfect Tradition.

Para. 21: Criticism of the Age of Learning and Politeness

303 AS barbarous and ignorant as we were in former Centuries, there was more effectual Care
304 taken by our Ancestors, to preserve the Memory of Times and Persons, than we find in this
305 Age of Learning and Politeness, as we are please to call it. The rude *Latin* of the *Monks* is still
306 very intelligible; whereas, had their Records been delivered down only in the vulgar Tongue,
307 so barren and so barbarous, so subject to continual succeeding Changes, they could not now be
308 understood, unless by Antiquaries who made it their Study to expound them. And we must at
309 this Day have been content with such poor Abstracts of our *English* Story, as laborious Men of
310 low Genius would think fit to give us; And even these in the next Age would be likewise 311
311 swallowed up in succeeding Collections. If Things go on at this rate, all I can promise Your
312 Lordship is, that about two hundred Years hence, some painful Compiler, who will be at the
313 Trouble of studying Old Language, may inform the World, that in the Reign of QUEEN
314 ANNE, Robert Earl of Oxford, a very wise and excellent Man, was made *High Treasurer*, and
315 saved his Country, which in those Days was almost ruined by a *Foreign War*, and a *Domestick*
316 *Faction*. Thus much he may be able to pick out, and willingly transfer into his new History,
317 but the rest of Your Character, which I or any other Writer may now value our selves by
318 drawing, and the particular Account of the great Things done under Your Ministry, for which
319 You are already so celebrated in most Parts of *Europe*, will probably be dropt, on account of
320 the antiquated Style and Manner they are delivered in.

Para. 22: Reason for wishing to fix the language: So that historians may be read in the future

321 HOW then shall any Man who hath a Genius for History, equal to the best of the Ancients, be
322 able to undertake such a Work with Spirit and Chearfulness, when he considers, that he will be
323 read with Pleasure but a very few Years, and in an Age or two shall hardly be understood
324 without an Interpreter? This is like employing an excellent Statuary to work upon mouldring
325 Stone. Those who apply their Studies to preserve the Memory of others, will always have some
326 Concern for their own. And I believe it is for this Reason, that so few Writers among us, of any
327 Distinction, have turned their Thoughts to such a discouraging Employment: For the best
328 *English* Historian must lie under this Mortification, that when his style grows antiquated, he
329 will only be considered as a tedious Relator of Facts; and perhaps consulted in his turn, among
330 other neglected Authors, to furnish Materials for some future Collector.

Para. 23: Extolling the virtues of the Earl of Oxford, possibly fishing for a pension

331 I DOUBT, Your Lordship is but ill entertained with a few scattered Thoughts, upon a Subject
332 that deserves to be treated with Ability and Care: However, I must beg leave to add a few
333 Words more, perhaps not altogether foreign to the same Matter. I know not whether that which

FIGURE 7.1. Continued

334 I am going to say, may pass for Caution, Advice or Reproach, any of which will be justly
335 thought very improper from one of my Station, to one in Yours. However, I must venture to
336 affirm that if Genius and Learning be not encouraged under Your Lordship's Administration,
337 you are the most inexcusable Person alive. All Your other Virtues, My Lord, will be defective
338 without this; Your Affability, Candor, and good Nature; that perpetual agreeableness of 339
340 Conversation, so disengaged in the midst of such a Weight of Business and Opposition; Even
341 Your Justice, Prudence, and Magnanimity, will shine less bright without it. Your Lordship is
342 universally allowed to possess a very large Portion in most Parts of Literature; and to this You
343 owe the cultivating of those many Virtues, which otherwise would have been less adorned, or
344 in lower Perfection. Neither can You acquit yourself of these Obligations, without telling the
345 Arts, in their turn, share Your Influence and Protection: Besides, who knows, but some *true*
346 *Genius* may happen to arise under Your Ministry, *exortus ut aetherius* Sol. Every Age might
347 perhaps produce one or two of these to adorn it, if they were not sunk under the Censure and
348 Obloquy of plodding, servile, imitating Pedants. I do not mean by a true Genius, any bold
349 Writer who breaks through the Rules of Decency to distinguish himself by the singularity of
350 Opinions; but one, who upon a deserving Subject, is able to open new Scenes, and discover a
351 Vein of true and noble thinking, which never entered into any Imagination before: Every
352 Stroke of whose Pen, is worth all the Paper blotted by Hundreds of others in the compass of
353 their Lives. I know, My Lord, Your Friends will offer in Your Defence, that in Your private
354 Capacity, You never refus'd Your Purse and Credit to the Service and Support of learned or
355 ingenious Men; and that ever since You have been in publick Employment, You have
356 constantly bestowed Your Favours to the most deserving Persons. But I desire Your Lordship
357 not to be deceived: We never will admit of these Excuses, nor will allow Your private
358 Liberality, as great as it is, to attone for Your excessive publick thrift. But here again, I am
359 afraid most good Subjects will interpose in Your Defence, by alleging the desperate Condition
360 You found the Nation in, and the Necessity there was for so able and faithful a Steward, to
361 retrieve it, if possible, by the utmost Frugality. We may grant all this, My Lord; but then, it
362 ought likewise to be considered, that You have already saved several Millions to the Publick,
363 and that what we ask, is too inconsiderable to break into any Rules of the strictest good
364 Husbandry. *The French King* bestows about half a dozen Pensions to learned Men in several
365 Parts of *Europe*, and perhaps a dozen in his whole Kingdom; which, in the whole, do probably
366 not amount to half the Income of many a private Commoner in *England*; yet have more
367 contributed to the Glory of that Prince, than any Million he hath otherwise employed. For
368 Learning, like all true Merit, is easily satisfied, whilst the False and Counterfeit is perpetually
369 craving, and never thinks it hath enough. The smallest Favour given by a Great Prince, as a
370 Mark of Esteem, to reward the Endowments of the Mind, never fails to be returned with Praise
371 and Gratitude, and loudly celebrated to the World. I have known some Years ago, several
372 Pensions given to particular Persons (how deservedly I shall not enquire) any one of which, if
373 divided into smaller Parcels, and distributed by the Crown, to those who might, upon occasion,
374 distinguish themselves by some extraordinary Production of Wit or Learning, would be amply
375 sufficient to answer the End. Or if any such Persons were above Money, (as every great *Genius*
376 certainly is, with very moderate Conveniences of Life) a Medal, or some Mark of Distinction,
377 would do full as well.

Para. 24: Closing the letter

378 BUT I forget my Province, and find myself turning Projector before I am aware; although it be
379 one of the last Characters under which I should desire to appear before Your Lordship,
380 especially when I have the Ambition of aspiring to that of being, with the greatest Respect and
381 Truth,

382 My Lord,
382 Your Lordship's
383 most Obedient, most Obliged,
384 and most Humble Servant
385 J. Swift

FIGURE 7.1. Continued

language is extremely immoral and that (b) it is in need of correction. On the one hand, Swift is drawing discursively on the *pure language myth*; on the other hand, if he is playing the role of the satirist, it is precisely this myth that is under attack. Is there any evidence here or in what the Milroys call the "polite preamble" (1999: 27) that we should doubt the sincerity of his complaint?

First of all, what the Milroys omit from their quotation of the second paragraph is highly significant. Who are "the Pretenders to polish and refine [English]"? What does Swift mean with the ironic use of the infinitives "to polish and refine [English]"? And in running the "true" statement <A corrupt language is inferior>, derived from the metaphor A MORALLY PURE LANGUAGE IS A PERFECT LANGUAGE in the sequence "[I complain] that its daily Improvements are by no means in proportion to its daily Corruptions", he deliberately opposes one set of language improvers to his own assessment of the overall situation. So his real criticism is aimed not so much at the language itself as at the supposed improvers, and the implication is that the "improvements" lie within the discourse of polishing and refining the language, that is, within the ideology of politeness (which I will discuss in more detail in chap. 8). Contemporary readers of Swift will have had little difficulty in identifying these "improvers" as Swift's erstwhile friends and contemporary political enemies Joseph Addison, Richard Steele and Daniel Defoe.

Second, when he takes it upon himself to make the complaint "in the Name of all the Learned and Polite Persons of the Nation", we either logically equate "learned persons" with "polite persons"—persons with good breeding, persons with polished behavior, persons who are born to be polite—or we assume that there are learned persons who are not polite. The first interpretation introduces a note of insincerity into the text, which would fit his role of satirist; the second entails that there are indeed nonpolite learned persons and, furthermore, implies that his aim will be to attack them.

Presumably, the Milroys, in using the expression "polite preamble", are making use of some of the twentieth-century meanings evoked by the lexeme *polite*: that Swift is flattering the Earl of Oxford, that he is attempting to avoid discord, that he is displaying deference to the Earl of Oxford, and so on. However, these interpretations of the lexeme *polite* are very different from those that were common in the eighteenth century. In addition, whether or not the letter was sent privately to the earl, it was still published as an open letter with a very different audience in mind: Swift's habitual readers.

It is quite feasible to argue that the preamble is anything but polite in the modern sense, although it may have met constraints on the eighteenth-century interpretation of the lexeme. The "very judicious Persons", who in line 5 are said to have confirmed Swift's sentiments, remain unnamed throughout the whole text, and they agree with him that "nothing would be of greater Use towards the Improvement of Knowledge and Politeness, than some effectual Method for *Correcting, Enlarging, and Ascertaining our Language*" (lines 6–8). Later sections of the *Proposal*, however, indicate that those who have apparently made this suggestion are, by implication, those same former friends and present political opponents: Joseph Addison and Richard Steele (and possibly also Daniel Defoe, who was the first to have made a proposal similar to Swift's in his *Essay upon Projects* in 1697). "Politeness", in the early eighteenth-century sense of the term, meant "polished" (from the French *poli*), and it was habitually associated with the good breeding and classical education of the landed gentry and higher echelons of the aristocracy. Knowledge would be the kind of knowledge that was beyond the reach of the rest of society, including the rising middle classes.

The final two sentences of the "preamble" appear to represent lavish praise of the Earl of Oxford's concerns for matters that appear to be outside the great affairs of state:

> I confess, the Merit of this Candor and Condescension is very much lessened, because Your Lordship hardly leaves us room to offer our good Wishes, removing all our Difficulties, and supplying all our Wants, faster than <u>the most visionary Projector can adjust his Schemes</u>. And therefore, My Lord, <u>the Design of this Paper is not so much to offer You *Ways and Means*, as to complain of a *Grievance*, the redressing of which is to be Your own Work, as much as that of paying the *Nation's Debts*, or opening a Trade into the *South Sea*</u>; and though not of such immediate Benefit as either of these, or any other of Your glorious Actions, yet perhaps, in future Ages, not less to Your Honour.

The first underlined sequence is an oblique reference to Swift's former friend, the Whig writer Daniel Defoe. Contemporary readers will have been familiar with Daniel Defoe's *An Essay upon Projects*, so that suggesting that a visionary projector cannot adjust his schemes as quickly as the Earl of Oxford can provide for everyone's wants is an ironic suggestion that the Tories get things done whereas the Whigs just make projects. The second underlined sequence equates the problem of the language to "paying the Nation's Debts" or "opening up a Trade into the South Sea", which can hardly be taken seriously.

What, then, is the status of Swift's *Proposal* as a complaint "that our Language is extremely imperfect"? The first two paragraphs of the text leave us good reason to doubt that this was his real aim in writing it. If this is the case, can we reasonably say that Swift meant everything he wrote? If his real intent is not to complain about the English language, can we interpret it in such a way as to reveal his underlying intent? Note, first, the veiled reference to Defoe in the first paragraph and to other Whig writers in the second. To fully understand the text, we need to locate it as part of a significant type of discourse in the first 10 to 15 years of eighteenth-century London society, and this will be the topic of the following section.

4. CONTEXTUALISING THE *PROPOSAL* SOCIOHISTORICALLY

The years in Swift's life that are significant as a background to his writing the *Proposal* are from 1696, when he left his post at Kilroot and returned to England to resume his work as secretary to Sir William Temple at Moor Park near London, to 1712, when the *Proposal* was written. It can be safely assumed that he met Daniel Defoe during his time at Moor Park, or at least that he was well acquainted with Defoe's writings, in particular the *Essay upon Projects*. After Sir William's death in 1699, he returned to Ireland to take up a post with a very small congregation some 20 miles outside Dublin. The small size of the congregation meant that his duties in the parish were light enough to enable him to travel to London frequently over the next ten years, where he made friends with Richard Steele and Joseph Addison. The connections between Defoe, Swift, Addison and Steele were as writers, friends and, perhaps more important for Swift, as members of the Whig Party. Swift is known to have contributed articles to the *Tatler* before deserting the Whigs for the Tories in 1710. In 1710 he also accepted the editorship of the *Examiner*, the Tory pendant to the *Spectator*. From 1710 on, Swift was closely connected with the Tory government that was ousted in 1714 on the death of Queen Anne and the accession to the throne of the Hanoverian king George I.

The first decade of the eighteenth century witnessed a concerted effort on the part of a number of writers (e.g. Shaftesbury, Addison, Steele and Swift himself) to define and exemplify polite behaviour as a culturally and socially desirable goal, intimately linked not only with forms of linguistic behaviour, but also with the chimera of a fixed, prestigious standard language. Shaftesbury went so far as to develop a philosophy of politeness to which those who wished to belong to polite society should ascribe (cf. chap. 8), and in the two short-lived but enormously popular periodicals the *Tatler* and the *Spectator*, Addison, Steele and other contributors commented on a wide range of topics that exemplified forms of polite behaviour and opinion.

The final decade of the seventeenth century and the first decade of the eighteenth century were also characterised by strong connections between politicians and literary activists,[2] with Defoe, Addison and Steele firmly in the Whig camp and Pope, Arbuthnot, Gay and St. John in that of the Tories. Robert Harley, who was raised to the peerage as the Earl of Oxford and Mortimer on 23 May 1711, was also well known for his literary interests, and during his early career in Parliament Harley made use of Defoe's skills as a political writer in 1703. He is known to have also made use of Swift's talents

---

2. Steele, for example, also stood for and was elected to parliament in 1713, and Robert Harley, with whom Swift worked closely, dabbled in literature in the first decade of the eighteenth century and, as a Whig politician, was familiar to this circle of Whig writers. Fitzmaurice (2000) is an excellent source of information on the politics of social networks and the interconnections between writers and politicians around the time when Swift published the *Proposal*.

as a pamphlet writer. Harley also started his political career as a Whig but defected to the Tory Party before taking office as lord high treasurer in 1711. Swift's career as a political satirist was closely bound up with Harley's as a politician, and in November 1712 an assassination attempt on Harley known as the Bandbox Plot was forestalled by the prompt intervention of Swift.

The *Proposal* was thus written at a time of political upheaval between the Whigs and the Tories, and political topics were discussed in issues of the *Examiner* and the *Spectator*, as well as in pamphlets such as this one, in efforts to gain support for one side or the other. The issues, however, were generally disguised behind a smokescreen of irony and satire, which would have been relatively easily to interpret for contemporary readers, although not for readers today. Part of that smokescreen consisted of accusations about the language used by Swift's opponents and allusions to their claims to belong to polite society and their advice to others on how to become "polite". In the previous section we located an oblique reference to Defoe and what may very well have been a criticism of Addison and Steele. If we lose sight of the veiled political invective in the *Proposal*, we lose much of its underlying significance when it is looked at from within the sociohistorical framework of the last years of the reign of Queen Anne. It is thus useful to search in the *Proposal* for possible references to these writers.

4.1 Veiled criticism: The smokescreen of complaining about language

The unusual thing about the *Proposal* is that it is one of the few texts to which Swift actually appended his name, which indicates that it was important for him to reach a reading public that could both immediately identify his status as the author and also put a name to the unnamed "pretenders", "projectors" and "judicious persons" obliquely referred to in the text. In Swift's other politically satirical writings, to which he did not append his name, he is a master in suggesting a tone of irony and non-literalness without the reader being able to pin the narrative voice down.[3] At some point in the overall text, however, the irony reveals itself explicitly.

The point at which the curtain is drawn aside to reveal Swift's ironic intent in the *Proposal* is the sentence underlined in paragraph 9 from lines 131 to 136:

> I HAVE never known this great Town without one or more *Dunces* of Figure, who had Credit enough to give Rise to some new Word, and propagate it in most

---

3. A perfect example of his technique can be found in *A Modest Proposal: For Preventing the Children of Poor People in Ireland from Being a Burden to Their Parents or Country, and for Making Them Beneficial to the Public*, in which the non-seriousness of his proposal is revealed in the following sentence: "I grant this food may be somewhat dear, and therefore very proper for Landlords, who as they have already devoured most of the Parents, seem to have the best Title to the Children." It is as if the narrative voice is declaiming on a stage in front of the audience with the curtains drawn behind him. At this sentence, the curtains are pulled aside to reveal the real intention of the narrative voice and then are hurriedly drawn again.

Conversations, though it had neither Humor, nor Significancy. *If it struck the present Taste, it was soon transferred into the Plays and current Scribbles of the Week, and became an Addition to our Language*; while the Men of Wit and Learning, instead of early obviating such Corruptions, were too often seduced to imitate and comply with them.

Swift has often been criticised for inconsistencies in the *Proposal* but the sentence highlighted above indicates his immense care to make sure that his ironic tone comes across (cf. the example from Swift's *Modest Proposal* discussed in note 3 of this chapter). The reference to Addison is almost explicitly made in the noun *Addition*, so that the allusion to the major "dunce", "scribbler", or "playwright" of the week could scarcely be more obvious. The "current Scribbles of the Week" thus becomes a derogatory comment on the *Spectator*. Swift's opponents become responsible for introducing new words into the language and for propagating their use in conversation. The criticism, however, is also directed at those who are facile enough to accept such words, "the Men of Wit and Learning", on the basis of the claim that they represent "the present Taste". In the enormously popular periodicals the *Tatler* and the *Spectator*, which did indeed appear weekly (cf. "current Scribbles of the Week"), Addison, Steele and other contributors commented on a wide range of topics that exemplified forms of polite behaviour and opinion. By extension, therefore, Swift can be interpreted as criticising the contemporary craze for politeness.

In his brief sketch (in par. 5) of how the Latin language first reached a state of perfection, but then fell into a period of decay, he refers to the "great Corruption of Manners" (lines 77–78) induced by the borrowing of words from other languages (i.e. Swift is writing within the **contamination through language contact myth** presented in chap. 5). The crucial word here is "Manners", since this was precisely what he saw the contributors to the *Spectator* attempting to prescribe in the periodical. In paragraph 6, in which he explicitly makes use of the discourse of the **pure language myth** by referring to notions such as perfection and decay with respect to Latin, he again reverts to the ironic, humorous mode in adding (somewhat gratuitously, since he is writing about Latin here): "And the *French* for these last Fifty Years hath been polishing as much as it will bear" (lines 81–82). As I shall argue in chapter 8, the concept of politeness (understood here as "polishing") had indeed been introduced into England since the Reformation from France, and it would appear that this is one of the major butts of his irony, since politeness and manners are precisely what he sees his political opponents as supporting. This again becomes clear in lines 83–84 when he suggests that "the Affection of some late Authors" is "to introduce and multiply *Cant* Words, which is the most ruinous Corruption in any Language". It would thus appear that Swift's purpose is not so much to complain about the state of the English language, but rather to aim verbal invective at his political opponents. The fact that he chose to use the framework of the language myths that had been current for several centuries creates an effective smokescreen to obfuscate his political and literary intentions.

In paragraph 8, lines 123–124, we meet with an apparent inconsistency in Swift's text unless we are prepared to take the reference to "Patterns of Politeness" as irony. Paragraph 8 purports to expose some of the corruptions that were introduced into the English language after the death of Queen Elizabeth up to the Restoration period. Swift runs the following "true" propositions within the discourse of the ***pure/perfect language myth***:

- <A corrupt language is inferior>
- <A corrupt language must be avoided>
- <A corrupt language reflects the corruption of its users>
- <An infected language has caught a disease>
- <An infected language needs to be purified>

The text reads as follows. Sequences in italics represent those points in the text in which the "true" statements are run, and the underlined sequence signals the possible introduction of irony:

> *From the Civil War to this present Time, I am apt to doubt whether the Corruptions in our Language have not at least equalled the Refinements of it; and these Corruptions very few of the best Authors of our Age have wholly escaped During the Usurpation,* such an Infusion of Enthusiastick Jargon prevailed in every Writing, as was not shook off in many Years after. *To this succeeded that Licentiousness which entered with the Restoration, and from infecting our Religion and Morals, fell to corrupt our Language;* which last was not like to be much improved by those who at that Time made up the Court of King *Charles* the Second; either such who had followed Him in His Banishment, or who had been altogether conversant in the Dialect of those *Fanatick Times*; or young Men, who had been educated in the same Company; *so that the Court, which used to be the Standard of Propriety and Correctness of Speech, was then, and, I think, hath ever since continued the worst School in England for that Accomplishment; and so will remain, till better Care be taken in the Education of our Nobility,* that they may set out into the World with some Foundation of Literature, in order to qualify them for Patterns of Politeness.

"From the Civil War to this present Time" indicates the period of time in which Swift considers the basic views of the Whigs—that is, support of Puritanism and nonconformist and Low Church religious practices—to have held sway.[4] He includes within his stricture the court of Charles II, and concludes that the language of the court generally, which at one point he refers to as "the Dialect of those Fanatick Times", is no longer "the Standard of Propriety and Correctness of Speech". His wish is that young nobles should be "sent out into the World with some Foundation of Literature, in order to qualify them for Patterns of Politeness". It is difficult to trace the note of irony here, but if we accept his rejection of the fad for politeness, then this can

---

4. He conveniently leaves out the short period in which James II attempted to reinstate the Catholic Church.

only be meant ironically, which automatically leads to the whole passage being interpreted by the reader in this way.

Three later passages confirm this interpretation, one in paragraph 12 beginning at line 163 and continuing till line 173, the second at the beginning of paragraph 13 from line 176 to line 179, and the third at the beginning of paragraph 21 from line 303 to line 305. The first sequence is particularly interesting since it makes a further oblique reference to the *Spectator*:

> SEVERAL young Men at the Universities, terribly possessed with the fear of Pedantry, run into a worse Extream, and think all Politeness to consist in reading the daily Trash sent down to them from hence: This they call *knowing the World*, and *reading Men and Manners*. Thus furnished they come up to Town, reckon all their Errors for Accomplishments, borrow the newest Sett of Phrases, and if they take a Pen into their Hands, all the odd Words they have picked up in a Coffee-House, or a Gaming Ordinary, are produced as Flowers of Style; and the Orthography refined to the utmost.... To this we owe that strange Race of Wits, who tell us, they Write to the *Humour of the Age*: And I wish I could say, these quaint Fopperies were wholly absent from graver Subjects.

The ironic tone is unmistakable in the phrase "terribly possessed with the fear of Pedantry", and "the daily Trash sent down to them from hence" is an explicit reference to copies of the *Spectator* that were regularly sent to students at the universities of Oxford and Cambridge from the capital. Swift reveals this by actually quoting two phrases used in the *Spectator*, no. 3 (March 1711) which "several young Men at the Universities" take to be equivalent to politeness: "knowing the World" and "reading Men and Manners".

The second sequence follows immediately after the invective levelled against the *Spectator* in paragraph 12:

> BUT I am very much mistaken, if many of these false Refinements among us, do not arise from a Principle which would quite destroy their Credit, if it were well understood and considered. For I am afraid, My Lord, that with all the real good Qualities of our Country, we are naturally not very Polite.

Swift's statement here needs no further explanation. His opinion of the Whig craze for politeness, especially as represented in the *Spectator*, is firmly criticised. The irony in the third sequence leaves no doubt in my mind that Swift did not think favourably of this craze:

> AS barbarous and ignorant as we were in former Centuries, there was more effectual Care taken by our Ancestors, to preserve the Memory of Times and Persons, than we find in this Age of Learning and Politeness, as we are pleased to call it.

This only strengthens the interpretation of his reference to politeness in paragraph 8 as irony, which logically leads to an ironic interpretation of the whole complaint made to the Earl of Oxford.

4.2 Swift's use of the language myths

It can hardly be doubted that the *Proposal* is framed as a linguistic complaint, but apart from the occurrence of the verb "complain" in line 22, paragraph 1, and in line 27, paragraph 2, no further reference is made in the text to its status as a complaint. The close look at the text in the previous subsection reveals that the complaint is levelled less at the language itself than at the language usage of sets of persons who are never explicitly named, but are very obviously, and sometimes pointedly, implied at a number of points throughout the text. To give the text the appearance of a complaint letter, however, Swift makes great use of many of the language myths that have been discussed in previous chapters. My interpretation of his use of the *pure/perfect language myth* in the sequence looked at from paragraph 8 as an example of irony shows that we would be well advised not to ascribe to Swift automatically a belief in those myths. Quite possibly, he uses them because he assumes that his readers are likely to believe them and that they would be far more likely to read the pamphlet if it were framed as a complaint about the language. So it would be interesting to look a little more closely at the use he makes of the myths.

In paragraphs 3 and 4, several of the myths familiar to us from chapter 5 occur. Swift even adds a further "true" statement derived from the metaphorical blend to refer to language in lines 32–33 of paragraph 3 when he assumes that the Earl of Oxford will agree with the reason that "our Language is less Refined than those of *Italy, Spain,* or *France*": <A pure language is refined>. The *pure/perfect language myth* then frames a reference to Latin in line 33. There is an interesting contradiction in what he writes here, however. He maintains that Latin was never used "in its Purity" in Britain, but he then denies that that it was "ever so vulgar in *Britain,* as it is known to have been in *Gaul* and *Spain*". How are we meant to interpret this? The only explanation is that Latin as a vernacular tongue did not remain in Britain, whereas it was used as a vernacular in those countries in which Romance languages developed out of Latin.

There is a brief reference to "barbarians" in paragraph 3 (lines 36–37): "The *Roman* Legions here, were at length all recalled to help their Country against the *Goths,* and other barbarous Invaders". A reference to the mixing of languages appears in paragraph 4 (lines 45–47 and 56–58): "*Edward the Confessor* having lived long in *France,* appears to be the first who introduced any mixture of the *French* Tongue with the *Saxon;* the Court affecting what the Prince was fond of, and others taking it up for a Fashion, as it is now with us" and "so that our Language, between two and three hundred Years ago, seems to have had a greater mixture with *French* than at present". But neither case is referred to in connection with the *barbarians myth* or the *contamination through contact myth*. There is a hint of negative criticism in the suggestion that people took up the mixture of French and English from Edward the Confessor "for a Fashion", and this is one of the points that Swift makes later about the "additions to the language" introduced by writers like Steele, Addison and Defoe.

Paragraphs 5, 6 and 7 contain references to the *pure/perfect language myth* ("THE *Roman* Language arrived at great Perfection before it began to decay", line 81, paragraph 6; "the Purity of the *Greek* Tongue may be allow'd to last", line 95, par. 7) and to what we could call the *myth of decay and death*, which is driven by a "true" statement that we could add to those in fig. 5.1 in chapter 5: <A mature/perfect language will finally decay and die>. However, Swift does not consider the issue of language decay and death to be worth spending much time over. As he says, "Whether our Language or the *French* will decline as fast as the *Roman* did, is a Question that would perhaps admit more Debate than it is worth" lines 69–70, paragraph 5. There is a clear link between the *pure/perfect language myth* and the *decay and death myth* when Swift mentions that "THE *Roman* Language arrived at great Perfection before it began to decay" and then says of English that it "is not arrived to such a Degree of Perfection, as to make us apprehend any Thoughts of its Decay" (lines 86–87).

Swift also makes use of the discourse associated with the three other myths referred to in chapter 5, the *barbarians myth*, the *good climate/soil myth* and the *pure language of the South and the corrupted language of the North myth*. In the case of the first of these three myths, the *barbarians myth*, there is no evidence to suggest irony. In the case of the second myth, the irony is clearly signalled, but Swift uses the third myth, the *pure language of the South and the corrupted language of the North myth*, to mock the Restoration poets. The first of these three myths is represented marginally in paragraph 13, lines 179–182: "This perpetual Disposition to shorten our Words, by retrenching the Vowels, is nothing else but a tendency to lapse into the Barbarity of those Northern Nations from whom we are descended, and whose Languages labour all under the same Defect." However, it is difficult to tell whether the statement is meant seriously or not.

The *pure language of the South and the corrupted language of the North myth* is echoed at the end of the following sequence (par. 10, lines 137–142):

> There is another Set of Men who have contributed very much to the spoiling of the *English* Tongue; I mean the Poets, from the Time of the Restoration. These Gentlemen, although they could not be insensible how much our Language was already overstocked with Monosyllables; yet, to save Time and Pains, introduced that barbarous Custom of abbreviating Words, to fit them to the Measure of their Verses; and this they have frequently done, so very injudiciously, as to form such harsh unharmonious Sounds, that none but a *Northern* Ear could endure.

The criticism of the Restoration poets fits into Swift's overall plan to attack the Whigs, and his comment on the disharmonious quality of the sounds produced in their verses is highly reminiscent of William of Malmesbury's scathing criticism of the language of the North, which Higden inserts into his *Polychronicon*. The problem is that Swift simply uses the myth to poke fun at the poets, which indicates that, of all the myths discussed in chapter 5, this local myth is the most deeply ingrained.

The *good climate soil myth* occurs in the following text sequence:

> Now, as we struggle with an ill Climate to improve the nobler kinds of Fruit, we are at the Expence of Walls to receive and reverberate the faint Rays of the Sun, and fence against the *Northern* Blasts; we sometimes by the help of a good Soil equal the Production of warmer Countries, who have no need to be at so much Cost or Care. It is the same thing with respect to the politer Arts among us; and the same Defect of Heat which gives a Fierceness to our Natures, may contribute to that Roughness of our Language, which bears some Analogy to the harsh Fruit of colder Countries. (par. 13, lines 187–192)

The "nobler kinds of fruit" which the people of Britain have to struggle to grow by putting up fences to keep out the cold winds and building walls to reflect the light of the sun are compared to "the politer Arts among us". The humour in the passage is created by the remark that trying to grow those nobler fruits is an expensive pastime and is only worth it if the soil is good. The harsh climate also has the effect of giving "a Fierceness to our Natures" and, says Swift, may make our language rough. However, note Swift's subtle use of the modal verb "may" here. He does not state unequivocally that the climate *is* responsible for the language; he simply entertains the possibility. Since we already know what Swift really thinks of the "politer Arts" practised by those he is attacking, it is difficult to take this passage as anything other than tongue-in-cheek humour. Obviously, he is familiar with the *good climate/ soil myth*, but the passage reveals that he mocks those who believe it.

There is enough evidence in the *Proposal* to suggest that the language myths he uses for his surface argument (i.e. the complaint) should not be taken at face value. This is important to bear in mind since Swift also introduces another language myth, which the Milroys take very seriously in constructing their complaint tradition, the *myth of the immutability of language*, assuming that a perfect language should not be changed. The myth is referred to several times in the text, but it is inconsistent both with the idea of language decay and death and also with the idea that English has not reached perfection. How can English reach perfection if it does not change? Setting up this new language myth is equivalent to setting up yet another straw man in an attempt to divert his readers from his true intent in the *Proposal*, or, rather, to allow his readers to see through the argument to construct his other readings. In the following section, I shall discuss some of these alternative readings.

5. ALTERNATIVE READINGS OF SWIFT'S *PROPOSAL*

In the first paragraph Swift states that his proposal to correct, enlarge and "ascertain" (= fix) the English language is aimed at the "Improvement of Knowledge and Politeness", and he rates its significance as being on a par with "paying the *Nation's Debts*, or opening a Trade into the *South Sea*", which I have interpreted as a typical Swiftian, tongue-in-cheek exaggeration that the reader is not meant to take seriously. What might have been his purpose in linking the complaint with such a blatantly nonserious comment?

Recall from the beginning of section 4 that the Tory Party had just assumed office after a long period of Whig domination, with the Earl of Oxford taking over the position of lord high treasurer and first minister to the queen. Swift had also switched his political allegiance from the Whigs to the Tories about the same time. Was he currying favour and looking for a pension from his friend and patron Robert Harley? The final two paragraphs of the letter (paras. 23 and 24) would certainly support this interpretation, and I shall return to this second alternative reading of the text below.

In the second paragraph, as we have seen, Swift repeats his complaint "in the Name of all the Learned and Polite Persons of the Nation", which echoes Defoe's suggestion in 1697 for a project to institute a language academy similar to the Académie Française. Defoe had suggested that the work of the projected academy "should be to encourage polite learning" and "to polish and refine the English tongue". Immediately after his complaint Swift berates "the Pretenders to polish and refine [the language]", who have "chiefly multiplied Abuses and Absurdities". Defoe was an active Whig, and one of his notable achievements was the publication of the periodical *A Review of the Affairs of France, and of All Europe* from 1704 till 1713. There is an oblique reference to contributions to that periodical in paragraph 19 when Swift mentions that "about a Year ago" he had "communicated to the Publick, much of what I had to offer upon this Subject [the "design" to prevent English from changing], by the hands of an ingenious Gentleman, who for a long Time did thrice a Week divert or instruct the Kingdom by his Papers". The *Review* did indeed appear three times a week, and Swift had contributed a series of articles to it during 1711 with the title "The British Visions: or, Isaac Bickerstaff's Twelve Prophecies for the Year" under the pseudonym of Isaac Bickerstaff. The pseudonym (sometimes written with a final "e") was Swift's invention, but it was also used by Richard Steele in the *Tatler*, another Whig periodical to which Swift contributed. The character was also appropriated by the *Spectator* when it began to appear in 1711, which prompts Swift to state in paragraph 19 that Bickerstaff "is supposed to pursue the same Design at present under the title of the *Spectator*". Needless to say, the strong implication is that this is not the case.

Rereading the *Proposal* from this point of view leads to the conclusion that, although it may have been, on the surface at least, a complaint letter, it was really intended as a political tract aimed at Swift's former allies in the Whig Party, above all, Addison, Steele and possibly also Shaftesbury and Defoe, who we may take to be the "Pretenders to polish and refine [the language]". The language issue was thus merely the pretext on which to hang a set of rather obscure political "bickerings" (cf. the name Bickerstaff itself). What it displays, however, is the potency of the "language as a cultural achievement" ideology in the early eighteenth century. Standard English truly was considered to be a *Kultursprache.* Is there any evidence for this interpretation? Yes, indeed, and it appears in paragraphs 9 to 13 of the *Proposal,* which I have already commented on above.

A further subtext occurs in paragraph 23, which offers a second alternative reading. We know that Swift frequently tried to convince the Tory government to grant him an ordination within the Church of England, but without any success. After the accession to the throne of George I in 1714 and the return to power of the Whigs, Swift accepted the position of dean of St. Patrick's Cathedral in Dublin and stayed in that office until his death in 1745. Gaining a living in England or receiving a state pension were professional and economic priorities for Swift in 1712, and his hopes rested on Robert Harley, the newly created Earl of Oxford. The following sequence from the penultimate paragraph of the *Proposal* (par. 23, lines 363–376) supports this hypothesis:

> The *French King* bestows about half a dozen Pensions to learned Men in several Parts of *Europe,* and perhaps a dozen in his whole Kingdom; which, in the whole, do probably not amount to half the Income of many a private Commoner in *England*; yet have more contributed to the Glory of that Prince, than any Million he hath otherwise employed. For Learning, like all true Merit, is easily satisfied, whilst the False and Counterfeit is perpetually craving, and never thinks it hath enough. The smallest Favour given by a Great Prince, as a Mark of Esteem, to reward the Endowments of the Mind, never fails to be returned with Praise and Gratitude, and loudly celebrated to the World. I have known some Years ago, several Pensions given to particular Persons (how deservedly I shall not enquire) any one of which, if divided into smaller Parcels, and distributed by the Crown, to those who might, upon occasion, distinguish themselves by some extraordinary Production of Wit or Learning, would be amply sufficient to answer the End. Or if any such Persons were above Money, (as every great *Genius* certainly is, with very moderate Conveniences of Life) a Medal, or some Mark of Distinction, would do full as well.

Swift's example of the French king giving pensions to "learned Men in several Parts of *Europe*" is an allusion to his expectation that, if the project he is proposing to Harley (which was really Defoe's idea in 1697) is accepted, he too should be given a pension. He backs this up with the comment, "I have known some Years ago, several Pensions given to particular Persons (how deservedly I shall not enquire)", which might very well be a reference to a state pension received by Defoe, which Defoe himself later denied having received. In any event, the message is clear that Swift is suggesting that he be given a state pension but that he would settle for some other form of recognition: "a Medal, or some Mark of Distinction, would do full as well."

6. SWIFT AND AFTER

Whether or not the *Proposal* is considered to be the "great classic of complaint literature", Swift's open letter to the Earl of Oxford certainly illustrates the degree to which he was able to use the standard language question as a smokescreen to hide behind while indulging in political infighting. It is also significant that language can become such a convenient instrument precisely because it is part of the ideological discourse of politeness. Swift may not have believed in that discourse, but he was clearly able to put it to good use.

Certainly, the idea of an emergent standard language at the beginning of the eighteenth century was able to stir the emotions of a whole range of writers, most of whom wrote in the name of "politeness" and "polite society". Milroy is right when he says that the lay conception of English henceforth was that of a cultural achievement and that looking at English in that way has caused a great deal of harm in the form of social discrimination since the early eighteenth century for millions of people in Britain. But he overlooks the way in which language became a political issue. In omitting this aspect of language in the early eighteenth century, the Milroys have raised Swift to a rather dubious status as the first writer in a complaint tradition, while conveniently forgetting that the myths created around the English language produced "complaints" well before the eighteenth century. It is precisely those myths that Swift uses as part of his satire and political polemic in the *Proposal*. In omitting the fact that they were dealing with the greatest satirist in English, the Milroys run the risk of creating yet another myth, which we might call, for argument's sake, the ***myth of complaining about English***.

Of course, this does not mean that such a myth exists, although the latest political battle over the cultural status of standard English that was fought in the 1980s and early 1990s and will be the subject of chapter 10, was essentially a battle fought over such complaints. It was couched in terms of the educational needs of the new National Curriculum, but it was once again based on the old belief that language is a cultural achievement, a *Kultursprache*, the product of an advanced civilisation. Language is not created by culture; it helps to create culture. It is an ever-changing sociocognitive ability that each and every one of us has, in whatever form. We can construct cultural artefacts and aesthetic verbal masterpieces with language, and although that does not make it the product of culture, it certainly makes it one of the most potent means by which we can create culture. As we shall see in chapter 10, the battle over English in the National Curriculum was not fought through to the end. What now exists is rather an uneasy truce.

To take Swift literally is an extremely risky undertaking. To quote the extract from a popular song sung in the eighteenth century quoted at the top of this chapter: "As for the Dean, you know what I mean. / If a printer will print him, he'll scarce come off clean."

Chapter 8

Polishing the myths

The commercial side of politeness

> The Pretenders to polish and refine [our Language], have chiefly multiplied
> Abuses and Absurdities.
> —Jonathan Swift, *A Proposal for Correcting, Improving and
> Ascertaining the English Tongue*, 1712

1. THE OBSESSION WITH POLITENESS

My interpretation of Swift's *Proposal* in chapter 7 reveals that his complaint
is not primarily what James Milroy calls "the battle against evil and corruption"
if "evil and corruption" are perceived as decay in the standard of English
used by his contemporaries. In the *Proposal* Swift explicitly uses a nexus of
myths about the English language discursively to belittle his political opponents. Within the metaphor of language as a living organism, a state of maturity must be reached before decay can set in, and Swift explicitly states in the
Proposal that English has not yet reached that state. One could of course
argue that maturity is not equivalent to perfection, and this would open the
way to interpreting Swift as suggesting that the English language, now that it
has reached maturity, needs to be perfected. But this would hardly be
equivalent to saying that Swift is complaining about English, despite his open
declaration in the second paragraph of the *Proposal* that this is his intent.

This chapter is an adaptation and extension of an article written for publication in the journal *Pragmatics* 9(1), 5–20, titled "Language and politeness in early eighteenth century Britain".

The complaint as such is levelled more at his political enemies and erst-while friends Joseph Addison and Richard Steele. Framing the *Proposal* as a complaint creates a convenient smokescreen to veil his political invective, and his major goal is to criticise, in a political framework, the claims made by these writers in the *Tatler* and the *Spectator* to present examples of polite behaviour. The "improvements" that Swift berates lie within the discourse of polishing and refining the language, the ideology of politeness. My focus in this chapter will thus be on how the nexus of myths that he uses in the *Proposal* are part of a wider discourse beginning at the end of the seventeenth century through which the ideology of politeness is constructed. I argue that the myths are "polished" to support this ideology, and my wider purpose is to show how the ideology itself became part of a redefinition of social class in Britain during the eighteenth century that had a crucial impact on attitudes towards language in the nineteenth and twentieth centuries. I am thus concerned with a brief but very significant phenomenon in the cultural history of the English language, the eighteenth-century obsession with polite-ness and the prescriptive grammarian's urge to "fix", or, as Swift would say, "ascertain", the English language.

Milroy and Milroy (1999) have called the urge to standardise English "the ideology of the standard", and in line with the blueprint set out in chapter 1, we could say that "the time was ripe" for this discourse archive to emerge. But we need to see the emergence of the archive as being driven by the obsession with politeness (Watts 2002, 2003a), which, at least from the point of view of language, converged on the nexus of language myths discussed in chapter 5. In forging and interweaving these ideologies in the eighteenth century, creative writers, literary critics, grammarians and other writers on language were involved in constructing the emergent standard language as a "natural" fea-ture of polite society. In doing so, they paved the way for the unnatural, social construction of oral "standard English". Contrary to what we might assume if we run the conceptual metaphor suggested in figure 5.1 in chapter 5, the movement towards standardising English was not a natural process. "Polite society" was an unnatural construct. As Swift claims in the *Proposal*, "with all the real good Qualities of our Country, we are naturally not very Polite".

One illustration of what is meant by the expression "polishing the myths" can be found in Samuel Johnson's work in the mid-eighteenth century. Johnson, the "father" of the English dictionary, was not just a dictionary writer; he was also a poet, an essayist and a literary critic. In 1747, when Johnson was gathering his ideas and materials for the dictionary, he pub-lished *The Plan of a Dictionary of the English Language*. In this plan, or, as Swift might say, "project", he states that the major aims of the dictionary are "to preserve the purity and ascertain the meaning of our English idiom" and "to fix the English language". The two aims are firmly embedded within the **language purity myth** and the **immutability myth**. To achieve these aims, it was his intention to select "the words and phrases used in the general intercourse of life, or found in the works of those we commonly stile *polite* writers". Both myths are guided by the eighteenth-century concept of politeness, although in the first 60 years of the century, "polishers" of the language were more concerned with written than with oral language. Like many other critics in the first half of the eighteenth century, Johnson assumed that English had already achieved a level of purity and perfection, and they were concerned that it should be prevented from changing, since "all change is of itself evil, which ought not to be hazarded but for evident advantage". The "polite writers" to whom Johnson refers are at one and the same time, in his eyes, "the best writers", although we learn next to nothing in *The Plan of a Dictionary of the English Language* about what makes them "best". Beyond this, however, the dictionary also aims to achieve the equivalent of Boileau's proposal to the Académie Française that "they should review all their *polite* writers, and correct such impurities as might be found in them, that their authority might not contribute, at any distant time, to the depravation of the language".

When it was published in 1755, the *Dictionary* took a more liberal view of change in language, and no attempt was made to "correct impurities" in any "polite" writer's work. Looked at from our present-day perspective, it seems preposterous to imagine that a linguist should castigate an author for mistakes in his grammar or lexis, let alone claim the right to correct any such "mistakes". But throughout the eighteenth century, criticism of the "best" authors—the "polite" authors—by grammarians and other language "experts" was relatively common. We can perhaps excuse Johnson, since he was himself a poet and essayist, but when we read in Bishop Robert Lowth's *A Short Introduction to English Grammar* (1761) the statement that "It will evidently appear from these Notes, that our best Authors for want of some rudiments of this kind [i.e. rudiments of English grammar] have sometimes fallen into mistakes, and been guilty of palpable errors in point of Grammar. (viii–ix)", we can perhaps be excused for inferring that grammarians placed themselves above the "best authors". The notes that Lowth refers to are copious notes placed at the foot of most of the pages of the grammar illustrating and explaining for the benefit of the nonpolite reader "mistakes" made by authors such as Pope, Addison, Milton and even the *Authorised Version of the Bible*.

Nor should we underestimate the influence of grammarians on authors. Arnovick (1999: 45–47) discusses Swift's "corrections" in his use of the modal verbs "will" and "shall" in the manuscript versions of his humorous *Directions to Servants* (1731). She attributes this to the influence of the prescriptive grammarians of the early eighteenth century:

> Swift's practice of revising and correcting questionable usage substantiates the usage quandaries troubling eighteenth-century writers. The dean's uncertainty also underscores the practical need shared by others writing English. Their requirement is satisfied by the grammars. Where common use is proscribed, correct use is prescribed and praised.

But who were the "polite" writers referred to by Johnson and Lowth? What did the term "polite", here in reference to writers, mean throughout the eighteenth century? Why were grammarians so concerned that their "best" authors should write "polite language", and what gave them the authority to decide on this? What effect did this insistence on authority have on the emergence of standard English? Why is it important, in tracing out these cultural developments in the emergence of the standard, to consider works of literature and the work of literary critics? To be able to answer any of these questions, we first need to understand how the term "politeness" was understood in the eighteenth century, and to acquire that understanding, we need to reach back into the seventeenth century.

2. THE ORIGINS OF EIGHTEENTH-CENTURY POLITENESS

Defoe's *Essay upon Projects*, which played a prominent part in the reinterpretation of Swift's *Proposal* in chapter 7, suggests that the society to be set up in England along the lines of the Académie Française should be composed of "none but persons of the first figure in learning". Unlike Johnson, however, he does give us some hints as to what he means by "best" by indicating those persons who should *not* be chosen as members of his proposed society.

He specifies that the work of this society

> should be to encourage polite learning, to polish and refine the English tongue, and advance the so much neglected faculty of correct language, to establish purity and propriety of style, and to purge it from all the irregular additions that ignorance and affectation have introduced; and all those innovations in speech, if I may call them such, which some dogmatic writers have the confidence to foster upon their native language, as if their authority were sufficient to make their own fancy legitimate. (Defoe 1697, in Bredvold, Root and Sherburn 1932: 3)

From the aims of the society as set out here by Defoe (see the underlined phrases in the above quotation), it would appear that he places the blame for the faults that need to be corrected on the shoulders of the presumed authority of certain "dogmatic writers", thus giving us a clear example of a writer in his role of critic passing moral judgment on fellow writers on the grounds of incorrect language and innovations in speech. So polite, or polished, language can be equated with correct language, purified language, language in which no change is condoned. Like Swift, but more seriously than Swift, Defoe uses the discourse of the *pure language myth* and the *immutability myth*. He also sets up and runs the following additional metaphorical blends, which turn out to be crucial throughout the eighteenth century:

1. A CORRECT LANGUAGE IS A POLISHED LANGUAGE
2. A POLISHED LANGUAGE IS A REFINED LANGUAGE
3. A POLISHED LANGUAGE IS A POLITE LANGUAGE

The myth constructed from these blends will henceforth be called the ***myth of the polite language***. Thus, as early as Defoe (1697), we recognise a nexus of closely associated myths guiding an ideological discourse on standardisation that was soon to develop into a discourse archive during the course of the eighteenth and nineteenth centuries (cf. Milroy & Milroy 1999; Watts 1999b and 2002). This discourse was destined to become the lynchpin of the "history of the language" discourse.

Defoe's conditions for admission into his proposed "society" give us further clues as to the meaning of "politeness" and "polite language" at the beginning of the eighteenth century:

> Into this society should be admitted none but persons eminent for learning, and yet none, or but very few, whose business or trade was learning. For I may be allowed, I suppose, to say we have seen many great scholars mere learned men, and graduates in the last degree of study, whose English has been far from polite, full of stiffness and affectation, hard words, and long unusual coupling of syllables and sentences, which sound harsh and untuneable to the ear, and shock the reader both in expression and understanding. (3)

Persons well known for their learning may become members of Defoe's proposed society, but not scholars from Oxford and Cambridge Universities, since their language is reprehensible by his standards. From what he says above, we can conclude that polite language must be fluent, easy to understand and without unnecessary syntactic complexity. It must be "easy" and "melodious" on the ear, and it must not shock the reader either in what it expresses or in the way it is expressed. In addition, it is not to be acquired in the major seats of learning.

Defoe then goes on to talk about the "spoilers and destroyers of a man's discourse", and he asks his reader "a little to foul his mouth with the brutish, sordid, senseless expressions which some gentlemen call polite English, and speaking with a grace". Those who claim to speak "polite English" but who lower themselves to use "brutish, sordid, senseless expressions" have "the character of a gentleman with a good estate, and of a good family, and with tolerable parts", but they do not cut a polished figure "for want of education". There are, we might say, gentlemen and gentlemen, and the difference lies in the degree to which each group uses polite English. However, we might wonder where a member of the landed gentry is to acquire the art of speaking and writing polite English if not at the universities.

To summarise Defoe's thoughts on his proposed language society, "polite" learning is closely associated with "polishing" and "refining" the English language and with establishing "purity and propriety of style", and it is placed in opposition to "ignorance and affectation" and to "innovations in speech".

I argue in this chapter that the term "polite" in the early eighteenth century in Britain, particularly when it was connected with language use, was manipulated in a socially selective way—that politeness was an attribute of the legitimate language variety within the early-eighteenth-century linguistic marketplace in Britain, access to which was equivalent to access to high social status. It was, in other words, part of an embryonic ideological discourse of standardisation. I shall also argue that determining who was a member of "polite society" was likewise in the hands of those who had already gained access. Defoe makes this quite explicit at one point:

> I would therefore have this society wholly composed of gentlemen, whereof twelve to be of the nobility, if possible, and twelve private gentlemen, and a class of twelve to be left open for mere merit, let it be found in who or what sort it would, which would lie as the crown of their study, who have done something eminent to deserve it. (Defoe 1698, in Bredvold et al. 1932: 4)

The nobility and the gentry are qualified to decide what should be deemed "polite English", and the implication is that they should also decide on which 12 scholars are worthy of admission to the society, thereby completing their number.

Before continuing, however, we need to define what Defoe understood by terms such as "nobility" and "gentlemen", as they will be used in this chapter to refer to what we call "social classes" today. The "nobility" included those members of society with inherited titles who possessed the hereditary right (and often the obligation) to appear at the royal court and to sit in the House of Lords (and this included the bishops of the Church of England). The term "gentry" was used to refer to a social class of hereditary land-owners with or without inherited titles (although many of them received knighthoods) but without any obligation to attend at the royal court and generally with no hereditary right to sit in the House of Lords. The gentry, who will be central to my argument in this chapter, thus constituted a powerful rural-based landowning class with no necessary affinities to the section of society that is often referred to as the "bourgeoisie".[1] The term "bourgeoisie" is certainly not coextensive with the gentry (although there might have been overlaps) and is more frequently used to refer to the wealthy urban middle classes of cities such as London, Bath and Norwich. The term "middle classes" was not generally used in the eighteenth century, but our modern term can certainly be used to refer to wealthy citizens who, through their wealth and influence, however these were acquired, had been

---

1. German writers often to refer to the gentry as the *Kleinadel* ("lower nobility") but this is inappropriate inasmuch as many of the gentry did not possess hereditary titles, having risen through the ranks of the yeomanry in the late medieval and early modern periods of English history.

steadily gaining in social prestige since Elizabethan times and were to compete with the gentry for social standing throughout the eighteenth century.

In the following sections, I also show how the concept of politeness in early-eighteenth-century Britain had already been subtly changed from the second half of the seventeenth century, when it was taken over from French conduct writers such as La Bruyère, the Abbé de Bellegarde and Antoine de Courtin (cf. Ketcham 1985: chap. 2).

3. THE *HONNÊTE HOMME* AND DESCARTES' PHYSIOLOGICAL METAPHOR

In his *Discours de la Méthode*, first published at Leiden in 1637, René Descartes postulated that human beings consist of a body and a soul (or mind, depending on how one translates the French lexeme *âme*) and that it was the soul/mind that distinguishes humans from animals. To conceptualise the relationship between body and soul/mind more clearly, Descartes used the metaphor of the moving machine, or automaton, which in the seventeenth century was undoubtedly driven by clockwork with springs, cogwheels, and so on, to refer to the movements, gestures and postures of the human body. The movements made by the animal automaton were under the control of "interior passions". The major distinction between animals and humans, however, resided in the human capacity for thought and language. For Descartes, this was the *âme*, which was not like a "pilot in his ship" (Descartes 1973: 159) but was independent of the body and would therefore not die with it.

The French conduct writers in the last 20 to 25 years of the seventeenth century adapted Descartes' metaphor to Cicero's concept of the *honestus vir* (*honnête homme*, "honest/upright man") and postulated a direct relationship between the mechanical functioning of the individual human body and the state of a person's soul. Ketcham (1985: 50) quotes the following passage from the English translation of the Abbé de Bellegarde's *Reflexions upon the Politeness of Manners*, which appeared in 1698 under its original French title *Réflexions sur la politesse des mœurs, avec des maximes pour la société civile, suite des Réflexions sur le ridicule*:

> There's so great a Correspondence betwixt those Springs that move the Heart, and those that move the Countenance; that we may judge by this outward Dial-plate, how the Clock-work goes in the Soul. (1717: 40)

The harmonious correspondence between the body and the mind/soul—the perfect union between an individual's outward behaviour (the body) and her character (the mind/soul)—was called "politeness" or "modesty", and the disharmony or disjunction of body and soul/mind was called "affectation" (cf. Ketcham 1985: 50). De Bellegarde defines "affectation" as follows:

> Affectation is the falsification of the whole Person, which deviates from all that is Natural, whereby it might please to put on an ascititious Ayre, wherewithal to become Ridiculous. . . . People corrupted with this Vice, have nothing natural in their way of Talking, Walking, Dressing, turning their Eyes or Head, these are Motions unknown to other Men. (1717: 58, in Ketcham 1985: 50–51)

Politeness is therefore a "natural" quality, and its opposite is affectation. Both are revealed in an individual's actions and, above all else, in her words. So from the very outset language use is taken as an indicator of that harmony between body and soul known as "politeness".

But there is a major problem with this definition. If politeness is natural and the harmonious union between the body and the soul, would we not have to say that a person with an evil soul, whose behaviour "naturally" reflects this character, is also polite? To counteract this argument, the conduct writers posit that the perfect union between body and soul is a virtue, not a vice. Hence, only if an individual is naturally good can we talk of "politeness".

De Bellegarde goes one step further and posits that the virtue of politeness should "have its Principle in the Soul, as being the Product of an accomplish'd Mind, centring on it self, and Master of its Thoughts and Words" (1717: 2, in Ketcham 1985: 51). In other words, to rescue the concept of politeness, we need to make a distinction between the soul and the mind, such that the soul (which could be roughly correlated here with the notion of character) is the product of the mind, but only after this has been refined or polished (i.e. has become "accomplish'd"). This suggests that the raw product, like a diamond, has to be polished to turn it into a "soul", and, as we shall see, it can only be polished if the individual is a member of the gentry or aristocracy. The rising middle classes, and most certainly the labouring classes, were excluded from any possibility of being polished—of having a soul and becoming "polite".

Once again, however, this contradicts the principle that politeness is natural. Polishing one's mind or having it polished is a social process of education and acculturation. The kind and degree of accomplishment that is the goal of the process is socially and ideologically constructed. It is determined not by the individual himself but by repeated habitual interactions with others, with the result that it is socially reproduced.

In fact, de Bellegarde contradicts his earlier assertions about the ideal harmony between the "accomplished", self-possessed mind and exterior behaviour in the examples he gives, which display individuals almost wholly concerned to please others by carrying out actions (including forms of verbal behaviour) intended to influence those others. He gives a second definition of the polite individual as one who "puts on all Appearances, and transforms himself into all Shapes, the better to gain his Point" (1717: 2), the purpose being to "purchase the Esteem and Affection of Men" (1717: 39). This commercial idea will be taken up again later, as it lies at the crux of the development of the concept of "politeness" in eighteenth-century Britain.

In the conduct writers, and in particular in de Bellegarde's work, we can identify the following self-contradictory and somewhat confusing aspects of politeness:

1. Politeness is the ideal union between the character of an individual and her external actions (e.g. the language which that individual uses).
2. Politeness is the ability to please others through one's external actions (e.g. through the language one uses).
3. Politeness is a natural attribute of a "good" character.
4. Politeness is a socially acquired state of mind which is adjudged to have reached a state of being "polished" and of thereby being in conformity with a set of socially accepted forms of behaviour.

The contradictions evident here make it possible to argue that an individual is born polite, that there is a natural connection between his soul/mind and bodily actions (including language). On the other hand, it is just as easy to argue that a person may acquire the ability to please and influence others whatever the circumstances of his birth. The contradictions also make it very easy to argue that politeness can be acquired only if one is socialised into the "correct" set of socially accepted norms, that is, if one is born into the appropriate social class. Those who are born outside that class can never acquire politeness. The attribution of "affectation" can always be used to categorise the behaviour of those who are not class members.

It is precisely this social interpretation of politeness that was mythologised when taken up by writers on language, morals, society and philosophy in Britain. The claim that politeness is a natural attribute of certain individuals and not of others is used to exclude the latter from the ranks of the former. In eighteenth-century Britain, politeness is thus caught up in a subdiscourse that we may call the "ideology of gentrification". Within this discourse, language behaviour was interpreted as one of the most significant markers, if not the most significant marker, of politeness. "The ideology of gentrification" becomes inextricably linked through the language myths with what Milroy and Milroy (1999) have called "the ideology of standard English". The link became so strong that "standard English" was ultimately almost synonymous with "polite English" or "the English of polite society", and even found its way into some of the prescriptive grammar books of the eighteenth century.

4. GENTRIFYING PHILOSOPHY

We saw in section 2 that Defoe excluded as members of his projected "society" for the "polishing" and "refining" of the English language all university scholars unless they were specifically elected by those in authority, the first 24 members chosen from the ranks of the nobility and the gentry. The exclusion of scholars from Defoe's putative society can be explained as follows. Throughout the seventeenth century, from the time of Francis Bacon, conflict had arisen between, on the one hand, those following a purely scholastic, syllogistic mode of argument in "scientific investigation" in which, in the tradition of the Renaissance, the ancients were credited with having already discovered the principal "laws of nature and the universe", and, on the other hand, those who were interested in questioning nature directly by experimentation, observation and manipulation. The former, the scholastics, were associated with the universities, whereas the latter, the experimenters or the "virtuosi", were associated with or became members of the Royal Society of London, which was granted its charter by Charles II in 1662.

From the outset the Royal Society, although it did not explicitly set itself up in opposition to the universities, saw itself as the heir to Bacon's utopian House of Salomon in the *New Atlantis,* in which he forecast "the Triumph of the new empiricism" (Cope & Jones 1958: xii). Some of the founding members of the Royal Society, like John Wallis and John Wilkins, were associated with the universities, but the majority were private individuals, most of them from the gentry and some from the nobility. Thomas Sprat, in his *History of the Royal Society*, has the following to say about its composition:

> But, though the *Society* entertains very many men *of particular Professions*; yet the farr greater Number are *Gentlemen,* free and unconfin'd. By the help of this there was hopefull Provision made against *new corruptions* of Learning, which have been long complain'd of, but never remov'd: The *one,* that *Knowledge* still degenerates, to consult present profit too soon; the *other,* that *Philosophers* have bin always *Masters, & Scholars;* some imposing, & all the other submitting; and not as equal observers without dependence. (1667: 67)

By "philosophers" Sprat is referring here to academic scholars, and the guarantee against both the degeneration of knowledge and its esoteric isolation in the universities is the preponderance of "gentlemen" in the Royal Society. "Natural philosophy" was therefore the domain of gentlemen scholars, of intelligent, inquisitive and enthusiastic amateurs rather than professional academics, and that is precisely the point of view that Defoe puts forward in his project for a society for the polishing and refining of the English language.

At a later point in the *History of the Royal Society* Sprat, giving a historical account of the development of learning from the classical period to the seventeenth century, suggests the following reason for learning being "the first thing, that was constantly swept away, in all destructions of Empire, and forein inundations" (118):

> It is, because *Philosophy* had been spun out, to so fine a thread, that it could be known but only to those, who would throw away all their whole Lives upon it. It was made too subtile, for the *common,* and *gross* conceptions of men of business, it had before in a measure been banish'd, by the Philosophers themselves, out of

the World; and shut up in the shades of their walks. And by this means, it was first look'd upon, as most *useless*; and so fit, soonest to be *neglected.* Whereas if at first it had been made to converse more with the senses, and to assist familiarly in all occasions of *human life*; it would, no doubt, have been thought needful to be preserv'd, in the most *Active,* and *ignorant* Time. (118–119)

Writing on behalf of the Royal Society, Sprat perceived a need to make philosophy accessible to those who were not professional scholars, and this meant using a style of language that he defines as a "natural way of speaking", "preferring the language of Artizans, Countrymen, and Merchants, before that, of Wits, or Scholars" (113).

However, with an increasing number of members coming from the ranks of the nobility and the gentry, what Sprat and his fellow members of the Royal Society in its early days must have thought of as a popularisation of philosophy had effectively become a "gentrification" of philosophy by the end of the seventeenth century. This meant taking philosophy out of the scholar's study and putting it into the "polite" world of the gentleman's drawing room, making it, in fact, part of what it meant to be "polite". This is nowhere more obvious than in the works of Anthony Ashley Cooper, the 3rd Earl of Shaftesbury, whose work spans the period from 1699 to 1710 and consists of essays that were collected and published together in 1711 under the title *Characteristics of Men, Manners, Opinions, Times: An Inquiry Concerning Virtue or Merit.*

Shaftesbury's argument is that humans, as individuals, are driven towards their own "self-good", but that, since they are also social animals, conflict between "private interest" and "public good" leads to what he calls "vicious affection". As a consequence "a creature cannot really be good and natural in respect of his society or public, without being ill and unnatural towards himself" (Shaftesbury 1711: bk. 1, pt. 2, sec. 2, in Bredvold et al. 1955: 249). In section 3 I put forward four definitions of politeness as defined by the conduct writers. I also argued that the third and fourth of these definitions contradict each other. If politeness is a natural attribute of a good character (definition 3), the "good" can only be adjudged as good in conformity with a set of socially accepted forms of behaviour (definition 4). In other words, politeness may be the natural attribute of a good character, but it can only be termed politeness if it is a socially acquired state of mind. Precisely this contradiction emerges in Shaftesbury's definition of public good as against private good:

When in general all the affections or passions are suited to the public good, or good of the species, as above mentioned, then is the natural temper entirely good. If, on the contrary, any requisite passion be wanting, or if there be any one supernumerary or weak, or anywise disserviceable or contrary to that main end, then is the natural temper, and consequently the creature himself, in some measure corrupt and ill. (251)

Hence, if all of an individual's "affections or passions" benefit the public good, then that individual's "natural temper" (or, to use Descartes' term, that person's *âme*) is good. If anything is missing from a perfect fit with the "public good", it does not matter whether or not the person's "affections or passions" benefit his private good, that person is "in some measure corrupt and ill". In Shaftesbury's terms, being "corrupt" or being "ill" is a quality that does not fit the "public good"; it is, in other words, not legitimate. "Corrupt" or "ill" language is thus language which does not fit the public good, language which is not legitimate.

But what does this have to do with politeness in Shaftesbury's philosophy? In book 3 of *Characteristicks of Men, Manners, Opinions, Times (Miscellany)*, Shaftesbury creates a fictive narrator, an alter ego commenting on and supporting Shaftesbury's philosophy. In chapter 2 of the *Miscellany* the narrator states that Shaftesbury's, and his, aim is "to advance philosophy (as harsh a subject as it may appear) on the very foundation of what is called agreeable and polite" (267). On the basis of this credo, he suggests a "joint endeavour":

> Our joint endeavour, therefore, must appear this; to show "that nothing which is found charming or delightful in the polite world, nothing which is adopted as pleasure or entertainment, of whatever kind, can any way be accounted for, supported, or established, without the pre-establishment or supposition of a certain taste". (267)

Shaftesbury's philosophy is thus aimed at the "polite world", and it is also educational and moralistic. Taste is a large part of what it means to be a polished member of society, but that taste is not simply taste in outward appearances and behaviour but also taste in morals:

> Let us therefore proceed in this view, addressing ourselves to the grown youth of our polite world. Let the appeal be to those whose relish is retrievable, and whose taste may yet be formed in morals, as it seems to be already in exterior manners and behaviour. (272)

In addition, decorum and grace in outward appearance, movements and behaviour are all attributes of politeness, as is a love of beauty, symmetry and order. At a number of points in his writings Shaftesbury also explicitly links gentility (i.e. being a member of the social class of the gentry) with politeness. All these elements are present in the following quotation from the *Miscellany*:

> Whoever has any impression of what we call gentility or politeness is already so acquainted with the decorum and grace of things that he will readily confess a pleasure and enjoyment in the very survey and contemplation of this kind. Now if in the way of polite pleasure the study and love of beauty be essential, the study and

love of symmetry and order, on which beauty depends, must also be essential in the same respect. (273)

The process of gentrifying philosophy, however, leads to a conception of language use in which decorum, grace, beauty, symmetry and order are now the main features defining polite language, or the language of polite society. Shaftesbury shifts the focus of a "natural way of speaking" to the language behaviour of polite society, which includes all these attributes, and in effect provides a programmatic blueprint for dealing with language and politeness throughout the rest of the eighteenth and well into the nineteenth century. Precisely what kind of behaviour, including language behaviour, counted as exemplars of "decorum", "grace", "beauty", "symmetry" and "order" could be decided only by members of the social classes of the gentry and the nobility themselves.

Legitimate forms of language were thus socially constructed and reproduced by members of polite society, but at the same time what counted as "politeness" could also be reconstructed. As the eighteenth century progressed, forms of legitimate language usage were conceptualised as prescriptive rules of language behaviour and were transformed into the rules of "standard English".

To summarise, then, polite language was the language of all those who propagated the values outlined in Shaftesbury's "Miscellany" and behaved in accordance with them:

a. It was a socially marked language.
b. It was the language of the "best authors".
c. It should be fluent and easy to understand.
d. It should be without unnecessary syntactic complexity.
e. It should be "easy" and "melodious" on the ear.
f. It must not shock the reader.
g. It should represent the aesthetic and moral values given above.
h. It could not be acquired at the universities.
i. It should not change but should retain the presumed purity of English.

In the course of the eighteenth century, literary critics and grammarians took it upon themselves to "police" polite English, or, in sociolinguistic terminology, to codify polite English, in an effort to standardise it. In case there should be any doubt that this was the case, consider the following statement by Shaftesbury's alter ego critic:

For this reason we presume not only to defend the cause of critics, but to declare open war against those indolent supine authors, performers, readers, auditors, actors or spectators who, making their humour alone the rule of what is beautiful and agreeable, and having no account to give of such their humour or odd fancy, reject the criticising or examining art, by which alone they are able to discover the true beauty and worth of every object.

For Shaftesbury and his contemporaries politeness was to be freed from courtly society and urbane civilisation and to become a set of moral values associated with the landed gentry. In other words, it became a quality marking out social class distinctions. The stage was set for a distinction between standard and nonstandard English along the lines of social class and wealth.

5. COMMERCIALISING THE *MYTH* OF THE POLITE LANGUAGE

The ideology of politeness, of course, concerns many more forms of social behaviour than simply language usage, but its greatest effect can be seen in the codification of English throughout the eighteenth century. The beginnings of this codification can be traced back at least as far as the first half of the sixteenth century, but a focus on written text rather than oral language production seems to dominate the first half of the eighteenth century. Driven by the obsession for politeness, it was inevitable that standardisation should rapidly crystallise into an elitist social discourse. Both McIntosh (1998) and Watts (1999b, 2002 and 2003a) use the term "gentrification" to refer to those changes in language that had become social class distinctions by the middle of the century. McIntosh suggests that "the presumption of a system of social rank is deeply implicated in the language itself" (McIntosh 1998: 23), and he ventures the tentative opinion that it "may sometimes have served to exclude unschooled writers from the circles of influence and power" (24). But at the same time he also allows for the possibility that those same forces may have helped the "unschooled" to gain access to circles of power through the acquisition of the standard. I would argue that the mechanism of social exclusion is likely to be more accurate.

In the course of the eighteenth century, emergent standard English is socially constructed as the "legitimate language", a term taken from the work of Pierre Bourdieu within his wider concept of the marketplace. Bourdieu's marketplace refers to all human activity in any social grouping and in any form of social interaction. Despite the obvious fact that the lexeme *marketplace* here is a metaphor taken over from the field of bargaining, buying and selling, Bourdieu did not want it to be understood metaphorically. His point was that in all interaction we give and take, paying for and receiving tribute for the value of that which is taken or given.

The marketplace can be understood either as an emergent concept, one which is constructed in every instance of interaction, or as a concept governing ways in which we interact socially. It is both an opus operatum and a modus operandi, what has been achieved and the mode of achieving it. Bourdieu's theory of practice is thus a theory of what goes on in every emergent marketplace. The marketplace of human interaction can be defined in three ways:

1. It is material or economic, a marketplace in which payment is made by the mutual exchange of equally valued objects or by the symbol of those objects in the form of money.

2. It is social or cultural, one in which payment is made in terms of human relations between the participants, the emergent formation of a range of personal identities, the acquisition and application of forms of knowledge and mental and physical skills, including language.
3. It is symbolic, one in which payment is made in terms of perceived or acquired social status, power, prestige, influence, and so on.

To function in the material marketplace one needs forms of material capital. For example, one needs a product to exchange for some other product or its symbolic monetary value; one needs finance, the means of production and a labour source; one needs to acquire profit; and so on. The sociocultural marketplace is determined by forms of sociocultural capital such as social connections, relational networks, forms of knowledge (including language), mental and physical skills, acquired competences and forms of identity. The forms of capital required in the symbolic marketplace are abstract qualities such as social status and prestige, power, influence and, significantly, language abilities. All three kinds of marketplace are in operation concurrently in any social interaction, and most of the values paid for and received in both the sociocultural and the material marketplaces are derived from forms of symbolic capital, language being one of the most central. So there is a constant flow from an underlying set of symbolic values that fuel interaction in the material and sociocultural marketplaces, and there is a constant give and take between sociocultural and material marketplaces. We can envisage this in the form of a dynamic model such as figure 8.1.

Various kinds of resource are necessary to acquire these forms of capital, the major type of resource in the area of symbolic capital being language.

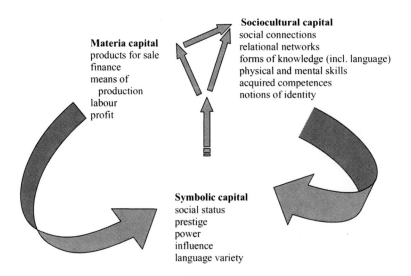

Materia capital
products for sale
finance
means of
    production
labour
profit

Sociocultural capital
social connections
relational networks
forms of knowledge (incl. language)
physical and mental skills
acquired competences
notions of identity

Symbolic capital
social status
prestige
power
influence
language variety

FIGURE 8.1. Bourdieu's concept of the marketplace

However, the types of resource necessary to acquire capital can vary in their forms, and each form can have a greater or lesser value than another form. In the case of language, highly valued forms of language give the user of those forms access to economic and cultural marketplaces. The most highly valued form of linguistic capital, in Bourdieu's terms, is "legitimate language": that language which has acquired a place of preeminence through forms of institutional discourse.

Individuals can be socialised into the ways in which they should comport themselves within any one marketplace, whether economic, cultural, or symbolic. The "feel" for a situation which an individual needs to gain to react accordingly is referred to by Bourdieu as the *habitus*. Bourdieu and Passeron (1994: 8) state that "language is the most active and elusive part of the cultural heritage", thereby implying that the "linguistic *habitus*" is one of the most salient kinds of *habitus* in social interaction and one of the most difficult to change.

The term "legitimate language" refers not only to a highly valued, officially sanctioned linguistic code, but also to the forms of discourse that characterise the social institution concerned. In the case of the social classes of the gentry and the nobility in the eighteenth century, the legitimate language code is constructed as "standard" English, and the legitimate forms of language behaviour are those that define the *habitus* of the gentleman, polite language. The other principal behavioural attributes of the *habitus* are also constructed socially, and, together with the "legitimate language", they serve as a means to admit members to the social classes of the gentry and the nobility or, alternatively, to exclude them.

However, as we saw in sections 2–4, between the time Sprat published his *History of the Royal Society* in 1667 and the time Defoe published his *Essay upon Projects* some thirty years later, a fundamental social reconstruction had taken place in the conceptualisation of the "legitimate language". The reconstruction entailed the emergence of the ***polite language myth***, which formed a central part of a mythical construction involving of the idea of the gentleman and of polite society. In the following three subsections I shall outline how this myth was developed discursively in a sociocultural and sociopolitical sense to become a dominant naturalised discourse (or what Fairclough [1995] would call a hegemonic discourse) in eighteenth-century Britain, one that survived till late in the twentieth century. Its main lynchpin was the "ideology of standard English".

5.1 Establishing the idea of a social order: The *Tatler* and the *Spectator*

Once a nexus of myths such as those I have identified has been discursively created, it needs to be diffused and accepted throughout the relevant sections of society, where it becomes a naturalised form of discourse. Within the class of the gentry and the Whig aristocracy, Shaftesbury's writings were influential in triggering this process of discursive diffusion, as were the writings of Addison, Defoe, Steele and many others, even Swift. But to be generally accepted as a hegemonic discourse, the diffusion has to spread down to other levels of social structure. In the case of the eighteenth century, the rising middle classes needed to embrace the myths and accept the discursive underpinnings of the new ideology. The ideology of politeness had to be popularised through different forms of discourse to gain acceptance, and the ideal means of doing this was through the periodicals printed in London but enjoying enormous popularity well beyond the confines of the capital.[2] In this subsection I shall briefly discuss the construction of social values represented in the Whig literary periodicals from 1709 on, in particular in the *Spectator*, and then, in subsection 5.2, show how "grammar" and "politeness" were explicitly connected in the transference from the *polite language myth* to the *legitimate language myth* in the work of Hugh Jones (1724), whose grammar, the first "colonial" grammar of English, was published in London but written in Williamsburg, Virginia. Subsection 5.3 focuses specifically on the full-scale commercialisation of standard English in grammars, dictionaries, pronouncing dictionaries and handbooks of style in the last 30 to 40 years of the eighteenth century.

The *polite language myth* focused on the social values defining the gentry that were set up by Shaftesbury and dealt with in section 4: "decorum", "grace", "beauty", "symmetry" and "order". These values were nowhere more clearly presented than in the two literary periodicals the *Tatler* and the *Spectator,* the first initiated by Richard Steele, the second initiated by Addison. Addison and Steele were regular contributors to both periodicals, and they were both literary figures (playwrights) as well as critics. But rather than criticise other authors, it was their purpose to hold up a critical social mirror to London society. Their major concern was to popularise the social, moral and aesthetic values of society—in other words, to bring Shaftesbury's philosophy out of the drawing rooms of the landed gentry and into the coffee houses and onto the tea tables of the metropolis. They very rarely mention the terms "polite" or "impolite" explicitly, but as Fitzmaurice (2000: 201) puts it,

> The combination of authority and expertise results in the citation of the *Spectator* as representative of the best in English prose and thus as a candidate for the model *par excellence* of polite language of the period. By the second half of the century, quotations from the periodical, with Addison invariably identified as the source

---

2. Cf. Swift's comment in the *Proposal* on university students reading the "daily Trash" sent down to them from London: "SEVERAL young Men at the Universities, terribly possessed with the fear of Pedantry, run into a worse Extream, and think all Politeness to consist in reading the daily Trash sent down to them from hence: This they call *knowing the World*, and *reading Men and Manners*. Thus furnished they come up to Town, reckon all their Errors for Accomplishments, borrow the newest Set of Phrases, and if they take a Pen into their Hands, all the odd Words they have picked up in a Coffee-House, or a Gaming Ordinary, are produced as Flowers of Style; and the Orthography refined to the utmost".

of the quotation, come to be the staple fare offered by grammars characterising polite language. This kind of citation presents the linguistic aspect of good manners and behaviour. The grammarians cite and change the *Spectator*'s language to demonstrate how elegant language might be improved by grammatical correctness.

Thus one of the main aims of both these Whig periodicals was to reach as large a reading public as allowed by the constraints of daily printing and of dissemination from within London in the early eighteenth century. McCrea (1990: 34) suggests that

> whether Addison and Steele explain the great philosophers, associate activities that we now separate, or domesticate satire, the touchstone for their work remains their commitment to popularity. Pursuing popularity, they cast themselves in the role of explainers and demystifiers.

But whereas McCrea argues that the modern, professional English department in the twentieth century—and here I presume he means "department of English literature"—needed to compartmentalise and specialise its language to forge an academic niche for itself, literature and literary language for Addison and Steele were very much public matters. Their commitment to as large a readership as possible led them to espouse a form of "plain English" that would be understandable to their readers. It was a variety of English in which words are taken "to be the 'representation of speech', and speech to be the representative of truth" (McCrea 1990: 42).

Ketcham (1985: 5) points out that the conventions of tolerant irony, a "sympathetic respect for the commonplaces of life" and the centrality of the family as the generator of human affection were actually created by the *Spectator* essayists

> to establish rather than question an idea of social order. They do not test conventions or test language in order to examine their inadequacies or hidden potentials. Instead they create conventions which will, in turn, create a self-confirming system of values. We do not find incisive thinking in the *Spectator* nor ironic undermining of expectations, but we find a social structure being created out of a literary structure.

This is an eminently important point. If literary structure is constructed out of "polite language", then social structure is determined by the principles of politeness. Once polite social structure has been constructed, the only appropriate literature to represent it will be "polite literature"—literature that does not shock the reader, that displays the aesthetic values of "decorum and grace", "the study and love of beauty" and "the study and love of symmetry and order", and that retains the purity of the English language. Hence, the conventions constructed by the *Spectator* help to create what Ketcham calls "a self-confirming system of values". The ideology of politeness actually con-structs not only the ideological discourse of the standardisation of English but also the eighteenth-century canon of what written texts deserve to be con-sidered literary.

The essays of the *Spectator*, Ketcham says, "reflect assumptions about the structures of social life which in turn reveal changing images of social man in the early eighteenth century" (1985: 3). Ketcham argues that Addison, Steele and the other contributors to the *Spectator* were actively trying to "establish rather than question an idea of social order" (5) and that they were doing so not to test or comment on social conventions or the language in which they were purveyed, but actually to establish those conventions. The way in which the character of Mr Spectator is constructed and allowed to comment on and act as a filter through which the reader could judge a variety of forms of social behaviour supports Ketcham's argument and detracts from McCrea's interpretation that they were only angling for popularity.

The touchstone of Ketcham's "sympathetic respect for the common-places of daily life" (5) is the continual attempt to relate outward behaviour to inward character. It is clear, therefore, that the principle of politeness as rep-resenting a natural connection between an individual's character and actions (including her variety and style of speech) is the main component in a con-scious strategy by Addison and Steele to construct the idea of social order. This, in turn, is closely linked to the attempt to gentrify philosophy, as is explicitly stated in the *Spectator*, no. 10:

> It was said of *Socrates*, that he brought Philosophy down from Heaven, to inhabit among Men; and I shall be ambitious to have it said of me, that I brought Philosophy out of Closets and Libraries, Schools and Colleges, to dwell in Clubs and Assemblies, at Tea-Tables, and in Coffee-Houses.

The periodicals of the second and third decades of the eighteenth century in Britain were immensely influential in helping to construct social conventions, particularly those of "politeness" as I have defined the term in this chapter. They were in fact one of the major sites for the cultural reproduction of polite behaviour and its intimate connection with social class differentiation and the emergence of standard English as a class "dialect". I shall now illustrate the effects of this potent and, in terms of the recent vitriolic debate over standard English in Britain (cf. Honey 1997), problematic connection by briefly looking at Hugh Jones's 1724 grammar of English.

5.2 Institutionalising the ideology of politeness/standard English

Discursively constructing an ideology from a nexus of interconnected myths is one thing, but transforming the discourse into a discourse archive constituting "the law of what can be said, the system that governs the appearance of statements as unique events" (Foucault 1972: 129) is another. As we saw in chapter 3, a discourse archive represents a hegemonic discourse that is open to reproduction, transformation and change. It disguises its discontinuity through statements that disperse the elements involving that discontinuity and that simultaneously construct an impression of cohesion and continuity. When statements founded on myth become naturalised discourse, they acquire a symbolic power (in Bourdieu's terms) that hides the essential discontinuity of the overall discourse.

This is precisely what happened in the discourse of standard English, which fed upon the ideology of politeness and, in so doing, created the discursive means through which that ideology was able to transform itself. This process can be observed throughout the eighteenth century with the overall effect that by the turn of the nineteenth century a belief in standard English had successfully been constructed, and the conceptualisation of politeness had changed in the process. This development can be observed in the extraordinarily rapid institutionalisation of the "legitimate" language, standard English, after 1750 in the education system and, in particular, in the very large numbers of grammars, dictionaries, pronouncing dictionaries and books teaching good style that flooded the market. In the process, the notion of the "polite language" gradually slipped into the background. However, in a little-known grammar published in 1724 by Hugh Jones, all of the myths are still explicitly in evidence.

Jones's *Accidence to the English Tongue* was published in London, although Jones describes himself in the frontispiece as "lately Mathematical Professor at the College of *William* and *Mary,* at *Williamsburgh* in *Virginia,* and Chaplain to the Honorable the Assembly of that Colony". It is therefore not clear whether Jones had returned to Britain at the time his grammar was published or was still in Virginia. The grammar encompasses just 69 pages, which are divided into five parts: 1. "Of English Letters" (pp. 2–15); 2. "Of English Syllables" (pp. 15–19); 3. "Of English Words" (pp. 20–38); 4. "Of English Sentences" (pp. 39–41); and 5. "Of English Discourse, or Speech" (pp. 42–69).

Just more than a third of the grammar was thus devoted to what Jones calls "English Discourse, or Speech", and even a brief look at the topics of part 5 and the way in which Jones presents those topics reveals that, apart from a description of discourse as being composed of sentences and a list of rhetorical tropes with examples, they are in fact rules of how to behave linguistically in a socially acceptable way.

Carew's praise of the "copiousness" of the English language as represented in its dialects is supplanted in Jones's *Accidence* by the discourse of "right English". He even goes so far as to suggest that the "polite Londoner" would find great amusement in listening to people conversing in rural dialects. The telltale word is, of course, "polite". Jones goes on to classify the variety of dialects as a "Confusion of English", but in listing five principal types of

English, he also includes the "Proper, or London Language", meaning not, of course, the English of the East End of London, but rather the English of the royal court. This is a return to the strictures of George Puttenham's *Arte of English Poesie* (cf. chap. 5), in which he advises the budding poet to follow the example of the royal court. In the Whig domination of politics from 1688 till 1712, the court was decidedly not chosen as a model by those writing on English, not even in Swift's *Proposal*. For Jones, the "polite Londoner" can be assumed to be a member of the gentry, and the language variety that Jones goes on to praise is the English of polite society.

The subsection titled "Of Delivery" immediately adopts a prescriptive tone:

> In Delivery you must regard 1st, the Quantity, 2dly, the Accent; 3dly, the Emphasis.

On p. 22 Jones tells his reader that

> it is to be wished, that a Publick *Standard* were fix'd; as a *Touchstone* to true *English*, whereby it might be regulated, and proved, which alone might give License to *Person*, and *Occasion* to make *Addition*, or *Corrections*.

Jones makes a difference here between a "Publick *Standard*" and "true *English*". The form, or grammar, of the language, "a Publick *Standard*", should be used to evaluate whether individual speakers and writers are using the language "truly", that is, in a way that is socially acceptable. Note here also that Jones, like Defoe, would like to see English "regulated, and proved", although he does not make it entirely clear who should be responsible for fixing the standard. From p. 51 till the end of the text Jones's grammar abounds with descriptions of socially acceptable forms of linguistic behaviour and the rules that individuals should follow to produce them, all of which help to construct discursively the myth introduced in this chapter, the ***polite language myth***.

In *The Evolution of English Prose, 1700–1800: Style, Politeness, and Print Culture*, McIntosh (1998) is primarily interested in tracing the cultural developments in print culture in eighteenth-century Britain and showing how prose style became progressively less oral and more "classical" as the century wore on. But he also shows an acute awareness of the close connections between the ideology of politeness and the ideology of standardisation, as we can see from the following two extracts:

> If we think of "English" as a count noun, as a great bundle of different systems of verbal communication, written as well as spoken, with its various strands sortable by region, social class, age, gender, genre, and occasion, then the ordering of English can hardly be ignored. It affected syntax, semantics, word order, vocabulary, style. It introduced new conventions for polite and utilitarian prose, for the

genres preferred by women and men of sensibility, for dictionaries and for political tracts. (235)

Whatever it was that promoted politeness and precision in language may sometimes have served to exclude unschooled writers from the circles of influence and power. Exactly the same forces may sometimes have helped the unschooled to gain access to circles of influence and power by enabling them to write standard English. (24)

McIntosh also deals with the influence that prescriptive grammarians may have had on these developments, although he remains a little cautious here and suggests that we might need to treat the grammarians as being symptomatic of an acute linguistic awareness rather than as the direct or indirect causes of language change. However, Arnovick's analysis of Swift's use of "will" and "shall" (see section 1 of this chapter) indicates that they may not have generated a certain insecurity only in Swift's use of English; they may also have had more influence on the future shape of standard English than sociolinguists are prepared to admit. Such insecurities as Swift's may well have been satisfied by the glut of grammars published in the latter half of the eighteenth century, as we shall see in the following subsection.

5.3 Commercialising standard English, or polite English

Langford, who has charted the eighteenth-century English obsession for politeness and the ways in which it was interwoven with the obsession for commerce in England from 1727 to 1783, goes so far as to call the attempts of the new, upwardly mobile middle classes of society to achieve polite values a "revolution", which he describes as follows:

Nothing unified the middling orders so much as their passion for aping the manners and morals of the gentry more strictly defined, as soon as they possessed the material means to do so. This was a revolution by conjunction rather than confrontation, but it was a revolution none the less, transforming the pattern of social relations, and subtly reshaping the role of that governing class which was the object of imitation. The aspirants sought incorporation in the class above them, not collaboration with those below them. (1989: 63)

Langford describes politeness as "an ambiguous term" that was "naturally associated with the possession of those goods which marked off the moderately wealthy from the poor". Part of what it meant to be "polite" was to acquire the economic ability to purchase those goods. But Langford also defines "the essence of politeness" as "that *je ne sais quoi* which distinguished the innate gentleman's understanding of what made for civilized conduct" (71). During the course of the eighteenth century, as the "middling orders" of society became progressively wealthier and more able to buy the outward trappings of polite society, those above them in the social hierarchy began to stress this je ne sais quoi, which had little to do with wealth as such but hinged on what constituted "civilized conduct". Politeness was not part of the material capital one needed to be successful in the economic marketplace but was located in the symbolic marketplace and concerned with the social values that constitute capital in that marketplace, that is, values that were listed earlier in this chapter such as "social status and prestige, power, influence and...language abilities". The language abilities required are equivalent to Bourdieu's "legitimate language". Through the acquisition of this kind of capital, members of the "middling orders" hoped to gain access to the values of the sociocultural marketplace by establishing significant social connections and relational networks. Part of the value system of the sociocultural marketplace, however, consists of acquiring the requisite forms of knowledge and social competence.

However, as is clear from figure 8.1, material capital feeds into both the symbolic and the sociocultural marketplaces, so wealth and material assets should enable the possessor of those forms of capital to "buy" social status and prestige and to establish the requisite social connections needed for their entry into the social echelons of the gentry. On the other hand, two very prominent forms of symbolic capital were necessary to achieve this, the legitimate language and the "right" kind of education. The second of these could be acquired only at the public boarding schools and grammar schools providing a classical education, whereas the first could be "bought" in the form of pedagogical aids to self-instruction. For the vast majority of the middling orders, acquisition of the legitimate language, "polite language", was thus more feasible than gaining access to a classical education.

As publishing houses sprang up to cater to this burgeoning market, the craze for politeness inevitably became commercialised. Johnson's dictionary was encouraged, if not in fact commissioned, by the publisher Robert Dodsley, and it was Dodsley who also encouraged Robert Lowth to publish his *Short Introduction to English Grammar* in 1761. "Polite pronunciation" was made popular by Thomas Sheridan, the father of playwright Richard Sheridan, in the late 1750s and early 1760s. Sheridan took it upon himself to teach the upwardly mobile "middling orders" of Langford's social scale the "correct" (i.e. polite) way to pronounce English and offered a series of lectures on elocution and related matters to large audiences in different parts of the country in the late 1750s. At each of these lectures he offered the members of the audience the opportunity of putting their names down on a subscribers' list, committing themselves to buying the published version of the lectures. The lectures were finally published in London in 1762 by another ardent publisher of educational self-help books in the 1760s, the Scotsman William Strahan, under the title *A Course of Lectures on Elocution: Together with Two Dissertations on Language and Some Other Tracts Relative to those Subjects*. The list of more than 200 subscribers was dutifully added to the beginning of

A Course of Lectures on Elocution, which gives us fairly solid evidence that Sheridan more than covered the costs of the publication by selling the book in this way. Sheridan lectured to packed halls across the country, and an admission fee was charged, so he probably earned large sums of money just by holding the lectures; he need only have mentioned the subscribers' list very casually to have picked up enough subscribers at each lecture to finance the publication. Sheridan, then, was cashing in on the obsession for politeness. The number of names indicating that the subscribers were members of the landed gentry or the aristocracy was extremely small. Sheridan's work and John Walker's *Critical Pronouncing Dictionary and Expositor of the English Language* mark the beginnings of a discourse that was to construct what later became known towards the end of the nineteenth century and in the first half of the twentieth century as Received Pronunciation (RP), as the only socially acceptable form of speech—at least in Britain and the British Empire.

The ideology of politeness based on the ***polite language myth*** had come to dominate the discourse of standardisation to such an extent that even pronunciation could not escape its attention. So many grammars of English were published in the latter half of the eighteenth and well on into the nineteenth century, many of which went into large numbers of editions and reprints, that we are justified in considering the English language market in the second half of the eighteenth century to have been extremely lucrative (see also Belanger 1982; Fitzmaurice 1998; Percy 2004; Watts 2008).

6. POSTSCRIPT

It has been my aim in this chapter to trace out how the concept of politeness in Britain was developed from the French conduct writers and how it was conceptualised in the last 10 to 12 years of the seventeenth and the first 20 years of the eighteenth century. I have argued that the shift from Sprat's "natural way of speaking" as the recommended form of language to be used in the Royal Society in its early years to the gentrification of philosophy (hence also the gentrification of the language of scientific enquiry outside the universities) corresponds neatly to a shift towards the ***polite language myth*** which formed the basis of a discourse ideology of politeness. From the very beginning of its use in English the term "polite" was interpreted ambiguously to justify shifts in the behavioural patterns of the gentry and the nobility, later of the middle classes of society, and held up to those who aspired to membership in higher echelons of society as being a desirable form of social behaviour.

By the end of the eighteenth century the nexus of myths which were traced out in chapters 5 and 7 had been thoroughly absorbed into an ideology of standard English. The ideological discourse was social in that it propagated one form of language for the gentry and the aristocracy, and another for the rest of society. It constructed the hegemonic domination of the former class over the latter along parameters such as heredity, wealth, education and, significantly, language. Through the boom in publications on language from 1750 on, polite language became modelled in terms of grammar, style and lexicon along the lines of the classical languages Latin and Greek. Prescriptive grammars in the wake of Robert Lowth's *A Short Introduction to English Grammar* in 1762 were made to fit into a classical mould even though it was plain to all concerned that English did not have the same richness of morphological marking or syntactic complexity as Latin or Greek. English simply had to be as "classical", erudite, abstract and refined as the classical models, and the style of writing also had to reflect those models. All other forms of English were said to be "vulgar", indecent and disrespectful.

Knowledge of the classical languages and their literature was only to be gained at the public schools and grammar schools, and, with very few exceptions, access to these schools was restricted to the upper classes of society. As a result, the gap between the privileged and the underprivileged of society was not only strengthened; it was also widened and deepened. As we shall see in the next chapter, Olivia Smith (1984) considers that, taken together, the spate of prescriptive grammar books—along with James Harris's *Hermes* (1751), Samuel Johnson's *A Dictionary of the English Language* (1755), James Burnett's (Lord Monboddo's) *Of the Origin and Progress of Language* (1774–1792) and Thomas Sheridan's *A Dissertation on the Causes of Difficulties which Occur in Learning the English Tongue* (1762)—constitute a coherent theory of language in the late eighteenth century. It was a theory of polite, refined, classical written language in contradistinction to vulgar, "barbaric" language, and it was a highly politicised theory, allowing those in power to extend their hegemony over the underprivileged of society.

In effect, we are faced here with a dominant sociopolitical discourse on language that effectively constituted a discourse archive determining what could be said and written. In the following chapter, I argue that the ideology of politeness in the years between 1750 and 1850 is transformed into the ideology of the superiority of standard English via the ***legitimate language myth***. I discuss the struggle to maintain hegemony over this discourse archive throughout the first half of the nineteenth century. It was a discourse archive that survived right through to the end of the twentieth century and attempted to reassert itself through the struggle to reintroduce prescriptive grammar in the National Curriculum. In chapter 10, I aim to show that the discourses resisting this hegemonic discourse, in which both literary scholars and linguists were deeply involved, have so far been successful in challenging the archive, although it is not yet entirely clear what new language discourse will emerge or perhaps has already emerged.

One indication of the enduring significance of the eighteenth-century term "politeness" concerns the current discussion of what standard English is and what it is not, whether or not a unified form of standard English can or should be advanced for the teaching of written and oral English in the British National Curriculum and whether it is justified to represent linguists, literary scholars and sociolinguists as the "enemies of standard English" as John Honey has done. Honey's repeated definition of standard English as the language of "literacy and of educatedness" (1997: 35) smacks suspiciously of Hugh Jones's insistence on the connections between "learnedness", politeness and "true English" and can perhaps best be seen as a mask used to cloak the author's real intention of retaining and strengthening social elitism and exclusion.

Chapter 9

Challenging the hegemony
of standard English

If you would not put [these publications of the Defendant] into their hands,
would you into those of the lower classes, which are not fit to cope with the
sort of topics which are artfully raised for them?
—William Hone, *The Three Trials of William Hone*, 1818

1. "POLITE ENGLISH" AND SOCIAL STRATIFICATION AT THE END OF THE EIGHTEENTH CENTURY

The obsession with "polite" language in the eighteenth century led, as we saw in chapter 8, to a social stratification of language in which those situated in the upper echelons of the social strata were deemed, by definition, to speak and write "polite English". The *polite language myth* was manipulated discursively to distinguish between the ratified members of the gentry and the upper classes and those of the middling orders aspiring to enter the upper ranks. Little or no thought was given to the burgeoning masses of the lower and working classes of society, even though they had always constituted the majority of the overall population. By the end of the eighteenth century the population figures in Britain had almost doubled. In 1700 the population (excluding Ireland) numbered around 6 million, and in 1801 this figure had reached around 10.5 million, increasing the majority of the population in the middle and working classes even further.

Despite these indisputable demographic facts, however, those in power were more worried about a diminution of their ancestral rights and privileges when faced with the increasingly wealthy and more numerous members of the middle classes than about an increase in the size of the working classes. The dominant discourse became hegemonic; it needed to be constantly adapted to the changing social system of values and beliefs by which power structures were upheld (cf. Gramsci 1971). Throughout the course of the eighteenth century, the concept of the "polite language" was subject to subtle changes that were disseminated through processes of socialisation (cf. McIntosh 1998). Polite language came to be understood as a written form of language using the ornate syntactic structures of the classical languages Latin and Greek and a Latinate vocabulary. It became a matter of written style rather than oral usage.

The surge of prescriptive grammars, dictionaries, pronouncing dictionaries and handbooks on elocution and polite speech after 1750 was a largely middle-class phenomenon, and it is testimony to the self-conscious need among the middle classes to acquire "polite" forms of language. It had more to do with becoming "educated" than being simply "schooled".[1] The term "standard English" is rarely found throughout the literature on language during the eighteenth century although most of the prescriptive grammarians make a point in their work of disparaging and condemning what we now recognise as nonstandard varieties. The conceptualisation of a "legitimate" form of English different from those varieties that were not legitimate had not yet been fully developed. In addition, language had also become politicised in the final three decades of the eighteenth century. Radicals such as John Wilkes, Charles James Fox, William Beckford, John Horne Tooke, Thomas Paine, William Cobbett, Sir Francis Burdett and others campaigned in and out of Parliament for parliamentary reform—aiming ultimately at universal male suffrage—the reform of Parliament and parliamentary procedures. Some even went so far as to demand a more democratic distribution of land.

It was the language of the radicals rather than that of the lower and working classes that provoked the anger, ridicule and fear of the established classes. "Non-legitimate" language consisted of all forms of language, particularly written, which threatened established institutions and social privileges. The extension of the notion of "non-legitimacy" to nonstandard varieties began to develop only when the negative social consequences of the Industrial Revolution made themselves felt in the lower and working classes, in that

---

1. An "educated" person was one who had attended a public school or a grammar school (and often also one of the universities) to acquire a classical education in Greek and Latin, and was thus equivalent to a member of the gentry or the aristocracy, who had the means to give their children an expensive education. In this sense "educated" is almost translatable into "polite" with respect to the social conditions of the eighteenth and early nineteenth centuries. A "schooled" person was one who had attended an elementary school for the purpose of acquiring the ability to manipulate rudimentary mathematics and to read and write. Most members of the middling orders had acquired this form of schooling, although many had also attended grammar schools which aspired to give them the equivalent of a classical education.

section of the population that did not speak or write "polite English" and thus did not have a voice.

In this chapter I shall trace out the transformation of the ***polite language myth*** into the ***legitimate language myth***. The transformation rested on the growing awareness of two varieties of English, that which came to be constructed as the standard, on the one hand, and all those language varieties which were English but "vulgar", hence not standard, on the other.

In the following section I argue that the split between a legitimate language and non-legitimate forms of English arose from the social class distinctions encouraged by the ***polite language*** *myth* throughout the eighteenth century and that it resulted in the politicisation of language by the end of the century. I shall outline Olivia Smith's hypothesis (1984) that the second half of the eighteenth century was faced with a highly politicised hegemonic form of language theory. It was a language theory that excluded those who spoke or wrote English but did not conform to the conceptualisation of "polite English" constructed in the social classes of the gentry and the aristocracy, the language of middle-class radicals. In particular I shall be interested in the work of John Horne Tooke.

In sections 3 and 4, I sketch out some of the important protest movements among the English working classes in the first 50 years of the nineteenth century and link these to the development of standard English and a growing awareness on the part of the working classes of the significance of their own varieties of English. Since Crowley (2003) and Mugglestone (1995) have argued cogently that the rise of standard English can only be seen as a continuation of the politicisation of language from the end of the eighteenth century on, I shall only mention their work briefly in passing. However, one aspect of elevating standard English to the hegemonic sociopolitical position it occupied till at least the beginning of World War II was the role that linguistic theory played in the latter half of the nineteenth century by focusing its energy on giving English a history. It is here that we find the genesis of some of the myths presented in this book (e.g. the ***superiority of English myth***, the ***greatness myth*** and the ***longevity of English myth*** and its two submyths).

2. RADICALS, REVOLUTIONARIES AND LANGUAGE

To examine how these ambivalent attitudes towards standard English arose, we need to go back in time to the latter half of the eighteenth century and trace out the politicisation of language and language theory into the nineteenth century. Olivia Smith's 1984 book, *The Politics of Language 1791–1819*, is an ideal entry point for assessing the politicisation of language in the last two decades of the eighteenth century and outlining the development of a new myth, the ***myth of the legitimate language*** (henceforth the ***legitimate language*** *myth*), which grew out of the *polite language myth*. The new myth became a major force in the construction of a dominant ideology out of which arose a discourse archive that survived till the time of the Second World War in the twentieth century. Some of the "true" statements belonging to this archive are given below:

- <The British nation-state is monolingual>
- <Standard English is the only legitimate language of the British nation-state>
- <A command of standard English displays moral and intellectual strength>
- <All children should acquire a command of standard English>
- <All nonstandard forms are corrupt, incorrect, degenerate, politically subversive, and so on>
- <Those who continue to speak nonstandard forms of English
  - have an immoral character
  - are politically subversive
  - are degenerate>
- <Standard English is superior to other languages>
- <Standard English is a cultural commodity that should be acquired by all states subject to the British Crown>
- <Standard English is a cultural and instrumental commodity that can be sold to those speaking other languages>

The list of statements could easily be expanded, but, for the moment, the one I have provided suffices to show how powerful the discourse archive was. Some of the statements also justify the commodification of English and its geographical diffusion across the world, which will concern us in chapter 11. Most of the statements are obviously no longer valid, and from an objective point of view were never valid. Clearly, Britain is not (and never has been) a monolingual state. In fact, the second statement reveals an uncanny feeling that there must be other languages or language varieties that need to be excluded by propagating the ideological discourse driven by the *legitimate language myth*. The third, fifth and sixth statements are still valid for a number of people living in Britain, but they could scarcely be used any longer for political purposes.[2] The fourth statement is still valid, but we need to discuss what we mean by "a command of standard English". This and other questions will be dealt with in chapter 10.

2.1 "Refined" and "vulgar" language

How could this discourse archive have taken hold so quickly and have endured almost to the present? As we have seen, the second half of the eighteenth

2. In chapter 10, however, I present statements made by politicians during the National Curriculum "wars" at the end of the 1980s which are solidly based on a belief in the truth of these statements.

century is characterised by a tremendous increase in the number of works published in Britain on language, in particular prescriptive grammars of English (for details, see, e.g., Michael 1991, 1997). Although there are notable exceptions, the majority of these works were pitched at those desperately needing to acquire the ability to write "politely", a style replete with the ornate syntactic structures of Latin and Greek and a Latinate vocabulary. Their authors consistently proscribed and prescribed for the benefit of their readers. At the same time, Harris's *Hermes* (1751) sets out to define what Harris considered to be "universal grammar", a term that meant something very different from the way it is used in modern linguistics. A distinction was made in Harris's work and in the work of others (e.g. Monboddo 1774–1792) between structures and lexemes that could be seen as universal in meaning and usage and those that were simply used to describe past, future and present events. Universal language encoded timeless things, ideas and events, which had been released from the immediate needs of the present, since the timeless must represent universal truths. Olivia Smith (1984: 24) gives the following example of what Harris means by quoting a section from his discussion of the verbs. Harris (1751: 159–160) maintains that the indicative mode "exhibits the Soul in her purest Energies, superior to the Imperfection of Desires and Wants...[and] serves Philosophy and The Sciences, by just Demonstrations to establish necessary Truth; THAT TRUTH...which knows no distinctions either of Past or Future, but is everywhere and always invariably one."

Such language veers towards the abstract rather than the concrete. The classical languages are seen to have reached a state of perfection in which abstract concepts could be expressed in individual nominal structures (rather than verbs) and with complex syntax relying on logical connectives. Logical connectives themselves and other "particles",[3] as they were called, have no meaning but to express the logical connections between abstract concepts, and for this reason they are highly valued by Harris and others. The goal of a writer (rather than a speaker) is to achieve this degree of abstraction and perfection in English. Vulgar language, on the other hand, is tied to the here and now and to what Harris calls "Desires and Wants". From this perspective, it is entirely unable to express universal truths.

Such a theory drives a huge wedge between written and oral language, between the expression of the universal and the expression of personal opinion and the present situation, between those who have been trained through a classical education to imitate the apparent achievements of the classical languages in written English and those who have not had this training—in short, between the haves and have-nots. It becomes a theory of social

---

3. I refer to the distinction made in most prescriptive grammars in the eighteenth century between the parts of speech (i.e. nouns, verbs, adjectives, adverbs and participles) and the so-called particles, those words which were assumed not to have had intrinsic meaning but were used by authors to construct larger, more abstract syntactic units such as prepositional phrases, subordinate clauses, and so on (e.g. prepositions, articles, some adverbs, conjunctions and pronouns).

superiority and discrimination disguised as a theory of language, and it differentiates between those who are judged worthy to rule and those who are ruled. In the first section of this chapter, I touched on the significant population increase in the second half of the eighteenth century. With it, more and more members of the "middling orders" of society were seeking access to the ranks of the gentry, and more and more of the lower and working classes were also clamouring to have a voice in the management of the political affairs of the country. The theory that English was a "classical" language like Latin and Greek was used explicitly by politicians, who of course had a classical education, to exclude those of the middling orders who had not, as well as the lower and working classes, from having any say in the political running of Britain. In this way the *polite language myth* was politically transformed into the *legitimate language myth*. The only legitimate language was written standard English displaying the features of classical syntax and a classical lexicon.

Smith gives examples of petitions sent to Parliament in 1793, 1810 and 1817 favouring universal suffrage or at least an extension of the suffrage (Smith 1984: 30), which were either rejected on the grounds that the language was "highly indecent and disrespectful", or, if they *were* accepted, were not sent to the committee stage.[4] The 1793 petitions from Sheffield and Nottingham are taken from *The Parliamentary History of England from the Earliest Period to the Year 1803* (Vol. XXX, p 776):

> Your petitioners are lovers of peace, of liberty, and justice. They are in general tradesmen and artificers, unpossessed of freehold land, and consequently have no voice in choosing members to sit in parliament:—but though they may not be freeholders, they are men, and do not think themselves fairly used in being excluded the rights of citizens.[5]

Certain members of Parliament objected in the debate that there was nothing indecent about the wording of the petition, but they were given to understand that "persons coming forward as petitioners, should address the House in decent and respectful language" (XXX, 779). In other words, a petition had to be phrased in the correct classical style of the legitimate language, or it would be rejected on the grounds of a lack of decency and respect. There are also cases of petitioners who attempted to couch their petitions in what they perceived to be the acceptable style, only to receive the response in parliament

---

4. Parliamentary procedure in Britain involves the transference of a petition or a bill that has been accepted in principle by the House to the next procedural stage in which a parliamentary committee debates on the exact wording of the proposal before it is debated properly in the House of Commons. At the committee stage amendments and deletions may be proposed for debate in the House. American procedures are essentially similar, but the term used to define the procedure is "to send to committee" rather than "to send to the committee stage".

5. One possible explanation for the petition being couched in language that was seen as "highly indecent and disrespectful" might lie in the phrase "in being excluded the rights of citizens," in which the preposition "from" after the verb "excluded" has been left out.

that the language was not "the genuinely authentic language of the petitioners" but "the dictation of certain factious demagogues" (XXV, 91, quoted
in O. Smith 1984: 33). In other words, there was always a way in which those
in power could reject petitions from those not in power on the grounds of the
language of the petition alone.

2.2 John Horne Tooke and the challenge to the distinction between "refined" and "vulgar" language

The work of John Horne Tooke, in particular his *ΕΠΕΑ ΠΤΕΡΟΕΝΤΑ, or the
Diversions of Purley*, presented a serious challenge to the eighteenth-century
theory of language that assumed the existence of two forms of language in
Britain, the legitimate standard written language of the "educated" (i.e. "refined"
language) and the vulgar language of the uneducated. *Diversions* has also been
the subject of controversy in linguistic circles.

Horne Tooke—who was born John Horne and assumed the name Tooke
at the request of his friend and benefactor William Tooke, the owner of Purley
Lodge south of Croydon in Surrey—was the son of a poulterer in Westminster.
Despite his non-aristocratic origins, he nevertheless managed to gain entry to
Eton and went on to study at Cambridge. He took orders in the Church of
England and, despite opposition from both political parties on account of his
membership in the radical organisation "The Society for Supporting the Bill
of Rights", obtained his MA degree in 1771. He resigned his benefice in the
church in 1773 to take up the study of law and philology. Although Horne
Tooke was elected to Parliament only once, in 1801, for a relatively short
period (to the rotten borough of Old Sarum[6]), he was associated with radical
politicians such as Charles Fox, Thomas Paine and John Wilkes throughout
his life and was instrumental in setting up the "The Society for Supporting the
Bill of Rights" in 1769, pledging financial support for the radical politician
John Wilkes, who was in jail after being prevented from taking his seat in
Parliament after the Middlesex election[7] and was charged with organising
popular opposition to the government and to the restriction of democracy.
Horne Tooke was thus thoroughly conversant in the politics of his day. He

6. A "rotten" or "decayed" borough was a constituency numbering very few voters that had earlier been
a sizeable town but had since shrunk considerably in terms of population and significance. Rotten boroughs
were under the patronage of influential members of the aristocracy and were used to influence those who were
elected to Parliament upon payment of the required sum of money. Old Sarum was an extreme case in that it
had just three houses by the end of the eighteenth century but still had the right to send two MPs to Westminster.
In the case of John Horne Tooke, one can only assume that the patron for one of the two seats was a Radical.

7. Although Wilkes won the parliamentary election for the county of Middlesex in the general election
of 1768, he faced charges for owing debts, producing pornography and duelling. Before George III and his
prime minister could decide whether to allow Wilkes to take his seat or to deny his right to election and to make
him stand trial, Wilkes pre-empted the decision by giving himself up for trial to clear his name. As a result,
people rioted in London, and troops were called out; six people were killed. Wilkes became a hero and a martyr
to the cause of liberty. Further details may be found in Kent ([1899] 1971).

was also thoroughly conversant with the law, philosophy and, more important, with Anglo-Saxon.

The points mentioned in this very brief biographical sketch of Horne Tooke are significant in light of assessments made of his contribution to linguistics in Britain in the first 30–40 years of the nineteenth century. Scholars such as Aarsleff (1967), Land (1974), Culler (1976) and Bergheaud (1979) largely ignore the political import of the *Diversions* and advance the opinion that the book was one of the major reasons that the school of historical-comparative philology on the Continent did not really take hold in Britain till around the end of the nineteenth century. Crowley (2003) also hints at the significance of Horne Tooke's book in the development of a peculiarly British approach to historical linguistics which he calls "the history of the language". Even commentators on the *Diversions* in Horne Tooke's day and for some time after his death conveniently played down the strong political aspect of his writing. Only Olivia Smith (1984) and Lamarre (1998) have seriously entertained the political import of the text.

Diversions was published in two volumes, the first appearing in 1798 and the second in 1805. Both volumes are written in the form of a discussion. In Volume 1 the discussion is between Horne Tooke (H in the text); his mentor, William Tooke (T in the text); and the master of Jesus College, Cambridge, the Reverent Doctor Beadon (B in the text). In Volume 2 it is between Horne Tooke and Sir Francis Burdett, baronet (F in the text). As we might expect, the discussion format is not particularly conducive to the presentation of Horne Tooke's linguistic argumentation, but given the fact that the two types of language proposed by the literati and the classically educated were "refined" and "vulgar" language, it is certainly appropriate for presenting the arguments for and against such a sociopolitical division of language. If language had become politicised, so too had the study of language. This becomes crystal clear at the very beginning of Volume 2, which I quote at length here:

F.— But your dialogue and your politics, and your bitter Notes—

H.—Cantantes, my dear Burdett, minus via lædit.

F.—Cantantes, if you please; but bawling out the Rights of Man, they say, is not
singing.

H.—To the ears of man, what music sweeter than the Rights of man?

F.—Yes. Such music as the whistling of a wind before a tempest. You very well
know what these gentlemen think of it. You cannot have forgotten.
"Sir, Whenever I hear of the word RIGHTS, I have learned to consider it as
preparatory to some desolating doctrine. It seems to me, to be productive of
some wide spreading ruin, of some wasting desolation." —*Canning's speech.*
And do you not remember the enthusiasm with which these sentiments
were applauded by the House, and the splendid rewards which immediately
followed this declaration? For no other earthly merit in the speaker that
Œdipus himself could have discovered.

H.—It is never to be forgotten. Pity their ignorance.

F.—Punish their wickedness.

H.—We shall never, I believe, differ much in our actions, wishes or opinions. I too say with you—Punish the wickedness of those mercenaries who utter such atrocities: and do you, with me, pity the ignorance and folly of those *regular* governments who reward them: and who do not see that a claim of RIGHTS by their people, so far from treason or sedition, is the strongest avowal they can make of their of their subjection: and that nothing can more evidently shew the natural disposition of mankind to rational obedience, than their invariable use of this word RIGHT, and their perpetual application of it to all which they desire, and to every thing which they deem excellent.

F. — I see the wickedness of it more plainly than the folly; the consequence staring one in the face: for, certainly, if men can claim no RIGHTS, they cannot *justly* complain of any WRONGS. (1829/40: 301–302)

The section is a preface to Horne Tooke's explanation of the meaning of the lexeme *right*, and it is placed very squarely into the acrimonious debate on Thomas Paine's *Rights of Man*, and the repression of civil liberties in Britain following the Treason Act of 1795 and the two Habeas Corpus Suspension Acts in 1795 and 1798. Horne Tooke has Burdett, who had unsuccessfully presented several petitions for universal male suffrage to parliament, quote part of a parliamentary speech by George Canning. The procedure here is to focus on Canning's deliberate interpretation of *rights* as something connected to sedition and revolution and then to present an etymological interpretation of what Horne Tooke assumes to be the basic meaning of the word.

My own interpretation of the *Diversions* is that it was Horne Tooke's intention to challenge the theory of a dichotomy between a "refined" and a "vulgar" language when used, as it was, to justify the rigid class structure of society and the misappropriation by the minority class—the classically educated, the literati, the gentry and the aristocracy—of the right to participate in the democratic running of the country. The challenge was sociopolitical and directed at the ruling class, but it was fuelled by the quasi-linguistic underpinnings of this misappropriation. In looking at the *Diversions of Purley*, therefore, we are not confronted with a new theory of language, only with the dismantling of an old theory. Horne Tooke's challenge was directed at the discourse that was emerging from the **legitimate language myth**. Looked at from this point of view, the criticism of the *Diversions* made in the 1970s to the effect that it prevented the development of a new, unpoliticised approach to language was made from within a late modern archive in which politics and linguistics are seen as incompatible areas of study.[8] Even though the *Diversions* was studied with great interest for at least the first 40 years of the nineteenth century, it is not difficult to argue that this was precisely because of its import

---

8. Unless, of course, the researcher focuses on the study of discourse, which is the major thrust of the present book.

during a critical period of political repression, the denial of civil rights to a majority of the population and great personal suffering as a consequence of the immense social changes caused by the age of industrialisation.

But how did Horne Tooke go about mounting this challenge to the misappropriation of language by the ruling classes? There were two major principles put forward by the proponents of "refined" or polite language, which Horne Tooke, from his knowledge of philosophy, in particular the philosophy of John Locke, and his study of Anglo-Saxon, was able to dismantle. The process of dismantling those principles, however, represented neither a philosophical nor a linguistic approach to the problem. The major claim made by believers in a "refined" language was that the legitimate language, English, was the equal of the classical languages Latin and Greek, which were thought to have achieved a high degree of perfection. They were thought to have reached a level of abstraction, both in terms of the lexicon and the syntax, which allowed them to be used in the expression of abstract universal values. Such values were thought to be timeless and subject to the laws of propositional logic, that is, to be beyond human beings in a world of sublime objectivity. If a language provides the means of expressing those values, then it, too, has reached a point of sublime objectivity. As a corollary of this, those who were able to manipulate the "legitimate" language were thought to have achieved the means of controlling not only the language but also the sociopolitical and religious affairs of the state in which that language was spoken and, in particular, written. To acquire that ability, intensive exposure to classical Latin and Greek and their literatures was considered absolutely essential.

The first major principle that Horne Tooke challenged was the claim that the meaning of abstract terms could be understood only by those who had had such a classical education. Since they were terms of universal value, they could not be applied to the here-and-now situation of late-eighteenth-century Britain, and the only way to understand them was to study Greek and Latin literature intensively. Obviously, if this claim is granted, such abstract terms as "rights," "constitution," "sovereignty," and so on are open to any arbitrary interpretation as long as the interpretation given satisfies the needs of the classically educated ruling class. Horne Tooke, like most of his radical colleagues, saw the danger of allowing this interpretation of universality to hold. The second major principle challenged by Horne Tooke was the assumption made by the "educated classes" that particles such as prepositions, conjunctions and articles had meaning only when used in the construction of abstract propositions; that is, that they were entirely functional and could be manipulated by those who knew how to use them. Once again, this opens up the field entirely to those who had the experience of using them, and those who did not use them were said to have no notion of objective universal ideas.

Horne Tooke developed his own theory of language from book 3 of John Locke's *Essay Concerning Human Understanding* in which Locke maintains that words represent ideas in the mind and that human language is a means to convey these ideas as efficiently as one can. Horne Tooke makes the assumption that, if this is the case, then to communicate efficiently and swiftly, human beings "abbreviate" words to such an extent that those words can be used as relations between other words, and he reduces the classes of words to two, verbs and nouns, the more significant being verbs.[9] More important, however, he assumes, as does Locke, that the ideas entertained by the individual are bound to the moment of speaking; hence there can be no universal truths such as those insisted on by eighteenth-century language theorists. To prove his point, he uses his knowledge of Anglo-Saxon, Latin and Greek to show how both the particles and the "universal" terms have evolved etymologically from verbs and nouns.

Although some of his explanations are entirely plausible, others turn out to be demonstrably wrong or at least highly speculative. Nevertheless, the simple fact that he took many of those words that were assumed to be entirely abstract particles back to Anglo-Saxon nouns and verbs appeared plausible to his readers. As a result, together with his political position, which is always latently present in the *Diversions*, he must have convinced many of his readers not only of the correctness of his linguistic analyses but also, and more important, of the hollowness of the distinction between "refined" and "vulgar". It is here that Horne Tooke has a point, whatever the plausibility of his etymological derivations may be.

In the following section I consider why it was so important to try to break down this bogus distinction, why the attempt to do so did not succeed, and why the concern with language in nineteenth-century Britain was focused so strongly on English to the detriment of the study of human language in general. I refute the claim made by Aarsleff, Culler and Land that ΕΠΕΑ ΠΤΕΡΟΕΝΤΑ, *or the Diversions of Purley* was the reason for this delay in the reception of Continental ideas about language, and I do so on the grounds that such an opinion neglects the interplay between language and sociopolitical and socioeconomic factors and fails to see the significance of discourses on language driven by sets of beliefs articulated by language myths. I shall thus turn my attention to some of the most significant events of the period and sketch out the interplay between them and the ***legitimate language myth***.

3. LANGUAGE AND WORKING-CLASS MOVEMENTS AT THE BEGINNING OF THE NINETEENTH CENTURY

The sentiments of the working classes with respect to the lack of universal male suffrage are aptly summed up, perhaps a little melodramatically but at least honestly, by George Loveless, one of the Tolpuddle martyrs. After being

---

9. In doing this, Horne Tooke sometimes appears to carry out a primitive kind of grammaticalisation analysis. The concept of "grammaticalisation" is dealt with in Hopper and Traugott 1993. Briefly, the theory maintains that grammatical forms are derived historically from more concrete lexemes. For example, the "be going to" future in English is ultimately derived from the cognitive concept of MOVEMENT, the movement being abstract in the direction of future time.

sentenced in 1834 to transportation to Australia to serve a seven year prison sentence, Loveless scribbled the following short poem on a scrap of paper:

> God is our guide! From field, from wave,
> From plough, from anvil, and from loom;
> We come, our country's rights to save,
> And speak a tyrant faction's doom:
> We raise the watch-word liberty;
> We will, we will, we will be free!

In 1824/1825 the Combination Acts of 1799, which were passed to prevent workers from forming societies with the expressed aim of gaining better working conditions, were finally repealed, thus making the formation of trade unions technically legal. The failure of the 1832 Reform Act was that, although it did away with the system of rotten boroughs, gave parliamentary representation to the large cities and extended the vote, it did not grant universal male suffrage. This led to the formation of a number of societies to protect workers from reduced wages during the early 1830s. Six rural labourers from the village of Tolpuddle in Dorset banded together to form the Friendly Society of Agricultural Labourers, led by George Loveless, a Methodist preacher, and refused to work for less than 10 shillings a week. A local landowner by the name of James Frampton wrote to the prime minister, Lord Melbourne, to protest the foundation of the union and invoked an obscure Act of Parliament passed in 1797 preventing people from swearing oaths. The six men were arrested, tried and transported to Australia. They all became popular heroes, and their sentence was curtailed in 1836, with the exception of that of James Hammett, who was released in 1837.

What can we learn from this brief narrative account and from Loveless's poem? From the poem we can deduce, first, that at least George Loveless (and possibly also his brother James) was a competent writer. In all probability most of the other members of the group were also able to read and write. Second, in keeping with Loveless's specific religious orientation—Methodists were nonconformists (as were large sections of the working-class population)— his call for liberty is prefaced by the expression of the belief that the working-class movement for the vote and for fair pay for a fair day's work is guided by God. Third, Loveless addresses his poem to and on behalf of workers of all kinds ("from field [soldiers],[10] from wave [sailors], from plough [agricultural labourers], from anvil [skilled craftsmen], from loom [factory hands]". Fourth, the body of workers ("we") are patriotic and consider that their rights are simultaneously the rights of all citizens ("our country's rights to save"). Fifth, the persecutors are a "tyrant faction", a minority who reserve for themselves the right to dominate and persecute, and the voice in the poem

---

10. I interpret "field" in the context of the times to represent the field of battle here, rather than a field in the agricultural sense.

predicts their ultimate downfall ("doom"). Sixth, the watchword of the working classes is "liberty", a word that they were consistently told they did not understand. Finally, the poetic voice expresses and repeats the working classes' determination to be "free".

By the 1830s, the lower classes of society in Britain were well on the way to literacy, they had taken on an air of militancy that was sanctified by their religious beliefs, and they were articulate and defiant. The ranks of the establishment—politicians, landowners, factory owners, the educated, the literati and the established Church of England—had become the "enemy", and they seemed determined to prevent universal male suffrage at all costs.

The Napoleonic Wars had been a time of political repression, isolation from Europe, rapid industrialisation, immense social change, social unrest and internal migration. Yet despite all this, it was also a time of continuing demographic growth in which the population doubled between 1801 (roughly 10.5 million) and 1851 (roughly 20.8 million). Olivia Smith (1984: 159–160) points out that an overall demand for news increased from the early 1790s to 1815, and access to an increasing number of newspapers stimulated the increase in literacy in the lower and working classes of the population. This was also aided by technological developments in the printing presses, so that by the time the Napoleonic Wars ended in 1815, the reading materials available to the "schooled" rather than the "educated" were no longer restricted to chapbooks, broadsheets, ballads and religious tracts. Newspapers, cheap novels and instructional texts of all kinds considerably enlarged the amount of material there was to read. W. B. Stephens (1987, 1998) warns us not to assume illiteracy in the working classes before the advent of compulsory schooling in 1870, and by looking through parish registers across the country he estimates that more than 50 percent of the adult population had the ability to sign their name at the turn of the nineteenth century.

There is still a considerable amount of discussion among historians and economists as to when the Industrial Revolution began and the degree to which we are justified in calling it a "revolution" (cf. Hobsbawm 1962; Ashton 1948; Deane [1969] 1979; Crafts 1985). But regardless of when it began and whether it deserves the nomenclature "revolution", industrialisation had the effect of transforming the natural and demographic physiognomy of large parts of Britain, particularly the north of England, a large swathe of Scotland to the south of Perth stretching from Glasgow across to Dundee and Edinburgh and including large parts of Ayrshire, the Midland counties of England (Staffordshire, the north of Worcestershire and west of Warwickshire), the East Midland counties of England (Leicestershire, Nottinghamshire and Derbyshire) and southern and northeastern Wales. Improvements in agricultural production after land enclosures (which peaked between 1760 and 1830) simultaneously began to push up population figures, but at the same time to force many labourers off the land. The improvements in the transportation system (better roads and the building of a system of canals) meant not only that produce could be moved more easily and rapidly from one place to another, but also that surplus labourers could move from their traditional homes to the rapidly industrialising areas of the country where work was available. Harnessing steam-generated power had begun in the early eighteenth century, but by the 1780s it was used for production purposes, thus mechanising, in particular, the hand production of textiles. The mining of coal from newly located coalfields meant that iron could be smelted more easily for the production of iron and steel products. All of this led indirectly to an increase in the population, particularly among the working classes, and to large-scale internal migration from the countryside to burgeoning industrial centres such as Manchester, Sheffield, Leeds, Bradford, Nottingham, Birmingham, Wolverhampton, Glasgow and Lanark. Large-scale industrialisation began in the textile industries of Lancashire, Yorkshire, Nottinghamshire and Leicestershire.

The major disruptive effect of industrialisation was felt more keenly in the north of England than elsewhere, and nowhere more sharply than in the handloom industry.[11] Some vandalism of machines had occurred in reaction to the demise of the handloom industry during the first decade of the nineteenth century, but not as an organised form of working-class protest. The Luddite movement was an organised, violent response to political repression and ruthless economic exploitation by the moneyed classes in the wake of the 1799 Combination Acts, and in particular after the election of Spencer Perceval as Prime Minister in 1809.[12] The Luddite movement, which began in Nottingham in March 1811 with demonstrations and frame-breaking,[13] did not begin its activities as a premeditated political organisation, but the harsh retaliatory reactions of the authorities soon led to a high degree of disciplined planning and coordination among its members. Luddism spread quickly into Lancashire and Yorkshire, where it took on more menacing forms including full-scale attacks on targeted mills. The government retaliated by billeting no fewer than 12,000 troops in the troubled areas, more than the number of troops fighting in Spain in the Peninsular War. Against this show of armed force, the Luddite movement fizzled out in 1812. As a result of the riots, Parliament passed the Frame Breaking Act in 1813, making industrial sabotage a capital offence. First convictions were made at a trial in York, after which 17 men were executed and many more transported to Australia.

Luddism, however, was only the tip of the iceberg. The end of the Napoleonic Wars led to a slump in industrial production, particularly in the iron industry, unemployment in the wake of hordes of demobbed soldiers and

---

11. One should also note that in the north there were significantly fewer people who had the right to vote than in the south.

12. Perceval was a declared opponent of Catholic emancipation and of the reform of Parliament. He was assassinated in May 1812 by a man with a personal grievance against him, and although no connection with the Luddite movement was ever proved, the violence of the years 1811 and 1812 is evidence of the dire political situation of Britain at the beginning of the nineteenth century.

13. "Frame-breaking" is a term used to denote the wilful destruction of various kinds of mechanised frames used in the textile industry, for example, stocking frames, water frames and different forms of steam-driven power looms.

widespread famine. Industrial unrest flared up at regular intervals and was always violently repressed. But, as Olivia Smith points out (1984: chap. 5), radical politicians and writers and the mass of the middle and working classes had a much clearer idea of their rights and, more significant, of their own abilities after 1810 than during the 1790s. It is certainly no exaggeration to suggest that the writings of John Horne Tooke, Thomas Paine, William Cobbett and others had given to the masses who had never had the dubious benefit of a classical education a surprising amount of self-confidence. And their self-confidence was boosted rather than suppressed by the almost hysterical repressive action taken by government after government to retain their own assumed privileges to govern and wield power over others. Horne Tooke, in particular, had deflated the claim made by the "refined" circles of society to be in possession of the legitimate form of English. For the time being, however, even though steady progress was made in wearing down the effectiveness of this discourse, it managed to hold its ground by adapting the *legitimate language myth* to the changing social system of values and beliefs by which those power structures were upheld. The crucial test that "vulgar" language was not vulgar but just as fit to express ideas, as creative and as valid a form of English as "refined" language, was about to take place. Prior to this crucial test, so-called vulgar language had proved its literary worth in the writings of the Coleridge/Southey school of poets, although this was not widely recognised at the time. It now had to prove itself as an instrument of effective, non-parliamentary, political opposition.

4. WILLIAM HONE, PETERLOO AND THE CHARTIST MOVEMENT

4.1 The three trials of William Hone

If there was ever a litmus test to prove the solidity of "vulgar" language by the "refined" section of society, it was in the activities of William Hone and his acquittal at the trials held against him at the Guildhall in London, on 18–20 December 1817.[14] The three charges made against Hone were (1) for publishing *The Late John Wilkes's Catechism of a Ministerial Member* (1817); (2) for parodying the litany and libelling the prince regent in *The Political Litany* (1817); and (3) for publishing the *Sinecurist's Creed* (1817), a parody on the Athanasian Creed.

Hone was born in Bath in 1780 into a strictly religious family in which his only education was learning to read from the Bible. The family had a small number of other books, among which were Bunyan's *Pilgrim's Progress*, Foxe's *Book of Martyrs* and Milton's *Paradise Lost*, which Hone read avidly

---

14. The first part of this section on William Hone is based on chapter 5 of Olivia Smith 1984.

throughout his childhood. The family moved to London in 1783, and at the age of 10 William was placed in an attorney's office. However, after two and a half years working in a solicitor's office in Chatham, Hone decided that the law was not where his interests lay. He had begun to think independently, and at the age of 16 he joined the London Corresponding Society, which set universal male suffrage as its goal.

After his marriage at age 20, he tried his hand in the printing and publishing trade and published his own first work, *Shaw's Gardener*, in 1806. Olivia Smith (1984: chap. 5) maintains that Hone was able to profit from the fact that he wrote, printed and distributed his own work without the intervention of publishing houses and printing presses, although this must have restricted the print run drastically. In all probability, he had already attracted the attention of government agents by the publication in 1816 of *The Important Results of an Elaborate Investigation into the Mysterious Case of Eliza Fenning*. The book sets about dismantling the case against Elizabeth Fenning, a cook who was accused of murdering her employer's family with arsenic in 1815. She was tried and executed on the flimsiest of evidence despite brave attempts by Hone in his *Traveller* newspaper to save her. The book is a masterpiece of investigative journalism that completely demolishes the case for the prosecution.

By the end of 1816, Hone had thus become a thorn in the flesh of the government and the legal system and an obvious political target. Hence it was no surprise, when he set up the *Reformist's Register*, which ran from February to October 1817, and published the three parodies based on religious texts mentioned above, one of which he had written himself (*The Sinecurist's Creed*), that three *ex officio* informations[15] were filed by the attorney general, Sir William Garrow, against him. Hone was forced to wait for five months without knowing whether he would be tried, and the scheduling of a trial for each published tract on three consecutive days shortly before Christmas 1817 was an open act of intimidation by the authorities. The charge against Hone was that the texts were blasphemous and were a danger to public morals. Hone decided to defend himself, and he had prepared himself well, bringing books and political tracts with him into the courtroom every day. Hone's defence was based on the argument that using a religious text to create socio-political parody did not constitute a case of blasphemy. All attempts made by the prosecution (and by the judge) to prove that the language of the parodies was couched in vulgar language were nullified by the simple fact that a number of the most popular and significant texts in the canon of English literature would also have to be considered vulgar insofar as they were written in a non-legitimate variety of English. In addition, Hone's argument also touched the sensibilities of the jury with respect to the language they used on an everyday basis (cf. Hone [1818] 2009). Hone was acquitted of each of the three charges made against him.

---

15. The legal term is "an *ex officio* information", and the plural is "informations".

Olivia Smith (1984: 176) makes a valid point in her assessment of the importance of these three trials, which I quote in full:

> Hone's three trials articulate the political and social pressures which such writers encountered. Hegemony of language gains an unusually discernible form as the Attorney-General and the Judge attempt to prove that Hone's language is sufficiently indecent and improper to be criminal. Although the vocabulary to describe vulgar language tended to shift from "barbaric" and "vulgar" to "indecent" and "improper" between the 1790s and 1817, the concept remained largely the same and served the same purpose of defining the inadequacy of various classes according to their language. Had Hone lost his trials, such vague concepts would have gained legal currency, becoming evidence of criminality in themselves.

Fortunately for the future development of varieties of English, no legal status was attributed to the equation "vulgar language=criminality", but this does not mean that the promoters of the *legitimate language myth* were defeated. There was a long, stony road ahead for those arguing against the concept of a legitimate language, and the equation itself was explicitly made, not quite in the terms I have given here, by Conservative politician Norman Tebbitt as late as 1985, as we shall see in chapter 10. The major advance in Hone's acquittal of the charges made against him was that such an equation could no longer acquire legal status.

4.2 The shame of Peterloo

In 1818 Hone published an account of his three trials, but he wisely decided not to publish any further parodies based on religious texts, in spite of his acquittals. The overall situation in the country, however, was still exceptionally tense. In the wake of the Luddite riots, secret societies of workingmen sprang up throughout the North, angered and embittered at government repression and the refusal to grant suffrage. Physical violence was resorted to on a number of occasions. In early June 1817, a group of workers in the village of Pentrich in Derbyshire decided to take matters into their own hands. Most were out of work after being laid off by the Butterley ironworks as a consequence of the decrease in production after the end of the Napoleonic Wars. Led by an unemployed stockinger named Jeremiah Brandreth, a small force of men armed with a few pikes, scythes and guns set off on what was to be an abortive march to Nottingham by way of the Butterley works. They were faced down by a factory agent and a few police constables at the works and managed to get through to Giltbrook but were scattered by a group of 20 soldiers. Retribution was, as usual, heavy. Twenty-four were sentenced, three to transportation to Australia to serve out a 14-year prison sentence and 11 for life; the three ringleaders, including Brandreth, were publicly hanged and then beheaded in Derby.

With historical hindsight, however, the most significant incident from a sociocultural/sociopolitical perspective was the Peterloo Massacre[16] on 16 August 1819. It was of central importance in defining future relationships between the mass of the lower middle and working classes and the all-powerful upper middle and upper classes (who constituted a small minority of the overall population of Britain). I shall go one step further in this subsection and argue that the Peterloo Massacre was also a decisive factor in the development of what had by then become the ideology of the legitimate language. After this shameful demonstration of military violence on the part of the authorities, the government was faced with two options. Either it could refrain from further use of violent repression and cooperate constructively to find a solution to the burning question of parliamentary reform, or it could step up the violence and increase the gulf between the polite, refined sector of society and the vulgar. The first reaction would have required it to admit that the central issue in social class distinctions was not language but the hugely unequal distribution of wealth and the political disenfranchisement of more than three quarters of the population. The second reaction, which was the path that was taken, retained the bogus distinction between refined and vulgar language and adopted the tactics of hegemonic discourse to insist on a unique "standard language". This second path helped to consolidate a discourse archive that lasted well into the twentieth century. However, before I present my arguments, we first need to sketch very briefly what happened on 16 August 1819.

Discontent at the totally inadequate parliamentary representation for the industrial north of England was not only channelled into the occasional desperate local outbreak of violence such as that at Pentrich, recounted at the beginning of this subsection. It also led to the peaceful organisation of groups agitating for parliamentary reform. The Lancashire cotton industry was, as we have seen, hit hardest by the change from handloom weaving to factory-based power-loom production, and the towns and villages around Manchester were urbanising at an alarming rate. Despite a population of almost one million, Manchester had no parliamentary representatives; there were merely two MPs for Cheshire and two for Lancashire. The Manchester Patriotic Union was formed to petition for more adequate representation in Parliament, and, more generally, for a wholesale reform of the parliamentary system. To this end the union organised a demonstration to be held in Manchester on 2 August and to be attended by delegations from the greater Manchester area. The radical orator Henry Hunt was invited to speak to the crowd on the question of parliamentary reform. The organisers chose as their venue a large stretch of wasteland called St. Peter's Field, which was scheduled for development to link up the two ends of Peter Street, Manchester (see fig. 9.1). There was a certain amount of symbolic significance in the choice of venue. It

---

16. The term "Peterloo" was coined by the radical Manchester newspaper, the *Monchester Observer*, in an analogy with the slaughter at the Battle of Waterloo and based on the fact that it took place on St. Peter's Field.

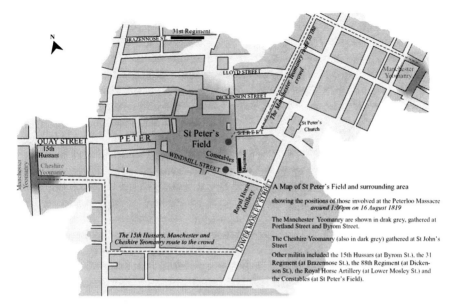

FIGURE 9.1. A map of St. Peter's Field showing the positions of those involved around 1 P.M. on 16 August 1819

was relatively central in Manchester and big enough to support a large crowd. Such a venue documented the intention of the organisers to make their feelings and wishes heard publicly and in the open.

Manchester magistrates informed Lord Portland, the home secretary, about the planned demonstration, and a letter to Henry Hunt was intercepted and copied. The crucial sentences in the letter are given as follows:

> Nothing but ruin and starvation stare one in the face, the state of the district is truly dreadful, and I believe nothing but the greatest exertions can prevent an insurrection. Oh, that you in London were prepared for it. (quoted in Reid 1989: 115)

Amazingly, the Home Office interpreted this to mean that an insurrection was actually being planned, and the local magistrates were instructed to ban the demonstration.

The organisers, on the other hand, were determined to make sure that the demonstration was orderly and nonviolent. Arms of any description were strictly forbidden, and the different groups from different locations around Manchester were allotted different parts of St. Peter's Field in which to stand. They were drilled prior to the demonstration on how they should dress, how they should march to Manchester and where they would be stationed. The drill was interpreted by spies as military training for an insurrection. The demonstration was originally planned to take place on 2 August, but was put off for organisational reasons till 9 August, when it was banned by the local authorities. On learning that the meeting was not for the purpose of electing an MP for Manchester but to discuss the intention of doing so, the home secretary, Lord Portland, criticised the grounds on which the local authorities had taken their decision, and the demonstration was finally held on 16 August. This gave the authorities sufficient time to organise an inordinately large military presence, including cavalry from the Cheshire Yeomanry and the Manchester and Salford Yeomanry. Hustings were set up on two farm carts in the middle of the field, and when Hunt arrived St. Peter's Field was packed.

Observing from a house on the corner of Windmill Street and St. Peter's Field, the magistrates saw Hunt mount the hustings, whereupon they gave orders that he and three others should be arrested. Because of the thickness of the crowd, letters were sent to the commanders of the two yeomanry cavalry units that military assistance would be required, whereupon riders from the Manchester and Salford Yeomanry charged to St. Peter's Field, knocking down a woman and her two-year-old child and, as a consequence, killing the child. On reaching the field they literally cut their way through to the hustings to make the arrests. The crowd began to disperse, and rioting occurred in the streets for most of the day. Fifteen fatalities were reported, 11 of them in St. Peter's Field, and between 400 and 600 are estimated to have suffered injuries.

The following aspects of the organisation of the demonstration need to be borne in mind:

1. The demonstration was a well-planned and thoroughly rehearsed event designed to attract attention to the demands made by the organisers. It was neither a desperate local resort to violence by a group of malcontents such as the Pentrich rising, nor was it deliberately organised violence in the face of a desperate situation such as the Luddite machine wrecking and riots.
2. The demands made were for (a) adequate parliamentary representation for the Manchester area, (b) universal male suffrage, (c) a secret ballot rather than openly casting one's vote at the hustings, (d) repeal of the Corn Laws and (e) annual parliaments.
3. Inviting Henry Hunt to chair the meeting was equivalent to documenting the national scale of the grievances against government's refusal to consider parliamentary reform. Arresting Hunt before he even had a chance to speak, convicting him of sedition and then sentencing him to 30 months in Ilchester prison exceeded the letter of the law.
4. Although it is debatable whether Lord Sidmouth's reinterpretation of the purpose of the meeting actually did constitute an annulment of the decision of the local authorities to ban the meeting, there was no pressing need to disperse it, since it was obviously not an armed insurrection. Ordering Hunt and the organisers to be arrested while he was on the hustings rather than after the demonstration was an act of folly, given the fact that an estimated 60,000 people were packed into St. Peter's Field and the roads leading to it.

The ideology of the legitimate language, however, can only be indirectly connected to such sociopolitical incidents and events as the Peterloo Massacre. It is clear that the government had an option as to how to act at and after Peterloo, and, with hindsight, made the wrong choice in advising the magistrates to arrest Hunt and the organisers. Not only were the prisoners tried and convicted of sedition, but the government clamped down swiftly and ruthlessly on any further claims to reform Parliament by passing the so-called Six Acts on 23 November of the same year. The six acts were (1) the Training Prevention Act (or Unlawful Drilling Act), to prevent people from attending a meeting for the purpose of receiving training or drill in weapons; (2) the Seizure of Arms Act, to empower magistrates to search any private property for weapons; (3) the Misdemeanours Act, to speed up the administration of justice by reducing the opportunities for bail; (4) the Seditious Meetings Prevention Act, to prevent public meetings concerned with "church" or "state" matters; (5) the Blasphemous and Seditious Libels Act (or Criminal Libel Act), to provide more punitive sentences; and (6) the Newspaper and Stamp Duties Act, to stiffen the taxes on publications that formerly escaped duty.

The Blasphemous and Seditious Libels Act, which tried to prevent texts such those published by Hone, did not attempt to redefine the terms "sedition", "blasphemy" and "libel", but to increase the sentences drastically. However, this did not prevent Hone from publishing one of his finest and most audacious parodies in December of that year, *The Political House that Jack Built*, lampooning the government and the prince regent for the tragedy of Peterloo. One wonders how Hone escaped the rigours of the law, until one realises that the text is cleverly built into the simple frame of the children's rhyme *The House that Jack Built*. It is not therefore blasphemous, nor does it incite others to insurrection of any kind (i.e. it is not seditious), but it does come quite close to libel at times, particularly in its representation of the prince regent.

My argument is that social class distinctions and the politics based on social class at the end of the eighteenth century and the beginning of the nineteenth hinged on language and education, and the argument runs as follows:

1. Throughout the 1790s, the social class in power, the gentry and the aristocracy, attempted, often unsuccessfully, to convict people of libel and sedition on the grounds that their writings constituted examples of vulgar language that was liable to corrupt their readers.
2. Their justification was that only those who had received a classical education and displayed refined language were capable of governing the country.
3. After the end of the Napoleonic Wars and under immense pressure from below to reform Parliament and introduce universal male suffrage, the politicolinguistic justification for upholding a distinction between themselves and the lower middle and working classes began to waver. As a result, the

political repression that was partly justified by being in a state of war up to 1815 was simply intensified and extended to maintain those class distinctions. But, at the same time, it became increasingly difficult to provide a linguistic justification for the distinctions themselves.

4. After Horne Tooke and Hone, the authorities were unable to define what "vulgar" language was and were thus unable to sustain a distinction between the legitimate language and illegitimate forms of language without reverting to outright violence and repression.

However, before the concept of the legitimate language could be put to use as a symbol of national pride and unity, the ruling classes were faced by the challenge of Chartism, as we shall see in the following subsection.

4.3 Chartism and the fear of armed revolution

The Chartist movement from 1838 to 1850 was arguably the largest organised movement in the first half of the nineteenth century campaigning for the attainment of universal male suffrage and the *full* reform of Parliament (which was not achieved in the Reform Act of 1832) and in resisting government repression. It was named after the *People's Charter* drawn up by William Lovett of the London Working Men's Association in 1838. The charter had its forerunner in the *People's Charter... giving a Condensed View of the Great Principles of Representative Government, and the Chief Objects of Reform* drawn up by the Metropolitan Political Union in 1832. The model for both documents was Magna Charta, and the 1838 charter contained the following six central aims:

1. Annual Parliaments.
2. Universal Suffrage.
3. Equal Voting Districts.
4. No Property Qualifications.
5. Voting by Ballot.
6. Payment of Members. (LWMA 1848: 7)

The most comprehensive history of Chartism has been written by Malcolm Chase, who makes the following comment about the fear of the Chartist movement in the eyes of polite society and the political establishment:

Clearly something remarkable was taking place as 1838 drew to a close. Seldom had the constitutional right to bear arms been so loudly asserted or the language of physical force so widely used. It was one of the hardest winters in recent memory and the economy was in depression. Yet a highly politicised movement had emerged, distinguished first and foremost by its self-possession. (2007: 41)

It is no exaggeration to say that the mood in the country as a whole was one of fearful apprehension. Armed insurrection seemed on the brink of turning into stark reality. Chartist organisations had sprung up all over the country, not just in the industrial areas, but even in the quiet rural backwaters of what was considered to be the most prosperous parts of the country. The movement was nothing if not well organised. At its head was a charismatic Irishman named Fergus O'Connor, who also financed a radical newspaper, the *Northern Star*, based in Leeds, which quickly became the mouthpiece for Chartism.

The year 1839 saw the establishment of a National Convention, whose purpose it was to put together a petition to be presented to Parliament based on the People's Charter. Chartists themselves fully expected that Parliament would accept the petition, but, as the year wore on, the authorities began to clamp down on allowing Chartists to hold large meetings. In April Henry Vincent, an important member of the convention, dared local magistrates at Newport to arrest him while making a speech at a meeting that had been declared illegal. The magistrates did not oblige, but the next time he was in Newport, a pitched battle took place between Vincent's supporters and special constables. He was arrested on 7 May in London, after which the organisers decided that the convention could be more safely held in Birmingham. Between May and 12 July, when the National Petition was debated in the House of Commons, more violence broke out in Llanidloes and Longton, and more convention members were arrested and imprisoned. The petition itself had almost 2 million signatures, which in a population of roughly 14 million represented one seventh of the total population of Great Britain, which in itself was no mean feat. Parliament debated a proposal by Thomas Attwood "that a committee of the whole House take into consideration the National Petition" (M. Chase 2007: 84), but after a lukewarm debate in a half-empty House the proposal was turned down. The vote was 235 votes to 46.

The response to Parliament's rejection of the petition was not only to dampen the confidence of Chartists but also to incite the more militant members to argue in favour of strikes, a nationwide armed insurrection, or both. Riots occurred in Birmingham, Bury and other places, and in November an armed march was organised into Newport. The reaction of the authorities was severe and punitive, with death penalties (later converted into transportation to Australia), transportation and prison sentences. Chase points out that "local circumstances explain each of the riotous outbreaks, but the overall effect was to increase apprehension that Chartists were intent on fomenting major upheaval" (2007: 95).

The movement continued its activities throughout the 1840s, culminating in a second Petition in 1848, which was said to have 5 million signatures. In reality, however, the total number of signatures was later calculated at a little more than 1.9 million after dual signatures, signatures that were obviously forged, children's signatures, women's signatures and those of people who had died in the meantime were struck out. The petition was accompanied by a mass meeting of Chartists on Kennington Common on 8 April, the intention being that it should be escorted to the House of Commons by those attending. Instead of the expected 400,000 on the Common, it is estimated that there were only roughly 150,000 present, and O'Connor, who had since won a seat in the House of Commons, agreed with the Metropolitan Police Force that the petition would be conveyed to Parliament in a number of hansom cabs. The fate of the petition was then in the hands of O'Connor himself. However, when the motion to present the petition to Parliament was due, O'Connor, who had lost his patience with a fellow MP and challenged him to a duel and then was constrained to apologise before the House, withdrew the motion in a fit of pique! So ended the People's Charter. Chartism itself lingered on for a few more years and petered out in 1852.

Apart from the clause demanding annual parliaments, however, all the clauses of the charter have now been fulfilled. The Ballot Act was passed in 1872; equal voting districts were agreed on in 1884, and the Representation of the People Act in the same year abolished property rights for voting; payment of MPs was introduced in 1911; and full universal suffrage (of men and women) was introduced in Britain in 1918. In this sense the charter was successful. So why was it first turned down, and what was it about Chartism that frightened the authorities so much? Chartism was a political movement, but it was never a political party, although a few Chartists were able to gain seats in the House of Commons. This was, perhaps, its weakness, one that the trade union movement managed to avoid although it, too, was never a political party. Chartism displayed an alarming degree of organisation and a bold and decisive command of written English; it was characterised by a high level and surprising degree of verbal articulation, fluency and eloquence in the field of political agitation. At the time, it was also thought to be characterised by a willingness to use force to achieve its ends, although Chase's book shows the degree to which this was caused more by fear among the middle and upper classes of society than by official policy decisions. I will argue in the final section, however, that the fear of the Chartist movement was driven by the politicised, class-dominated theory of language developed in the latter half of the eighteenth century.

5. FROM THE LEGITIMATE LANGUAGE TO THE STANDARD LANGUAGE

The ideology of the legitimate language, set in motion and driven by the *legitimate language myth* led to a bipartite division of language in Britain. On the one hand, we have the so-called refined language of the educated, those who had received a classical education, which was of course equivalent to those who had the money to afford such an education: the propertied gentry and aristocracy and those of the middle classes who had achieved newfound wealth in the first stage of the Industrial Revolution. On the other hand, we have the so-called vulgar, barbaric language of the mass of the lower middle classes and the working classes: the language of those who possessed no property and did not have the means for anything but very elementary schooling. Radical politicians and young intellectuals from the middle classes, however, realised very early on in the 1770s and 1780s that this distinction was a bogus one and was only held rigidly in position to protect the property rights of the upper orders. In point of fact, the ornate, classical style of writing could often be shown to contain very little of substance, and even to lead to tautologous repetition. Horne Tooke frequently calls it the language of "imposture". But as long as this distinction between two different kinds of writing could be upheld and used to discriminate against those who were not able to produce a classical style of writing, language itself had irrevocably become politicised. Language was the outward sign of a person's origins and good breeding. Horne Tooke's work must be seen from the political perspective of a radical who was bent on exposing the sham of this distinction. This was the significance of his work, and this was the attraction of his challenge to the established theory of language.

Since it was a theory that supported the argument that only the propertied class with a classical education was fit to govern the country, language became one of the key issues. The more the theory was challenged, the more the established classes attempted to defend it with repressive measures. Horne Tooke's work must nevertheless have had a great effect on his radical readers if one judges by the newfound political and linguistic confidence displayed by supporters of the reform of Parliament after the Napoleonic Wars. Cobbett successfully challenged the theory through his *Grammar of the English Language* in 1819, which he wrote specifically for labourers and rustics. One hundred thousand copies had been sold by 1834, indicating the popularity that the grammar enjoyed and the effect it had on improving the writing and speaking of those who had had a rudimentary education, and it was precisely that class of underprivileged workers which drew up the People's Charter and were so eloquent in defence of their rights during the 1830s and 1840s. In a word, despite the continued repression by the government, the propertied classes were ultimately at a distinct disadvantage.

The solution was subtle. It was to admit that the written language of the "vulgar" was not in fact vulgar, but that it was politically subversive and a danger to national unity within Britain. Only by accepting what rapidly came to be called standard English could one reconstitute the unity that had been lost. Standard English was thus adapted to new social conditions such that it was no longer the property of the upper middle and upper classes, but was the symbol for a unified nation—albeit still under the political dominance of those classes.

The legitimate language thus became the national language and soon the imperial language, which could be commodified and sold to others who wanted to possess it. Crowley (2003) deals with this stage in the history of

English in great detail, so I will forgo a repetition of his arguments. However, it is significant that in the second half of the century there was a renewed interest in the assumed origins of the English language (i.e. the standard language). As Olivia Smith says, "Such an understanding of language forms the background of Tooke's re-evaluation of Anglo-Saxon and 'mere' native English. He insists that early authors and Anglo-Saxon are the proper foundations for understanding English: English is a continuation of Anglo-Saxon 'with a very little variation of the written character'" (1984: 124).

I argued in chapter 2 that the number of translations of *Beowulf* increased from 1850 onwards and peaked in the final two decades of the century (cf. fig. 2.1). In addition, there was a veritable spate of historical grammars of English, some of which I quoted in chapter 1. And it is in precisely this work that the *superiority of English myth*, the *longevity of English myth* and the *greatness myth* first appear in all their strength. We have seen that many of the other myths dealt with in this book go back several centuries, and some of them may even be universal. The myths with which I began my investigation, however, are rooted in precisely this hegemonic transformation of the *polite language myth* into the *legitimate language myth*.

It is also significant that standard English as a written variety of the language lost its power as an indicator of social superiority and class, and, as it did so, great efforts were made to replace it with a so-called oral form of standard taken from the accents of upper-class boys attending public schools, the (eventually) Received Pronunciation or RP. Once again enough work has been carried out on this phenomenon by Mugglestone (1995) and J. Milroy (1999, 2002) to warrant leaving it out of our discussion here. The hegemonic linguistic discourse throughout the nineteenth century and right up to the Second World War was based on the myth that the "best" kind of English was standard English. It formed a powerful discourse archive that did not come under pressure until the late 1950s. Curiously enough, echoes of an attempt to turn the clock back and return to a conceptualisation of English based on notions of "educatedness" and social class reappear in the "standard English wars" generated by the development of the National Curriculum, which is the topic of chapter 10.

Chapter 10

Transforming a myth to save an archive

When polite becomes educated

> From her radio and television appearances it seemed [Mrs Rumbold] found repugnant our insistence that a child's dialect is not inaccurate in its use of grammar and should be respected.
>
> —Brian Cox, *Cox on Cox*, 1991

1. FROM *HOMO SOCIALIS* TO *HOMO CULTURALIS*

Within the last 30 years, linguists have experienced the so-called pragmatic turn in linguistics. So we may be forgiven for missing out on the fact that literary studies have also experienced a number of their own "turns" in the late modern era. The turn in literary studies that promises to produce the most fruitful forms of collaboration between linguists and literary theorists in helping to deconstruct "the history of the language" discourse and solving the "question of good speech" once and for all is what I will call the "cultural turn". The cultural turn represents an attempt to embed the study of literature (and of course the same goes for the study of language) into the study of cultural movements in general. The pragmatic turn is a turn toward the uniquely dialogic nature of language, toward the social process of meaning making, toward the acceptance of the simple truism that it is human language that turns *homo socialis* into *homo culturalis*.

It is human language that enables social groups to construct a past with all its myths and histories and to project a future with all its hopes and utopias. It is human language that allows individuals, as members of social groups, to communicate with one another, to reason, hypothesise, construct ideologies, exert power and dominate others. And it is human language that allows individuals to attempt to express the inexpressible, to imagine and fantasise, to weave webs of creation.

Chapters 8 and 9 trace out the process by which a set of individual myths all deriving from the *linguistic homogeneity myth* were focused on the discursive construction of an ideology of politeness that, from the outset, was imbued with ideas of social superiority. It was an ideology that fed easily into the embryonic ideology of the standard language and was fostered throughout the eighteenth century by the commercial production of books on English, on the one hand, and the emergence of Britain as a maritime colonial power, on the other. The onset of the Industrial Revolution in the last quarter of the eighteenth century propelled the ideology of the standard language forward until social unrest in Britain during and in the wake of the Napoleonic Wars and the second stage of the Industrial Revolution created the necessity to construct the standard language discursively as a unifying catalyst in the attempt to prevent a sociopolitical revolution in Britain. In this way, the eighteenth century *polite language myth* was transformed into the *legitimate language myth* in the nineteenth-century construction of the nation-state, in which a homogeneous language spoken by all was to be linked with a homogeneous political system and a homogeneous religion. The nation-state was to exemplify a homogeneous "culture".

As we saw in chapter 9, however, the ideology of the legitimate language that emerged from both myths constituted a dominant language discourse that became highly politicised in the first half of the nineteenth century by the strong challenge offered by radical thinkers, writers and politicians. As unofficial representatives of the disenfranchised mass of the lower middle and working classes, they did not take kindly to being excluded from political decision making on the grounds that their style of written English was classified as "vulgar" by those above them in the rigid social class structure that characterised Britain at the turn of the nineteenth century. They spoke and wrote English plainly and directly, avoiding what Horne Tooke called the "imposture" of the "refined" and "educated" sections of society. We also saw in the previous chapter that the assumed rights and privileges of the propertied classes were based on a bogus sociolinguistic distinction between refined and vulgar varieties of English.

In the wake of the Napoleonic Wars and the unprecedented industrialisation of Britain and in the face of the painful socioeconomic and sociocultural transformation of the country, an unbending insistence on those rights led to wholesale poverty, massive exploitation of the working classes and serious outbreaks of violence. With hindsight, however, the threat of armed insurrection on a national scale seems to have been relatively insignificant, and it is hard for us to fathom the latent, almost permanent fear of the upper middle and upper classes of society in the face of an ever more confident and growing mass of disenfranchised citizens. As noted in chapter 9, one solution would certainly have been to grant universal suffrage and to reform the parliamentary system to stamp out the rampant political corruption inherent in it. But it is easy to make those suggestions now, from our own late modern archive, and not at all easy to see things from the perspective of a population trying to grapple with new and frightening problems.

From a sociolinguistic perspective, the answer appeared to be the adaptation of the ideology of the legitimate language in the face of the new social conditions, and, as Crowley (2003) has shown, to re-create standard English as a socially unifying force to which every citizen in Britain, at least in theory, had access. The problem was that access to it was never equal, which is witnessed by the shift of focus from the written standard language to a proposed oral standard (see Crowley 2003: chap. 5), which did not seriously change the permissible and impermissible statements of the discourse archive. Certain forms of language were "refined", hence socially acceptable, and others were "unrefined" or "vulgar", hence unacceptable. As we shall see in this chapter, the discourse archive itself (which had its beginnings in the late eighteenth century) began to be challenged and to break down only in the 1950s. One last, rearguard action on the part of politicians in the late 1980s attempted to reverse this trend, and I shall deal with this challenge here. My assessment at the end of the chapter is that it failed and that it also leaves sociolinguists seriously questioning what is meant by the term "standard language".

2. LANGUAGE AND POLITENESS, LANGUAGE AND "EDUCATEDNESS"

The link between politeness and language in Britain was one of the major cultural forces in the formation of the powerful ideology of standard English. Even as late as 1920, Thomas Nicklin, in a book titled *Standard English Pronunciation with some Notes on Accidence and Syntax*, makes the following set of statements:

> I will venture to contend that it is the right of everyone born in these islands, whatever the profession and whatever the property of his parents, to be taught to speak that English dialect which marks an educated man [i.e. standard English]. Nothing can be more disastrous than that the accidents of history, which have led to this dialect of the educated appearing to be a special prerogative of the well-to-do, should be regarded as irretrievable. The democratic spirit must demand for every child, however humble his parents' occupation, that he shall be taught that one common dialect which can be understood everywhere, and which is the modern representative of all that has been greatest in English learning, statesmanship, oratory, poetry, and politeness. (1920: 10–11)

The term "politeness", here and elsewhere in Nicklin's book, is to be understood in the way it was defined in chapter 8. However, in the quotation from

Nicklin it is now explicitly connected through the ideology of standard English to education, learning, oratory and poetry,[1] indicating a further transformation of the *politellegitimate language myth* into the *myth of the educated language*. The connection between Nicklin's defence of standard English and the notion of education can be clearly seen here, although modern proponents of "educatedness" have masked their endorsement of the socially exclusive nature of standard English through the argument that it is the language of the educated. In doing so, being educated in this late modern sense also means being socially exclusive, although in a way that is rather different from the late-eighteenth-century sense.

In the second edition of *Standard English and the Politics of Language*, Crowley adds an extra chapter to bring the reader up-to-date on what we may call the "state of the standard English question". The first edition took the reader up to the end of the 1980s and the bitter dispute between Conservative politicians, the media and self-appointed guardians of the language, on the one hand, and linguists, education theorists and teachers, on the other. In this chapter, I shall use the metaphorical term the "National Curriculum wars", a bold step and one that goes beyond what Tony Bex and I called a "widening debate" in 1999, but one that I feel is adequate to define the feeling of verbal warfare on the subject of English in the National Curriculum in the late 1980s and early 1990s.

The '90s saw the lukewarm reception of the Kingman Report, the embarrassment over the Cox Report,[2] and the final implementation of the National Curriculum in England and Wales.[3] The definition of standard oral English, however, has still not been adequately tackled, and when we read such linguists as Quirk, Greenbaum, Leech and Svartvik in their grammar (1985) referring to

---

1. To be fair to Nicklin, though, the socially exclusive nature of this alliance of concepts is roundly rejected by him.

2. The Kingman Report was the final report made by the Committee of Inquiry into English Language Teaching chaired by Sir John Kingman, which was set up in 1986 by the secretary of state for education and science in the Conservative government of the time, Kenneth Baker. Its terms of reference were:

   1. To recommend a model of the English language, whether spoken or written, which would:
      (1) serve as a basis of how teachers are trained to understand how the English language works;
      (2) inform professional discussion of all aspects of English teaching.
   2. To recommend the principles which should guide teachers on how far and in what ways the model should be made explicit to pupils, to make them conscious of how language is used in a range of contexts.
   3. To recommend what, in general terms, pupils need to know about how the English language works and in consequence what they should have been taught, and be expected to understand, on this score, at age 7, 11 and 16.

   The Cox Report was produced by the Cox Committee set up by the Conservative government under the chairmanship of Brian Cox, professor of English at the University of Manchester. The Cox Committee was set up immediately after the publication of the Kingman Report to develop a curriculum for English teaching "for all pupils, whatever their first language" (Thompson 2000: 33).

3. One might even argue that the Kingman Report was given the cold shoulder by the Conservative government at the time, and it is known that Mrs Thatcher's immediate reaction to it was that it should be rejected. As it was, its acceptance and publication were not welcomed by those who felt very strongly that the form of "grammar" teaching common in the schools of the 1950s should be reintroduced.

"Standard English" as educated English or even Trudgill (1995) referring to it as "the variety which is normally spoken by educated people", they sound suspiciously like eighteenth-century proponents of "educatedness". Crowley is acutely aware of the dangers here, and he reminds us of what Raymond Williams argued in *Communications*: "At the roots of much of our cultural thinking is our actual experience of speech. In Britain the question of good speech is deeply confused, and is in itself a major source of many of the divisions in our culture" (Williams 1962: 102). The argument that I wish to trace out and deconstruct in this chapter is the perhaps not so subtle transformation of the eighteenth-century discourse of politeness, by way of a prior transformation into the discourse of the legitimate language, into a discourse of educatedness.

In effect this transformation was really only a subtle shift in the conceptual meanings of the lexeme *educated* itself. To say that someone was "educated" in the latter half of the eighteenth century and throughout the nineteenth century implied that he or she (usually, of course, "he") had been exposed to a thorough training in Latin and Greek, classical literature and rhetoric. To say that someone was "schooled" meant that that person had been given enough rudimentary instruction and training at school to be able to read and write passably and to apply the fundamental principles and functions of mathematics in his everyday life. Until the post–World War II era, "schooling" did not really mean much more than this. It was not meant to prepare young people for adult life in other respects despite the fact that subjects such as history, geography, the natural sciences, physical education and foreign languages had been added to the syllabus.[4] The major problem was that, until well into the 1960s, the "educated" were still thought of as the privileged sector of society (whether or not they had come from middle-class or working-class homes), as those who had enjoyed a public school or grammar school education, or as those who constituted the "top 5 percent" of the population who went on to study at one of the universities.

In my essay "From polite language to educated language" (2002), I showed how, in the modern discourse on standard English, polite language, particularly with reference to the socially legitimate version of the spoken language, was subtly transformed into the language of the educated, and Crowley gives evidence of how this came about with the extension of universal education in the nineteenth century. In doing so, the myth forming the nucleus of this hegemonic discourse, the ***polite/legitimate language myth***, lost none of its socially divisive force. To give evidence for this point of view, I shall first consider the teaching of English in schools throughout England and Wales and show how the transformation from polite to educated language came to the

---

4. Teaching children with the aim of preparing them for the vagaries of adult life and the difficulties of choosing a trade or a profession was certainly the goal of a number of excellent, dedicated teachers throughout Britain, but the overall tenor of elementary education till the age of 14 (in pre–World War II days), 15 (in the postwar period until the 1960s) or 16 (from the 1960s on) was not particularly conducive to such teaching goals.

fore during the National Curriculum wars in the 1980s, in which both literary scholars and linguists were deeply involved.

3. COMPREHENSIVE SCHOOLS AND THE TEACHING OF STANDARD ENGLISH

From a linguistic point of view, there are good reasons to focus on the heated debate over the teaching of English in the National Curriculum in the 1980s and early 1990s. As far as the media, the Conservative government of the time and certain sections of society were concerned, the declared goal of the National Curriculum with respect to the teaching of English was a return to the rote learning of prescriptive grammar rules and stylistic prescriptions, and a rejection of the creative, communicative learning and understanding of language as a multiplicity of dialectal varieties and different registers. In section 5 we shall take a closer look at Honey's book *Language Is Power: The Story of Standard English and Its Enemies* (1997), in which he promotes the equation of standard English with the language of the educated and devalues the university as an educational institution.

The idea of comprehensive schools at the secondary level of education in England and Wales was proposed by the post–World War II Labour government under Prime Minister Clement Attlee as an antidote to the social segregation of schoolchildren that took place as a result of the so-called 11+ exam, in which those who passed had a right to a place at a grammar school and those who did not were constrained to attend so-called secondary modern schools and technical schools. It was also the avowed aim of the postwar Labour government eventually to abolish the institution of the fee-paying public schools. In the postwar era this project became a highly politicised, controversial and hotly debated issue in the field of state education. Pedagogical arguments for the introduction of comprehensive education were overshadowed by the political arguments of the opposition, who predicted that it would lead to a dangerous levelling and lowering of educational standards and that it was a denial of parents' rights to choose the kind of school their children attended.[5]

The Attlee government, however, did not have time to implement this educational project before it was voted out of office in 1951 by Winston Churchill's Conservatives. During the following 13 years of Conservative government, a few comprehensive schools were introduced by local authorities, particularly in rural areas where it was more economic to concentrate schoolchildren at different levels of achievement in one rather than several schools, and in urban areas controlled by the Labour Party. In the years after 1964, following the victory of the Labour Party under Harold Wilson,

---

5. In reality, of course, the only people who had this option were those with money.

local authorities were instructed to draw up plans as to how they intended to introduce comprehensive education. Most of the secondary modern schools were transformed into lower schools catering to all pupils from age 11 to age 16, and the old grammar schools were transformed into upper schools (or sixth-form colleges) catering for pupils who wanted to continue their education to higher levels. In fact, however, only the high achievers were accepted into upper schools, which effectively continued the old system of social segregation. By the time of the first Thatcher government in 1979, this process, with certain exceptions, had been largely completed, despite the short interregnum of the Conservative government under Edward Heath from 1970 to 1974.

The shift towards comprehensive education coincided, not totally by accident, with a second pedagogical debate in the school system with regard to the teaching of English. Towards the end of the 1950s opposition was increasingly raised in pedagogical circles against the rote learning of prescriptive grammar in English.[6] A number of research studies in the early 1970s (e.g. Doughty, Pearce & Thornton 1971; Tough 1976) had shown that there was no correlation between the prescriptive teaching of grammar and the acquisition of communicatively adequate oral skills and correctness in writing standard English. Pupils who had not set their sights on higher academic levels of education turned away from the study of standard English instead of considering it as an added medium through which to express themselves and to discover the world around them. More creativity and flexibility in teaching English were called for, and the general goal of English teaching became not the mastery of grammar but the means of developing the pupil's personality and communicative abilities. The grammatical parsing of sentences devoid of context, the correct representation in written form of what was spoken (i.e. dictation), the training of correct spelling, and the writing out of stylistic rules to avoid what were generally referred to as "incorrect", "ungrammatical" expressions were given up in favour of open discussion, forms of debate, creative writing, the study of other varieties of English and familiarity with different registers of English.

In the eyes of critics within and outside the education system in the early 1970s, this meant that one generation of schoolchildren in the period after 1964 had been educated with no formal training in grammar, spelling, style and the lexicon. By the time of the Thatcher government of the 1980s, two to three generations of schoolchildren had not been exposed to prescriptive ideals of correctness—to what were traditionally considered to be the components of a homogeneous standard language. It also meant that two to three generations of teachers had been trained without the necessary experience to teach these supposedly important aspects of language. As is usual in such

6. Again not totally by accident, this revolution in the teaching of English coincided with the rise of modern linguistics at the end of the 1950s and the beginning of the 1960s.

general debates, the criticism completely ignored the fact that many of these teachers had found creative ways and means to direct pupils' attention to grammar, spelling and style.

Conservative politicians in the Heath administration from 1970 to 1974 became convinced that the new approach towards the teaching of English was a thorn in the flesh of the whole education system, and no one more than the minister for education at the time, Margaret Thatcher. But the conversion of the old segregational forms of education into different types of comprehensive education had progressed too far to be reversed without a huge financial outlay on the part of the state. In addition, in 1974 the Heath government called an early general election at the end of a long miners' strike that had crippled the supply of energy within Britain, and it was ousted by the Labour Party under Harold Wilson.[7] While still in power, however, the Heath government set up a committee under the chairmanship of Sir Alan Bullock to take a critical look at the state of English teaching and to present a report to the government. The Bullock Committee met from 1972 to 1974, but the report, titled *A Language for Life*, was not published till 1975 when Labour had returned to power. In addition, it contained no recommendations that the "old" form of teaching English should be reinstated, but endorsed the new policy.

The Conservative government that returned to power in 1979 with Margaret Thatcher as prime minister allowed itself enough time to prepare a new attempt to reform the school system in England and Wales. After Sir Keith Joseph had transferred from his cabinet position of secretary of state for industry in 1981 to take over the Ministry of Education, he developed the idea of a National Curriculum for England and Wales and discussed it in detail with Thatcher. During the period from 1974 to 1979, when the Conservatives were in opposition, Thatcher and Joseph had worked closely together on Conservative policies for the future, and it is quite conceivable that the idea for a National Curriculum was mooted during this time. However, no formal proposal to present a bill on education to Parliament was made during Thatcher's first term in office. In 1986 Kenneth Baker took over the Ministry of Education, and during that year the Great Education Reform Bill (known as the Gerbil) was published. Throughout England and Wales education was split into four phases, called "key stages", with an exam at the end of each phase on the subjects that were compulsory throughout the curriculum from age 5 to age 16: mathematics, science, English, technology, history, geography, art, music, and physical education. The exams were called standard assessment tasks (SATs), and pupils were examined at ages 7, 11, 14 and 16. The Education Reform Act became law in 1988.

7. Wilson retired from office in 1976, when the premiership passed to the newly elected leader of the Labour Party, James Callaghan.

4. PLANNING THE REINTRODUCTION OF GRAMMAR INTO THE NATIONAL CURRICULUM

Three working groups were then set up by Secretary of State for Education Baker to cover the three core subjects: English, mathematics and science. The working group for English, the Committee of Inquiry into the Teaching of the English Language, was chaired by mathematician Sir John Kingman, vice chancellor of the University of Bristol. The mandate defined by the Department of Education and Science was to report on the teaching of English in England and Wales and to suggest a model of English that would be of use for the second working group chaired by Brian Cox, who was then professor of English at the University of Manchester and who had also been a member of the Kingman Committee. The mandate of this working group was "to prepare proposals for English in the National Curriculum" from age 5 to age 16 (Cox 1991: 4), and it was asked to build on the Kingman Report.

The Kingman Report was submitted on 17 March and published on 29 April 1988. It did not meet with the approval of the government, and the prime minister seriously considered rejecting it because it not only failed to recommend a return to formal prescriptive grammar teaching as this had been practised up to the end of the 1950s but also suggested that such a move might hamper what the panel saw as the real goal of a national curriculum in English: the ability to communicate adequately in the spoken and written word.[8] Brian Cox's working group was established on the day of the publication of the Kingman Report. The seminal publication on the activities of the working group and the difficulties that it encountered in having the final report published at all is Cox's detailed critical analysis of all the issues involved (*Cox on Cox: An English Curriculum for the 1990's* [1991]), which I will look at in some detail in this section.

Presumably because the Cox working group was set up the same day the Kingman Report was published and because press reports indicated that neither Thatcher nor Baker was happy that the report had not taken into account their conceptualisation of how grammar should be taught, Cox suggests that "the press presumed that I was to lead a Group which would make firm recommendations on grammar, in contrast to the equivocations of Kingman" (1991: 14). He reminds his readers that he had been a member of the Kingman Committee and that he fully endorsed the report it produced, which he considered to consist of "carefully balanced descriptions of the place of English in the curriculum" (14) rather than "equivocations".

---

8. It is interesting to note that the quality presses were somewhat ambivalent in their appraisal of the Kingman Report. The newspaper *Today* was fully in support of the proposal, the *Guardian* was cautiously in support, the *Observer* took a middle-of-the-road position, and the *Times* avoided any evaluative commentary. The popular press, needless to say, came out in support of government criticism, producing statements that were calculated to fan the flames of dissension.

The group worked very quickly and submitted its final report in the middle of May 1989. Cox reports as follows on the way the report was received:

> Mr Baker very much disliked the Report. He had wanted a short Report, with strong emphasis on grammar, spelling and punctuation, which would have been easy for parents to read. In contrast, as I have already said, I was most anxious to persuade the teaching profession to implement our recommendations with good will, and so I felt it essential to explain our assumptions in detail. I understand that Mrs Rumbold [minister of state at the Department of Education and Science] also found our Report distasteful. I was never asked to discuss the final Report with her or Mr Baker, so I cannot be sure about her reasons, but from her radio and television appearances it seemed she found repugnant our insistence that a child's dialect is not inaccurate in its use of grammar and should be respected. (1991: 11)

A number of points are very revealing here. The "strong emphasis" that Mr Baker wanted on grammar, spelling and punctuation indicates that the standard *written* language was what he equated with standard English. Schoolchildren, in accordance with this conceptualisation of standard English, should be trained to accuracy and correctness rather than encouraged to explore standard English as an added variety of the language which children can and should use creatively and communicatively. The *legitimate language myth* can be seen here as the driving force behind the promotion of standard English, nota bene in its written form, as the only valid language in the state education system.

The first inference that one can draw from the ideological discourse of the standard language, as represented by Mr Baker and the rest of the Conservative cabinet, is that the language of those wielding political power is the only valid language, not just because it is the language of the education system but also because it is the language of the power holders themselves. This was precisely the attitude of governments during the 1790s and 1800s, against which Horne Tooke wrote the *Diversions of Purley*. The second inference is that, given the need to use standard language in oral communication in the school system, oral standard English is put on an equal footing with written standard English. The real issue, however, is how we define oral standard English, and the Conservative government's stress on spelling, punctuation and "correct" grammar is evidence of a lack of awareness that this problem should be tackled at all.

The second point concerns those who are addressed by the report. Mr Baker assumes, somewhat unrealistically, that the target group is parents, whereas Cox and his committee, far more realistically, assume the target group to be teachers of English. Baker and Rumbold criticised the report for being too detailed, but the criticism itself and the identification of parents as the target group amount to not much more than a popular political statement. One senses here a lack of respect for the quality of English teachers on the

part of Baker and Rumbold. Obviously a government report is public property, but teachers are more directly implicated in carrying out the recommendations of a report than parents are ever likely to be. It is they, not the parents,
who need to benefit more from careful detail concerning the reasoning behind
the report.

The next point concerns the fact that Cox was never asked to discuss the
report with Baker and Rumbold, and Cox himself speculates on the possible
reasons for this. Apparently Rumbold, in her radio and television appearances, found the "insistence that a child's dialect is not inaccurate in its use of
grammar and should be respected" repugnant. The phrase that looms large
here is "inaccurate in its use of grammar", which indicates that it was precisely misguided ideas about what grammar is that lay at the heart of the
matter. The *legitimate language myth* comes out in all its strength in Cox's
statement that a child's dialect also has grammar and his implication that
many of the reports in the popular print and television media imagine that
only standard English can have a grammar. In Rumbold's eyes (and no doubt
in the eyes of the Conservative government in general), dialects are simply
"inaccurate"; they are debasements of the legitimate standard language. The
second inference that can be drawn is that university academics specialising in
language are themselves misguided if they argue otherwise, or even if their
data support the linguistic regularity of dialect. The step from accusing a
speaker of bad grammar to accusing her of bad character and creating a
causal link between the two is small, as is evident in countless academic discussions on the subject (e.g. Milroy & Milroy 1985; Milroy 2002; Crowley
2003; Cameron 1995). Cox (1991: 34) gives the example of Norman Tebbitt,
a prominent member of Thatcher's cabinet who was later to become chairman
of the Conservative Party, saying on Radio 4 in 1985 that "the decline in the
teaching of grammar had led directly to the rise in football hooliganism".[9]
Cox goes on to suggest that "correct grammar was seen by him as part of the
structures of authority (such as respect for elders, for standards of cleanli-
ness, for discipline in the schools) which in recent decades had fallen into
decline" (34).

Cox suggests that three major interest groups were fighting for control
over the National Curriculum English programme: journalists, politicians
and professional teachers. I would add a fourth group consisting of academics
concerned with language and teaching, who were treated by journalists and
politicians with as much contempt as were the teachers. It is clear from what
we have seen of the way in which both the Kingman Report and the Cox
Report were received in the media and by the government that the journalists
and politicians considered "grammar" to be associated somehow with the
correct use of standard English, or even with the correct use of the written

9. A certain amount of caution is in order here, however. Has Cox simply transferred Tebbitt's original
statement into indirect speech, or has he interpreted the gist of Tebbitt's statement as amounting to a causal
connection between bad grammar and hooliganism?

language, and that any space given to dialects in the state school system was to be cut out in favour of the teaching of standard language. These are the discursive reflexes of an unshakable belief in the *legitimate language myth*, and the major bone of contention is labelled "grammar".

How did the Cox group conceptualise "grammar", and how did they envisage teachers dealing with the structure of English in the classroom? The central point that Cox makes in his chapter on "Grammar in the classroom" is the following (1991: 36): "When grammar fell into decline much of value was lost: a certain analytic competence, and with it the valuable ability to talk and write explicitly about linguistic patterns, relations and organisation." But he follows this in the very next sentence with an important caveat: "The reintroduction of the teaching of grammar does not mean that teachers need to neglect the subjective, the creative, personal and expressive, for our ability to express ourselves depends on craft, and craft involves understanding of the forms of language." Cox does not explicitly present a definition of grammar in *Cox on Cox*. But he distances himself from the idea that "English grammar is a fixed form, stable and unchanging, which obeys logical rules" (36), or that it should be equated with the "correct" structure of standard English only. Other varieties of English also have their grammars. This is particularly important when he mentions, among four points in which grammar can be of relevance in English language teaching, the fact that it should be able "to describe the considerable differences between written and spoken English" (37). The recommendations made in the report are that teachers should be familiar enough with terminology (which exists at other levels in the study of language) to invite pupils to comment actively on structure and to think about differences; that pupils should be given an opportunity to increase their awareness of the structures of language so that these can be used creatively; that the goal of any discussion of structure is to "create predictable and new meanings" (37); that there is always variety in language, which pupils should be encouraged to talk about; and that language is always in the process of changing.

These ideas are anathema to those who believe in such language myths as the *superiority of English myth*, the *immutability myth*, the *perfect language myth*, the *pure language myth* and, of course, the *legitimate language myth*, all of which form the core of the discourse archive on language that was constructed in the nineteenth century and began breaking down only at the end of the 1950s.

In the early 1990s, the government asked Professor Ronald Carter of the University of Nottingham to design training materials for future teachers of English who had not received much formal language training. Carter and his colleague Michael McCarthy had argued that standard oral English was different in many respects from standard written English (Carter & McCarthy 1988; Carter 1990; see also Carter 1999). Expecting pupils to produce the same kind of English in debate, oral discussion and conversation as they would when writing thus constitutes a misrepresentation of standard English, particularly when varieties of oral English show a wide range of structures (by individuals as well as groups) that vary according to the speaker, the person the speaker is addressing and the context of the communicative situation. On the basis of materials from the Cambridge and Nottingham Corpus of Discourse in English (CANCODE) compiled by Carter and McCarthy, Carter set about producing the LINC (Language in the National Curriculum) programme. However, the review of the programme at the end of 1991 revealed that the government was dissatisfied with the materials on the grounds that they were not formal enough, not decontextualised and, above all, that they did not always follow the "rules of standard English". The government, therefore, decided what was "correct standard English" and not a trained applied linguist! There was a great deal of public dispute over the government's decision not to allow the materials to be published. The government even placed a Crown copyright on them to prevent publication. The materials have since been used widely and successfully in teacher training courses.[10] A report in the *Daily Telegraph* of 28 June 1992—which refers to the LINK programme rather than the LINC programme—shows very clearly where the fault lines ran between the government and the press, on the one hand, and teachers and academics, on the other:

> And although the DES [Department of Education and Science] will not publish the document, it is being distributed to teacher training institutions, where its voodoo theories about the nature of language will appeal to the impressionable mind of the young woman with low A-levels in "soft" subjects who, statistically speaking, is the typical student in these establishments.

The tone of this short extract unmistakably shows the contempt with which journalists in the early 1990s held the teaching profession and academics. Theories about language such as those by Carter and McCarthy on the difference between written and oral standard English are dismissed as "voodoo theories" and those who are training to be English teachers at teacher training establishments are said to be "impressionable" and to have low A-level marks in "soft" subjects.[11]

From 1995 on, a series of books was published by Routledge on teaching at the level of the secondary school, and among them was Davison and Dowson's collection of essays *Learning to Teach English in the Secondary School: A Companion to School Experience*. The editors deal in their own article in the collection with the recent history of the National Curriculum debate and the Kingman Report, and they quote the following somewhat damning statement by John Richmond in 1992. According to Richmond, the

---

10. The political and ideological debates surrounding the LINC materials can be found in Carter 1996 and 1997.

11. In addition, a distinct note of male chauvinism is injected into the opinion presented here by referring to trainee teachers specifically as young women.

Kingman Report had "failed to deliver the two simple linked nostrums expected of it: that the most important thing teachers need to know about language concerns the grammar of sentences; and that children come to command language by being taught the grammar of sentences in advance" (Richmond 1992: 17, quoted in Davison & Dowson 1998: 39).

The National Curriculum wars, then, were characterised by disparaging public statements made in the press and by a government that considered itself to know what correct standard English was. The truth of the matter was that the attempt to turn back the clock to the 1950s relied on committee after committee and work group after work group of academics, teachers and language experts who were expected to back up the government's conceptualisation of standard English. That attempt failed despite vilification in the press, threats not to publish reports, the deliberate editing of the reports to bring them more in line with the government's policies on language and even the prohibition on publishing. It failed because the discourse archive had begun to break down at least 20 years prior to the planning of the National Curriculum.

Politicians, however, had what they thought was one strong trump card up their sleeve in the linguist John Honey, whose 1997 book, titled *Language Is Power: The Story of Standard English and Its Enemies*, will be the focus of the following section.

5. JOHN HONEY AND THE NOTION OF EDUCATEDNESS

At the beginning of the twenty-first century "standard English" is in crisis. Terms such as "BBC English", "RP", the "Queen's English", "Oxford English", "polite language", "refined language", or others that might be used to refer to "standard English", once so highly valued in the dominant language discourse archive of the nineteenth century and the first half of the twentieth century, have come increasingly under pressure in the last 40 years. Curiously enough, the pressure has come from those we might have expected to be its guardians: teachers, university lecturers, writers and poets. We could of course look at the "crisis of the standard" from the opposite point of view and consider that liberal attempts made by schools and writers to construct a creative attitude towards the standard based on the wide range of varieties of English have fallen into discredit with the media, government and frustrated self-proclaimed defenders of standard English.

However we look at it, the impression we gain is that the wars over "standard English" can no longer be conducted in a civilised fashion. Those who imagine themselves to be in control of the legitimate language seem to have willingly entered a state of war, which in the first decade of the new millennium has been temporarily suspended in a state of uneasy truce. The metaphors used on both sides of the debate are taken more and more frequently from the source domain of war or storm. Crowley (1999: 271), for example, begins his epilogue to Bex and Watts (1999) with the following sentence: "And so the standard English debate *rumbles* on." In a review of Bex and Watts (1999), Cameron (2000) expresses the opinion that it is now a matter of "war", not of civilised debate. And John Honey goes furthest with the title of his 1997 volume on standard English: *Language Is Power: The Story of Standard English and Its Enemies.*

It is Honey's book that will be looked at in more detail in this section. In chapter 8, I traced out the conceptualisation of politeness which was used to propagate the **polite language myth** from the time of the "Glorious Revolution" in 1688 to roughly 1720 and beyond. There is an uncanny similarity between that period of history and the period from 1960 to the present. In the first case the conceptualisation of the "standard" depends on vertical social differences built on the principle of "politeness", and since 1960 similar vertical social differences have been built on the principle of educatedness. But there is one essential difference between the two periods of history: in the eighteenth century the principle of politeness was ultimately victorious, whereas since 1960 the principle of educatedness as a way of measuring the standard language has functioned less and less efficiently.

The central concept in Honey's book, which was published just before the landslide victory of Tony Blair's "New Labour" over the Conservative Party in the 1997 general election, is "educatedness". The book has been heavily criticised in several reviews. Three examples from Crowley's epilogue to Bex and Watts (1999) can serve as examples of the severity of this criticism. Referring to a passage from Honey's book that reads "Critics have pointed out that from his emotionally frigid home background (he came from a poor family, and won his way to grammar school and Cambridge) [Raymond] Williams learned to love 'the People' rather than actual people" (1997: 115), Crowley first notes immediately after the first word "critics" that none are specified. He then goes on to make the following assessment:

> Honey is too skilled a rhetorician not to know what he is doing with such words, though whether he understands academic standards is again called into doubt. In case he does not know, it should be made clear that such attacks on (dead and thus not able to be libelled) fellow members of the profession, have no place in academic debate. This is not a question of falling standards, but of shamefully fallen standards of decency and professionalism. (281, n1)

Honey argues that "Standard English" has two forms, written and spoken, and that they "share a common, ideal structure" (Crowley 1999: 273). However, Crowley notes that the valid point made by the Milroys that written language is altogether different from oral language for the simple reason that the written channel is different from the spoken channel is simply evaded by Honey: "Honey's answer is simply to duck such complicated research and to resort, in a common tactic in these debates—frequently used by conservative politicians for example—to received social attitudes and beliefs (one might say prejudices)" (273). His assessment is made on the basis of the following quotation from Honey:

> It is important, though, to emphasise here that many educated people, including some respectable linguists [who are, as we might expect, not named], and also huge numbers of ordinary and not particularly educated people, act as though they believed that those forms of spoken English which are the most acceptable for a number of functions, especially functions associated with formality, are the forms which most clearly reflect written forms. (1997: 122–123)

Crowley (1999: 279) completes his contribution to Bex and Watts by stating that "It is in fact a great pity that the standard English debate is marred by the sort of conceptual confusions and political posturings (no matter how poorly expressed) which I have outlined by looking at one contribution to the debate [i.e. Honey's book]."

At the beginning of his book Honey quite explicitly uses the metaphor of the battlefield—"Standard English is now a battlefield" (1997: 1)—to offer a virtually tautologous definition of standard English shortly afterwards: "By Standard English I mean the language in which this book is written" (3). He then resorts to the adjective *educated* repeatedly to strengthen and justify his argument. Honey's major argument is that there is a natural connection between proficiency in standard English and levels of education. The argument is so central—and also so similar to the argument put forward by politicians of the 1790s and early 1800s—that I shall focus on it specifically in this section. His first proposal (p. 33) is that "educatedness" and "literacy" are closely connected, and that the connection creates access to what he calls the "mainstream" of society: "Standard forms are the expression of a complex of values associated with being in the mainstream of society, and with educatedness, which is in turn associated with literacy." Unfortunately, Honey never defines what he understands by the "mainstream of society", but the argument is in any case circular: standard English is in use in the mainstream of society, so if you do not have proficiency in standard English, you cannot be in the mainstream. It is also purely exclusive: "we" in the mainstream will exclude "you" from it on the grounds that you do not speak (write?) standard English, and, as with the eighteenth-century concept of politeness, members of the mainstream may at any time shift the goalposts so that you will never be admitted to the select few. I assume that the select few here are the "educated". Those who are not proficient in standard English are not educated and may therefore not be admitted to the mainstream. This is an almost direct transference from the *polite language myth* and the *legitimate language myth* to the *educated language myth*, supporting the ideological discourse of "standard English".

This subtle shift in myths is made explicit six pages further into the text (p. 35): "Standard English is perceived by all—and resisted by some—as the language of literacy and of educatedness." If everyone perceives "standard

English" to have this status, how can there still be some who resist? Honey is implicitly making a distinction between good, commonsensical people who accept the equation "standard English = literacy + educatedness" and a small, misguided band of people who wish to reject acceptance of the equation. The equation itself is thus presented as fact. Unfortunately for Honey's argument, the band of unbelievers is rather larger than he imagines and includes teachers, lecturers, writers, education theorists and others. In addition, surely he would hardly wish to suggest that the "enemies" of "standard English" are not also "educated" and "literate".

In both these quotations, being literate is also equated with having proficiency in the "standard language". But if we take Koch's complex model of literacy used in chapter 3 as the basis for my concept of inscribed orality, it is incumbent on us as linguists, sociolinguists and educationists to admit to the extreme complexity of a term such as "literacy". Am I literate if I can just about read comics and the popular press, instructions on medical prescriptions, and cooking recipes, but never read novels, histories, academic monographs? Am I literate if, as was the case with many people in the late Middle Ages, I can read simple texts but cannot write? Am I literate if, as a nuclear physicist, I read complex treatises on physics but have never read a novel and know next to nothing about literary texts in general? Am I literate if I spend all of my free time participating in Internet chat groups, receiving and sending e-mails, or setting up blogs? We cannot now know how Honey would have classified these cases, but my interpretation of the way in which he seems to use the term "literacy" implies a connection to the reading of literature, in all probability of the high-brow variety rather than true-love stories, adventure stories, detective stories and Western pulp fiction. Without a clear definition of what Honey understands by "literacy", which is never given to us throughout the whole book, it is meaningless to equate literacy with "standard English".

Honey's next move (p. 39) is to introduce grammar into his argument: "There is a long-standing and now overwhelming association, right across British society, between the use of the grammar, vocabulary and idioms of standard English, and the concept of 'educatedness'." He subtly conceals the significance attributed to the term "grammar" here by combining it with "vocabulary" and "idioms". However, the discussion of the tug-of-war that went on between the Conservative government in the second half of the 1980s and the Kingman and Cox Committees as to what the term "grammar" should mean in the National Curriculum for English and, in the course of his book, Honey's attacks on theoretical linguists proposing a descriptive rather than a prescriptive approach to syntax are enough to convince the reader that grammar refers to standards of "correctness" and a prescriptive approach to the structures of English represented in the parsing exercises given up in the early 1960s. Throughout the book, Honey also makes sweeping statements such as the one above, entirely unsupported by concrete evidence, in an effort to make it seem that any right-thinking person must also think the same way, and that those who think differently are either subversive or perhaps a little deranged. This is a form of rhetoric based on the assumed rightness and commonsense of hegemonic discourse that has become so naturalised that it is considered to represent fact and does not need to be bolstered up by any further evidence. By now, it should be possible to see through Honey's rhetoric and recognise most of the language myths that lie at the basis of his discourse, **perfection, homogeneity, purity, legitimacy, immutability**.

Part of Honey's tactic is to ridicule linguists' insistence on objectivity so that he can appear to be taking a modern, sociolinguistic stance by admitting that language varieties are never "neutral". The aim of this strategy is to avoid criticism that his support of "standard English" is in any sense partisan—which of course it is, as is obvious from his repetition of the connection between "standard English", literacy and educatedness (p. 114): "She [Janet Batsleer] is right, of course, that standard English is not a neutral norm: it is the badge of literacy and educatedness."

Honey has his own private enemies throughout the book, and two of these are James and Lesley Milroy. In the following quotation (p. 122), he says that the Milroys don't understand why so much of the public admires literate forms, and he offers the following reason for this: "Their lack of understanding of the basis of popular respect for literate forms is due to their failure to recognise the popular association of standard English with educatedness and competence."

The "popular respect for literate forms" that Honey refers to here in fact transforms the more abstract notion of literacy into a concrete example of what he means by the term: "literate forms", exemplars of literature. This is a small step away from the grammarians of the eighteenth century using the best writers of the day to illustrate their grammar rules and even to upbraid them for making mistakes. He has also smuggled in the notion of "competence" alongside "literacy", "grammar" and "educatedness" as being represented by standard English.

Honey refers to educatedness in close association with standard English every few pages of his book, and as he progresses he manoeuvres himself into a position in which, by his own admittance, standard English is a value-laden term to categorise those who are, in his sense, "literate" and educated. But what does Honey understand by "education" and being "educated"? What is his ulterior motive in writing the book apart from maligning fellow linguists for wrongheadedness? Throughout the whole book, Honey never defines the terms that he uses. We search in vain for a definition of "education" or "educatedness", although in one passage he does give his readers an insight into how he understands the category "educated people":

> In October 1995 I published in the journal *English Today* evidence drawn from more than fifteen years of recording examples of educated people who use the supposedly "incorrect" forms—"to my wife and I", "between you and I", "for we British", etc. My fifty examples came from *prominent literary figures*, from *university professors* (including *well-known professors of English*), *distinguished Oxbridge theologians* ("for we who are in chapel today"), *politicians* (including several party

leaders, and three education ministers) like Paddy Ashdown, Lord (David) Owen, George Walden ("the likes of you and I"), Sir Rhodes Boyson, Paul Channon and Margaret Thatcher. (1997: 161, italics mine)

The odd thing about this quotation is that what "educated people" frequently say, even if—from a technical, prescriptive point of view—ungrammatical, must, according to Honey, be allowed to be good standard English. I would argue that the phrases he quotes involving use of the nominative form of the first-person pronouns singular and plural (*I* and *we*) are perfect examples of variability lending support to the argument against homogeneity.

However, Honey's scale of values to define the class of the educated includes university professors, famous literary figures, Oxbridge theologians and politicians, so it is not quite coterminous with those who might have deserved this etiquette in the eighteenth century. As we saw in chapter 8, this would have included the gentry and the aristocracy. But it does contain a liberal sprinkling of those who wielded power in late-twentieth-century Britain. The problem is that it is out of step with the course taken by the public education system in England and Wales in introducing a National Curriculum. The significance of standard English in that system is not disputed, since the argument in educational circles is that every child should have access to and be taught to use standard English in written form just as long as she is not prevented from using her own oral style of English in or outside the classroom.

Perhaps Honey's real aim throughout the book is expressed just two pages later (1997: 163) when he argues explicitly for the setting up of "a form of authority" to watch over standard English. He does not explicitly call it an "academy", but it is perfectly clear that this how he intends it to be understood: "So what the English language needs is a form of authority that can easily be appealed to for guidance as to the uses which are acceptable compared with those which are not—an authority based not on an individual's irrational likes and dislikes but on the consensus of educated opinion." The wheel has turned full circle since Defoe first made the suggestion in 1697 that a body of people should be set up to "encourage polite learning". The members of Defoe's "society", as he called it, should be members of "polite society"; those who would provide guidance in Honey's putative "authority" should be "educated" people. They should, in other words, be "prominent literary figures", "university professors", "distinguished Oxbridge theologians" and "politicians". Linguists, sociolinguists, sociologists, cultural theoreticians and, one might also presume, professors of education, as well as a host of other progressive persons (whether educated or not) would, in all probability, be immediately barred from deciding on what constitutes the chimera of standard English. The discourse and the basis on which it was originally constructed—the *linguistic homogeneity myth*, the *purity myth* and the *perfection myth*—have been continually reproduced and reconstructed institutionally from the beginning of the eighteenth century to the present. Under the roof of the *legitimate language myth,* which promoted an immutable standard English, the *polite language myth* has simply been reproduced as the *educated language myth*.

It is not totally clear by the time we reach the end of Honey's book exactly how he conceptualises the notion of "educatedness". We have seen that he frequently uses it in conjunction with "literacy", which, as I pointed out above, does not mean for Honey simply the ability to read. It comes rather closer to the term "literate" as this was used in the eighteenth century to refer to "knowledgeable in the classical languages and their literatures". However, as he uses the term so often in conjunction with "standard English", it is obviously a term of importance to him. In poring over all the references to the term, one is left with a degree of uncertainty as to whether Honey is simply of the opinion that every child in Britain should have the opportunity to achieve a good education, which would mean, in terms of the National Curriculum, a good grounding in the full range of subjects that would enable the student to specialise in certain subjects after the age of 16. I suspect that the old elitism of the eighteenth and nineteenth centuries still forms part of the concept for Honey, and this comes out very clearly in his use of Latin etymologies to back up his argument that most writers use certain Latinate words wrongly in English. One of the classic cases here is his lampooning of the "wrong" use of the lexeme *decimate*. Honey makes sure his readers are aware of his knowledge of Latin in explaining that "decimate" refers to taking out one in every 10 of a set of objects, and refers to a seventeenth-century law of decimation, by which a tenth of some citizens' payment was taken. He deplores the modern use of the term to mean "destroy utterly" and makes the comment that "with the decline in the widespread knowledge of Latin among the educated of the late twentieth century, the one-in-ten meaning of decimate was lost" (1997: 154). One is left with the impression that Honey would like to see Latin make a comeback in the schools and universities of Britain, and that what he means by "educatedness" is not very far from what it meant at the beginning of the nineteenth century.

6. WHAT *IS* STANDARD ENGLISH?

There is still considerable confusion over what is meant by the term "standard English" and, in particular, "standard oral English". The breakdown of the "legitimate language archive" in Britain has created a situation in which it has become crucial to know exactly what is meant by these terms. And in defining "standard English", it is crucial that every effort be made to ensure that it is not reinvested with the political and sociocultural baggage it has gathered over the last two centuries.

Crowley tries to define what he understands by "standard oral English" in the final chapter of the second edition of *Standard English and the Politics of Language* (2003: 266), but it is not altogether convincing. He discusses the issues of standard English in the wake of the National Curriculum wars, and he concludes that confusion still reigns in the ways in which the term is defined and operationalised for the purposes of language teaching. On the final page of the book, he gives a fictional example to illustrate how he understands "spoken Standard English". He sets up a fictional situation in which two people are attempting to communicate. The first speaker is a migrant to England who has been learning the language for a short period of time, and the second is a first-language speaker of English. Both have difficulty in understanding one another, but despite comprehension difficulties and with a high level of tolerance and a readiness to exploit whatever language resources they have, they manage to make sense to one another. Crowley calls this an instance of "spoken Standard English", and his reasoning is as follows:

> It is "standard" not in the sense of a level of excellence fixed in advance, but in the sense of making and having something in common. It is "standard" in the sense of being able to share sense and meaning through common effort and participation. And in case it be forgotten, "common" is the etymological root of both "communication" and "community". Looked at in this way "standard spoken English" is what each of us creates every time we use any of the various spoken forms of English and make meaning with them. (266)

However much we might sympathise with it, the definition remains problematic. How can it be said that something is "standard" because the participants in the interaction can "share sense and meaning through common effort and participation"? The definition does not conform to any of the more conventional meanings that Crowley himself gives for the lexeme *standard* in an earlier chapter of the book. It certainly takes into consideration much of the argumentation in the present book that human language is reconstructed at the emergent moment of communicative social practice, although the lexeme *standard* has not been used to refer to such situations. The more usual reference to "standard English" is to a variety of English rather than to the use of language in communication. Trudgill (1999) uses it in this sense, and he insists that the only linguistic difference between standard English and other varieties of English is that it is neither a regional variety nor a social variety.[12]

Looked at from the perspective of varieties of English, standard English is not East Anglian English or Tristanian English. It is not Geordie, or Scouse, or Brummie, or Jamaican Creole. But it should also not be equated with such general terms as "American English", "British English", or "Australian English". There is a wide range of varieties of each of these broad categories, as is also the case in Katie Wales's term "Northern English" (2006) or even the term "East Anglian English" that was used above. The thrust of the "legitimate language discourse", however, has historically aimed at constructing

---

12. He makes the valid point that it can be used in any register or style and that lexical variation is simply an indication of a change in style or register but not an indication of a shift in the variety of English. He lists a small set of syntactic or morphological criteria by which standard English can be distinguished from other varieties.

standard English as superior to, better, more polished and more refined than any other variety of English. It has accepted without question the conceptual metaphor A LANGUAGE IS A HUMAN BEING, in evaluating language varieties as if they were individual human beings. The suggestion was even made by John Honey that standard English is "neutral".

It is certainly true that, as a variety of English, it has a far larger lexicon than other varieties, but this is a result only of the fact that it has long been in use in a wide number of social registers and domains as the means for written communication. There are no other levels of linguistic description that would merit the kinds of evaluation proffered by those who still believe in the discourse archive created through the discourse of the legitimate language.

The broad term "English" refers to an extremely wide range of language varieties, some of which might be considered more prototypical, others less so. There is also no definitive boundary between what is classified as "English" and what is classified as another language. From a historical point of view we can ask whether Old English really *is* English and whether its obvious affinities with Old Norse do not take it out of the system of English. Or we can question whether Tok Pisin, which is so obviously derived from English, is not now something totally different.

Three caveats need to be made before we proceed:

1. Varieties may shade into one another.
2. Speakers may use elements of more than one variety when engaged in oral communication.
3. Varieties can be distinguished from one another in terms of the linguistic constructions that go to make them up.

On the basis of caveat 3, varieties of English may be distinguished in terms of lexical, phrasal, syntactic, morphological, phonological and prosodic criteria, but from a purely linguistic perspective only syntactic and morphological criteria are central in distinguishing between varieties. This implies that different styles, registers and genres of whatever variety we focus on differ in terms of lexicon, phraseology, phonology and prosody, but not in terms of morphology and syntax.

A concrete example would be the use of the distinction between past tense "was" and "were" for singular and plural subjects.[13] Assume that the two speakers hold to this distinction consistently but use different lexical and phonological constructions in doing so:

1. Can they be said to speak a standard form of English but each with a different accent? or
2. Can they be said to speak two different varieties of English?

---

13. I am simplifying matters here quite considerably, since if two varieties differed according to these criteria, they would be sure to differ in other ways as well. For the moment, however, I will let the simplification stand.

If we now assume that one of the speakers upholds the distinction consistently, but the other uses either "was" or "were" consistently with both singular and plural subjects, as in "they was here", can the former be said to speak a standard form of English, whereas the latter speaks a nonstandard variety? I suggest that in this second case we would indeed be more likely to say that speaker 2 speaks a nonstandard variety of English than in the first, regardless of his accent. But the term "nonstandard" has by now come to refer to such evaluative yardsticks as "better than", "superior to", "more refined than", and to make the distinction between "standard" and "nonstandard" is to evaluate on social grounds.

Now let us return to the first situation once again and assume not only that the sole distinguishing feature between the two is accent, but that one of the speakers also uses an RP accent. Would this increase the likelihood of suggesting that this speaker is the standard English speaker and the other is not? In the Britain of the 1950s this would in all probability have been the judgment. In the Britain of the early third millennium, this is far less likely to occur. And if those making the judgment are not from Britain, the likelihood would be even smaller.

All types of linguistic construction can be used in identifying different varieties, but there is a cline along which the degree of distinguishing features is salient, as follows:

phonology/prosody < lexicon/phraseology < syntax/morphology (where < indicates that the constructions to the right are more salient than those to the left)

Phonology and prosody are important, particularly as a first approximation to the geographical and social provenance of the speaker. The choice of set phrases and lexical items used is the next most salient feature, and syntax and morphology are the most salient. In a word, "standard English" is simply a variety of English, once the phonological/prosodic level is suppressed, and when the phonological/prosodic level is faded in again, it serves as a marker of geographical and possibly also social provenance.

So, rather than agree with Crowley that "'standard spoken English' is what each of us creates every time we use any of the various spoken forms of English and make meaning with them", I suggest that varieties of language in all oral language contact situations are by their very nature nonstandard precisely because they are always variable and heterogeneous. In emergent social practice in the oral medium both below the level of consciousness and also below the level at which codification and functional expansion are in operation (although not necessarily at lower levels of social structure), we are faced with processes of *nonstandardisation*.

Ultimately, the problem is the word "standard" itself. If we take a standard to be something that is conventionally agreed upon in a community as being the measure to which all instantiations (e.g. of length, weight, volume, temperature) must conform, and if we apply this to language, then our understanding of language is governed by the myths of *homogeneity*, *immutability* and *perfection* and we have no means of accounting for innovations, spontaneity, creativity and flexibility of speech. Like all varieties of English, standard English is absolutely open to innovation, change, creativity and development. This is even the case in the written medium.[14] If we take a standard to be a rallying point (a banner around which those fighting for a cause gather), and if we apply it to language, then our understanding of language is governed by the myths of *legitimacy* and *greatness*. If we force legitimacy on others, we constrain them to use only one form of language or to exclude them from participation in the state. And if we take a standard to be an agreed-upon level of achievement that must be reached, and if we apply this to language, then our understanding of language is governed by the myths of *perfection* and *purity*. No language variety ever achieved perfection since languages do not achieve anything, and no speaker can ever command a language perfectly since all language varieties, when they are used by their speakers, are constantly open to innovation and change.

Standardisation processes strive for a unitariness and homogeneity which it is impossible to achieve in oral social interactions, a striving for some form of purity, a set of top-down, imposed standards which must be met in language, a conformity with educatedness (whatever that means today) or with politeness (whatever that meant in the eighteenth century). Non-standardisation processes aim at attaining mutual understanding, a tolerance of the Other, the will to negotiate meanings, the acceptance, sometimes even encouragement of creativity and innovation, the readiness for what was not expected and the simple enjoyment of face-to-face communication. Non-standardisation is *not* simply the opposite of standardisation. The benchmarks for successful communication in one situation are so totally different from those in the next that perhaps any notion of a standard is inappropriate. Socially, however, speakers will continue to construct differences between standard and nonstandard varieties, on the basis of language myths, and sociolinguists should be aware of the need to deconstruct those myths.

---

14. I have noted a recent tendency in first-language speakers towards English writing <lead> ([lɛd]) instead of <led> on analogy with <read> ([ɹɛd]). It has long been the custom to use the backformation "orientate" from "orientation" rather than "orient". There are many other examples that I could adduce here, but all of them point to the simple fact that the written language is also subject to variation and change.

Chapter 11

Commodifying English and
constructing a new myth

Our speech, as spoken in common life, is wonderfully terse and pithy; your
average Englishman will never waste his breath more than he can help. His
tongue is well fitted to be the language of the world in future years.
—T. L. Kington-Oliphant, *The Old and Middle English*, 1878

1. THE EMERGENCE OF A MODERN MYTH

Two chapters in this book have dealt with modern myths (or potential
modern myths) about English, both of them originating in sociolinguistic
research on English. The first of these, the ***creolisation of English myth***,
dealt with in chapter 4, appears to have been spread beyond the academic
confines of linguistics. The other, a potential myth about the beginnings of
the complaint tradition, has not yet spread discursively beyond the framework of historical arguments concerning the ideology of the standard language (cf. work by James and Lesley Milroy). However, at least two other
books, Deborah Cameron's *Verbal Hygiene* (1995) and Rosina Lippi-Green's
English with an Accent (1997), have argued from a similar perspective that
lay attitudes towards language inevitably reveal value judgments about
speakers and groups of speakers and about the varieties of language used
by them.

The present chapter deals with a third "modern myth", the ***myth of
English as the global language***, which can be shown to derive from the
superiority of English myth and the ***legitimate language myth***. It originated in
the middle of the nineteenth century and is well established as the driving

force behind a present-day modern hegemonic discourse both within and beyond English-speaking nation-states that promotes the acquisition of English on a global scale. It is not the aim of the present chapter to evaluate the pros and cons of the discourse, but warning voices have been raised consistently that it promotes a covert modern form of imperialism (Phillipson 1992; Canagarajah 1999; Pennycook 1994), that it represents a danger to the continued existence of minority languages as well as to bi- and multilingualism as a rich form of linguistic coexistence (Skutnabb-Kangas [1984] 2007, 2003; Mühlhäusler 1996) and that it encourages a return to forms of neocolonial discourse (Pennycook 1998; Alim, Awad & Pennycook 2009). As one would expect, these critical analyses of the presence of English in the world have not gone unchallenged (cf., e.g., Berns et al. 1998; Davies 1996; Alatis & Straehle [1997] 2006; Crystal 2000).

Although my purpose in this chapter is not to take sides in this dispute, it is still interesting to note that those who *have* taken sides refer to the term *myth* in its negative sense of an "untruth", a "fiction", a "fabrication", as a story below what we take to be faithful to fact in a hierarchy of believability (see chapter 1). Davies (1996), for example, implies in the title of his review article of Phillipson's book on linguistic imperialism that it purveys the "myth of linguicism", and he accuses Phillipson of "trivialising history in favour of myth". Phillipson counters that Davies' review article itself spreads "myths" about his book. Neither Phillipson nor Davies defines the term "myth", and the implication made by both is that creating and spreading myths is simply unscientific. My position, however, is that every discourse on language is ultimately based on myths representing beliefs about language, and I argue that the discourse has become hegemonic enough to represent "the law of what can be said, the system that governs the appearance of statements as unique events" (Foucault 1972: 129), and that as such it constitutes a potential new discourse archive. Linguists, applied linguists and sociolinguists, like everyone else, are very much the prisoners of this archive, which leads them to resent or oppose any challenge from an alternative discourse.

Despite my attempt to retain "neutrality" in the debate, I still wish to argue that one particular current hegemonic discourse determining "the law of what can be said" about English in Foucault's sense is based on a mythical construction, which needs to be unearthed and reexamined—without the myth being branded as an untruth. I shall attempt to walk this argumentative tightrope in the present chapter. The attempt begins by stating that when the English language becomes a commodity, to be given a price and to be traded like every other commodity in a Bourdieuan material as well as symbolic marketplace, the *superior language myth* and the *legitimate language myth* are open to transformation into the *global language myth*. I am certainly not suggesting that those who have not acquired English as an additional language have no right to do so. Any such claim would represent a violation of the human right to learn and use whatever languages the individual wishes to learn and use. Languages do not have a price—or rather they should not have a price—and may thus be freely acquired by anyone who has the will, the time and the energy to learn them. But the *global language myth* has long since extended beyond the confines of academia, and it informs language policies in a wide range of nation-states, to the extent that such policies seriously need to be questioned.

In the following section of this chapter I outline how the *global language myth* began to emerge in the middle of the nineteenth century, and I trace its progress into twentieth-century discourses on English. I then give a brief account of the historical development of English in colonial and imperial settings, and explain what I mean by the term "the commodification of English". To illustrate some of the latent dangers of running the global archive on the status of English, I focus in some detail on a more local example of the development of a linguistic ideology concerning English in a setting with which I am intimately familiar, the changing situation of English in Switzerland. Finally, I shall criticise attempts to construct varieties of English as homogeneous systems, English as a Lingua Franca (ELF) and English as an International Language (EIL). I argue that, in attempting to construct such varieties as systems to teach, the danger reemerges of returning to the myths of homogeneity and legitimacy that characterise the ideology of "standardisation". This goes against the grain of variability, hybridity and heterogeneity, which is one of the major themes of this book.

2. ENGLISH—"THE LANGUAGE OF THE WORLD"?

If we look at the quotation from Kington-Oliphant's *The Old and Middle English* given as the leitmotif for this chapter, we note a distinct air of self-congratulatory arrogance and self-assured confidence, which is redolent of the ideological discourse driven by the *superiority of English myth*. In that myth, English is constructed as an imperial language preeminent among others, a language that, because of its assumed superiority, is destined to become "the language of the world". Kington-Oliphant's use of the term "Englishman" not only encourages the inference that the term stands metonymically for the inhabitants of the British Isles; it also strongly implies that speakers of languages other than English are in the habit of wasting their breath. The only fact that can be put forward in Kington-Oliphant's favour is that he refers to the oral language spoken in "common life" as being "terse and pithy" rather than to forms of written, "educated" standard English.

The opinion that English is "fitted to be the language of the world in future years" is by no means an isolated occurrence in discourse on English in the second half of the nineteenth and throughout the twentieth century. A search through grammars and histories of English from around 1850 reveals, from the middle and up to and beyond the end of the nineteenth century, an increasing number of references predicting the emergence of English as a world language. As early as 1850 we find the following statement by R. G. Latham in his book *The English Language* (p. 576): "Transplant the other [Teutonic dialect] to England, let nine centuries pass over it, and it becomes a language too, and a language of more importance than any which was ever yet spoken in the world, it has become English." At this point in the text Latham is discussing the two "Teutonic" languages German and English. The reference to English as a world language is oblique rather than direct, but the discursive trajectory of the statement is clear enough.

In 1875, A. H. Keane, in a handbook on the history of English meant for use by teachers and students of English, goes so far as to state blatantly that English may already be called a "world-language":

> In truth, the English language, which by no mere accident has produced and upborne the greatest and most predominant poet of modern times, as distinguished from the ancient classical poetry (I can, of course, only mean Shakespeare), may, with all right, be called a world-language, and, like the English people, appears destined hereafter to prevail with a sway more extensive even than its present, over all the portions of the globe. (170)

The "destiny" of English is expressed discursively in terms of the wielding of power ("to prevail with a sway more extensive than its present"), and Keane's vision is one of linguistic domination "over all portions of the globe". Imperial competition with other languages (e.g. French, Spanish and German) seems to be the determining factor in the evaluation of English here, which is the first step not only towards making the language and the culture it is thought to represent part of the prestige of the British nation-state, but also increasing its selling power as a commercial commodity.

The Scotsman John M. D. Meiklejohn is a little more cautious and ascribes the prediction that English will become the world language to "the great German grammarian Grimm", among others, although he is silent on which of the two Grimm brothers, Jacob or Wilhelm, is meant. The prediction, however, is much the same as Keane's but without the undertone of cultural competition and domination: "Hence the great German grammarian Grimm, and others, predict that English will spread itself all over the world, and become the universal language of the future" (1886: 322).

If we move into the twentieth century we even find Otto Jespersen in 1905 falling prey to the English-as-a-world-language myth in *The Growth and Structure of the English Language*: "Only two or three centuries ago, English was spoken by so few people that no one could dream of its ever becoming a world language" (1905: 246). By the end of the First World War, the discourse, well established by this time, had taken on the perspective of speakers of other first languages[1] who might wish (perhaps even need) to acquire English as a

---

1. I deliberately use the terms "first language", "second language", "other language", often in combination with the noun "speaker(s)", to avoid involving myself in the acrimonious debate over the dubious validity of terms such as "native speaker" and "non-native speaker".

second language. This represents an inevitable development from the "English-as-a-world-language" theme since, if English is to achieve the status of a world language, it will have to be used by large numbers of speakers and writers who do not have English as their first language. A classic example of this development is provided as early as 1919 by Ernest Classen:

> By common consent, the opinion of the foreigner concerning English is that it is a very practical language, easy to learn, and one in which one can with the utmost ease and convenience give expression to fine shades of thought. Now, although the foreigner very often gravely underestimates the difficulties in mastering English, yet his opinion that it readily lends itself to the expression of new turns of thought, and that it is a most flexible and adaptable instrument, is probably just, whilst his view that it is easy to learn holds promise of its future as a world language. (1919: 260)

The quotation from Classen indicates that "foreign"[2] languages had become part of the school syllabuses of most European nation-states by the end of the nineteenth century. In terms of Bourdieu's marketplace, represented diagrammatically in figure 8.1, these languages had, in other words, acquired a certain value as sociocultural capital that could afterwards be converted into symbolic capital and thence into material capital. Knowledge of and the ability to use a second language had become, in Classen's terms, an "instrument", meaning knowledge that could be put to good use in enhancing one's social status, power and influence, which in turn gave the "possessor" of the language the means of increasing his material well-being. Languages had become abstract commodities, which could be put on sale in the sociocultural and symbolic sectors of the marketplace, and the means through which those commodities could be sold to others (e.g. teaching materials, teaching methods, teacher training courses) became part of what we might call the "language industry". Languages as commodities began to develop different social, cultural and instrumental values with respect to one another.

In Classen's day, after the horrifying and devastating four years of the First World War, the "language industry", which had begun in state school systems, still hankered after the acquisition of cultural and sociopolitical prestige. For example, learning French meant learning "refined", "educated" French and using it not simply to be able to speak to those who had French as their first language, but to read the cultural monuments of the French

---

2. I place the term "foreign" in quotation marks here to indicate that learning languages other than the standard variety of the language of the nation-state meant learning a language outside or beyond the cultural values of that state. All outsiders were thus "foreigners", and if they had, as their first language, one that was "outside" the confines of the nation-state, that language was regularly classified as a "foreign language". Several problems are immediately created by the use of this term. For example, what would Welsh or Scots Gaelic be called within the framework of the British nation-state? What about Gujerati, Bengali, or Urdu? Or what would a co-official language of a state be called, as in the case of French, German, Italian or Rhaeto-Rumantsch in Switzerland? Obviously in both cases the term "foreign language" is entirely inappropriate.

nation-state. The model for teaching foreign languages was built very solidly on the ways in which the classical languages Latin and Greek had always been taught. Languages were learned because they were *Kultursprachen*, and if they were not considered to be *Kultursprachen*, what was the purpose of learning them at all? Learning languages as differently valued commodities in the marketplace was, as yet, in conflict with learning languages as the carriers of national culture.

Despite these factors, however, the quotation from Classen also contains some revealing characteristics of the "English-as-a-world-language" discourse. The "foreigner", by which term Classen means someone living outside an English-speaking country with another first language, is said to find English "easy to learn", "practical" and "a most flexible and adaptable instrument". Classen finds it necessary to modify the perception that learning the English language is easy. For example, he suggests that learners of English as an additional language "gravely underestimate the difficulties in mastering" it, thus hinting at his belief that most of them will never be able to acquire English as a *Kultursprache*. But although he doubts the validity of the opinion that English is easy to learn, he nevertheless considers that this opinion "holds promise of its future as a world language", an opportunistic stance if ever there was one. The major characteristics of the discourse, which are still to be found in the nonacademic discourse of English as a global language, are the following:

1. that English is easy to learn
2. that English is a practical language
3. that the desire to learn English is instrumentally motivated.

It is precisely these characteristics which are most frequently given by present-day learners of English as a second language as their motivation for wishing to acquire the language, and not the desire to immerse themselves in the cultural achievements of the English-speaking world, as we shall see in section 4. We note here an important contradiction: on the one hand, "foreign-language teaching" in public state education systems has always stressed the need to acquire the language being learned as a *Kultursprache*; on the other hand, learning a "foreign" language is seen to enhance an individual's sociocultural, symbolic and hence material capital, which entails learning to speak and use it. The commodification of language is closely associated with commercial interests, with a new kind of metaphorical conceptualisation of language as a valuable human resource. The commercial and colonial history of Britain, however, tended to overstress the significance of "refined" English in an effort to underscore the racial and social differences between colonisers and colonial subjects. The English that colonial subjects needed to acquire was meant to be matter-of-fact, instrumental and concerned with the pragmatic problems of everyday life, and it was precisely this emphasis which was put to use in the phenomenal surge of private English-language schools in Britain after the Second World War.

3. THE COMMODIFICATION OF ENGLISH

Before I discuss how the incipient English-as-a-world-language myth of the late nineteenth century was transformed into the present-day ideological discourse of English as the global language, I need to turn the clock back to the eighteenth century and outline, in very general terms, the growth of the British colonial empire. The most salient feature of this growth was the ability of the Royal Navy to protect both Britain's far-flung colonies and its elaborate global system of trade. The trade network consisted of two major geographical axes, one in the Indian Ocean, the western rim of the Pacific and the South China Sea and the other in the North Atlantic. The former involved the export to Britain by the East India Company of cheap cotton from the Indian subcontinent and the trade in opium to China in exchange for tea, while the latter involved the exportation of slaves from West Africa to provide labour for the profitable sugar plantations in the West Indies. The loss of the American colonies after the American War of Independence in 1782 meant the loss of Britain's major source of cotton, but this was more than compensated by the trade along the Pacific route.

To secure the markets in all these goods, it became necessary for Britain to assert political control over its various geographical locations and their indigenous inhabitants. This, of course, was nothing new. The Spanish had developed the system of colonisation in the Americas since the end of the fifteenth century, often involving the wholesale extermination of local populations. Asserting colonial control also entangled Britain in a long series of wars throughout the eighteenth century, principally against France, but, in addition, it provided ready-made markets for the exportation of goods manufactured in Britain.

One of the most potent ways of securing the colonies and the markets they offered was to export "British" cultural values, and the most important of these was the English language itself. This, in turn, automatically generated the question of what variety of English should be "exported". In the North American colonies, which had been colonised as early as the late sixteenth and early seventeenth centuries, waves of settlers had come from different parts of the British Isles creating the ideal conditions for the koïneisation of dialects in contact. Ireland had been colonised earlier in the sixteenth century, but the number of settlers in Ireland was never enough to guarantee the development of koïnés.[3] Settlers from Britain continued to immigrate to North America, even after the War of Independence, but the next waves of settlers to the colonies from Britain are not to be found until the early years of the nineteenth century in South Africa, Australia and later in New Zealand. Once again conditions favouring koïneisation were created (Britain & Trudgill

---

3. The first demographically significant wave of settlers to Ireland came (largely but not entirely) from the south of Scotland at the beginning of the seventeenth century.

1999; Moore 2008; Gordon 2004). With the exception of Kenya and present-day Zimbabwe (formerly Rhodesia[4]) towards the end of the nineteenth century, the remainder of the British possessions and colonies spread over the world were administered by civil servants sent out from London rather than settled.

The vast majority of colonial administrators were "educated" rather than simply "schooled", since colonial administration tended to provide a living for the second sons of the gentry and the aristocracy who had been exposed to a system of education in the public schools and universities, in which knowledge of the classical languages Greek and Latin was at a premium. Gramsci (1971: 40) suggests that schooling, which, in eighteenth-century Britain as in pre–Second World War Italy, simply meant a rudimentary training in mathematics and in reading and writing the mother tongue, was part of a hegemonic discourse which aimed at socialising children into the acceptance and maintenance of the status quo. So, in Gramsci's sense, colonial administrators were given administrative positions to uphold British hegemony in the colonies, not to teach the indigenous population English. Their own English would have been "polite", or at least aspiring to be "polite", according to the changing conceptions of politeness in the eighteenth and early nineteenth centuries (cf. chapters 8 and 9).

If the "natives", as the indigenous population were almost invariably and disrespectfully called, acquired any proficiency in English, it was generally pidginised forms of the language, which were enough to carry out the day-to-day, on-the-spot running of the affairs of the colony but conveniently prevented the "natives" from acquiring a "legitimate", educated variety of English. "Polite", "educated" or standard English was reserved for official business involving the indigenous population rather than to effect efficient communication with them. Although moves to "school" the indigenous population of the colonies were not really begun until the latter half of the nineteenth century, the model for that schooling, standard English, was already firmly in place by the end of the eighteenth century. Its prestige and preeminence were enhanced by its acceptance, in the nation-state ideology and amongst the "educated" elite, as the "one" legitimate homogeneous language. In achieving this status, it automatically became the only legitimate language for the purposes of "schooling".

Before the advent of compulsory schooling, missionary schools focused on educating the indigenous population in their first language, since their primary concern was to convert the local inhabitants to Christianity. This led to a spate of grammars, writing systems and educational materials in the local languages, but retaining first language teaching throughout all levels of the education system was never a viable option once colonial administrative systems had decided to introduce compulsory education. It was convenient for

---

4. Or Southern Rhodesia during the period of the Federation of Rhodesia and Nyasaland.

colonial administrators to uphold the distinction between education and schooling and to provide schooling only for the vast majority of the indigenous population. However, the need to employ local administrators from among the local population led to the encouragement of a small number of selected pupils who were willing to go on to the secondary level of education in which English was the language of instruction throughout the curriculum. At that level, teachers, the majority of whom were recruited in Britain, needed to develop more pragmatic methods of teaching than those in use in the public schools and grammar schools, and the teaching of English itself naturally developed matter-of-fact, down-to-earth forms of instruction that were adequate to the task of teaching English. This experience was invaluable when the perceived need to learn English as an instrument of communication rather than as a *Kultursprache* burgeoned after the Second World War. English had by then indeed become a commodity, a resource that could be bought and sold like any material good.

Teaching English as a "foreign" language in the far-flung British Empire was focused largely on British India from the second half of the nineteenth century through to the end of the Second World War, India taking the place of the American colonies as the "jewel in the crown" of the Empire. It was also the only area in the non-English-speaking colonies in which tertiary education played any significant role in English-language teaching.[5] From the beginning of the twentieth century the so-called direct method of teaching foreign languages, developed in Germany and France around 1900, was adopted for use in extending the teaching of English as a foreign language, and more emphasis was placed on the oral use of language based on conversation and phonetic analysis (cf. Palmer 1921, 1924; R. Smith 2003) and, from the mid-1940s on, the major syntactic structures of the language (Fries 1945).

American involvement in foreign-language teaching became most prominent at the time of the Second World War and resulted in the U.S. Army Specialized Training Program. Much of the technology and many new teaching methods used in this programme were taken up after the end of the war and put to great use in the teaching of English as a second language. The involvement of the United States in a market that had been in the hands of the British in the years between the two world wars gave an enormous boost not only to the significance of English throughout the world but also to the exponential growth of the EFL/ESL market. Private English language schools catering to those who wished to acquire English in a first-language-speaking environment sprang up in Britain in the late 1950s and throughout the 1960s, particularly along the southern coast and in London, to be followed by similar institutions in the United States, Canada, Australia and, at a much later stage, New Zealand. The commodity "English language competence" was

---

5. The seminal work on the history of English language teaching is A. P. R. Howatt's *A History of English Language Teaching* (1984), on which the following paragraphs are based.

suddenly in great demand; this in turn generated a surge of interest in applied linguistics as a postgraduate course of study at the universities designed to produce experts on second-language teaching, EFL/ESL teachers and course writers; and finally publishers began to cash in on the demand for a wide range of English-language teaching materials. Semi-government organisations operating abroad such as the British Council and the American Field Service realised that English language teaching could be a lucrative addition to the cultural programmes already on offer.

The decolonisation of Africa after 1960 resulted in English being chosen as the official language of the new states (cf. Phillipson 1992), which gave the boom in EFL/ESL a further impetus in experimenting with the new teaching methods and course materials. However, it took some time for these to be adopted or used as models for the teaching of other languages as a second or additional language in state education systems, although it was certainly clear that English as a foreign language in the public school systems of western Europe, then later in Asia, South America and, after 1990, post-communist eastern Europe, would eventually take over these methods and materials. For example, in Switzerland, which will be the locus of a case study on the spread of English and the imminent dangers of that spread in the following section, the introduction of communicative teaching methods in English began to enter the cantonal school systems in the second half of the 1970s. Those teaching methods have by now been adopted almost wholesale for English, but not for the teaching of languages such as French, German, Italian, Spanish or Russian.

Teaching English as a second language has led to a sudden spread of English across the world, but the myth that English is the global language raises a range of problems that I will deal with in section 5. In particular, the costs of favouring English as the first additional language in most nation-states of Europe exceed the ability to produce enough speakers of English to feed the perceived needs of the "global market". Those costs, as we shall see in section 4, are not only in terms of finance, but also in terms of local cultural values.

4. THE PRICE OF ENGLISH IN SWITZERLAND

The present section surveys the discursive construction of beliefs, through forms of written discourse, that aim to promote the teaching of English in Switzerland above the teaching of the other national languages. I argue that the question of whether to introduce English as an obligatory school subject in the cantonal school systems of Switzerland has become a political issue. I also wish to argue that sociolinguists and applied linguists in Switzerland need to focus on the variations of the *English as the global language myth* that have been created discursively in order to find ways of leading all the parties in the discussion back to a responsible form of debate. To begin with, however, readers need some basic information on Switzerland itself to be able to follow the argument.

4.1 Background information

Switzerland is composed of 26 cantons, each with its own educational system, although these systems are coordinated on the federal level by the so-called *Schweizerische Konferenz der kantonalen Erziehungsdirektoren* (Swiss Federal Committee of the Directors of Education). The Swiss constitution provides for four official languages, German, French, Italian and Rhaeto-Rumantsch,[6] three of which are offered as second (or additional) languages in the state education systems of the country. Until recently English has also been an option as an additional language. Previous policy favoured French as the first obligatory additional language in the German- and Italian-speaking cantons, and German as the first obligatory additional language in the French-speaking cantons. In the Italian-speaking Canton of Ticino and Italian-speaking areas of the Canton of Grisons, German was favoured as a second additional language. Since the mid-1990s, however, there has been a movement to instate English as an obligatory additional language throughout the country, which has generated a great deal of heated discussion, in particular because cantons in the eastern part of Switzerland have recently declared it to be the first obligatory additional language in the curriculum, thereby demoting the two official languages French and Italian.

The pressure to introduce English is based on a set of beliefs concerning language, language learning and the peculiar role that English has come to acquire not only in Switzerland but across the world. The insistence on English is driven by a discourse ideology based on the ***English as the global language myth***. The English language is understood to be a commodity that can be bought at a price, but ultimately the price may be too high, even for Switzerland. If the acquirer of the commodity, in this case, knowledge of and ability to use the English language, values it highly, she will be prepared to pay a reward for it in some way, either in financial terms or in terms of some other appropriately high value or set of values, which may be sociocultural or political.

As we saw in figure 8.1, to function in Bourdieu's material marketplace one needs forms of material capital. One needs a product to exchange for some other product or its symbolic monetary value; one needs finance, the means of production and a labour source. The sociocultural marketplace is determined by forms of sociocultural capital such as social connections, relational networks, forms of knowledge (including language), mental and physical skills, acquired competences, forms of identity, and so on. The types

---

6. Rhaeto-Rumantsch is in effect a semiofficial language in which information concerning federal matters is published, but which is not used in parliamentary debates.

of capital required in the symbolic marketplace are abstract qualities such as social status and prestige, power, influence and language abilities. All three kinds of marketplace are in operation concurrently in any social interaction, and most of the values paid and received in both the sociocultural and the material marketplaces are derived from forms of symbolic capital, language being one of the most central. So there is a constant flow from an underlying set of symbolic values which fuel interaction in the material and sociocultural marketplaces, and there is a constant give-and-take between sociocultural and material marketplaces. The price for acquiring the ability to use English will be economic, social and cultural, and the symbolic value of English in instances of social interaction will also be economic, social and cultural. Ultimately, this train of thought leads to the conclusion that the use of human language in social interaction, whatever "language" we are referring to, can never be valueless or "neutral".

Ideologies are constructed and reproduced through forms of discourse, discourse being an institutionalised mode of thinking, instantiated in social interaction between individuals. Such interaction may be through the medium of written or oral language, but it may also make use of other systems of signifying (e.g. pictorial, gestural, etc.), thereby allowing us to talk in the singular of a discourse to refer to one institutionalised mode of thinking in contrast to others. A discourse is thus a set of communally shared beliefs representing "truth" for the community concerned, but not necessarily for another community. The shared beliefs themselves may then be referred to as an ideology. However we define ideologies, it is crucial to see them as sets of ideas that are shared by the members of a community.

4.2 Locating the transformation: Two significant official documents

In my essay "Discourse theory and language planning" (2001), I deal explicitly with two important Swiss documents as realisations of two kinds of discourse pertaining to the spread of English in Switzerland. In chapter 1, I offered two definitions of "ideology", one by Hodge and Kress (1993: 6) in which ideology is seen as "a systematic body of ideas, organized from a particular point of view" and the second by Seliger (1976: 14), who sees it as "sets of ideas by which men posit, explain and justify ends and means of social action, and specifically political action, irrespective of whether such action aims to preserve, amend, uproot or rebuild a given social order". Both approaches to the study of ideology should be considered together here, particularly that which concerns the notion of "political action". The construction of "a systematically organized presentation of reality" leads to a shared belief in that "reality", within which explanation and justification of social and political action may be grounded.

The first of the two documents is a report submitted to the Swiss *Bundesrat* (Federal Council)[7] in 1989, titled *Zustand und Zukunft der viersprachigen Schweiz* ("The present state and the future of quadrilingual Switzerland") by a work group under the chairmanship of the late Professor Peter Saladin of the University of Berne. In this first document alarm is expressed at the low degree to which Swiss citizens speaking different national languages are capable of interacting verbally with compatriots using one of the other national languages apart from their own. The foreword to the report covers 26 pages and constructs a vision of English (which is not indigenous to Switzerland) that runs throughout the rest of the document. English is presented as an ominous presence threatening the harmonious coexistence of the four national languages within Switzerland. It is presented as competing with French, German and Italian for a place in the educational systems of Switzerland as a second language. I shall call this document the "Saladin report".

The second document is a report titled "'Gesamtsprachenkonzept': Welche Sprachen sollen die Schülerinnen und Schüler der Schweiz während der obligatorischen Schulzeit lernen?" ("'Overall concept for languages': Which languages should schoolchildren in Switzerland learn during their obligatory period of schooling?") published in 1998. It was commissioned by the Swiss Federal Committee of the Directors of Education and was prepared by a small group of experts under the chairmanship of Professor Georges Lüdi of the University of Basle. I shall henceforth refer to this document as the "Lüdi report". The report recommends the obligatory introduction of English in all cantonal education systems and astutely leaves it up to each individual cantonal education system to decide which languages other than the first language should be introduced and in what order. The report was written and presented at a time when the director of education of the Canton of Zürich had already announced the intention of the cantonal government to carry out a school project called "Projekt 21" over a six-year period introducing the teaching of English in first grade through a didactic method known as embedding. The ultimate goal of the project was to assess the feasibility of introducing English before French as a first additional language throughout the whole canton as part of the primary school syllabus and to do this as early as possible in the curriculum. The "Lüdi report" was written with this fact in mind and with the knowledge that during the 1990s intense pressure was exerted on the government of the Canton of Zürich, largely by industrialists, bankers and professional groups but also by parents, to promote the teaching of English above that of French. For this reason, the report has to be read with an eye to what is not said as much as to what is said.

---

7. The *Bundesrat* is the highest executive organ of government within the Swiss political system. It consists of seven federal councillors representing the numerically most powerful political parties in the country. In this respect it is somewhat different from a cabinet, whose members are chosen from among the political party (or parties) responsible for governing the country. Each year, the president and vice president of Switzerland are chosen from among these seven federal councillors to serve for the period of one year.

Two important points can be made here concerning these two documents. First, it is significant that, within the space of only nine years, a discourse that promotes the multilingual nature of Switzerland through its four national languages and constructs the advance of English as a threat to the harmonious coexistence of those languages should be challenged by an alternative discourse promoting English in addition to the first language in preference to other national languages. Second, it is already implicit in the "Saladin report" that the driving force behind this movement lies in commerce and industry, and that the "Lüdi report" only echoes the perceived need for English in an increasing globalisation of the economy. I will call these two discourses the "discourse of multilingual Switzerland" and the "discourse of global English".

The debate has remained on the political and educational agenda since at least 1998 and the appearance of the "Lüdi report", and there is evidence that it had begun well before that date. It has been carried on through parliamentary petitions, political speeches, television debates and discussion programmes, lectures given on the occasion of annual book fairs such as the "Salon du livre" in Geneva, in articles on the pros and cons of early English and an earlier start to additional language learning, in newspapers as diverse as the *Neue Zürcher Zeitung*, the *Blick*, the *Bund*, the *Weltwoche*, *Le Matin*, the *Tribune de Genève*, in letters to the editor, and so on. Much of the discussion has tended to simplify the issues somewhat, and this has led to an almost unquestioning and dangerously naive belief in some of the ideologies represented in these competing discourses.

4.3 Competing ideologies

What ideologies do the discourses instantiate, and is there another alternative discourse that can be identified in Switzerland involving the English language? To answer those questions we need to take a look at the discourse of multilingual Switzerland. Nyffenegger (2003) describes her search through all the letters to the editor printed in the *NZZ*, the *Blick*, the *Tribune* and the *Matin* from 1994 to 2003. She first asks how important the topic of English in Switzerland actually was to the readers of these newspapers during this time period, and the results are extremely sobering. Letters to the editor from 1994 to 2003 reveal that English in Switzerland was not a particularly burning issue. Only two of the four newspapers feature letters concerning English in more than 1 percent of the overall number of letters per year, the *NZZ* in 1997 (at the time when Projekt 21 was mooted) and in 2000, and the *Tribune* in 1994 and in 2000. Nyffenegger then assesses the overall percentage of letters to the editor in each of the newspapers with respect to whether the writer appears favourable to or against the spread of English in Switzerland or whether no overall attitude can be discerned. Over the whole time period, there was only one year in which favourable attitudes dominated, and that was 1997 at the promotion of Projekt 21 in Zürich. In 2003, the final year of the time period chosen, 20 letters voiced negative opinions, with only three in favour of the spread of English and one noncommittal letter. Throughout the time period between 1994 and 2003 there was no overall movement towards a favourable opinion of English; if anything, there has been an increase in the number of negative opinions expressed.[8]

Nyffenegger also teases out the counterarguments against the spread of English and the arguments in favour of English. The arguments against English are listed in table 11.1. Out of a total of 229 negative opinions voiced overall, 81 are within the framework of the discourse of multilingual Switzerland in which English is seen as a threat to some imagined sense of "Swiss identity" involving the peaceful coexistence between the language areas and the presupposed but hardly realistic multilingual nature of the country. Fifteen represent political arguments against English and 13 raise explicitly educational issues.

The surprising thing about these statistics, however, is that 79 negative opinions are framed within another kind of discourse, this time driven by the *pure language myth* and a fear that linguistic standards will be lowered. 36 instantiate a variation of this language ideology which also imputes negative character traits to those who insist on using English and introducing supposed impurities. Cameron (1995) calls this solidly represented lay attitude towards

TABLE 11.1. Arguments against English

English is a danger to Swiss identity	29
English makes German/French "impure"	27
English is a threat to German or French	24
English should be translated	19
Using English impedes comprehension	18
English prevents people from learning French/German "properly"	17
Using English is "stupid"/"bad behaviour"	15
Using English is a sign of Anglo-American dominance	15
English is not used correctly (is abused)	10
Using English terms is euphemistic	10
English is superfluous	7
English is ridiculous	7
Using English is a sign of "snobbery"	7
Using English terms displays lack of diversity	7
Teaching English too early is expecting too much of pupils	7
Teaching English is at the expense of teaching French/German	4
Teaching English is at the expense of teaching other subjects	4
English is a difficult language	2

8. One has to bear in mind, however, that only a small percentage of letters sent to newspapers by the general public ever get published, the choice lying with the editor in charge. Letters are often chosen because they fit some current news topic, and they may thus reflect the editor's predilections rather than an overall sense that the topic is of interest to the reading public at large. This is of course an eternal problem in investigating letters to the editor as a data source in the print media. Nevertheless, the low number of published letters dealing with this topic that do appear in print still indicates the low salience of the topic, regardless of the editorial influence.

language "verbal hygiene", and it is based on the *pure language myth*. The discourse of verbal hygiene encompasses 115 of the total of 229 negative opinions overall, i.e. 50 percent, a fact that we should certainly not ignore, since English appears to have become the scapegoat to justify those lay beliefs.

Nyffenegger lists a total of only 104 arguments in favour of English in letters sent to the editor during the period between 1994 and 2003. The overall number of favourable arguments voiced is only 32 percent of all positive and negative arguments put together, and this is in need of some explanation. Even if the hypothesis that writers of letters to the editor are hardly representative of popular opinion is taken into consideration, it is still highly unlikely that positive opinions nationwide with respect to English will reach much more than 50 percent, if that.[9] The pro-English arguments contained in the letters can be listed as in table 11.2.

Out of a total of 104 positive opinions voiced overall, 39 are connected in one way or another to the world of work and to the idea that English is important in the global economy. It is also implied and exclusively stated elsewhere in the discourse of global English that a knowledge of English is connected to higher salaries. Thirty-seven arguments in favour of English refer to its assumed status as a lingua franca across the world and even within Switzerland. Nine argue that English is an easy language to learn, four of these focusing on the early introduction of English. Fourteen arguments appear to be directed against the discourse of verbal hygiene, which indicates that the ideology underlying this discourse is more salient to the general population than has

TABLE 11.2. Arguments for English

English can be used/is used as a lingua franca throughout the world	30
English is necessary for the development of the global economy	15
English is necessary in the world of work	10
The argument that English endangers the purity of German/French is grossly exaggerated	10
English can be used as a lingua franca in Switzerland	7
There is a demand for English	6
Certain documents are untranslatable	6
English is an easy language	5
English is easy to learn at an early age	4
English is a creative language	2
Using English saves translation costs	2
English does not exclude other languages	2
English is "cool"	2
Prescription of national languages serves those in power	1
English is an enrichment	1
English is an open system (?)	1

9. A number of other M.A. theses written at the end of the 1990s and throughout the 2000s, however, present findings very similar to those analysed by Nyffenegger, which strengthens the likelihood that we are faced with a relatively high degree of representativity (cf., e.g., Regli 2008; Grosse 2009).

hitherto been assumed. Finally, four arguments are based on a positive personal evaluation of the English language.

If we lump together the 39 arguments in favour of English at work and the 37 in favour of learning English because of its supposed lingua franca function on the grounds that they present slightly different aspects of the discourse of global English, we have a total of 76 arguments out of the overall total of 104. In addition, we still have 14 arguments countering the discourse of verbal hygiene. In Nyffenegger's work, based, as it admittedly is, on a narrow database of letters to the editor over a period of 10 years, we have evidence to support the two dominant forms of language discourse pertaining to English in the 1990s and the early part of this decade that emerge from a close analysis of the Saladin report and the Lüdi report. In addition, the 76 arguments in favour of English seem to support at least points 2 and 3 emerging from the quotation from Classen given in section 2.

The third point derived from Classen, that English is an easy language to learn, certainly occurs in Nyffenegger's analysis but not nearly as frequently as might have been predicted. The belief itself, however, is definitely part of the overall discourse of English as the global language, since, if English is perceived to be an easy language to learn, this inevitably leads to the assumption that English *is* an easy language, thus fitting it to assume the role of the global second language. From a linguistic point of view this belief borders on the absurd. Whether or not a language is easy to learn is a purely subjective assessment on the part of every individual learner, and can in no way be attributed to some inherent quality of the language. Obviously, many learners of English do find it "easy", but there are equally as many who find it "difficult". In 1994, the writer of a letter to the editor in the *Tribune de Genève* considers that English has *[une] grammaire relativement simple* ("a relatively simple grammar"), an assessment which is echoed six years later in 2000 by another writer to the same newspaper who considers that *il s'agit d'une langue relativement simple* ("we're dealing here with a relatively simple language"). This kind of statement, however, turns out to refer to the morphological structure of verbs and noun phrases. A teaching focus on the written medium and on the production of grammatical correctness rather than on communicativity is bound to make English appear "easier". Arguments that language A is simpler, more beautiful, manlier, more logical, and so on than language B are not linguistic, but belong to the discourses founded on language mythology. They are nevertheless important, and they link back to the conviction generally held that the "price" of English in Switzerland will be worth it.

4.4 "The earlier, the better" and the need for English in the global market

Another set of arguments often put forward by educationists to encourage the early learning of English does not concern us centrally in this chapter, but it is nevertheless worth noting. The assumption is made that learning a second language at an early age is more likely to lead to the successful acquisition of that language in later life and that there is a cutoff age beyond which it is not possible to acquire additional languages to anything like native-speaker level. Quite apart from the fact that the native-speaker, or first-language-speaker, level might be considered a luxury in acquiring a global language and that this aim tends to be restricted to the acquisition of an additional language as a *Kultursprache*, the assumption is based on outdated theoretical positions from the late 1960s and 1970s that have been seriously challenged in the meantime.[10]

The major argument used in the Swiss discourse in favour of an early introduction of English into the cantonal school systems is that it is absolutely necessary in the world of business and global commerce. Without a knowledge of English—so runs this argument—school leavers will not be in a position to take up employment in a wide range of professions in which English is required and for which higher salaries can be expected. There is certainly a need for English in companies and firms that have regular business contacts with other parts of the world in which either English is the first language or English is used as a means of international communication. But we still need to retain a realistic assessment of precisely which Swiss businesses have a need for English-speaking employees and at what levels in the employment hierarchy the positions involving knowledge of English lie. In the vast majority of cases, active use of oral or written English is to be found at various levels in the managerial structure of firms, in export contacts, or in highly specialised international research teams. Grin has pointed out in a number of important articles (e.g. 2000, 2001, 2003) that it is certainly true that knowledge of English does entail a higher salary at present, but he argues that the financial advantage of English is likely to drop over time. The principle of supply and demand would decrease the financial value of English if the educational segment of the sociocultural marketplace were to produce more young people with an active knowledge of the language.

4.5 Consequences of the discourse of English as a global language

Most of the arguments in favour of introducing English as an obligatory subject in the curriculum, and introducing it early on, are geared to the needs of state education systems. Learning a language at school, however, is very different from acquiring a second language in a natural setting. Why is this so? First, the amount of time given over to the learning of a second language at school is constrained by the rest of the curriculum and, in the majority of

---

10. One of the major theories used to bolster up such assumptions is Lenneberg's Critical Period Hypothesis, which goes back to the late 1960s and deals only with first language acquisition.

Swiss schools, often leads to a maximum of three to four lessons a week over the school year. Second, the size of primary school classes motivates against pupils' having an adequate opportunity to use what they may have acquired. Third, a very large number of primary school classes are now composed of the children of migrant families speaking neither the official languages of Switzerland nor English. As a consequence, not all children have the same levels of ability in German (or French or Italian). Fourth, in classes of 25 pupils or more, learning motivation and learning ability are very widely distributed. Fifth, the teacher needs to feel confident, alert and flexible in his mastery of the second language.

The "more English–more financial opportunities" angle of the discourse of global English also rests on the assumption that English is used actively across the world as a lingua franca. Some say that speakers use English across the language borders of Switzerland to avoid having to use one of the Swiss national languages. Most statements of this kind, however, are lacking in empirical evidence (cf. Andres & Watts 1993). In addition, the four-year research project for the Swiss National Science Foundation called "Language Contact and Focussing: The Linguistics of English in Switzerland," under the supervision of Peter Trudgill, David Allerton and me managed to find examples of English being used in this way, but only in situations in which speakers of German, French and Italian were involved or in companies in which either English speakers or speakers of languages other than the Swiss national languages were involved. A more systematic, close-grained analysis of those data also shows that the use of English posed problems of communication that went beyond participants' differential abilities to use the language actively. English, in other words, can be shown to take on different kinds of symbolic value in both the sociocultural and the material marketplaces and to pose problems for those who still believe that it can function as a neutral language.

The dominant discourse driving the introduction of early English is the discourse of global English. It is based on the *English as the global language myth* and is fuelled by the perceived needs of the Swiss economy and Swiss business and industry. It is hardly surprising that the cantons in the eastern part of the country, led by the Canton of Zürich, have been most active in implementing early English. However, we have already seen that there is another kind of discourse which challenges the dominant discourse more seriously than the discourse of multilingual Switzerland, and that is the discourse of verbal hygiene. This indicates that the *pure language myth* is not totally compatible with the *English as the global language myth*, although it is compatible with the *legitimate language myth* discussed in chapter 9.

Nyffenegger's research into attitudes expressed in letters to the editor and research carried out by others on the status of English in Switzerland (Regli 2008; Grosse 2009) reveals a very strong current of opinion that English represents a contaminating influence on the languages of Switzerland. The strength of this ideological discourse is borne out by Nyffenegger's statistics, which reveal that even those who argue in favour of early English still feel that this discourse is in some way salient. The discourse of verbal hygiene is based on the **pure language myth**, on a mythical Golden Age in which language is perceived to have reached a zenith, after which any change in the language represents change for the worse rather than for the better. It assumes that languages can be acquired or learned perfectly and that the most perfect speakers and writers are first-language speakers. It assumes that borrowing from English (e.g. in advertising, in job descriptions, in in-group language used by the young or in the media) automatically contaminates the language. This is even the case for the German dialects in Switzerland referred to as Swiss German, and by making such statements believers in the discourse of verbal hygiene automatically raise those dialects to the status of a "language".

The following is a small selection of negative comments from the *Tribune de Genève*, the *Neue Zürcher Zeitung* and the *Blick* on the influence that English is assumed to exert on French, German and Swiss German, all of them emotionally ideologically loaded:

- *ce terme barbare* (this barbarous term)
- *l'épidémie semble avoir contaminé un large éventail d'organisations et de firmes.* (The epidemic seems to have contaminated a large range of organisations and firms.)
- *Je trouve insupportable le charabia anglo-conquérant que l'on nous sert à toutes les sauces.* (I find the Anglophone conquering gibberish that is served up to us with all kinds of sauces insupportable.)
- *sprachliche Missgeburt* (linguistic miscarriage)
- *Es gibt nichts Schlimmeres als dieses Kauderwelsch.* (There's nothing worse than this hotchpotch.)
- *Die schrittweise Durchmischung des Schweizerdeutschen mit amerikanischem Slang ist nun offenkundig.* (The gradual contamination of Swiss German with American slang is now clear.)
- *Was die Jugend und zum Teil auch die Erwachsenen für Wörter rauslassen, schreit zum Himmel. Ich finde, es wäre Sache der Eltern, den Kindern klar zu machen, wie man korrekt spricht.* (The kinds of words youths, and to some extent adults, produce are abominable. It ought to be the parents' job to teach their children how to speak correctly.)

There is a wealth of metaphorical material in these comments, attesting to the strength of negative evaluation by the letter writers:

INTRODUCING ENGLISH INTO LANGUAGE X IS A BARBARISM
INTRODUCING ENGLISH IS INTRODUCING A DISEASE
INTRODUCING ENGLISH IS INTRODUCING UNPALATABLE FOOD
INTRODUCING ENGLISH IS A MISCARRIAGE

In the sociocultural marketplace, we need to acquire the following forms of capital:

- social connections
- relational networks
- forms of knowledge (including language)
- mental and physical skills
- acquired competences
- notions of identity

If we assume that a near-first-language ability in English is an acquired competence and also a form of knowledge which will benefit the social status of the learner, we need to consider in what professional areas this might be the case. Clearly, in academia this is so. But in the academic world, other mental skills and other forms of knowledge are also required. In a similar way, the professional area of commerce and industry requires not just knowledge of English but knowledge of the working of the financial, production and labour markets. In addition, and in particular in this area of professional activity, social connections and relational networks are vitally important, and although it might be true that knowledge of English could help to create those connections, this need not always be the case.

The price of English in Switzerland, then, is high in terms of financial investment but equally high in terms of the acquisition of the necessary skills in English that will create synergies with the material marketplace. The price might also be too high for Switzerland in terms of the overall sociopolitical structure of the country. Introducing English at an early age before any of the other national languages is not likely to create French-English, German-English or Italian-English bilingualism throughout the Swiss population. It is also not likely to help the development of forms of Swiss identity—which do exist—or to promote social connections over the language borders within Switzerland. The prime movers behind early English are industrialists, bankers, managers and CEOs in multinational companies, and their major motivation is to prevent having to spend money on in-company courses in English. Let us assume for the moment that they have a point in arguing that English should be taught obligatorily in the school system. If the price of introducing it early is too high and if the assumptions on which the ideology of "the earlier, the better" are muddle-headed—which current research indicates—it can still be introduced at a later stage in the school curriculum, as has always been the case, and still produce more speakers of English than at present.

The commodity for sale is English, but not just any form of English, rather near-first-language competence in English. Buying that product requires a very large financial investment since it entails, in its turn, the following conditions:

1. a marked increase in overall motivation to learn English (and not just among children who would be expected to be highly motivated in any case, but also

among those who are unlikely—for socioeconomic reasons—to be successful at school). This can be achieved only in much smaller classes;

2. the training of primary school teachers to the level of near-first-language competence in English;

3. the development of teaching materials that are adequate to teaching English to young children (four-, five-, or six-year-olds?) and are adapted to the needs of Swiss primary school students rather than the general non-native learner of that age;

4. adequate provision for transition from primary to secondary education, involving once again teachers with near-first-language competence in English.

The cantonal education systems in Switzerland are at present a very long way from satisfying any of these conditions, and the financial outlay that fulfilling them would entail far exceeds the usefulness of attempting to reach the idealistic goal of producing generations of graduates with near-first-language competence in English, particularly since those goals can be argued to be discursively produced ideologies driven by the *English as the global language myth*.

Switzerland is a rich country, but it is a model case of a transformation in language-teaching policies that has taken place in just 20 years. I have argued here that the price is too high for Switzerland. So how high will it be for countries that do not have the financial resources that Switzerland has? One of the solutions to this conundrum is that language teaching need not focus on producing near-first-language speakers of English, but should be satisfied with producing speakers who can get by in situations in which English might indeed be the only language that they can use to communicate. This is an eminently sensible point, but, as we shall see in the next section, it leads to such concepts as English as a Lingua Franca, which tends to be conceptualised as if it were a homogeneous system.

5. PROBLEMS IN THE ASSUMPTION THAT ENGLISH IS THE GLOBAL LANGUAGE

The discourse constructing the belief that English is not just *a* global language but rather *the* global language rightly assumes that English is currently needed in the "global marketplace". The pressure that has been put on education authorities in Switzerland to make English an obligatory subject in all cantons is not at issue. Even before the Lüdi report, English was offered in the vast majority of schools, so the final step of making it obligatory was a small and probably logical one.

There is no way of knowing, at the present time, whether the pool of people with competence in English will increase in size. But if it does increase, this will effectively lower the value of the commodity, not increase it. A detailed survey of precisely where English is needed in the world of work in

Switzerland, listing not only which institutions make use of the language but also at what levels in their professional hierarchies it is required, has not yet been made. My hunch is that, if and when such a survey is made, the result will be much more sobering and will reveal that higher levels in the hierarchy require it more than others. Obviously, this depends on the industry concerned. For the tourist industry, it does indeed seem sensible to have competence in English at all levels. For banking, however, there are many areas in which it will not always be necessary, even though it may be desirable. At present, at least in Switzerland, more research needs to be carried out on the language ecologies of different industries and the companies and organisations making up those industries.

Switzerland has served as an example in this chapter for some of the consequences of a blind belief in the discourse of the global language. However, it is at least a country in which four official languages are in use, and the awareness of multilingualism is higher than in most other European states. The major problem in the *English as the global language myth* is that no one seems to have defined adequately what is meant by the term "global language". If it simply means that English can be found as a first or additional language in one function or another in most parts of the world, this is certainly true. If it means that English can be used to communicate with others anywhere in the world, it is blatantly misleading. In countries like Switzerland, this second interpretation seems to be favoured, particularly among those who construct and institute language policies for schools!

This is not at all surprising if we consider the way in which the language is promoted by ESL/EFL organisations. One such organisation, which can be found on the Internet at www.anglik.net, purports to be an "online resource for students of English as a second or foreign language". One of the sections on the Web site is "The History of the English Language", which is a potted version of most histories of English currently on offer. At the end of the section is a subsection on Global English in which we read: "English has now inarguably achieved global status." To provide evidence for this somewhat wayward claim, a number of "facts" are listed, which include statements to the effect that more than 90 countries use English as an official language, that the working language of the Asian trade group ASEAN is English, that it is the de facto working language of 98 percent of the world's chemists and physicists, that it is the official language of the European Central Bank, and that Indian and black parents in South Africa want their children to be educated in English.

The vast majority of those 90 countries with English as their official language are former British colonies, and although they may have chosen English, this fact throws virtually no light on the percentage of the population who can actually speak and use English with ease. The Asian trade group obviously chose English because it was already a second language in a number of ASEAN countries (e.g. Singapore, Malaysia, India) and because business tends to be carried out globally in English. It is true that the scientific community has shifted quite considerably to English, but these are very specialised registers of English and the claim bears no relation to whether the physicists and chemists writing in English are able to use the language orally. The South African example can be explained historically through the competition between English and Afrikaans in South Africa.

However, it is not so much what is said, but rather how it is said that is unsettling. No one doubts the spread of English, but it tends to be confined to specific registers that need a "global" language for international communication to take place. From this point of view, the idea that English is a global language is not in dispute. The tone in which these facts are listed, however, leaves one with a feeling that those who are making the claims are jubilant, almost triumphant. This is evident in the following paragraph from the subsection (my underlining):

> One of the <u>more remarkable aspects of the spread of English around the world</u> has been the extent to which Europeans are adopting it as <u>their internal lingua franca</u>. English is spreading from northern Europe to the south and is now <u>firmly entrenched as a second language in countries such as Sweden, Norway, Netherlands and Denmark</u>. Although not an official language in any of these countries if one visits any of them it would seem that <u>almost everyone there can communicate with ease in English</u>. Indeed, if one switches on a television in Holland one would find as many channels in English (albeit subtitled), as there are in Dutch.

The "spread of English around the world" is characterised as "remarkable", and the statement that Europeans are "adopting it as their internal lingua franca" is patently untrue if one descends from the level of politics, academia and big business, in which, obviously, some form of lingua franca is needed, to the level of less well educated people. For example, Preisler (1999) shows how large portions of the Danish population (particularly those older than 40) have little or no knowledge of English and feel discriminated against when English is introduced into Danish advertising and public notices. It is simply not true that "almost everyone [in Sweden, Norway, Netherlands and Denmark] can communicate with ease in English". Although a European survey of attitudes towards languages carried out in 2001 reveals that English is seen to be a useful language by 43 percent of informants, the ratios of acceptance of English differ quite spectacularly by country, from 89 percent in Sweden to just 6 percent in Spain. Yet on the basis of such flimsy evidence the following statement is confidently made on the Web site: "English has without a doubt become the global language." And so English is now not merely *a* global language; it is heralded as *the* global language—it has no rival. The phrase "without a doubt" is not a statement of fact, but one of belief. One could argue, of course, that if the Web site has been set up for teachers of English, this kind of message simply expresses a feeling of elation that these teachers will never be out of a job!

However, we are still no nearer explaining what is understood by the term "global English". It cannot mean that wherever one goes in the world, one can use English. Mercifully, this point has not yet been reached—not by a long way. It might mean that English has swept the board in terms of its choice as a second language in state education systems, but this is not true either. French still has pride of place in a number of states. It could mean—and here we might be on the right lines—that English is rapidly taking over as the language in which the world financial system, world trade, international politics and worldwide scientific collaboration are carried out. As Crystal (1997) notes, English has been used as the only language in a large number of international organisations for some time now, particularly since the Second World War. This is most noticeable in air-traffic control, but this was a result of American domination when civil aviation became big business after World War II, and the English used is, of necessity, a very restricted register.[11] Crystal writes clearly and cogently on the subject of global English, making the point that English always seems to have been "in the right place at the right time". However, he, too, has been criticised for using a style that belies a note of triumph. In addition, his figures of second-language speakers of English across the world are somewhat exaggerated in that, if English is taught as the only additional language in the school curricula of non-English-speaking states, this does not automatically mean that the whole population of the country has had some instruction in English, let alone that the whole population can be counted as second-language speakers of English.

It is understandable, to some extent, that EFL/ESL teachers should feel secure, or even jubilant, that they are never likely to be out of a job for very long in the face of the current demand for English. Despite the exaggerated estimates of the number of second or additional language learners of English, they still far outstrip the numbers of first-language English speakers, and the language is indeed in use in situations in which people have no other language to communicate with each other; it is frequently used as a lingua franca. This has prompted some researchers to propose that there might be similarities in the way English is used as a lingua franca by non-first-language speakers.

The research programme mentioned in section 4.5, financed by the Swiss National Science Foundation and supervised by Trudgill, Allerton and Watts, set up the bold hypothesis that a variety of English that we tentatively called "Swiss English" might be in the process of formation through German, French and Italian speakers using English within Switzerland as a lingua franca. Three doctoral dissertations resulted from the analysis of the data collected during the course of the research, and very little evidence was unearthed to enable us to uphold the hypothesis of a focusing process toward a Swiss form of English. Rosenberger (2009) carried out a detailed statistical analysis

---

11. Cf. Welskopf 2008.

of the data and discovered only three constructions that might be taken to be typically Swiss. There were two problems with this result, however: (1) those three constructions could also be found in other European data corpora of ESL/ELF; (2) the material displayed a bewildering range of non-first-language English constructions, many of which were idiosyncratic, as they were restricted to one individual speaker at a time.

In chapter 3, Rosenberger deals with the topic of "English as an International Language and English as a Lingua Franca". He first discusses the old distinction between "native speakers" and "non-native speakers", and, like most other critics, comes to the reasonable conclusion that a language cannot belong to anyone, but is, on the contrary, open to everyone to use. English is not the possession of English speakers, and in a situation in which we are far outnumbered by speakers of English as a second or additional language, any attempt to claim ownership borders on the absurd. However, in the area of English language teaching, whose goals must surely be to enable the learner to acquire sufficient English to achieve whatever her aims are, a number of distinct goals can be discerned.

If the purpose is to equip the learners with a linguistic competence which is almost equal to that of first-language speakers,[12] the learning will be aimed at the acquisition of the *Kultursprache*, and there are various pedagogical ways in which this goal can be reached. If the purpose is to enable learners to use the English language instrumentally in whatever kinds of interaction with first-language speakers they are engaged in, then the learning will be aimed at the acquisition of English as a second language or some form of English for specific purposes. Communicativity and the development of a pragmatic awareness of how to use English in different environments will be focused on in this teaching scenario.

Most learners in the modern global context, however, will need English to communicate adequately either with first-language speakers or with other speakers of English as an additional language, in which case the learning will be focused on English as a lingua franca. Communicativity will be needed, but pragmatic awareness may present problems, since in a non-first-language interaction, each partner may tend to use English to instantiate his own cultural expectations. In this kind of situation, cross-cultural issues become significant.

The argument in favour of teaching English as a lingua franca is either based on the assumption that a lingua franca is a simplified form of language,

---

12. A fair number of students who have studied under my supervision have turned out to command a proficiency in spoken and written English that is fully equal to that of the average first-language speaker and, in some cases, well beyond the average. I may say that this is *not* to be attributed to my teaching, but to the students' astounding ability to adapt fully to the English-speaking cultures in which they functioned. In all cases, these language acquirers did not begin to learn English till at least age 10 or 11, this being the perfect answer to the claims made by supporters of the the-earlier-the-better ideology that this is an impossible achievement.

which again feeds into the question of what we understand by pidgins and creoles, or that it is a form of language designed to function in specialised situations such as trading and business—that is, that it represents various types of English for specific purposes. Widdowson (1997: 144) takes the latter approach and suggests that English, with its international status, has now become a *virtual* language. It is there for anyone to use, and as soon as it is used for some purpose, it is adapted accordingly to the needs of the people involved. "The virtual language," he writes, "has spread as an international language: through the development of autonomous registers which guarantee specialist communication within global expert communities."

Rosenberger argues that this view "empties the concept of ESP [English for specific purposes]" (2009: 51). As we can see, the focus of attention has now narrowed to the following nexus of English learning scenarios: English as an international language, English as a lingua franca and English for specific purposes. Whether or not we accept Widdowson's point, it at least avoids the temptation to construct a new variety of English based on principles of simplification and levelling. This, as Rosenberger cogently argues, is what appears to have happened in the case of English as a lingua franca; certain researchers have postulated that, instead of teaching English, the English language teaching community should focus more narrowly on teaching English as a lingua franca (Jenkins 2000, 2003, 2004; Jenkins & Seidlhofer 2001; Modiano 1999; Seidlhofer 2004). Such a position, however, is tenable only if there really is a variety of English that, on an international level, could be shown to be English as a lingua franca.

In her book *The Phonology of English as an International Language* (2000), Jenkins attempts to identify English as a lingua franca as a new variety with respect to phonology, but what she really does is to suggest a set of core features that would (or could) constitute the phonology of it. Rosenberger raises the counterargument that this is equivalent to discursively constructing (or trying to construct) English as a lingua franca, and that it ignores the simple linguistic fact of variability and heterogeneity in all situations of emergent social practice. I wish to go a step further and suggest that it also reopens the desire to construct a homogeneous variety of English—that it has not freed itself from the **homogeneity myth**. To construct an English as a lingua franca variety requires a huge effort of codification and valorisation that is hardly supported by the kinds of eighteenth- and nineteenth-century myth that drove the powerful language ideological discourses from then up to the twentieth century. The failure of the Conservative government of the late 1980s to turn the clock back and insist on the use of a "correct" version of standard English for the National Curriculum was a clear indication of a change in the discourse archive (cf. chap. 10). The standard language today is simply one variety of English among a myriad of other varieties and is just as prone to innovation and change as those varieties.

How does this discussion bear on the issue of global English? Let us assume for the moment that a global language is indeed one in which the world financial system, world trade, international politics and worldwide scientific collaboration are carried out. It also includes the need or the ability of individuals and groups of individuals to move quickly from one point in the world to another in search of work, or simply to satisfy a craving to see other parts of the world. What more natural development could there be than that the same language as is in use in the global domains listed above should also be used to function as a mobility factor? This does not mean that English is spoken everywhere and by everyone, nor does it mean that it is uniquely in use to facilitate communication in the global scenarios sketched out above. Nor does it mean that it is the only global language. It most certainly does not mean that this was the destiny of English; no language has a destiny. Despite the metaphor, no language is a human being.

The *English as the global language myth* appears to have triggered off a language discourse that very quickly became hegemonic, although it began its appearance as early as the mid-nineteenth century. It would also appear to be the case that a new archive governing the law of what can be said has also emerged, so much so that national language policies with respect to English are founded on ideological principles that learning English will enable the learner to communicate with anybody in the world, will guarantee better and financially more lucrative job opportunities and at the same time will not present the learner with insuperable difficulties. Policy makers appear to take no notice of counterarguments with respect to the possible negative influences on the official indigenous languages, nor do they concern themselves with the fact that such principles as "the earlier the better" are no longer scientifically supported. Worst, however, they seem to ignore the extravagant costs of such policies. At the same time, those linguists in control of influencing the discourse of English as *the* global language (not merely *a* global language) are resorting to the old *homogeneity myth*, backed up by the *superiority of English myth*. They have a responsibility to reconsider their motivations to ensure that the global status of English is considered from a more realistic and matter-of-fact perspective.

Chapter 12

▬

Myths, ideologies of English
and the funnel view of the
history of English

> History is the version of past events that people have decided to agree
> upon.
>
> —Napoleon Bonaparte

1. FROM CONCEPTUAL METAPHORS TO
DISCOURSE ARCHIVES: THE FUNCTION
OF THE MYTH

I begin this final chapter as I ended the first, with figure 1.2, which has been
slightly reorganised from bottom to top as figure 12.1. Conceptual metaphors
to account for and understand language are the first stage of the process
whereby language ideologies are constructed. If those ideologies become part
of a dominant hegemonic discourse, a discourse archive is constructed in
which, as Jan Blommaert says in his book *Discourse*, macrosociological forces
and formations "define and determine what can be said, expressed, heard,
and understood in particular societies, particular milieux, particular historical periods" (2005: 102).

It has been my aim in the present book to show how language myths,
derived as they are from statements made on the basis of a small number of
conceptual metaphors about language, have functioned discursively to produce ideologies of the history of the English language. I have ranged widely
from the Anglo-Saxon period through the period of transition from Anglo-
Saxon to Middle English, to one of the central texts in the fourteenth century,

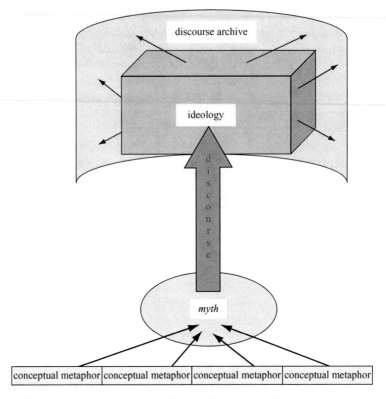

FIGURE 12.1. From conceptual metaphors to discourse archives

Higden's *Polychronicon*, to the explanations for the Great Vowel Shift and a reanalysis of Swift's famous *Proposal*. I then dealt with the changing conceptualisation of politeness in the eighteenth century to show how it became central to the dominant discourse of language in that century and operated as a means of establishing and cementing social class distinctions that lasted well into the twentieth century. The close association of polite language with the upper levels of the class system was not only instrumental in developing standard English; it also helped to establish it as the legitimate language in Great Britain in the first half of the nineteenth century. Some of the sociopolitical consequences of that development were dealt with in chapter 9. My next step was to move into the recent past, the late 1980s, when the myth of the legitimate language reared its head once again, this time in the guise of the *educated language myth*, and I ended with some of the current problems generated by the term "global language".

The aim of this book has not been to write yet another history of English, but rather to show how different histories of English have actually helped to construct language myths which are at the basis of a dominant discourse on what modern English is and how the history of the language should be taught. Admittedly, from a historical point of view there are rather large gaps in my analysis of this discursive trajectory through the course of time. The fifteenth, sixteenth and seventeenth centuries have been largely ignored, as has the end of the nineteenth and most of the twentieth century. A great deal of interesting material still has to be examined, particularly in the fifteenth century, which might not only reveal evidence for the myths I have proposed but also enable us to discover potential new myths. In all probability, new myths will interconnect in interesting ways with the myths suggested here. It may be objected that, since the larger myths governing the modern-day presentation of the history of English are dominated by a discourse which arose in the latter nineteenth century and continued into the twentieth century, this particular gap is problematic. However, I have quoted quite liberally from some of those texts at various places in the book. In addition Crowley (2003), Mugglestone (1995) and James Milroy (1996, 1999, 2000, 2002) have already gone over most of this ground, which would make a repetition of their work somewhat unnecessary.

The myths discussed in the present volume form three distinct but interconnected groups. In the first group, we find myths that sprang up in the latter half of the nineteenth century in the wake of the construction of the nation-state in Europe (cf. the first section of chap. 5). In chapters 2 and 3 I have dealt with the two aspects of what I have called the *longevity of English myth*, the *ancient language myth* (chap. 2), and the *unbroken tradition myth* (chap. 3). The nation-state concept did not suddenly appear in the nineteenth century but was formed gradually through the emergence of such powerful European states as Great Britain, France, Spain, the Austro-Hungarian Empire, Russia and Prussia, three of which (Spain, France and Britain) were engaged in an embittered struggle for colonial domination on a worldwide scale throughout the eighteenth century. In addition, apart from domination in the areas of trade, the economy and the establishment of overseas colonies, one of the other components of the nation-state concept that emerged in all its force in the nineteenth century, as a powerful determiner of how the nation-state was actually to be defined, was the standardisation and national diffusion of certain languages: Spanish, English, German and French. The age of politeness in Britain spawned the notion of the "polite language", a powerful social myth that, at least in Britain, was all important in focusing the efforts on the codification and standardisation of the English language (cf. the discussion of the *polite language myth* in chap. 8). The confluence of the concept of the nation-state with one national standard language and one national religion led to the emergence of another myth, the *legitimate language myth*, in the nineteenth century.

The second nexus of myths presented in chapters 5 and 7 is composed of a set of interlinked myths that go back several centuries, some at least as far as the twelfth century, and most of them common to the language myths developed in other European countries. In fact it is highly likely that some of these myths are inherent in perceptions of language in general, particularly when different languages come into contact with one another. The *pure language myth* and the *perfect language myth*, obviously very closely related, are not restricted to perceptions of English. I have ample evidence of this myth in frequent statements by Swiss-German dialect speakers bemoaning the loss of "pure" Basel German, "pure" Zürich German or "pure" Bernese German! Closely related to these myths are those that tell the stories of the dangers of language contact and warn that such contact involves contamination (the *contamination through contact myth*), or even decay and death (the *decay and death myth*). The notion of contamination through contact springs from the conviction that the language brought into contact with one's own must in some sense be inferior to it, a belief that derives from the *barbarians myth*, the barbarians, of course, being the culturally inferior group. This myth reaches far back to the world of ancient Greece and is probably evidence of a universal set of perceptions wherever a language community feels threatened from outside. When this nexus of myths is infused with the urge to standardise a language by making it "polite", "refined", or "legitimate", it generates the fear of language change and the *immutability myth*. Once again, this language myth is not restricted to English.

In a sense, therefore, the nexus of myths presented in chapter 5 (and those that Swift satirises in chap. 7) are almost universal. Two myths in this group, however, appear to be peculiar to the English-speaking world, the *good climate/good soil myth* (one that is derived from the conceptual metaphor A LANGUAGE IS A PLANT) and the *pure language of the South and the corrupted language of the North myth*. It is of course conceivable that the former myth may turn up in examining the myths of other languages, although I have no data to confirm this hunch.

The third group of myths consists of more modern stories with a mythical character, like the *English as a creole language myth* (chap. 4) and the *English as the global language myth* (chap. 11). If we look closely at these new myths, there is some substance to the claim that they may have been started by linguists themselves. In the case of the *English as a creole language myth*, which has now generated lay interest in the discourse, this is definitely the case; it has now reached beyond the confines of the academic community. In the case of the *English as the global language myth*, we can be less sure of our facts, although it is certainly the case that a number of significant sociolinguists have contributed to promoting this idea.

2. THE FUNNEL VIEW OF THE HISTORY OF ENGLISH

My major interest in unearthing and deconstructing the myths has been to argue in favour of histories of language other than the conventional ones of the standard. The canonical way of dealing with the history of English is to start with "Old English", a term which I have assiduously tried to avoid using, and then to move through the familiar periodisation of Middle English, Early Modern English and Late Modern English. The end product of the process is inevitably a focus on the modern standard language, and the starting point a range of varieties of Anglo-Saxon.[1] The perspective on the history of the language is thus rather like a funnel, in which a number of varieties are poured in at the wide top of the funnel and standard English comes out of the narrow neck (cf. fig. 12.2). The fate of the original varieties poured in at the top and others that may have arisen at a later stage are generally not taken into consideration.

The funnel view constitutes a modern archive of "what can be said, expressed, heard, and understood" (Blommaert 2005: 102) about the history of English. The contributions to Watts and Trudgill (2002) argue for a wider range of histories to cover these varieties, and a focus on alternative histories of English is highly likely to challenge canonical views of the history of English. Other publications, including the use of media such as television, have already begun to challenge the hegemony of the dominant version of the history of English (McCrum, Cran & MacNeil 1986; McArthur 1998; Elmes 1999; Crystal 2002). One way to crack open the archive is to focus more consciously on a range of alternative histories and to investigate the language ideologies that constitute the canonical version. The discourse leading from myth

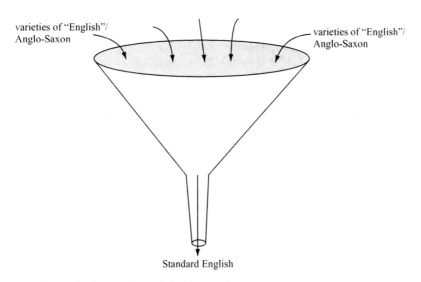

varieties of "English"/
Anglo-Saxon

varieties of "English"/
Anglo-Saxon

Standard English

FIGURE 12.2. The funnel view of the history of a language

1. Even in the period of "Old English" there is also a tendency to assume that the literary West Saxon variety of the tenth and eleventh centuries was a "West Saxon" standard language, and this is all too often generalised to cover the whole area in which Anglo-Saxon was spoken.

to ideology in figure 12.1 is itself historical, and it rests on or is driven by myths. So the present book has not been a "new" history of English, but rather a blueprint as to how to challenge and deconstruct the underlying myths.

One excellent example of a book-length alternative history—which presents itself as a "social and cultural history"—is Wales's book *Northern English*. At one stage in her argument, Wales makes a very perceptive point about the neglect of "the provincial voices rooted in the oral traditions of ballad, song and music-hall", and she develops this point further as follows:

> Both kinds of histories [linguistic and literary] on the one hand assume mistakenly that literacy and the written standard killed off both oracy and dialect writing (although the relationship between the standard, the production of dialect and the representation of dialect was complex); and on the other hand underestimate the strength and potency of Northern English as living speech used by both working class and middle classes. Indeed, I would go further and say that it is significantly because of this vibrant body of literature, and later the music-hall to which it is related, that Northerners themselves became more conscious than ever before of their own regional identities and differences: dialect was not only spoken but consciously performed and enacted for both entertainment and edification on a scale hitherto unknown. This in turn promoted still more creativity and, increasingly, local civic pride. (2006: 128–129)

Wales's point is well taken here. Not only were songs sung, tales told, humorous and semi-serious ditties performed, drama enacted, and narrative and poetry written in dialect; they are still being sung, told and written in nonstandard varieties at the beginning of the twenty-first century. A whole set of vibrant, successful or tragic lives have been lived by other Englishes both within Britain and throughout the world in the speakers and writers of those varieties, and although we know this to be the case, as sociolinguists we have tended to turn the other way.

One brief illustration must suffice here to indicate the rich vein of "nonstandard" Englishes and the alternative stories that can be revealed by unearthing them and by looking at them against the background of the language myths governing the dominant discourse of the history of English. Songs from the North of England that were common in the nineteenth century may still be heard today in certain cultural niches such as folk clubs, ceilidhs and folk festivals. One such song is commonly known as "The Oldham Weaver". Wales reminds us that the song is printed out in full in chapter 4 of the novel *Mary Barton* by Elizabeth Gaskell, and she notes that it was circulating in (at least) 13 different versions at the time that Gaskell wrote the novel (2006: 122 n. 5). She suggests that it was composed after the Battle of Waterloo.[2] However, we know that a poem called "Jone o' Grinfilt" was

---

2. I have my doubts as to whether it makes much sense to talk about folk songs being "composed". Most of the time, we simply do not know how they came into existence and were diffused among the community.

written in 1805 by Joseph Lees in the Oldham dialect of Lancashire telling the story of a naïve man called Jone (or John) living in the village of Greenfield who believed that the border between Lancashire and Yorkshire was the border between England and France. On the assumption that the French were across the Pennines in Yorkshire, he sets out for Oldham to enlist in the army. Some time later a song was circulated with the title "Jone o' Grinfilt junior", but there is no obvious topical connection between the poem and the song apart from the hint that the song was about the son of the naïve hero of Lees' poem.

"Jone o' Grinfilt junior" began to circulate sometime after 1815 and was frequently given the title of "The Oldham Weaver", "The Hand-loom Weaver", or "The Poor Cotton Weaver". Its topic is the hard times encountered by hand-loom weavers when steam-driven power looms were first introduced, forcing the wholesale shift of workers into the mills. The song, still sung today, goes under the title "The Four Loom Weaver".

Wales suggests that Gaskell's inclusion of the song was politically moti-vated to attract the reader's attention to the continuing deprivations of workers in the cotton industry in the 1840s. Chapter 4 of *Mary Barton* is cen-tred on Mary's visit to old Alice Wilson, who invites her to tea. Alice's female lodger, a young woman called Margaret, comes down from a room upstairs to join the party. The narrator describes the poverty of Alice's house and has Alice tell the two young women of how she left her girlhood home in the hills to find work in Manchester but never had an opportunity to go home for a visit. Alice then suggests that Margaret should sing "Th' Owdham Weaver" for Mary on the grounds that "she can make me cry at any time by singing [it]". At this point, the narrator addresses the reader directly, using the sec-ond-person pronoun "you", as follows:

Do you know "The Oldham Weaver"? Not unless you are Lancashire born and bred, for it is a complete Lancashire ditty. I will copy it for you.

She uses the standard English title of the song when she addresses the reader, while allowing Alice to use what we take to be the local dialect in addressing Mary and Margaret. However, had Gaskell made a more consis-tent attempt to represent the dialect in the characters' speech, the second word in the title would be spelt something like <weyver>. At other points in Alice's story preceding the performance of the song, concessions are made to the dialect, for example, "I was very *frabbit* with him" (where Gaskell glosses *frabbit* as "peevish" for her readers), "she *were* always ailing, and he *were* always in trouble", "I never *seed* such a *bonny* bit anywhere", and so on. But, in general, the conversation is held in standard English, in particular when Mary Barton speaks.

The text of the song is then given in a dialect version with two concessions to the standard English reader, in which *clem* is glossed as "to starve with hunger" and *pick ower* is glossed as "to throw the shuttle in hand-loom weaving". After the song the narrator again addresses the reader, admitting that it may sound humorous, but stressing that the humour is "near to pathos":

> The air to which this is sung is a kind of droning recitative, depending much on expression and feeling. To read it, it may, perhaps, seem humorous; but it is that humour which is near akin to pathos, and to those who have seen the distress it describes it is a powerfully pathetic song. (Gaskell 1849: chap. 4)

As Gaskell knows only too well, very few of her readers will have seen "the distress it describes". The two metadiscursive addresses to the readers immediately prior to and following on from the text of the song thus indicate that the narrator is aware that she is giving her middle- and upper-class readers access to "unknown England".[3]

Novel writers who were concerned to expose the "state of England question"—Elizabeth Gaskell, Benjamin Disraeli and many others—were faced with a dilemma. Their attempts to reproduce dialect in the written medium, if too sweeping, would, in the eyes of the publishers, have put off potential readers.[4] Gaskell's way out of the dilemma in chapter 4 of *Mary Barton* is to represent her characters with a few strokes of dialect and to refer the reader directly to the dialect text of the "The Oldham Weaver" commenting briefly on its content. This is almost equivalent to a polite nod of recognition in the direction of dialect speakers, but without any doubt, it reveals that the only legitimate language in which one could write was, even in the first half of the nineteenth century, standard English. By extension, dialect, or any other form of nonstandard English, was illegitimate and subject to censure, much of which carried moral overtones taken from the *polite language myth*. Those who were unable to sympathise with the plight of the working classes and their obvious deprivations looked upon them as morally depraved, socially inferior and in dire need of education and conversion to the "true" religion.

3. MYTHS AS STORIES

My account of the myths that drive the discourses of English began with my argument in the first section of chapter 1 that myths are communally told and shared stories that help members of the community to socially construct their worlds by "languaging" them and orienting their own individual lives to

---

3. The reference here is to a collection of descriptions made by social explorers into the depressed areas of industrial England edited by Peter Keating, with the title *Into Unknown England 1866–1913: Selections from the Social Explorers.*

4. Cf. Wales's discussion of the connections Emily Brontë made between dialect and "poverty, coarseness and religious fanaticism" related to her uncompromising representation of the Yorkshire dialect of the dales area in the character of Joseph in *Wuthering Heights* (2006: 121 n. 3).

the perceived history of the community. Our own individual worlds and our changing identities within them are created through the telling of stories, but we are not generally aware of the fact that narration always contains an element of fiction.

For the sociolinguist, the stories that create the myths are not always easy to locate as concrete instantiations of social practice, although we know that they occur within the verbal interaction that takes place in a whole range of communities of practice in which we are ratified members. But in our present-day world, compared with the information we have inherited from the past, we have the inestimable advantage of being able to broadcast and record oral performances of discussions, arguments, casual conversations, school lessons and university lectures, parliamentary debates, and so on in which evidence of the myths may be found. For example, one story told in the corpus of conversations recorded from my own family concerns a man who was an inveterate user of the discourse marker *you know*, so much so that the storyteller felt it necessary to point out that, because they did not know his name, he and his mother would refer to him as "Mr You-know". This sparked off a lively impromptu discussion of discourse markers, in which the participants, my own family members, who were all from the south of England, expressed their distaste at the use of certain discourse markers which they perceived to be from the North. They did so quite openly and without realising that they themselves occasionally used instantiations of those very same discourse markers during the ongoing conversation (cf. Watts 1989). The story was one small instantiation of the ***pure language of the South and the corrupted language of the North myth***. A further small instantiation of the same myth is evident in the story told by Lesley Milroy (1999) of a woman from the North who found it extremely difficult to find employment in London on account of her northern accent. The example given in chapter 10 (from Cox [1991: 34]) of the Conservative politician Norman Tebbitt implying or openly stating in a programme on Radio 4 in 1985 that "the decline in the teaching of grammar had led directly to the rise in football hooliganism"[5] was a small instantiation of a whole nexus of myths—the *legitimate language myth*, the **barbarians myth**—in which the failure to learn standard English had led to a moral decline involving hooliganism and violence.

Small stories of this kind could be narrated almost endlessly. They are not hard to find, and they offer the evidence that is required to substantiate the existence of the myths. The myths themselves cannot be said to represent objectively truthful accounts of the past, nor can we expect each telling of a myth to be the same. But they do contain a grain of truth, and as such they are an eminently useful means of accounting historically for present attitudes

---

5. See chapter 11, note 9, in which I express diffidence at stating that these were the words actually used by Tebbitt and that they have simply been transferred into direct speech by Cox. Without access to the original recording of the radio programme, I am obliged to hedge a little here. However, this does not alter the interpretation that the gist of Tebbitt's argument is an instantiation of the *legitimate language myth*.

towards language. Myths tend to hover somewhere in the space between total objectivity and total fiction. For many, they may be represented as closer to truth than fiction, whereas for others, their fictional character may be much stronger. But the beliefs instantiated by myths still need to be taken seriously if hegemonic discourses on language are driven by those beliefs. In the previous chapter, for example, it is not enough to admit to the spread of English across the world if one does not at the same time analyse the effects of an unquestioning belief in English as *the* global language. Such beliefs can indeed lead to misguided language policies involving English (as shown by the example of Switzerland given in chapter 11) and to a conviction in countries in which English is the official language spoken by first-language speakers that one does not need to acquire languages other than English (as evident in the current dramatic situation with second-language teaching in the United Kingdom school systems).[6]

If we hear or read a set of beliefs about language that are difficult to accept, we frequently classify the narration of those beliefs as a "myth", thus using the term to refer to an untruth or a fabrication. This was the case in chapter 11 in Davies' review article (1996) of Phillipson's book *Linguistic Imperialism*, which accuses him of spreading the myth of linguicism. He objects quite strongly to the inference that he made in reading Phillipson's book that the Applied Linguistics Department of the University of Edinburgh[7] is the academic nerve-centre training ESL/EFL personnel for the British Council. I can feel a certain sympathy for Davies's point, but his use of the term "myth" implies that linguicism is a fiction, an untruth, something that is discursively constructed by Phillipson and others. Within the discourse of review writing, it is almost a term of abuse. Phillipson, on the other hand, is no better, and he, too, uses the term "myth" to counter Davies's criticism with the same set of negative connotations.

One important point that I have explicitly made in this book is that myths are stories that instantiate sets of communally shared beliefs. Fiction adheres to a myth by virtue of the fact that it *is* a story, a narrative act. Myths are certainly not lies—although Davies does not appear to be accusing Phillipson of lying. The grain of truth in a myth constitutes the central belief around which the story is woven and elaborated. We may not agree with the stories that are woven and elaborated, nor with the dominant discourses that are driven by such beliefs, but it is still up to us to discover the grain of truth.

Let us take Davies' use of the expression "the myth of linguicism". If we assume that there is a modern *myth of linguicism*—that people have been discriminated against socially and politically on the basis of the language variety they speak—there must surely be some truth in the myth.[8] To find evidence

---

6. I use the plural here to indicate that the education system for England and Wales is different from that of Scotland and that of Northern Ireland.

7. This is where Davies worked in 1996.

8. Obviously, such discrimination may also have other sources—differences of gender, ethnicity, religion, skin colour, and so on.

for the grain of truth, we first need to construct a meaning from the term "linguicism," which is coined in analogy to the term "racism". Skutnab-Kangas and Phillipson (1989: 455) have defined it, acceptably enough, as "ideologies and structures which are used to legitimate, effectuate, and reproduce unequal division of power and resources (both material and non-material) between groups which are defined on the basis of language". It is perfectly plausible to argue that discriminating against others socially and politically is a reprehensible act, regardless of whether the discrimination is based on language, gender, racial, ethnic, or religious differences. It is also perfectly reasonable to agree that the legitimation, effectuation and reproduction of the social structures through which power and resources are distributed should be questioned and, if found to be unjust, changed. So two questions need to be asked:

1. What evidence do we have that discrimination on the basis of language varieties has taken place or is taking place?
2. Is the discrimination made purely or largely on the basis of these linguistic differences?

The second question is a thorny one, since any act of social or political discrimination that sociolinguists may attribute to differences in language variety are often denied by the perpetrators and ascribed to other causes. This would mean that there is a certain relativity attached to the second question. But the first can be shown to hold in many of the myths dealt with in this book.

The three trials of William Hone in chapter 9 provide ample evidence to support the hypothesis that language was at the base of the attempted socio-political exclusion in 1817 of Hone and, through him, others of his social class. The attorney general, Sir Samuel Shepherd, goes to great lengths in each of the three trials to prove that the case of libel against Hone for publishing political satire based on commonly used texts in the established church is a question of moral and religious degradation and has nothing to do with class prejudices or with politics. But by suggesting that the lower classes are not fit to appreciate "the sort of topics which are artfully raised for them" by the original parodied Church texts, he also makes it perfectly plain that social repression of the lower classes is the real purpose of the trials. Hone is simply the scapegoat. Hone and his publishing activities are covertly represented as being a real danger to the hegemony of the "refined" language. The dogged way in which the three trials were carried through on three successive days despite the fact that the jury had acquitted Hone twice before the third trial is testimony to the authorities' desire to victimise him.

A more explicit example of linguicism is to be found in the explanation offered in *The Parliamentary History of England from the Earliest Period to the Year 1803* for the rejection by the House of Commons of the two petitions for voting rights from Nottingham and Sheffield in 1793. The comment made was that "persons coming forward as petitioners should address the House in decent and respectful language". Since the language of the petitioners was judged by members of Parliament not to be "decent and respectful", their petition for universal suffrage was rejected on linguistic grounds. This is an explicit case of linguicism, the object of which was to discriminate politically, and therefore also socially, against the lower classes of society by not allowing them access to the democratic parliamentary process of policy making and legislative procedures. There could surely be no more blatant case than this of an attempt to use discourse "to legitimate, effectuate, and reproduce unequal division of power and resources" and, on the basis of language, to exclude those with the "wrong" variety of language from enjoying the right to those resources. With regard to the second question in this case, Parliament could simply claim that the petitioners did not fulfil the social prerequisites to have the right to vote. But the point is that it was precisely those social prerequisites that the petitioners wished to change so that they might be able to enjoy that right. So if linguicism is a myth, there is in fact a very large grain of truth to it. In the case of many of the myths examined in this book, the grain of truth is difficult to find, although the reasons for "running" the myth discursively are to be found in the sociohistorical, sociocultural conditions of its emergence. In the following section I shall illustrate this by looking at the *longevity of English myth* in a little more detail.

4. ESTABLISHING THE "SUPERIORITY" OF ENGLISH

The first myth that we looked at in chapters 1 and 2 was used exclusively to raise English above other European languages. Its social function within the framework of the Victorian nation-state was to act as a catalyst for national unity in the wake of the social unrest and the perceived threat of armed insurrection by the working-classes after the Chartist movement fizzled out in the early 1850s (cf. chapter 9). The *longevity of English myth* consisted of two interlinked myths, the *ancient language myth* and the *unbroken tradition myth*.

In chapter 2, I seriously questioned the validity of the "story" that the *Beowulf* manuscript is the final manuscript in a line of lost manuscripts going back at least into the eighth century. As far as we know, there is—and in all probability was—only one manuscript of *Beowulf*, and even this manuscript was very nearly destroyed by the fire at Ashburnham House. Ingenious arguments have been put forward to support the "story", some linguistic, others stylistic and still others of a cultural-historical nature. Most arguments, however, were made without looking at the manuscript in meticulous detail, and they miss some very important factors which vitiate against the assumption of a long manuscript history. Kiernan (1996) has taken the trouble to examine the manuscript in detail, as has Westphalen (1967), and he raises a number of points in favour of the hypothesis that the surviving *Beowulf* manuscript was the only one prepared and that its preparation was scribe B's personal project. The evidence of the palimpsest put forward by Westphalen opens up the distinct possibility that scribe B was the author of at least the homecoming episode that links the two stories of *Beowulf*.

My own theory relies on palaeographical evidence to show that, in all probability, the manuscript has to be situated temporally in the first decade of the eleventh century rather than during the reign of Cnut from 1016 on. The following question thus arises: Why, in the face of the evidence to the contrary, do the majority of researchers still cling to the "story" of a long manuscript tradition? The answer that I proposed in chapter 2 is that the story is part of a myth constructed in the latter half of the nineteenth century which insists on a long history for the English language, the *ancient language myth*. The myth can be told only if we are prepared to accept that Anglo-Saxon was an early form of English. But whether or not this hypothesis is accepted, there is still another question: Why does the hypothesis as such need to be made? Where is the reason for elaborating the *ancient language myth* in the first place? The reason actually lies outside the content of the myth and is to be found in the fierce competition among European national standard languages (or *Kultursprachen*, languages with a literature). Part of the economic struggle for imperial domination between nation-states such as France, Spain, Great Britain and Germany in the nineteenth century consisted in being able to show whose language was superior to all the others. If Anglo-Saxon is counted as an early form of English, it has a longer and better documented literary history than any of the others, but only just. German[9] also has literary monuments going back at least into the ninth century. The *Hildebrandslied*, which like *Beowulf* was written in alliterative verse, exists in a manuscript codex dating from the 830s. The text is relatively short, by no means as long as *Beowulf*, but historians of English, the philologists of the nineteenth century, had a difficult time in claiming the greater longevity of English when compared with German. The myth thus validates the fierce competition between two nation-states in claiming the more ancient language. In the light of the uncertainties about *Beowulf*, one might wonder why modern historians of English still need to make those claims.

The other half of the longevity myth, the *unbroken tradition myth*, dealt with in chapter 3, is closely associated with the *ancient language myth*. Given the tenuous fact of the great age of English, the next challenge is to show that the language represents an unbroken tradition from the very first runic inscriptions all the way through to the present. The textual instantiations of the *Kultursprache* English can be shown to exist in all centuries as far back as the eighth century,[10] but the links are very tenuous, particularly in the period of transition after the Norman Conquest from Anglo-Saxon to Middle English.

---

9. Old High German is also more closely related to modern German than Old English/Anglo-Saxon is to modern English.

10. Even further back if one counts the inscriptions on stones such as the Ruthwell Cross.

If a cultural tradition is invoked, this part of the *longevity myth* does not hold up at all, since, as I showed in chapter 3, it is possible to discern a very clear break in continuity in terms of the dominant archive of Anglo-Saxon England and the period after the Conquest. There is an even cleaner break between the last of the Norman kings, Stephen, and the first of the Plantagenets, Henry II. My argument consisted in showing that an increased degree of what I call *inscribed orality* is evidence for the cultural breakdown of the archive. Once again, we need to question why it is still important to uphold this myth. Part of the reason is given in the second part of chapter 4, in which I demonstrate a linguistic continuity in terms of levelling processes and forms of simplification that reach back to the language contact period in the Danelaw between the Danish variety of Old Norse and Anglo-Saxon.

5. LINGUISTIC HOMOGENEITY VERSUS LINGUISTIC HETEROGENEITY

At the basis of all the myths presented in this book is the *linguistic homogeneity myth*. The myth assumes that a language should be a coherent, homogeneous system that all its speakers use, or at least should use. It expresses a teleology of language in which the end goal, the ultimate purpose of the process of historical development, should be some kind of perfection. But what would that perfection consist of? Must the language be free of any taint or blemish? If so, what kind of taint or blemish can a language have? Must the language be logically consistent? If so, linguists will admit that this can never be totally the case. Must it, in the terminology of Shaftesbury (see chap. 8), display decorum and grace and show perfect symmetry and order? If so, how would we define these qualities in reference to a language? Or must it simply be superior to all other languages?

Questions such as these have never been adequately addressed, largely because they cannot be adequately answered. But they remain set in people's minds as the ultimate goal(s) of the history of a language, and those who firmly believe in these goals use the myth, and all the other myths derived from it, to justify the means of achieving them. Imagine a world in which the goals of linguistic perfection and purity were achieved. Of what use would the perfect language be? It would still need to change and be adaptable to suit the needs of a changing world. Johnson's position in *The Plan of an English Dictionary* (1747) was that any change must inevitably be change for the worse. Reaching perfection, therefore, is equivalent to arriving in a static world in which no further change is possible.

So the *linguistic homogeneity myth* is a double-edged sword. It drives a discourse which aims at purity and perfection, but it leads to a situation in which stasis, not dynamism, is the ultimate goal. In the myths that we have looked at, homogeneity may be interpreted to mean that a language is a recognisable unity clearly distinguished from other linguistic systems, and, not infrequently, this implies an assumption of superiority over other languages. This attitude towards the homogeneity of languages is revealed in Higden's *Polychronicon*, and the myths that are derived from it are the ***pure language myth***, which holds that the language should retain its assumed purity when confronted by other languages; and the ***contamination through contact myth***, which holds that contact with other languages inevitably leads to loss of purity, that is, to contamination and ultimately to decay and death (the ***decay and death myth***), and that those who do not speak the language either have an inferior language or none at all (the ***barbarians myth***). The ***pure language myth*** is still with us today, and not just with respect to English (see chapter 11 on the assumed "purity" of the Swiss German dialects). It is closely linked to the ***contamination through contact myth*** by way of the assumed reasons for loss of purity (see the discussion of the discourse of verbal hygiene revealed by Nyffenegger's research in chapter 11).

Homogeneity also refers to a state of affairs in which all speakers of English have equal command of the linguistic system of the standard language and use it in their daily lives. A homogeneous system is a perfect system that answers to all the needs of the community of its speakers and writers (the ***perfect language myth***), but, as we have seen, it is also a static system, one in which, as Johnson's position implies, language change does not and should not take place (the ***immutability myth***). But such a language does not exist, nor can it or will it ever exist—at least not as a variety of *human* language. It remains a goal in the minds of those who would standardise language to the extent that, as a perfect, unchangeable system, it can serve as the one acceptable language variety of the nation-state. The conceptualisation of homogeneity as perfection leads to the automatic discrimination of those who speak some other variety, and the myth becomes transformed into the ***legitimate language myth***, with all its sociopolitical consequences, some of which were discussed in chapter 9. The perfect language, conceptualised as a totally harmonious and symmetrical system, refers to polite (or polished, "refined") language, which was then claimed to be the possession of the upper, polite segments of society (the ***polite language myth***). As such, it paved the way for the notion of the legitimate language of the nation-state and helped to construct the kinds of social class distinctions that dogged British society till the end of the twentieth century. It was instrumental in discriminating against all other languages and language varieties which were not legitimate. In summary, this is the product of the funnel view of the history of English.

The myth of linguistic homogeneity revealed in the fourteenth century by Higden's work had been in existence for a much greater length of time. It represents an attempt to establish English in opposition to other language varieties in competition with it, but because it did not emerge within the framework of an ideology of standardisation, it did not contribute to social stratification and sociopolitical discrimination. Once English was consciously subjected to the standardisation process in the eighteenth century, it became politicised as the single legitimate form of language. This new and pernicious kind of linguistic homogeneity was used to drive the *legitimate language myth*, and, in the twentieth century the *educated language myth*. The canonical discourse of the history of English, the funnel view, has since taken on the trappings of a discourse archive governing the law of what can be "said, expressed, heard and understood" to be the history of English.

The sociolinguistic view of language change, however, takes on board Weinreich, Labov and Herzog's principle of structured heterogeneity. My very first point in chapter 1 was to establish a mode within which I could see the myths as the product of a set of conceptual metaphors about language. I proposed to take what I call a *sociocognitive view of language* in which human language functions cognitively as a mediator between our own individual physical, social and mental worlds, on the one hand, and the expansion of those individual mental worlds in potentially infinite ways, on the other. Social structure cannot exist without human beings using human language with one another, and the cognitive constructions of language in individuals cannot exist if those constructions had not been acquired socially. This involves us in three paradoxes:

1. *The homogeneity/heterogeneity paradox*: A language is not, and never can be, a unitary, homogeneous system because the people using it need flexibility at all times to adapt it to the purposes of the current social practice. *Paradox*: There is an in-built heterogeneity in all human language. The language myths constructed cognitively to explain, justify and ratify the concept Language A are based on notions of perfection, purity and homogeneity.
2. *The unique distinguishability paradox*: Although Language A may share a large number of constructions or construction types with Language B, it nevertheless has a certain number of constructions that allow the researcher to proclaim it to be a unique language. *Paradox*: This does not prevent speakers of A or B from communicating freely and easily with one another, and it may also mean that those same speakers may not perceive A or B to be uniquely distinguishable from each other at all.
3. *The language-as-a-property paradox*: The language system is the property of its speakers. *Paradox*: Speakers who are not ratified members of the group may still pass as such if they have an equal command of the language variety and if the language variety shared by the group is taken as one of the group's fundamental defining properties.

Rather than contaminate the host language, language contact situations create the external motivations required for change, since *potential change* is inherent in the *pragmatic* concern to negotiate meaning in *social* interaction. This is not to deny that change is often encouraged by the internal structure of the language system, but no change can occur of its own accord. I go so far as to suggest that any instantiation of social practice between speakers sharing linguistic constructions is a language contact situation. If participants in social practice perceive themselves to be using the "same" language, the degree of comprehensibility among the interactants is likely to be high-to-very-high, but innovations may still be introduced by one or other of the speakers.

So why do we need to concern ourselves with language myths? After all, the myths help to construct a view of language that is anathema to the very notion of language change. I have argued in this final chapter that they have even helped to construct a discourse archive that historical sociolinguists must break away from. We can break out of that mode only by taking on a positive attitude towards the natural heterogeneity of language in which variability, innovation, creativity, flexibility and potential are emphasised. We need to know about the myths, as well as the ideologies and discourse archives that have been constructed from them, if we are to be able to present alternative histories of the whole range of varieties of English. But the myths will never go away. They will continue to exist and get in the way of an honest appraisal of English in all its amazing varieties. They will continue to influence people who maintain that they "speak English perfectly", or that the only valid English worth teaching to second-language learners is some form of standard English, or that there are better or worse speakers of English, or that there is some kind of connection between language variety and the speaker's moral character. We will never be able to overcome these lay conceptualisations of language, precisely because they are built on mythical beliefs, but, as sociolinguists, we need to know as much as we can about the myths themselves.

References

Aarsleff, Hans. 1967. *The Study of Language in England, 1780–1860.* Princeton, N.J.: Princeton University Press.

———. 1982. *From Locke to Saussure: Essays on the Study of Language and Intellectual History.* Minneapolis: University of Minnesota Press.

Alatis, James, and Carolyn A. Straehle. 2006. The universe of English: Imperialism, chauvinism, and paranoia. In Kingsley Bolton and Braj B. Kachru (eds.), *World Englishes: Critical Concepts in Linguistics,* Vol. 5, 250–270. New York: Routledge.

Alim, H. Samy, Ibrahim Awad, Alastair Pennycook (eds.). 2009. *Global Linguistic Flows: Hip Hop Cultures, Youth Identities, and the Politics of Language.* New York: Routledge/Taylor & Francis.

Ammon, Ulrich (ed.). 1989. *Status and Function of Languages and Language Varieties.* Berlin, N.Y.: Walter de Gruyter.

Anderson, Benedict. 2006. *Imagined Communities: Reflections on the Origin and Spread of Nationalism.* London: Verso.

Anderson, Peter. 1987. *A Structural Atlas of the English Dialects.* London: Croom Helm.

Andres, Franz, and Richard J. Watts. 1993. English as a lingua franca in Switzerland: Myth or reality? *Bulletin CILA* 58: 109–127.

Arnovick, Leslie. 1999. *Diachronic Pragmatics: Seven Case Studies in English Illocutionary Development.* Amsterdam: Benjamins.

Åsen, Ivar. 1864. *Norsk Grammatik.* Christiana: Mallings Forlagsboghandel.

Ashton, T. S. 1997. *The Industrial Revolution, 1760–1830.* Oxford: Oxford University Press.

Auer, Peter. 1995. Context and contextualization. In Jef Verschueren, Jan-Ola Östman and Jan Blommaert (eds.), *Handbook of Pragmatics,* 1–19. Amsterdam: Benjamins.

Babington, Churchill (ed.). 1865. *Polychronicon Ranulphi Higden Monachi Cestrensis: Together with the English Translations of John Trevisa and of an Unknown Writer of the Fifteenth Century.* 7 vols. London: Longman, Green, Longman, Roberts, and Green.

Bailey, Charles-James, and Kurt Maroldt. 1977. The French lineage of English. In J. M. Meisel (ed.), *Langues en contact–pidgins–creoles–Languages in Contact*, 21–53. Tübingen: Narr.

Barber, Charles. 1976. *Early Modern English*. Edinburgh: Edinburgh University Press.

Barber, Richard. 1981. *The Pastons: The Letters of a Family in the Wars of the Roses.* London: Folio Society.

Bauer, Laurie, Paul Warren, Dianne Bardsley, Marianna Kennedy and George Major. 2007. Illustrations of the IPA: New Zealand English. *Journal of the International Phonetic Association* 37(1): 97–102.

Bede. 1990. *Ecclesiastical History of the English People.* Trans. Leo Sherley-Price, rev. R. E. Latham and ed. D. H. Farmer. Harmondsworth: Penguin.

Belanger, Terry. 1982. Publishers and writers in eighteenth-century England. In Isabel Rivers (ed.), *Books and Their Readers in Eighteenth-Century England*, 5–25. Leicester: Leicester University Press.

Bell, Alan, and Peter Garrett (eds.). 2002. *Approaches to Media Discourse.* Oxford: Blackwell.

Bellegarde, Abbé de. 1717. *Reflexions upon the Politeness of Manners.* London. Originally published as *Réflexions sur la politesse des mœurs, avec des maximes pour la société civile, suite des Réflexions sur le ridicule*, 1698.

Bergheaud, Patrice. 1979. De James Harris à John Horne Tooke: Mutations de l'analyse du langage en Angleterre dans la deuxième moitié du XVIIIe siècle. *Historiographia Linguistica* 6: 15–45.

Berndt, Rolf. 1969. The linguistic situation in England from the Norman Conquest to the loss of Normandy (1066–1204). In Roger Lass (ed.), *Approaches to English Historical Linguistics*, 369–391. New York: Holt, Rinehart & Winston.

Berns, Margie et al. 1998. (Re)experiencing Hegemony: The Linguistic Imperialism of Robert Phillipson. Special issue of the *International Journal of Applied Linguistics* 8(2).

Bex, Tony. 2008. "Standard English", discourse grammars and English language teaching. In Miriam Locher and Jürg Strässler (eds.), *Standards and Norms in the English Language*, 221–238. Berlin: Mouton de Gruyter.

Bex, Tony, and Richard J. Watts (eds.). 1999. *Standard English: The Widening Debate.* London: Routledge.

Blakemore, Diane. 1992. *Understanding Utterances: An Introduction to Pragmatics.* Oxford: Blackwell.

———. 2002. *Relevance and Linguistic Meaning: The Semantics and Pragmatics of Discourse Markers.* Cambridge: Cambridge University Press.

Blommaert, Jan. 2005. *Discourse.* Cambridge: Cambridge University Press.

Boberg, Charles. 2000. Geolinguistic diffusion and the U.S.–Canada border. *Language Variation and Change* 12: 1–24.

Bolton, Kingsley, and Braj B. Kachru (eds.). 2006. *World Englishes: Critical Concepts in Linguistics.* Vol. 5. New York: Routledge.

Bonfiglio, Thomas P. 2002. *Race and the Rise of Standard American.* Berlin: Mouton de Gruyter.

Bourdieu, Pierre. 1977. *Outline of a Theory of Practice*. Trans. Richard Nice. Cambridge: Cambridge University Press.

———. 1991. *Language and Symbolic Power*. Cambridge, Mass.: Harvard University Press.

Bourdieu, Pierre, and Jean-Claude Passeron. 1994. *Academic Discourse*. Trans. R. Teese. Cambridge: Polity Press.

Boyle, Leonard, O. P. 1997. The Nowell Codex and the dating of *Beowulf*. In C. Chase (ed.), *The Dating of "Beowulf"*, 23–32. Toronto: University of Toronto Press.

Braudel, Fernand. 1949. *La Méditerranée et le monde méditerranéen a l'époque de Philippe II*. Paris: Librairie Armand Colin.

———. 1980. *On History*. Trans. Sarah Matthews: Chicago: University of Chicago Press.

Bredvold, Louis, Robert K. Root and George Sherburn (eds.). [1932] 1955. *Eighteenth Century Prose*. New York: Nelson.

Britain, David, and Peter Trudgill. 1999. Migration, new-dialect formation and socio-linguistic refunctionalisation: Reallocation as an outcome of dialect contact. *Transactions of the Philological Society* 97(2): 245–256.

de la Bruyère, Jean. 1688. *Les caractères*. Paris.

Bullokar, William. 1581. *Book at Large, for the Amendment of Orthographie for English Speech*. London.

Burnett, James, Lord Monboddo. 1774–1792. *Of the Origin and Progress of Language*. 6 vols. Edinburgh: J. Balfour & T. Cadell.

Camden, William. 1605. *Remains Concerning Britain*. London.

Cameron, Deborah. 1995. *Verbal Hygiene*. London: Routledge.

———. 2000. Review of Bex and Watts (eds.), *Standard English: The Widening Debate*. *Multilingua* 19(4): 425–430.

Campbell, Lyle. 2004. *Historical Linguistics: An Introduction*. 2nd ed. Edinburgh: Edinburgh University Press.

Canagarajah, A. Suresh. 1999. *Resisting Linguistic Imperialism in English Teaching*. Oxford: Oxford University Press.

Carew, Richard. 1769. *The Svrvey of Cornwall. And an Epistle Concerning the Excellencies of the English Tongue*. London: B. Law.

Carter, Ronald. 1990. *English in the National Curriculum: The Development of a National Curriculum in England and Wales*. London: British Council.

———. 1996. Politics and knowledge about language: The LINC project. In R. Hasan and G. Williams (eds.), *Literacy and Society*, 1–21. London: Longman.

———. 1999. Standard grammars, spoken grammars: Some educational implications. In Tony Bex and Richard J. Watts (eds.), *Standard English: The Widening Debate*, 149–166. London: Routledge.

Carter, Ronald, and Michael McCarthy. 1988. *Vocabulary and Language Teaching*. London: Longman.

Chambers, Jack, Peter Trudgill and Natalie Schilling-Estes (eds.). 2002. *Handbook of Language Variation and Change*. Oxford: Blackwell.

Champneys, Arthur Charles. 1893. *History of English: A Sketch of the Origin and Development of the English Language with Examples, down to the Present Day*. New York: Macmillan.

Chase, C. (ed.). [1981] 1997. *The Dating of "Beowulf"*. Toronto: Toronto University Press.

Chase, Malcolm. 2007. *Chartism: A New History*. Manchester: Manchester University Press.

Chomsky, Noam, and Morris Halle. 1968. *The Sound Pattern of English*. New York: Harper & Row.

Claiborne, R. 1983. *Our Marvelous Native Tongue*. New York: Times Books.

Clark, Cecily. 1958. *The Peterborough Chronicle 1070–1154*. Oxford: Oxford University Press.

Classen, Ernest. 1919. *Outlines of the History of the English Language*. London: Macmillan.

Clemoes, Peter, Simon Keynes and Michael Lapidge (eds.). 1987. *Anglo-Saxon England*. Cambridge: Cambridge University Press.

Clyne, Michael (ed.). 1992. *Pluricentric Languages: Differing Norms in Different Nations*. Berlin: Mouton de Gruyter.

Cobbett, William. 1819. *A Grammar of the English Language, in a Series of Letters*. London: Thomas Dolby.

Cooper, Anthony Ashley, the 3rd Earl of Shaftesbury. [1711] 1999. *Characteristicks of Men, Manners, Opinions, Times*. Ed. Lawrence E. Klein. Cambridge: Cambridge University Press.

Cooper, Christopher. 1685. *Grammatica linguae anglicanae*. London.

Cope, Jackson I., and Harold Whitmore (eds.). 1958. *Thomas Sprat, History of the Royal Society*. St. Louis, Mo.: Washington University Studies.

Coupland, Nikolas, Christopher Candlin and Srikant Sarangi (eds.). 2001. *Sociolinguistics and Social Theory*. London: Addison Wesley Longman.

Courtin, Antoine de. 1671. *Nouveau traité de la civilité*. Paris.

Cox, Brian. 1991. *Cox on Cox: An English Curriculum for the 1990s*. London: Hodder & Stoughton.

Crafts, Nicholas. 1985. *British Economic Growth during the Industrial Revolution*. Oxford: Clarendon Press.

Croft, William. 2001. *Radical Construction Grammar: Syntactic Theory in Typological Perspective*. Oxford: Oxford University Press.

Croft, William, and D. Alan Cruse. 2004. *Cognitive Linguistics*. Cambridge: Cambridge University Press.

Crowley, Tony. 1999. Curiouser and curiouser: Falling standards in the standard English debate. In Tony Bex and Richard J. Watts (eds.), *Standard English: The Widening Debate*, 271–282.

———, ed. 2000. *The Politics of Language in Ireland: A Sourcebook*. London: Routledge.

———. [1989] 2003. *Standard English and the Politics of Language*. Basingstoke: Palgrave Macmillan.

Crystal, David. 1997. *English as a Global Language*. Cambridge: Cambridge University Press.

———. 2000. On trying to be crystal-clear: A response to Phillipson. *Applied Linguistics* 21(3): 415–421.

———. 2002. Broadcasting the nonstandard message. In Richard J. Watts and Peter Trudgill (eds.), *Alternative Histories of English*, 233–244. London: Routledge.

Culler, Jonathan. 1976. *Ferdinand de Saussure*. London: Fontana.

Cumming, Susanna, and Tsuyoshi Ono. 1997. Discourse and grammar. In Teun A. van Dijk (ed.), *Discourse as Structure and Process*, Vol. 1, 112–137. Thousand Oaks, Calif.: Sage.

Daines, Simon. 1640. *Orthoepia anglicana: or, The First Principall Part of the English Grammar: Teaching the Art of Right Speaking and Pronouncing English, with Certaine Exact Rules of Orthography and Rules of Spelling.* London.

Dalton-Puffer, Christine. 1995. Middle English is a creole and its opposite: On the value of plausible speculation. In Jacek Fisiak (ed.), *Linguistic Change under Contact Conditions*, 35–50. Berlin: Mouton de Gruyter.

Dance, Richard. 2004. North Sea currents: Old English–Old Norse relations, literary and linguistic. *Literature Compass* 1(1): 1–10.

Danchev, Andrei. 1997. The Middle English creolization hypothesis revisited. In Jacek Fisiak (ed.), *Studies in Middle English Linguistics*, 79–108. Berlin: Mouton de Gruyter.

Davies, Alan. 1996. Ironising the myth of linguicism: Review article of Robert Phillipson *Linguistic Imperialism*. *Journal of Multilingual and Multicultural Development* 17(6): 485–496.

Davis, Graeme. 2006. *Comparative Syntax of Old English and Old Icelandic: Linguistic, Literary, and Historical Implications.* Bern: Peter Lang.

Davis, Norman. 1971, 1976. *The Paston Letters. Vols. 1 and 2.* Oxford: Oxford University Press.

Davison, Jon, and Jane Dowson. 1998. Battles for English 2: English and the National Curriculum. In Jon Davison and Jane Dowson (eds.), *Learning to Teach English in the Secondary School: A Companion to School Experience*, 35–54. London: Routledge.

Davison, Jon, and Jane Dowson (eds.). 1998. *Learning to Teach English in the Secondary School: A Companion to School Experience.* London: Routledge.

Dawson, Hope C. 2003. Defining the outcome of language contact: Old English and Old Norse. *OSUWPL* 57: 40–57.

Deane, Phyllis. 1969. *The Industrial Revolution in England 1700–1914.* London: Collins.

Defoe, Daniel. 1697. *An Essay upon Projects.* In Louis Bredvold, Robert K. Root and George Sherburn (eds.). [1932] 1955. *Eighteenth Century Prose.* New York: Nelson.

de Lacy, Paul (ed.). 2007. *The Cambridge Handbook of Phonology.* Cambridge: Cambridge University Press.

Department of Education and Science. 1975. *A Language for Life. Report of the Committee of Enquiry appointed by the Secretary of State for Education and Science under the Chairmanship of Sir Alan Bullock FBA.* London.

———. 1988. *Report of the Committee of Inquiry into the Teaching of English Language.* London.

———. 1988/1989. *Cox Reports 1 and 2.* London.

Descartes, René. [1637] 1973. *Discours de la méthode.* Montrouge: Librairie Générale Française.

Disraeli, Benjamin. 1845. *Sybil, or The Two Nations.* London. Henry Colburn.

Domingue, Nicole Z. 1977. Middle English: Another creole? *Journal of Creole Studies* 1: 89–100.

Doughty, P., J. Pearce and G. Thornton. 1971. *Language in Use.* London: Edward Arnold.

Dresher, B. Elan, and Nila Friedberg (eds.). 2006. *Formal Approaches to Poetry.* Berlin: Mouton de Gruyter.

Dumville, David N. 1987. English square minuscule script: The background and earliest phases. In Peter Clemoes, Simon Keynes and Michael Lapidge (eds.), *Anglo-Saxon England* 16, 147–180. Cambridge: Cambridge University Press.

Duranti, Alessandro, and Charles Goodwin (eds.). 1992. *Rethinking Context*. Language as an Interactive *Phenomenon*. Cambridge: Cambridge University Press.

Eckert, Penelope. 2000. *Linguistic Variation as Social Practice*. Oxford: Blackwell.

Eckert, Penelope, and Sally McConnell-Ginet. 2003. *Language and Gender*. New York: Cambridge University Press.

Ellis, Alexander. 1869. *On Early English Pronunciation, with Especial Reference to Shakspeare and Chaucer*. London: Trübner.

Elmes, Simon. 1999. *Talking for Britain: A Journey through the Nation's Dialects*. Harmondsworth: Penguin.

Emerson, Oliver Farrar. 1894. *The History of the English Language*. London: Macmillan.

Fairclough, Norman. 1989. *Language and Power*. London: Longman.

———. 1995. *Critical Discourse Analysis*. Boston: Addison Wesley.

Fauconnier, Gilles. [1985] 1994. *Mental Spaces*. New York: Cambridge University Press.

Fauconnier, Gilles, and Eve Sweetser. 1996. *Spaces, Worlds, and Grammar*. Chicago: University of Chicago Press.

Fauconnier, Gilles, and Mark Turner. 2002. *The Way We Think: Conceptual Blending and the Mind's Hidden Complexities*. New York: Basic Books.

Feldman, Jerome A. 2006. *From Molecule to Metaphor. A Neural Theory of Language*. Cambridge, Mass.: Bradford MIT Books.

Féry, Caroline, and Ruben van de Vijver (eds.). 2003. *The Syllable in Optimality Theory*. Cambridge: Cambridge University Press.

Fisiak, Jacek (ed.). 1995. *Linguistic Change under Contact Conditions*. Berlin: Mouton de Gruyter.

Fitzmaurice, Susan. 1998. The commerce of language in the pursuit of politeness in eighteenth-century England. *English Studies* 79: 309–328.

———. 2000. *The Spectator*, the politics of social networks, and language standardisation in eighteenth century England. In Laura Wright (ed.), *The Development of Standard English 1300–1800: Theories, Descriptions, Conflicts*, 195–218. Cambridge: Cambridge University Press.

Foucault, Michel. [1969] 1972. *Archaeology of Knowledge*. Trans. A. M. Sheridan Smith. New York: Pantheon.

———. [1975] 1977. *Discipline and Punish: The Birth of the Prison*. Trans. Alan Sheridan. New York: Vintage Books.

———. [1976] 1978. *The History of Sexuality: An Introduction*. Vol. 1. Trans. Robert Hurley. New York: Random House.

Freeborn, Dennis. 1992. *From Old English to Standard English: A Course Book in Language Variation across Time*. Ottawa, Canada: University of Ottawa Press.

Fries, Charles C. 1945. *Teaching and Learning English as a Foreign Language*. Ann Arbor: University of Michigan Press.

Gardner, R. G., and W. Lambert. 1972. *Attitudes and Motivation: Second-Language Learning*. Rowley, Mass.: Newbury House Publishers.

Gaskell, Elizabeth. 1849. *Mary Barton: A Tale of Manchester Life*. Leipzig: Tauchnitz.

Gellner, Ernest. 1983. *Nations and Nationalism*. Ithaca. N.Y.: Cornell University Press.

Geoffrey of Monmouth. 1966. *The History of the Kings of Britain*. Trans. and with an introduction by Lewis Thorpe. Harmondsworth: Penguin.

Giancarlo, Matthew. 2001. The rise and fall of the Great Vowel Shift? The changing ideological intersections of philology, historical linguistics, and literary history. *Representations* 76: 27–60.

Gil, Alexander. 1619. *Logonomia Anglica*. London.

Gordon, Elizabeth, Lyle Campbell, Jennifer Hay, Margaret Maclagan, Andrea Sudbury and Peter Trudgill. 2004. *New Zealand English: Its Origins and Evolution*. Cambridge: Cambridge University Press.

Görlach, Manfred. 1986. Middle English: A creole? In Dieter Kastovsky and A. J. Szwedek (eds.), *Linguistics across Historical and Geographical Boundaries: In Honor of Jacek Fisiak on the Occasion of his Fiftieth Birthday*, 329–344. Berlin: Mouton de Gruyter.

Gramsci, Antonio. 1971. *Selections from the Prison Notebooks*. New York: International Publishers.

Grillo, Ralph D. 1989. *Dominant Languages*. Cambridge: Cambridge University Press.

Grin, François. 2000. The economics of English as a global language. In H. W. Kam and C. Ward (eds.), *Language in the Global Context*, 284–303. Singapore: SEAMEO Regional Language Centre, Series No. 41.

———. 2001. Der ökonomische Wert der englischen Sprache. In Richard J. Watts and Heather Murray (eds.), *Die fünfte Landessprache? Englisch in der Schweiz*, 105–120. Zürich: v/d/f.

———. 2003. Economics and language planning. *Current Issues in Language Planning* 4(1): 1–66.

Grosse, Amanda. 2009. The presence of myths in early English-related discourse in Switzerland: An analysis based on eight interviews and a documentary film. M.A. thesis. Department of English, University of Bern.

Guzman, Trinidad. 1994. The Great Vowel Shift revisited. In Fernández Francisco Moreno, Miguel Fuster and Juan Jose Calvo (eds.), *English Historical Linguistics 1992*, 81–89. Amsterdam: Benjamins.

Hall, Robert, A., Jr. 1953. *Haitian Creole: Grammar, Texts, Vocabulary. The American Anthropologist. Memoir 74*. Washington, D.C.: American Anthropological Association.

Harris, James. 1751. *Hermes, or A Philosophical Inquiry Concerning Universal Grammar*. London: Nourse & Vaillant.

Harrison, William. 1577. On the languages spoken in this land. In Raphael Holinshed, *Chronicles of England, Scotland and Ireland*. London.

Hart, John. 1955. *John Hart's Works on English Orthography and Pronunciation, 1551, 1569, 1570*. Ed. Bror Danielsson. Stockholm: Almqvist & Wiksell.

Hasan, R., and G. Williams (eds.). 1996. *Literacy and Society*. London: Longman.

Henry, Archdeacon of Huntingdon. 1996. *Historia Anglorum: The History of the English People*. Ed. Diana Greenway. Oxford: Oxford University Press.

Higden, Ranulph (see under Babington, Churchill).

Hobsbawm, Eric. 1962. *The Age of Revolution in Europe*. London: Weidenfeld & Nicholson.

———. 1990. *Nations and Nationalism since 1780: Programme, Myth, Reality*. Cambridge: Cambridge University Press.

Hodge, Robert, and Gunter Kress. 1993. *Language as Ideology*. 2nd ed. London: Routledge.

Holinshed, Raphael. 1577. *Chronicles of England, Scotland and Ireland*. London.

Hone, William. 1816. *The Important Results of an Elaborate Investigation into the Mysterious Case of Eliza Fenning.* London.

——. [1818] 2009. *The Three Trials of William Hone: To which is added The Trial by Jury.* London. Facsimile reprint by Kessinger Publishing's Legacy Reprints.

——. 1819. *The Political House That Jack Built.* London.

Honey, John. 1997. *Language Is Power: The Story of Standard English and Its Enemies.* London: Faber.

Hopkins, A. G. (ed.). 2006. *Global History: Interactions between the Universal and the Local.* Houndsmills: Palgrave Macmillan.

Hopper, Paul J., and Elizabeth Closs Traugott. 1993. *Grammaticalization.* Cambridge: Cambridge University Press.

Howard, Ian. 2003. *Swein Forkbeard's Invasions and the Danish Conquest of England. 991–1017.* Woodbridge, Suffolk: Boydell Press.

Howatt, Anthony P. R. 1984. *A History of English Language Teaching.* Oxford: Oxford University Press.

Husserl, Edmund. 1970. *The Crisis of European Sciences and Transcendental Phenomenology: An Introduction to Phenomenological Philosophy.* Trans. David Carr. Evanston, Ill.: Northwestern University Press. Originally published in German as *Die Krisis der europäischen Wissenschaften und die transzendentale Phänomenologie: Eine Einleitung in die phänomenologische Philosophie,* ed. Walter Biemel. 1954. The Hague: Martinus Nijhoff.

Hymes, Dell (ed.). 1971. *Pidginization and Creolization of Languages.* Cambridge: Cambridge University Press.

Jary, David, and Julia Jary. 1991. *The HarperCollins Dictionary of Sociology.* New York: HarperCollins.

Jenkins, Jennifer. 2000. *The Phonology of English as an International Language.* Oxford: Oxford University Press.

——. 2003. *World Englishes: A Resource Book for Students.* London: Routledge.

——. 2004. ELF at the gate: The position of English as a lingua franca. *European English Messenger* 13(2): 63–69.

Jenkins, Jennifer, and Barbara Seidlhofer. 2001. *Bringing Europe's lingua franca into the classroom. Guardian Weekly.* Available at: http://www.guardian.co.uk/GWeekly-/Story/0,3939,475315,00.html

Jespersen, Otto. 1905. *The Growth and Structure of the English Language.* Leipzig: Teubner.

——. 1909. *A Modern English Grammar on Historical Principles, Volume 1.* Heidelberg: C. Winter Verlag.

——. 1933. *Essentials of English Grammar.* London: Allen & Unwin.

Johnson, Mark. 1987. *The Body in the Mind: The Bodily Basis of Meaning, Imagination, and Reason.* Chicago: University of Chicago.

Johnson, Samuel. 1747. *The Plan of an English Dictionary.* London: J. and P. Knapton.

——. 1755. *A Dictionary of the English Language.* Vols. 1 and 2. London: Dodsley.

Johnston, Paul A., Jr. 1992. English vowel shifting: One Great Vowel Shift or two small vowel shifts? *Diachronica* 9: 189–226.

Jones, Daniel. 1909. *The Pronunciation of English.* Cambridge: Cambridge University Press.

——. 1917. *An English Pronouncing Dictionary.* London: Dent.

Jones, Hugh. 1724. *An Accidence to the English Tongue*. London: John Clarke.

Joseph, John E. 1987. *Eloquence and Power: The Rise of Language Standards and Standard Languages*. London: Francis Pinter.

Kam, H. W., and C. Ward (eds.). 2000. *Language in the Global Context*. Singapore: SEAMEO Regional Language Centre, Series No. 41.

Kastovsky, Dieter, and A. J. Szwedek (eds.). 1986. *Linguistics across Historical and Geographical Boundaries: In Honor of Jacek Fisiak on the Occasion of his Fiftieth Birthday*. Berlin: Mouton de Gruyter.

Kastovsky, Dieter, and Gero Bauer (eds.). 1988. *Luick Revisited*. Tübingen: Gunter Narr.

Keane, A. H. 1875. *Handbook of the History of the English Language for the Use of Teacher and Student*. London: Longmans, Green.

Keating, Peter (ed.). 1976. *Into Unknown England 1866–1913: Selections from the Social Explorers*. Harmondsworth: Penguin.

Kemble, John Mitchell. 1837. *A Translation of the Anglo-Saxon Poem of Beowulf with a Copious Glossary, Preface and Philological Notes*. London: William Pickering.

Kent, C. B. R. [1899] 1971. *The English Radicals: An Historical Sketch*. New York: Lennox Hill.

Ker, N. R. 1957. *Catalogue of Manuscripts containing Anglo-Saxon*. Oxford: Clarendon Press.

Kerswill, Paul. 2002. Koinëization and accommodation. In Jack Chambers, Peter Trudgill and Natalie Schilling-Estes (eds.), *Handbook of Language Variation and Change*, 669–702. Oxford: Blackwell.

Ketcham, Michael. 1985. *Transparent Designs: Reading, Performance, and Form in the Spectator Papers*. Athens: University of Georgia Press.

Keynes, Simon. 1980. *The Diplomas of King Æthelred "the Unready" 987–1016*. Cambridge: Cambridge University Press.

Khan, Ali. 1992. *The Extinction of Nation States: A World without Borders*. The Hague: Martinus Nijhoff.

Kiernan, Kevin S. [1981] 1996. *Beowulf and the Beowulf Manuscript*. Ann Arbor: University of Michigan Press.

Kington-Oliphant, Thomas L. 1878. *The Old and Middle English*. London: Spottiswoode.

Kiparsky, Paul. 2003. Syllables and moras in Arabic. In Caroline Féry and Ruben van de Vijver (eds.), *The Syllable in Optimality Theory*, 147–181. Cambridge: Cambridge University Press.

———. 2006. A modular metrics for folk verse. In B. Elan Dresher and Nila Friedberg (eds.), *Formal Approaches to Poetry*, 7–49. Berlin: Mouton de Gruyter.

Klaeber, F. (ed.). 1950. *Beowulf and the Fight at Finnsburg*. Baltimore: Heath.

Klemola, Juhani, Merja Kytö and Matti Rissanen (eds.). 1996. *Speech Past and Present: Studies in English Dialectology in Memory of Ossi Ihalainen*. Frankfurt am Main: Peter Lang.

Koch, Peter. 1997. Orality in literate cultures. In Clotilde Pontecorvo (ed.), *Writing Development: An Interdisciplinary View*, 149–171. Amsterdam: Benjamins.

Kövecses, Zoltán. 2006. *Language, Mind, and Culture. A Practical Introduction*. New York: Oxford University Press.

Kristensson, G. [1967] 1988. *Survey of Middle English Dialects 1290–1350*. Lund: Lund University Press.

Labov, William. 1994. *Principles of Linguistic Change*. Vol. 1: Internal Factors. Oxford: Blackwell.

———. 2001. *Principles of Linguistic Change*. Vol. 2: *Social Factors*. Malden, Mass.: Blackwell.

Labov, William, Sharon Ash and Charles Boberg. 2006. *The Atlas of North American English*. Berlin: Mouton de Gruyter.

Labov, William, and Joshua Waletsky. 1997. Narrative analysis: Oral versions of personal experience. *Journal of Narrative and Life History* 7(1–4): 3–38.

Labov, William, Malcah Yaeger and Richard Steiner. 1972. *A Quantitative Study of Sound Change in Progress*. Philadelphia: U. S. Regional Survey.

Lakoff, George. 1987. *Women, Fire, and Dangerous Things: What Categories Reveal about the Mind*. Chicago: University of Chicago Press.

Lakoff, George, and Mark Johnson. 2003. *Metaphors we Live By*. 2nd ed. Chicago. University of Chicago Press.

———. 1999. *Philosophy in the Flesh: The Embodied Mind and Its Challenge to Western Thought*. New York: Basic Books.

Lakoff, George, and Rafael Núñez. 2000. *Where Mathematics Comes From: How the Embodied Mind Brings Mathematics into Being*. New York: Basic Books.

Lamarre, Paul. 1998. John Horne Tooke and the grammar of political experience. *Philological Quarterly* 77: 187–208.

Land, Stephen. 1976. Lord Monboddo and the theory of syntax in the late eighteenth century. *Journal of the History of Ideas* 37: 423–440.

Langer, Nils, and Winifred Davies (eds.). 2005. *Linguistic Purism in the Germanic Languages*. Berlin: Walter de Gruyter.

Langford, Paul. 1989. *A Polite and Commercial People: England 1727–1783*. Oxford: Oxford University Press.

Lass, Roger (ed.). 1969. *Approaches to English Historical Linguistics*. New York: Holt, Rinehart & Winston.

———. 1988. Vowel shifts real and otherwise: Remarks on Stockwell and Minkova. In Dieter Kastovsky and Gero Bauer (eds.), *Luick Revisited*, 395–410. Tübingen: Gunter Narr.

———. 1989. How early does English get modern? Or, what happens if you listen to orthoepists and not to historians. *Diachronica* 6(1): 75–109.

——— (ed.). 1999a. *The Cambridge History of the English Language*. Vol. 3: *1476–1776*. Cambridge: Cambridge University Press.

———. 1999b. Phonology and morphology. In Roger Lass (ed.), *The Cambridge History of the English Language*. Vol. 3: *1476–1776*. Cambridge: Cambridge University Press.

Latham, R. G. 1850. *The English Language*. London. Taylor, Walton & Maberly.

Lave, Jean, and Etienne Wenger. 1991. *Situated Learning: Legitimate Peripheral Participation*. Cambridge: Cambridge University Press.

Legge, M. Dominica. 1941. Anglo-Norman and the historian. *History* 26: 167.

Lehmann, W., and Y. Malkiel (eds.). 1968. *Directions for Historical Linguistics*. Austin: University of Texas Press.

Leitner, Gerhard (ed.). 1991. *English Traditional Grammars*. Amsterdam: John Benjamin.

Lenneberg, Eric. 1967. *Biological Foundations of Language*. New York: Wiley.

Lippi-Green, Rosina. 1997. *English with an Accent*. London: Routledge.

Llamas, Carmen, Louise Mullany and Peter Stockwell (eds.). 2007. *The Routledge Companion to Sociolinguistics*. London: Routledge.

Locher, Miriam, and Jürg Strässler (eds.). 2008. *Standards and Norms in the English Language*. Berlin: Mouton de Gruyter.

Locke, John. 1690. *An Essay Concerning Human Understanding*. 4 vols. London: Thomas Basset.

London Working Men's Association. 1838. *The People's Charter*. London.

Lowth, Robert. 1761. *A Short Introduction to English Grammar*. London: Dodsley.

Lüdi, Georges, et al. 1998. *"Gesamtsprachenkonzept": Welche Sprachen sollen die Schülerinnen und Schüler der Schweiz während der obligatorischen Schulzeit lernen?*. Bern: Schweizerische Konferenz der Erziehungsdirektoren.

Luick, Karl. 1964. *Historische Grammatik der englischen Sprache*. Oxford: Blackwell.

Macaulay, Ronald. 1994. *The Social Art: Language and Its Uses*. New York: Oxford University Press.

Mair, Christian (ed.). 2003. *The Politics of English as a World Language*. Amsterdam: Rodopi.

Map, Walter. 1983. *De nugis curialium: Courtiers' Trifles*. Ed. and trans. M. R. James, rev. C. N. L. Brooke and R. A. B. Mynors. Oxford: Oxford University Press.

Markus, Manfred (ed.). *Historical English: On the Occasion of Karl Brunners's 100th Birthday*. Innsbruck: Institut für Sprachwissenschaft.

McArthur, Tom. 1998. *The English Languages*. Cambridge: Cambridge University Press.

McCrum R., W. Cran and R. MacNeil. 1986. *The Story of English*. Rev. ed. London: Faber.

McIntosh, Angus, M. L. Samuels and Michael Benskin. 1986. *A Linguistic Atlas of Late Mediaeval English*. Aberdeen: Aberdeen University Press.

McIntosh, Carey. 1998. *The Evolution of English Prose 1700–1800: Style, Politeness, and Print Culture*. Cambridge: Cambridge University Press.

McLaren, Mary-Rose. 2002. *London Chronicles of the Fifteenth Century: A Revolution in English Writing*. Woodbridge: D. S. Brewer.

McRea, Brian.1990. *Addison and Steele Are Dead: The English Department, Its Canon, and the Professionalization of Literary Criticism*. Cranbury, N.J.: Associated University Presses Inc.

Meiklejohn, John M. D. 1886. *A Brief History of the English Language and Literature*. London: D. C. Heath.

Meisel, J. M. (ed.). 1977. *Langues en contact–pidgins–creoles–Languages in Contact*. Tübingen: Narr.

Michael, Ian. 1991. More than enough English grammars. In Gerhard Leitner (ed.), *English Traditional Grammars*, 11–26. Amsterdam: John Benjamin.

———. 1997. The hyperactive production of English grammars in the nineteenth century: A speculative bibliography. *Publishing History* 41: 23–61.

Michelet, Jules. 1833. *Histoire de la France*, Vol. 2. Paris: Champion.

Miège, Guy. 1688. *English Grammar; or the Grounds and Genius of the English Tongue*. London.

Milroy, James. 1992. *Linguistic Variation and Change*. Oxford: Blackwell.

———. 1996. Linguistic ideology and the Anglo-Saxon lineage of English. In Juhani Klemola, Merja Kytö and Matti Rissanen (eds.), *Speech Past and Present: Studies in English Dialectology in Memory of Ossi Ihalainen*, 169–186. Frankfurt am Main: Peter Lang.

———. 1999. The consequences of standardisation in descriptive linguistics. In Tony Bex and Richard J. Watts (eds.), *Standard English: The Widening Debate*, 16–39. London: Routledge.

————. 2000. Historical description and the ideology of the standard language. In Laura Wright (ed.), *The Development of Standard English 1300–1800: Theories, Descriptions, Conflicts*, 11–28. Cambridge: Cambridge University Press.

————. 2001. Language ideologies and the consequences of standardization. *Journal of Sociolinguistics* 5(4): 530–555.

————. 2002. The legitimate language: Giving a history to English. Prologue to Richard J. Watts and Peter Trudgill (eds.), *Alternative Histories of English*, 7–25. London: Routledge.

————. 2005. Some effects of purist ideologies on historical descriptions of English. In Nils Langer & Winifred Davies (eds.), *Linguistic Purism in the Germanic Languages*, 324–342. Berlin: Walter de Gruyter.

————. 2007. The ideology of the standard language. In Carmen Llamas, Louise Mullany and Peter Stockwell (eds.), *The Routledge Companion to Sociolinguistics*, 133–139. London: Routledge.

Milroy, James, and Lesley Milroy. [1985] 1999. *Authority in Language. Investigating Standard English*. London: Routledge.

Milroy, Lesley. 1999. Standard English and language ideology in Britain and the United States. In Tony Bex and Richard J. Watts (eds.), *Standard English: The Widening Debate*, 173–206. London: Routledge.

Modiano, Marko. 1999. Standard English(es) and educational practices for the world's lingua franca. *English Today* 15(4): 3–13.

Monboddo, Lord, see Burnett, James

Moore, B. 2008. *Speaking Our Language: The Story of Australian English*. Melbourne: Oxford University Press.

Moreno, Fernández Francisco, Miguel Fuster and Juan Jose Calvo (eds.). 1994. *English Historical Linguistics 1992*. Amsterdam: Benjamins.

Mugglestone, Lynda. 1995. *"Talking proper": The Rise of Accent as Social Symbol*. Oxford: Clarendon Press.

Mühlhäusler, Peter. 1996. *Language Change and Linguistic Imperialism in the Pacific Region*. London: Routledge.

Nevalainen, Terttu. 2006. *An Introduction to Early Modern English*. Edinburgh: Edinburgh University Press.

Nicklin, Thomas. 1920. *The Sounds of Standard English with some Notes on Accidence and Syntax*. Oxford: Clarendon Press.

Nixon, Graham, and John Honey (eds.). 1988. *An Historic Tongue: Essays in Honour of Barbara Strang*. London: Routledge.

Núñez, Rafael, and W. J. Freeman (eds.). 1999. *Reclaiming Cognition: The Primacy of Action, Intention and Emotion*. Thorverton, UK: Imprint Academic.

Nyffenegger, Susanne. 2003. Reactions to the spread of English in Switzerland: An analysis based on letters to the editor. M.A. thesis, Department of English, University of Bern.

Orchard, Andy. [1985] 2003. *Pride and Prodigies: Studies in the Monsters of the Beowulf-Manuscript*. Toronto: University of Toronto Press.

Orton, Harold, et al. 1962–71. *Survey of English Dialects: Basic Materials*. Introduction and 4 vols. (each in 3 parts). Leeds: E. J. Arnold & Son.

Paine, Thomas. [1791/1792] 1817. *The Rights of Man*. London: W. T. Sherwin.

Palmer, Harold. 1921. *The Oral Method of Teaching Languages: A Monograph on Conversational Methods*. Cambridge: Heffer.

————. 1924. *A Grammar of Spoken English*. Cambridge: Heffer.

Patterson, Annabel. 1994. *Reading Holinshed's Chronicles*. Chicago: University of Chicago Press.

Pennycook, Alistair. 1994. *The Cultural Politics of English as an International Language*. London: Longman.

————. 1998. *English and the Discourses of Colonialism*. London: Routledge.

Percy, Carol. 1997. Paradigms lost: Bishop Lowth and the "poetic dialect" in his English grammar. *Neophilologus* 81: 129–144.

Peyton, Victor. 1779. *Elements of the English Language*. London.

Phillipson, Robert. 1992. *Linguistic Imperialism*. Oxford: Oxford University Press.

————. 1997. Realities and myths of linguistic imperialism. *Journal of Multilingual and Multicultural Development* 18(3): 238–247.

————. 1999. Voice in global English: Unheard chords in Crystal loud and clear. *Applied Linguistics* 20(2): 265–276.

Philological Society. 1859. *Proposal for the Publication of a New English Dictionary*. London: Trübner.

Polomé, Edgar. 1980. Creolization processes and diachronic linguistics. In Albert Valdman and Arnold Highfield (eds.), *Theoretical Orientations in Creole Studies*, 185–202. New York: Academic Press.

Pontecorvo, Clotilde (ed.). 1997. *Writing Development: An Interdisciplinary View*. Amsterdam: John Benjamin.

Poussa, Patricia. 1982. The evolution of early standard English. The creolization hypothesis. *Studia Anglica Posnaniensia* 14: 69–85.

Preisler, Bent. 1999. *Danskerne og det engelske sprog*. Frederiksberg: Roskilde University Press.

Prescott, Andrew. 1997. "Their present miserable state of cremation": The restoration of the Cotton Library. In C. J. Wright (ed.), *Sir Robert Cotton as Collector: Essays on an Early Stuart Courtier and His Legacy, 391–454*. London: British Library Publications.

Pullum, Geoffrey K. 1991. *The Great Eskimo Vocabulary Hoax and other Irreverent Essays on the Study of Language*. With a foreword by James D. McCawley. Chicago: University of Chicago Press.

Puttenham, George. 1588. *The Arte of English Poesie*. London.

Quirk, Randolph, S. Greenbaum, G. Leech and J. Svartvik. 1985. *A Comprehensive Grammar of the English Language*. London: Longman.

Regli, Cécile. 2008. Myths in English-related discourse in Switzerland: An analysis based on newspaper articles, television discussions, and a group discussion. M.A. thesis, Department of English, University of Bern.

Reid, Robert. 1989. *The Peterloo Massacre*. London: Heinemann.

Rindler-Schjerve, Rosita (ed.), *Diglossia and Power*. Berlin: Mouton de Gruyter.

Rivers, Isabel (ed.). 1982. *Books and Their Readers in Eighteenth-Century England*. Leicester: Leicester University Press.

Roca, Iggy, and Wyn Johnson. 1999. *A Course in Phonology*. Malden. Mass.: Blackwell.

Rose, Gregory F. 1997. A look back at Kevin S. Kiernan's *Beowulf and the Beowulf Manuscript*—the Kiernan theory revisited: *Beowulf* at the court of Cnut? *Envoi* 6(2): 135–145.

Rosenberger, Lukas. 2009. *The Swiss English Hypothesis*. Tübingen: Francke Verlag.

Rothwell, W. 1998. Arrivals and departures: The adoption of French terminology into Middle English. *Modern Language Notes* 50: 144–167.

Saladin, Peter, et al. 1989. *Zustand und Zukunft der viersprachigen Schweiz.* Bern: Eidgenössisches Departement des Innern.

Scannell, Paddy. [1998] 2002. Media—language—world. In Alan Bell and Peter Garrett (eds.), *Approaches to Media Discourse*, 251–267. Oxford: Blackwell.

Schank, Roger C., and Robert P. Abelson. 1977. *Scripts, Plans, Goals, and Understanding: An Inquiry into Human Knowledge Structures.* Hillsdale, N.J.: Lawrence Erlbaum.

Schmid, Heinrich. 1982. *Richtlinien für die Gestaltung einer gesamtbündnerischen Schriftsprache: Rumantsch Grischun.* Chur: Lia Rumantscha.

Schreier, Daniel. 2003. *Isolation and Language Change.* Houndsmills: Palgrave Macmillan.

Schuchardt, Hugo. [1914] 1980. *Die Sprache der Saramakkaneger in Surinam.* Amsterdam: Johannes Müller.

Seidlhofer, Barbara. 2004. Research perspectives on teaching English as a lingua franca. *Annual Review of Applied Linguistics* 24: 209–239.

Seliger, Martin. 1976. *Ideology and Politics.* London: Allen & Unwin.

Sheridan, Thomas. 1762. *A Course of Lectures on Elocution together with two Dissertations on Language: and Some Other Tracts Relative to those Subjects.* London: A. Millar, R. & J. Dodsley, T. Davies, C. Henderson, J. Wilkie & E. Dilly.

Short, Ian. 1980. On bilingualism in Anglo-Norman England. *Romance Philology* 33: 467–479.

Silverstein, Michael, and Greg Urban (eds.). 1996. *Natural Histories of Discourse.* Chicago: University of Chicago Press.

Skutnabb-Kangas, Tove. 2003. Linguistic diversity and biodiversity: The threat from killer languages. In Christian Mair (ed.), *The Politics of English as a World Language*, 31–52. Amsterdam: Rodopi.

———. 1984. *Bilingualism or Not—the Education of Minorities.* Clevedon. Avon: Multilingual Matters.

Skutnabb-Kangas, Tove, and Robert Phillipson. 1989. "Mother tongue": The theoretical and sociopolitical construction of a concept. In Ulrich Ammon (ed.), *Status and Function of Languages and Language Varieties*, 450–477. Berlin, N.Y.: Walter de Gruyter.

Smith, Anthony D. 1971. *Theories of Nationalism.* London: Duckworth.

———. 1987. *The Ethnic Origins of Nations.* Oxford: Blackwell.

———. 1991. *National Identity.* Harmondsworth: Penguin.

———. 2004. *The Antiquity of Nations.* Cambridge: Polity Press.

Smith, Jeremy. 1993. Dialectal variation in Middle English and the actuation of the Great Vowel Shift. *Neuphilologische Mitteilungen* 94(3–4): 259–277.

Smith, Jeremy. 1996. *A Historical Study of English.* London: Routledge.

Smith, Olivia. 1984. *The Politics of Language 1791–1819.* Oxford: Oxford University Press.

Smith, Richard C. 2003. *Teaching English as a Foreign Language 1912–1936. Vols. 1 and 2.* London: Routledge.

Sprat, Thomas. 1667. *History of the Royal Society.* London.

Stanihurst, Richard. 1577. A treatise containing a plain and perfect description of Ireland. In Raphael Holinshed (ed.), *The Chronicles of England, Scotland, and*

Ireland, 1–69. London. Reprinted in Tony Crowley (ed.), *The Politics of Language in Ireland: A Sourcebook*, 31–37. London: Routledge.

Stephens, W. B. 1987. *Education, Literacy and Society: The Geography of Diversity in Provincial England*. Manchester: Manchester University Press.

———. 1998. *Education in Britain 1750–1914*. New York: St. Martin's Press.

Stockwell, Robert P., and Donka Minkova. 1988a. The English vowel shift: Problems of coherence and explanation. In Dieter Kastovsky and Gero Bauer (eds.), *Luick Revisited*, 355–394. Tübingen: Gunter Narr.

———. 1988b. A rejoinder to Lass. In Dieter Kastovsky and Gero Bauer (eds.), *Luick Revisited*, 411–417. Tübingen: Gunter Narr.

———. 1990. The early modern English vowels, more O'Lass. *Diachronica* 7: 199–214.

———. 1997. On drifts and shifts. *Studia Anglica Posnaniensia* 21: 283–303.

Swanton, Michael. 1996. *The Anglo-Saxon Chronicles*. London: J. M. Dent.

Sweet, Henry. [1873–74] 1888. *History of English Sounds from the Earliest Period*. London: Trübner.

Swift, Jonathan. 1712. *A Proposal for Correcting, Improving, and Ascertaining the English Tongue*. London.

———. 1729. *A Modest Proposal: For Preventing the Children of Poor People in Ireland from Being a Burden to their Parents or Country, and for Making them Beneficial to the Public*. London.

———. 1731. *Directions to Servants*. London.

The Parliamentary History of England from the Earliest Period to the Year 1803. Vol. XXX comprising the Period from the Thirteenth of December 1792 to the Tenth of March 1794, p. 776. London: T. C. Hansard.

Thomason, Sarah, and Terrence Kaufmann. 1988. *Language Contact, Creolization, and Genetic Linguistics*. Berkeley: University of California Press.

Thompson, Linda. 2000. *Young Bilingual Learners in Nursery School*. Clevedon: Multilingual Matters.

Tieken-Boon van Ostade, Ingrid (ed.). 2008. *Grammars, Grammarians and Grammar-writing in Eighteenth-Century England*. Berlin: Mouton de Gruyter.

Todd, Loreto. 1974. *Pidgins and Creoles*. London: Routledge & Kegan Paul.

Tooke, John Horne. 1798/1805. *ΕΠΕΑ ΠΤΕΡΟΕΝΤΑ, or, The Diversions of Purley*. 2 vols. London: J. Johnson.

Tough, J. 1976. *Listening to Children Talking*. London: Ward Lock.

Trench, Richard Chevenix. [1855] 1881. *English Past and Present: Eight Lectures*. London: Macmillan.

Trudgill, Peter. 1995. *Sociolinguistics*. Harmondsworth: Penguin.

———. 1999. Standard English: What it isn't. In Tony Bex and Richard J. Watts (eds.), *Standard English: The Widening Debate*, 117–128. London: Routledge.

Trudgill, Peter, and Jean Hannah. 2002. *International English*. 4th ed. London: Arnold.

Tschichold, Cornelia (ed.). 2003. *English Core Linguistics: Essays in Honour of D. J. Allerton*. Bern: Peter Lang.

Turner, Mark (ed.). 2006. *The Artful Mind: Cognitive Science and the Riddle of Human Creativity*. New York: Oxford University Press.

Valdman, Albert, and Arnold Highfield (eds.). 1980. *Theoretical Orientations in Creole Studies*. New York: Academic Press.

van Dijk, Teun A. (ed.). 1997. *Discourse as Structure and Process*. Vol. 1. Thousand Oaks, Calif.: Sage.

van Gelderen, Elly. 2006. *A History of the English Language*. Amsterdam: Benjamins.

van Lier, Leo. 2004. *The Ecology and Semiotics of Language Learning: A Sociocultural Perspective*. Dordrecht: Kluwer Academic.

Verschueren, Jef, Jan-Ola Östman and Jan Blommaert (eds.). 1995. *Handbook of Pragmatics*. Amsterdam: John Benjamin.

Vetter, Eva. 2003. Hegemonic discourse in the Habsburg Empire: The case of education. A critical discourse analysis of two mid nineteenth century government documents. In Rosita Rindler-Schjerve (ed.), *Diglossia and Power*, 271–307. Berlin: Mouton de Gruyter.

Voeste, Anja. 2008. *Orthographie und Innovation. Die Segmentierung des Wortes im 16. Jahr-hundert*. Hildesheim: Olms.

Wales, Katie. 2006. *Northern English: A Social and Cultural History*. Cambridge: Cambridge University Press.

Walker, John. 1781. *Elements of Elocution. Being the Substance of a Course of Lectures on the Art of Reading*. London: T. Cadell, T. Becket, G. Robinson and J. Dodsley.

———. 1791. *A Critical Pronouncing Dictionary and Expositor of the English Language*. London: G. G. J. and J. Robinson; and T. Cadell.

Wallis, John. 1653. *Grammatica linguae anglicanae*. London.

Wallmannsberger, Josef. 1988. The "creole hypothesis" in the history of English. In Manfred Markus (ed.), *Historical English: On the Occasion of Karl Brunner's 100th Birthday*, 19–36. Innsbruck: Institut für Sprachwissenschaft.

Wanley, Humfrey. 1705. *Librorum Vett. Septentrionalium, qui in Angliæ Biblioth. extant, Catalogus Historico-Criticus [Antiquæ Literaturæ Septentrionalis Libri Duo]. In his Catalogus Historico-Criticus*. London.

Watts, Richard J. 1989. Taking the pitcher to the well: Native speakers' perceptions of their use of discourse markers in conversation. *Journal of Pragmatics* 13: 203–237.

———. 1999a. The ideology of dialect in Switzerland. In Jan Blommaert (ed.), *Language Ideological Debates*, 67–103. Berlin: Mouton de Gruyter.

———. 1999b. Language and politeness in early eighteenth century Britain. *Pragmatics* 9(1): 5–20.

———. 2000. Mythical strands in the ideology of prescriptivism. In Laura Wright (ed.), *The Development of Standard English 1300–1800: Theories, Descriptions, Conflicts*, 29–48. Cambridge: Cambridge University Press.

———. 2001. Discourse theory and language planning: A critical reading of language planning reports in Switzerland. In Nikolas Coupland, Christopher Candlin and Srikant Sarangi (eds.), *Sociolinguistics and Social Theory*, 297–320. London: Addison Wesley Longman.

———. 2002. From polite language to educated language: The re-emergence of an ideology. In Richard J. Watts and Peter Trudgill (eds.), *Alternative Histories of English*, 155–172. London: Routledge.

———. 2003a. *Politeness*. Cambridge: Cambridge University Press.

———. 2003b. Was the Great Vowel Shift really "great"? A reappraisal of research work on an elusive linguistic phenomenon. In Cornelia Tschichold (ed.), *English Core Linguistics: Essays in Honour of D. J. Allerton*, 13–30. Bern: Peter Lang.

————. 2008. Grammar writers in eighteenth-century Britain: A community of practice or a discourse community? In Ingrid Tieken-Boon van Ostade (ed.), *Grammars, Grammarians, and Grammar-Writing in Eighteenth-Century England*, 37–56. Berlin: Mouton de Gruyter.

Watts, Richard J., and Heather Murray (eds.). 2001. *Die fünfte Landessprache? Englisch in der Schweiz*. Zürich: v/d/f.

Watts, Richard J., and Peter Trudgill (eds.). 2002. *Alternative Histories of English*. London: Routledge.

Weinreich, Uriel, William Labov and Marvin Herzog. 1968. Empirical foundations for a theory of language change. In W. Lehmann and Y. Malkiel (eds.), *Directions for Historical Linguistics*, 95–195. Austin: University of Texas Press.

Wells, John C. 1982. *Accents of English*. New York: Cambridge University Press.

Welsford, Henry. 1845. *On the Origin and Ramifications of the English Language*. London: Longman, Brown, Green & Longmans.

Welskopf, Margun. 2008. Language varieties and the air traffic control workplace. Ph.D. diss., University of Berne.

Wenger, Etienne. *Communities of Practice: Learning, Meaning, and Identity*. Cambridge: Cambridge University Press.

Westphalen, Tilman. 1967. *Beowulf 3150–3155*. Munich: Fink.

Whinnom, Keith. 1971. Linguistic hybridization and the "special case" of pidgins and creoles. In Dell Hymes (ed.), *Pidginization and Creolization of Languages*, 91–115. Cambridge: Cambridge University Press.

White, Philip. 2006. Globalization and the mythology of the nation state. In A. G. Hopkins (ed.), *Global History: Interactions between the Universal and the Local*, 257–284. Houndsmills: Palgrave Macmillan.

Whitelock, Dorothy (ed.). 1954. *The Peterborough Chronicle: The Bodleian Manuscript Laud Misc. 636*. Copenhagen: Rosenkilde & Bagger.

Widdowson, Henry. 1997. EIL, ESL, EFL: Global issues and local interests. *World Englishes* 16(1): 146–153.

Wildhagen's German–English, English–German Dictionary. 1972. 2 vols. Wiesbaden: Brandstetter.

William of Malmesbury. 2007. *Gesta pontificum Anglorum. Vol. 1: Text and Translation*. Ed. and trans. M. Winterbottom. Oxford: Oxford University Press.

Williams, Raymond. 1962. *Communications*. Harmondsworth: Penguin.

Wolfe, Patricia M. 1972. *Linguistic Change and the Great Vowel Shift in English*. Berkeley: University of California Press.

WordReference. Com Language Forums. http://forum.wordreference.com/showthread.php?t=240473 (accessed on December 8, 2007).

Wormald, Patrick. 1999. *The Making of English Law: King Alfred to the Twelfth Century*. Oxford: Blackwell.

Wright, C. J. (ed.). 1997. *Sir Robert Cotton as Collector: Essays on an Early Stuart Courtier and his Legacy*. London: British Library Publications.

Wright, Laura (ed.). 2000. *The Development of Standard English 1300–1800: Theories, Descriptions, Conflicts*. Cambridge: Cambridge University Press.

Wyld, Henry C. 1906. *The Historical Study of the Mother Tongue: An Introduction to Philological Method*. London: Murray.

————. 1913. *Evolution in English Pronunciation: A Public Lecture Delivered at the University of Liverpool on November 21st 1913*. Liverpool: University Press of Liverpool.

Zec, Draga. 2007. The syllable. In Paul de Lacy (ed.), *The Cambridge Handbook of Phonology*, 161–194. Cambridge: Cambridge University Press.

Zupitza, J. (ed.). 1882. *Beowulf: Autotypes of the Unique Cotton MS Vitellius A. xv in the British Museum, with a Transliteration and Notes. Early English Text Society* 77. London: Oxford University Press.

Index

Aarsleff, Hans, 216, 219
Abelson, Robert P., 5n2
accent, 133, 136, 141n2, 203, 234, 256–257, 295
acculturation, process of, 92, 190
action, social, 22, 270
actuation of changes, 153; problem, 153
Addison, Joseph, 170–174, 177, 180, 184, 199–201
address, metadiscursive, 294
Æthelræd II, 39–41, 50, 61–63, 65, 68–69, 72
Æthelredian Exemplar, 62, 65, 68–69
Afrikaans, 282
Alatis, James, 260
Alfred the Great, 39, 49, 59–61, 63, 65, 67, 121
Alim, H. Samy, 260
Allerton, David, 277, 283
American Field Service, 268
Anderson, Benedict, 115, 121
Anderson, Peter, 151
Andres, Franz, 277
Anglo-Norman (French), 25, 70, 73, 82, 83, 85, 89–90, 92, 95–96, 99, 107, 110, 121, 126, 132, 153, 160
Anglo-Saxon, 16, 20, 24, 30, 32, 37, 49, 54, 59–61, 68, 85, 87, 92–93, 95–96, 98–100, 103–104, 107–108, 110, 121, 139, 216, 218–219, 234, 287, 291, 299–300;

charters, 39, 54, 59, 66, 69, 122; codices, 34–35, 66; dialects, 107; diplomas (land grants), 59, 63, 65–66, 74, 122; glosses, 54; kingdoms, 67; land grants (see Anglo-Saxon diplomas); laws 54, 59–60, 66, 68–69, 121; literature, 50; manuscripts, 37, 39, 51; period/era, 29, 32–33, 39, 51–52, 54, 67n5; poetry, 39, 46, 54; quasi-standard, 72, 108; studies, 52; texts, 24, 29, 47, 54; translation, 54, 61; varieties of, 107, 121, 291
Anglo-Saxon Chronicles (ASC), 24, 31, 39, 55, 59–70, 72, 74, 76, 78, 84, 108, 121; decentralisation of, 69; disappearance of, 79–82; manuscripts of, 60–63; sociopolitical functions of, 69
archives, 17, 29–30, 55–56, 66–69, 72, 84, 121, 158, 187, 207, 212, 235–258, 260, 286; breakdown of, 20, 55, 59, 67n5, 69–78, 107, 254, 300; change of, 31, 54–55, 68–69, 202, 285; decentralisation of, 72; definition of, 18–21; disappearance of, 77; discourse, 3, 18–21, 26, 31, 34, 38, 50–52, 54–55, 60, 65, 79–82, 107–108, 121, 159, 184, 187, 201–202, 207, 212, 226, 234, 237, 246, 248, 256, 260, 285, 287–290, 302–303; disjunctive, 35;

CPSIA information can be obtained at www.ICGtesting.com
Printed in the USA
BVOW071154010712

294067BV00001B/7/P